PENGUIN CLASSICS

ADVISORY EDITOR: BETTY RADICE

THE REPUBLIC

PLATO (*c.* 427–347 BC) stands with Socrates and Aristotle as one of the shapers of the whole intellectual tradition of the West. He came from a family that had long played a prominent part in Athenian politics, and it would have been natural for him to follow the same course. He declined to do so, however, disgusted by the violence and corruption of Athenian political life, and sickened especially by the execution in 399 of his friend and teacher, Socrates. Inspired by Socrates' inquiries into the nature of ethical standards, Plato sought a cure for the ills of society not in politics but in philosophy, and arrived at his fundamental and lasting conviction that those ills would never cease until philosophers became rulers or rulers philosophers. At an uncertain date in the early fourth century BC he founded in Athens the Academy, the first permanent institution devoted to philosophical research and teaching, and the prototype of all western universities. He travelled extensively, notably to Sicily as political adviser to Dionysius II, ruler of Syracuse.

Plato wrote over twenty philosophical dialogues, and there are also extant under his name thirteen letters, whose genuineness is keenly disputed. His literary activity extended over perhaps half a century: few other writers have exploited so effectively the grace and precision, the flexibility and power, of Greek prose.

SIR DESMOND LEE was born in 1908 and was a scholar both at Repton School and at Corpus Christi College, Cambridge, where he gained a 'double first' in classics. He was a fellow and tutor at Corpus Christi, and a university lecturer there from 1937 to 1948. His lifelong association with the college continued after he became headmaster of Clifton College in 1948. In 1954 he left Clifton College to take up the position of headmaster at Winchester College where he remained until 1968. In 1959, 1960 and again in 1967 he was chairman of the Headmasters' Conference. Returning to Cambridge in 1968 he became Senior Research Fellow at

University (now Wolfson) College, and then from 1973 to 1978 President of Hughes Hall, Cambridge.

He is also the translator of Plato's *Timaeus and Critias* in the Penguin Classics.

Desmond Lee died in 1993.

RACHANA KAMTEKAR teaches philosophy at the University of Michigan. Her research focuses on ancient ethical and political philosophy, and she has written on the relationship between social justice and happiness in Plato, and on moral development and moral motivation in both Plato and the Stoics. She was educated at Stanford University and the University of Chicago. She previously taught at Williams College.

PLATO

The Republic

Translated with an Introduction by
DESMOND LEE

SECOND EDITION

PENGUIN BOOKS

PENGUIN BOOKS

Published by the Penguin Group
Penguin Books Ltd, 80 Strand, London WC2R 0RL, England
Penguin Putnam Inc., 375 Hudson Street, New York, New York 10014, USA
Penguin Books Australia Ltd, 250 Camberwell Road, Camberwell, Victoria 3124, Australia
Penguin Books Canada Ltd, 10 Alcorn Avenue, Toronto, Ontario, Canada M4V 3B2
Penguin Books India (P) Ltd, 11, Community Centre, Panchsheel Park, New Delhi – 110 017, India
Penguin Books (NZ) Ltd, Cnr Rosedale and Airborne Roads, Albany, Auckland, New Zealand
Penguin Books (South Africa) (Pty) Ltd, 24 Sturdee Avenue, Rosebank 2196, South Africa

Penguin Books Ltd, Registered Offices: 80 Strand, London WC2R 0RL, England

www.penguin.com

First published in this translation 1955
Second edition (revised) 1974
Reprinted with additional revisions 1987
Reissued with new Further Reading 2003

6

Copyright © H. D. P. Lee 1955, 1974, 1987
Further Reading © Rachana Kamtekar, 2003
All rights reserved

Set in 10.25/12.25 pt PostScript Adobe Sabon
Typeset by Rowland Phototypesetting Ltd, Bury St Edmunds, Suffolk
Printed in England by Clays Ltd, St Ives plc

Contents

PART III: EDUCATION: THE FIRST
STAGE (376)

PART IV: GUARDIANS AND
AUXILIARIES (412)

PART V: JUSTICE IN STATE AND
INDIVIDUAL (427)

PART VI: WOMEN AND THE
FAMILY (499)

PART VII: THE PHILOSOPHER
RULER (471)

PART VIII: EDUCATION OF THE
PHILOSOPHER (521)

PART IX: IMPERFECT SOCIETIES (543)

PART X: THEORY OF ART (595)

PART XI: THE IMMORTALITY OF THE SOUL AND THE REWARDS OF GOODNESS (608)

APPENDIX I: THE PHILOSOPHICAL PASSAGES IN THE *REPUBLIC*

Acknowledgements

My thanks are particularly due to a number of individuals. To Dr T. J. Saunders for a long and helpful criticism; to Mr Thomas Gould for both criticism and correspondence; to Professor W. K. C. Guthrie for comments on a number of particular points and for help with the bibliography. But I owe a particular debt to Professor H. D. Rankin, then Professor of Classics at Monash University, who arranged a seminar on translating the *Republic* which was attended by members of the Classics and Philosophy Departments of Melbourne and Monash Universities. This brought home to me very clearly the difficulties of those who use the *Republic* for teaching pupils who have no Greek, and it led me in particular to further discussion and correspondence with Dr John Howes of the Department of Philosophy at Melbourne. Dr Howes not only gave me a copy of his duplicated notes on the *Republic*, which contained many useful emendations of my version, but has also been kind enough to correspond with me about the more difficult philosophical passages, as well as to discuss them in galley proof. These passages owe much to his acute critical sense, and to a cooperation from which we have both learned.

To all those named I owe my grateful thanks for help generously given.

March 1974   DESMOND LEE

expedition was a disastrous failure and by 412 BC the men, ships, and money devoted to it were irretrievably lost. The strain of external disaster can sharpen internal conflict. There was constant opposition to the policies of the democratic leaders; to the better-off their external policy seemed folly and their internal policy exploitation of the rich for the benefit of the irresponsible masses. The shock of the Sicilian disaster gave the opposition, the 'oligarchs', their chance, and in 411 BC there was a revolution in which control passed to a Council of Four Hundred. This was succeeded a year later by the so-called Government of the Five Thousand, a constitution of which many moderates approved,[4] and which consisted, essentially, in limiting active citizen rights to those able to equip themselves with arms (the Athenian hoplite or infantryman was expected to provide his own arms), who proved to number about nine thousand, about a quarter to a third of the adult male population. The object was to keep political control in the hands of the more responsible elements in the population; but Athens depended on her sea-power, and could not deprive her poorer citizens, who served in the fleet, of a say in her affairs. The Government of the Five Thousand only lasted a year; the democratic constitution was then restored, and savage measures were taken by the democrats against their oligarchic opponents, so that the following six years have been described as a 'democratic terror'.[5] It was in this atmosphere of party bitterness that Plato reached his eighteenth year.

The final downfall of Athens came in 404 BC. It was again followed by an oligarchic revolution, this time carried through with the help of victorious Spartan arms. A commission of thirty was set up: in theory they were to frame a new constitution, but in practice they retained power in their own hands and used it to settle old scores, and any good they may have done initially in 'purging the city of wrongdoers' was forgotten in the savage tyranny that followed. It was a tyranny that lasted only eight months; the Thirty were driven out and subsequently killed, and the democratic constitution, in all essentials the same, restored. Athens was tired of extremists, and on the whole the restored democracy acted with sense and moderation. But it did one

thing which Plato could never forgive: in 399 BC it put Socrates
to death on a charge of impiety and corrupting the young. We
have Plato's own account, in his Seventh Letter, written when
he was an old man, of his experiences during these years when
he was a young man of about twenty-three to twenty-eight.
'I had much the same experience as many other young men. I
expected, when I came of age, to go into politics. The political
situation gave me an opportunity. The existing constitution,
which was subject to widespread criticism, was overthrown . . .
and a committee of Thirty given supreme power. As it happened
some of them were friends and relations of mine and they at
once invited me to join them, as if it were the natural thing for
me to do. My feelings were what were to be expected in a young
man: I thought they were going to reform society and rule justly,
and so I watched their proceedings with deep interest. I found
that they soon made the earlier regime look like a golden age.
Among other things they tried to incriminate my old friend
Socrates, whom I should not hesitate to call the most upright
man then living, by sending him, with others, to arrest a fellow-
citizen and bring him forcibly to execution; Socrates refused,
and risked everything rather than make himself party to their
wickedness. When I saw all this, and other things as bad, I was
disgusted and drew back from the wickedness of the times.

'Not long afterwards the Thirty fell, and the constitution was
changed. And again, though less keenly, I felt the desire to enter
politics. Those were troublous times, and many things were
done to which one could object; nor was it surprising that
vengeance should sometimes be excessive in a revolution. None
the less the returned democrats behaved, on the whole, with
moderation. Unfortunately, however, some of those in power
brought my friend Socrates to trial on a monstrous charge, the
last that could be made against him, the charge of impiety; and
he was condemned and executed.'

Plato was probably quite young when he first met Socrates –
at any rate, he represents him in his dialogues as being well
known to members of his family, for example Adeimantus and
Glaucon in the *Republic*. But whenever the meeting took place,
it was a turning-point in Plato's life. Socrates' position in

European thought is unique. He wrote nothing; yet through his followers, of whom others besides Plato wrote dialogues in which he figured, he has influenced subsequent thought as much as any other single person. In his later years, when Plato knew him, he devoted himself entirely to discussing ethical questions. The oracle at Delphi, in response to an inquiry by one of his admirers, had said that he was the wisest man in Greece. Socrates was sure that he was not, and set out to prove the oracle wrong. His method of doing so was to cross-question people he met about their beliefs, and about their ethical beliefs in particular, since for a Greek 'wisdom' had a strongly ethical meaning. And his questions would commonly take the form of asking people what they meant when they referred to common ethical qualities like self-control, or justice, or courage. He found that they did not really know, or at any rate could give no satisfactory account of what they meant; and to that extent he was wiser than they – he was aware of his ignorance, they were not. But the cure of ignorance is knowledge, and so, in addition to showing that conventional moral notions were frequently confused and contradictory, Socrates insisted on the importance in morals of knowledge. If only we *knew* what justice was, then, he argued, the problems of being just would be comparatively simple; and in quest of that knowledge he never ceased his constant examination of himself and of others.

But being cross-examined with the penetrating thoroughness of Socrates was not an experience which everyone enjoyed; and with all his uncompromising honesty and his essential piety, Socrates was hardly an orthodox character, and Athens had had enough of unorthodoxy. Socrates was linked in the minds of many Athenians with the scepticism and questioning of accepted beliefs which they blamed for their many misfortunes; what was needed, they felt, was a greater respect for the principles of conventional morality, not a questioning of them. In addition, many of Socrates' associates were of oligarchic sympathies, and this, though he was himself a man of no party, cannot have endeared him to the restored democracy. The amnesty declared after the defeat of the Thirty was honoured; but there were many who regarded him as an undesirable political influence.[6]

Whatever the immediate occasion of Socrates' trial or the details of his indictment, it was this mixture of feelings that led to his condemnation.[7]

But to Plato his condemnation meant a final disillusionment with contemporary politics. The passage from the Seventh Letter, already quoted, continues: 'When I considered all this, the more closely I studied the politicians and the laws and customs of the day, and the older I grew, the more difficult it seemed to me to govern rightly. Nothing could be done without trustworthy friends and supporters; and these were not easy to come by in an age which had abandoned its traditional moral code but found it impossibly difficult to create a new one. At the same time law and morality were deteriorating at an alarming rate, with the result that though I had been full of eagerness for a political career, the sight of all this chaos made me giddy, and though I never stopped thinking how things might be improved and the constitution reformed, I postponed action, waiting for a favourable opportunity. Finally I came to the conclusion that all existing states were badly governed, and that their constitutions were incapable of reform without drastic treatment and a great deal of good luck. I was forced, in fact, to the belief that the only hope of finding justice for society or for the individual lay in true philosophy, and that mankind will have no respite from trouble until either real philosophers gain political power or politicians become by some miracle true philosophers.'

This, in a few words, is the theme of the *Republic*, from which the concluding sentence is borrowed with some verbal alteration. Plato's decision to abandon a political career was finally taken during the ten years or so after Socrates' death. During those years he is said to have travelled, to Cyrene, to Egypt, and perhaps to Phoenicia; but much of his time must have been spent in Athens, as we are told that he served in the Athenian army in three campaigns. He also wrote his first dialogues, beginning with a defence of Socrates, continuing with others in which he explored the implications of Socrates' life and thought, and ending, probably, with the *Gorgias*, in which the life of philosophy and the life of politics are confronted and politics rejected; and the peculiar bitterness and emotional tension of this last dialogue show how difficult the decision had been.

In 388–387 BC Plato visited South Italy, perhaps in order to make the acquaintance of some of the Pythagorean philosophers living there. The Orphic–Pythagorean belief in the after-life and the Pythagorean emphasis on mathematics as a philosophic discipline certainly influenced him strongly, as can be seen in the *Republic*. From Italy he crossed to Sicily and visited the court of Dionysius I of Syracuse, where he learned something of tyranny at first hand. He also made the acquaintance of the tyrant's brother-in-law, Dion, who was deeply impressed with Plato's ideas about politics, and was later to try with him to turn the younger Dionysius into a philosopher ruler. But this visit to Syracuse did not last long. Plato is said to have offended Dionysius, who, according to one version of the story, sold him into slavery, from which he was redeemed by a friend.

He returned to Athens and there in about the year 386 BC founded the Academy, where he taught for the rest of his life. The Academy was founded as a school for statesmen. Plato had decided that nothing could be done with contemporary politics and contemporary politicians. He therefore decided to set up a school where a new type of politician could be trained, and where the would-be politician might learn to be a philosopher ruler. He probably did not expect any very immediate results; but he continued to hope, in his own phrase, that he might turn some statesmen into philosophers, and the Academy was always, under Plato, 'primarily a school of philosophic statesmen'.[8] It was not without a rival. A few years before, Isocrates had also founded a school at Athens. He was continuing the tradition started by the Sophists in the previous century. They were travelling teachers and lecturers, who appeared in the middle of the century in response to the demand for an education that went beyond the grounding in the works of the poets which formed the traditional Greek curriculum. They taught most things; but since success in life is what most men want, and since the ability to persuade your neighbour is always an important element in success, and was particularly important in the Greek

democracies, they all taught rhetoric, the art of self-expression
and persuasion. From this purely practical political interest
many of them proceeded to political and moral theory; Thrasymachus in Book I of the *Republic* is typical of this side of
their activity. And he was typical too in charging fees for his
instruction.[9] Isocrates himself criticized the Sophists of his day
for triviality and pretentiousness. None the less the rhetorical
training which he offered was a continuation of the educational
tradition which they started. He believed that a training in the
art of self-expression, in the art of composing and setting out a
coherent and persuasive argument, provided in itself an educational discipline that was, together with the literary studies
on which it was based, the best preparation for life. If it did not
teach morality directly, yet by inculcating standards of good
taste, and by the intellectual discipline which it involved, it
should give what was in effect a moral training. Isocrates therefore claimed that his methods turned out better men and better
statesmen than Plato's. And in fact a training in rhetoric
remained the standard form of higher education in the ancient
world.[10]

Plato's conception of higher education was quite different.
Briefly, he thought rhetoric superficial because it gave you the
means of expression without guarding you against its abuse.
The statesman must first know how society is to be run; exposition and persuasion come afterwards. For detail, we must
turn to the *Republic*, the product of Plato's early years in the
Academy. We cannot be certain of its exact date; but if we think
of it as having been written round about 375 BC we shall not be
far wrong. And the section on the education of the philosopher
(Part VIII in this edition) gives in substance the kind of study
that Plato thought suitable for the philosopher ruler, and the
kind of study – mathematics with an increasing stress on mathematical astronomy, and 'dialectic', comprising what we should
today call logic and philosophical discussion – that was in fact
pursued in the Academy. The *Republic*, in short, is a statement
of the aims which the Academy set itself to achieve.

The rest of Plato's life is only relevant to the reader of the
Republic in so far as it illustrates further the attitude to politics

already described. He never lost the hope of being able to turn a statesman into a philosopher. When Dionysius I died in 367 BC Plato's friend Dion, now chief minister in Syracuse, invited him to come and train Dionysius II, who was then twenty-eight, as a philosopher statesman. Plato went with hesitation and can have had few illusions about the difficulty of his task. His visit was not a success. Dionysius did not trust Dion, was old to enter on any course of training, and detested the mathematics Plato expected him to do. Dion was banished, and shortly afterwards Plato left. He had been there about a year. He returned in 361, on the invitation of Dionysius, who, in spite of his dislike of mathematics, seems to have liked Plato, or perhaps wanted to impress him. Plato hoped to reconcile Dion and Dionysius but he failed, and returned again to Athens after about a year. Dion resorted to force, and after various vicissitudes, during which he first tried to set up a constitution in which autocracy was tempered by legal checks and some degree of popular control, and then proceeded to repression and violence, he was finally assassinated in 354 BC. Plato did nothing to encourage him in these last years, though he continued to regard him with affection, felt his loss deeply, and regarded it as a disaster for Sicily. Dion was undoubtedly sincere, and a man of courage and enterprise; but he was something of a prig, and, like many political idealists, inclined to resort to force when the world refused to accept his ideals.[11]

Rather happier is the story of Plato's dealings with Hermias of Atarneus, of which we learn something in the Sixth Letter. Atarneus is in north-west Asia Minor, and Hermias had made himself a kingdom in that area. He had probably visited Athens, and been impressed by the teaching in the Academy. And when two members of the Academy, Erastus and Coriscus, returned to their native city of Scepsis, in his kingdom, he got in touch with them, and seems to have associated them in some way with him as advisers in his government. This is the situation assumed by the Sixth Letter, of which Hermias, Erastus and Coriscus are joint addressees, and it illustrates well 'what in Plato's view was the educational purpose of the Academy; it was to be a training-ground for rulers, not only maintaining a particular

political theory, but also furnishing practical guidance to such
of its members who had attained to political power'.[12] Hermias
is said to have turned his tyranny into a milder form of government on the advice of the philosophers, and to have handed
over Assos to them to rule in gratitude for what they had done.
It was at Assos that Aristotle joined them after Plato's death,
and when he in turn left to become tutor of Alexander the Great
he was carrying on the Platonic tradition.

All this took place during the last ten years of Plato's life and
shows his continued hope of finding the philosopher statesman.[13] And if he looked for him, at Syracuse and Atarneus, in
the courts of a tyrant, that was because he believed that political
control must always be in the hands of a minority, and where it
was concentrated in the hands of one man his conversion was
all that was necessary to bring philosophy to bear on the conduct
of affairs. With the continued hope of practical intervention
went the continued interest in theory; and Plato's last and
longest work, the *Laws*, is again about politics. It is the work
of his old age, said to have been left unrevised at his death in
347 BC. And though it makes more concessions to common
sense and practical possibilities than the *Republic*, it remains
very much akin to it in its general approach: those who have
read the *Republic* have read all the essential things Plato has to
say on basic principles. How he thought those principles could
be translated into action is less clear. Plato himself warns us in
several places in the *Republic* of the difference between theory
and practice (see esp. 472*a–d*, 592*a–b*), and it contains comparatively little about the detail of practical legal or constitutional arrangements (cf. 425*c–e*). In his later works, the
Politicus and *Laws*, he stressed the importance of law, and the
governmental and administrative arrangements in the *Laws* are
less austerely autocratic than those in the *Republic*. As Mr
Saunders has said, 'to suppose that Plato ever thought that the
Republic was attainable would be to suppose him capable not
merely of optimism or idealism but of sheer political naïveté';[14]
while Mr Crombie has similarly remarked that the *Republic* 'is
not intended to make a direct contribution to practical politics'.[15] It is better therefore to treat it as a statement of principles

whose application would vary with time and place and circumstance. Thus it may *in principle* be true that the position assigned to women in Greek society (and indeed in other societies) entailed a gross waste of the talents of 'one half of the human race' (*Laws* 781), and that if full use is to be made of them some means must be found to free women to a greater or lesser extent from the ties of family life; but what Plato thought to be possible *in practice* is to be found in the *Laws* rather than in the extremer statement in the *Republic*. It seems likely therefore that the *Laws* represents more nearly what, in practice, Plato at any time thought might be possible; there is a distinct similarity between what Dion at one point hoped to achieve and some of the provisions in the *Laws* (cf. p. xviii above). Plato believed indeed that politics was a sphere in which reason should operate; his fault was less that he failed to see that theory and practice must differ (though he did fail sometimes) than that he never allowed enough for the element of sheer unreason in politics and human affairs.

2. PLATO ON CONTEMPORARY SOCIETY

A good way to approach the *Republic* itself is to consider the actual types of Greek constitution of which Plato took account when he wrote it. These he deals with in Book VIII (Part IX in this edition), where he lists them as Timarchy, Oligarchy, Democracy, and Tyranny. The type of society which Plato calls timarchy is one which has no real parallel in modern experience, because it is, as he explicitly tells us, a sketch of the essential features of Spartan society. But for Plato Sparta was very important indeed, and some of the features of his own ideal society are borrowed from it. The Spartans were, briefly, a military aristocracy living among a subject population, the 'helots'. These helots were peasant serfs, cultivating the land for their Spartan masters; they could be called on to serve as light-armed troops in war, and might occasionally win their freedom, but in general they had neither rights nor privileges. Each year the magistrates declared war on them, so that to kill a Helot was an act of war and not of murder; and the Spartan secret police watched constantly for disaffection and killed mercilessly when they found it.

It was largely because they were a minority living thus in a subject population, which they always feared would revolt and which on several occasions did, that the Spartans followed their peculiar way of life. They were a military caste, in which the individual was rigidly subordinated to the community. Each citizen was a soldier, and education, marriage, and the details of daily life were all strictly regulated with a view to the mainten- ance of perfect military efficiency. 'When a child was born it was submitted to the inspection of the heads of the tribe, and if they judged it to be unhealthy or weak, it was exposed to die on the slopes of Mount Taygetos. At the age of seven years, the boy was consigned to the care of a state-officer, and the course of his education was entirely determined by the purpose of inuring him to bear hardships, training him to endure an exact- ing discipline, and instilling into his heart a sentiment of devotion to the State. The boys, up to the age of twenty, were marshalled in a huge school formed in the model of an army.'[16] Here they were under the instruction of young men aged twenty to thirty, who were not yet of age to be admitted to full citizen- ship. At twenty they entered on military service and were per- mitted to marry; but they must still live in barracks, and could only pay fugitive and stolen visits to their wives. At thirty they became full citizens, but though they might live at home, they must still dine together in common messes, to which each made a fixed contribution from the 'lot' which each Spartan owned, which he might not alienate, and which was cultivated for him by his helot serfs. 'Spartan discipline extended itself to women too ... The girls, in common with the boys, went through a gymnastic training; and it was not considered immodest for them to practise their exercises almost nude. They enjoyed a freedom which was in marked contrast with the seclusion of women in other Greek states. They had a high repute for chas- tity; but if the government directed them to breed children for the State, they had no scruples in obeying the command, though it should involve a violation of the sanctity of the marriage-tie.'[17]

No Spartan was allowed to possess wealth in the form of gold or silver, and they continued to use a clumsy iron coinage. Private luxury was forbidden, and Spartan simplicity was proverbial. The individual was entirely lost in the State; he had no life, no problems of his own. He lived in a camp, under military discipline, ready at any moment to fight for his country. It was not surprising that the Spartans were the most efficient soldiers in Greece, though they were not an aggressive people, but notoriously difficult to provoke to war.

These are the features of the Spartan system most relevant to a reader of the *Republic*. Its constitutional arrangements – a unique combination of hereditary kingship, popular election and magistrates, and council of elders – are comparatively unimportant, save perhaps in the respect paid to age and experience; membership of the Council was restricted to those over sixty, and in the *Republic* the status of full Guardianship cannot be reached till fifty. The Spartan system had many admirers in Greece; it had a completeness and aesthetic simplicity which appealed to the Greek mind, and made many Greeks admire it, though few would have wished to live under it. But if they admired they also criticized, and the criticisms Plato makes of timarchy are typical. He criticizes its exploitation of the lowest class as a wrong relation between ruler and ruled, liable to lead to serious disunity. He criticizes its intellectual limitations; Spartans thought little, and were proverbially slow-witted. They were also, in spite of their system, notoriously avaricious; and so timarchy is criticized for the institution of private property, forbidden in the ideal state, and the consequent growth of private greed. The Spartan and the timarchic society, in short, have the merits of discipline, respect for law, and courage, but are stupid, greedy, and brutal to their less privileged classes. Plato may to some extent have shared the admiration often felt by other Greeks for Sparta; but he was well aware of Spartan limitations.

The Spartan system was without parallel, except in Crete. But the other three types of social system which Plato mentions were common; indeed, one may generalize and say that in the fifth and fourth centuries BC the Greek cities were either democracies or oligarchies, interspersed here and there with tyrannies. During the Peloponnesian War the oligarchies had, on the whole, sided with Sparta, the democracies with Athens. And party differences, always acute in Greece, had been exacerbated by the suspicion that the other party was in league with the enemy. The suspicion was often justified, for both democrat and oligarch habitually put party first; and Plato's references to a party getting help against its opponents from outside (cf. 556e) and his deep horror of faction and disunity are a reflection of the bitterness of party strife, of which Thucydides has left the classic description. 'Both sides claimed to have the good of the community at heart, while both in fact aimed at political control, and in their struggle for ascendancy indulged in the worst excesses.'[18]

To Plato an oligarchy was a society in which power and prestige went with wealth; and since the wealthy are normally few, where power goes with wealth political control is in the hands of a minority. The days of hereditary aristocracy were long over, and though there were of course old families in most states (like Plato's own at Athens), birth had had to come to terms with wealth and, by itself, was, at the most, of limited political influence. So though Plato's characterization of oligarchy may be an over-simplification, it is not an unfair generalization to say that oligarchy in his day meant control by a wealthy minority. It was the controlling influence given to wealth that Plato particularly disliked. He had the deepest distrust of what would today be called the profit-motive and of the political influence of private wealth; and he thought that in an oligarchy (an 'acquisitive society') you were bound to get increasing exploitation of poor by rich, and an increasing degree of social maladjustment and disunity in consequence. He draws a picture of growing oppression met by growing bitterness and ending in revolution.

In his account of democracy Plato is drawing on his own experiences at Athens. And it is important to remember what a democracy in fifth- and fourth-century Greece was like. The Greeks lived in city-states, small communities consisting of a 'city' nucleus, with an area of agricultural land attached, from which the urban population drew all or most of its food-supply.

The populations varied in size, but were all small by the standards of a modern city. The population of Athens when Plato was born was perhaps 200–300,000, including men, women, and slaves; and Athens was by Greek standards large. In a democracy the vote was confined to the adult male citizen population. At Athens slaves may have numbered some 60–80,000, and there were perhaps 35–40,000 'metics', that is, residents who because they had been born elsewhere did not qualify for citizenship. The total voting population was about 35–45,000.[19] But within this body of voting citizens popular control was complete; for the Greeks never invented representative government, and the sovereign body at Athens was the Assembly, a mass meeting of all adult male citizens. Of course not all citizens bothered to attend regularly, and some whose homes were outside Athens itself found it difficult to do so. But in theory all could attend, and both in theory and in practice the Assembly was the sovereign body by which all political decisions must be taken. It was not practicable for it to meet too often (in theory it met ten times a year; in practice a good deal more often, though probably never more than once a week); and to carry on the business of state between meetings, to deal with much routine and financial business, and above all to draft business for meetings of the Assembly there was a Council of Five Hundred. This further sub-divided itself into Committees of fifty, each of which was responsible for carrying on public business during one-tenth of the year. But important as the Council's functions were, its powers were in practice limited by the rule that it should be chosen by lot from the citizen body, that membership was limited to one year, and that no citizen might hold membership more than twice. The Council thus never became a continuing body with a policy of its own: the Assembly remained supreme. Finally, the law-courts also were in popular control. Nearly all cases were tried before panels of jurors drawn by a system of mixed lot and election from the citizen body; and before these panels the magistrates could be tried for any irregularities committed during their year of office.

Such a complete system of popular control has never been known before or since. And it is important to remember that this, and not any form of modern representative government, is the background to Plato's comments on democracy. Its workings in fifth-century Athens and the criticisms then made of it have already been mentioned.[20] It involved, said Thucydides, 'committing the conduct of state affairs to the whims of the multitude',[21] and it has been described by a modern writer as government by perpetual plebiscite. But wide as the differences of background are, it would be quite wrong to dismiss Plato's criticisms of democracy as having no relevance today. If we are tempted to do so, we may perhaps remind ourselves that this is the first generation since his when a political leader can address and be seen by the whole electorate. What the ultimate effects of television will be we cannot yet say. But they have certainly brought political leaders far closer to the ordinary citizen, and opened up opportunities of a direct approach to the whole electorate that did not exist before in modern society.

What then are Plato's criticisms in the *Republic*? If we look first at the similes of the ship's captain (488*a–e*) and the large and powerful animal (493*b–e*), they seem to be twofold. First, that the people are bad judges in many political matters. The common man has no experience or expert knowledge of such things as foreign policy or economics, and to expect any very sensible judgement from him on such matters is to expect the impossible. He will judge on impulse, sentiment or prejudice, and though his heart may be sound (and Plato would have doubted whether even this was always true) his head will be muddled. This drawback might perhaps be overcome by good leadership. But here we come to the second criticism, that democracy encourages bad leadership. The people's judgement of their leaders is not always good, and they can't be trusted to make the best choice. But quite apart from that, the popular leader, dependent as he is for his position (and perhaps his income) on popular favour, will constantly be tempted to retain that favour by the easiest possible means. He will play on the likes and dislikes, the weaknesses and foibles of the public, will never tell them an unpleasant truth or advocate a policy that might make them uncomfortable. Like the modern advertiser and salesman, he is dependent on his public, and his position depends on selling them comfort and not telling them the truth. Sophist, salesman, and popular politician are on a par, and the people care little who their leaders are provided they 'profess themselves the people's friends' (558c). Popular leaders are as devoid of true knowledge as are the people they lead.

But that is not the whole story. The salient characteristic of democracy, we learn in Book VIII, is liberty – 'every individual is free to do as he likes' (557b). This gives democratic society a diversity and variety that are very attractive, but its effect is extremely disintegrating. There is a growing dislike of any authority, political or moral; fathers pander to their sons, teachers to their pupils, 'and the minds of the citizens become so sensitive that the least vestige of restraint is resented as intolerable' (563d). Where there is so little social cohesion dissension inevitably grows. Politically, it takes the form of a struggle between rich and poor which finally degenerates into class-war. The poor have no use for the rich except to squeeze taxes out of them; the rich retaliate, and 'the freedom which the democrat claims will be a freedom of the *two nations*, the rich and the poor, to fight it out between themselves who shall have the larger slice of the cake.'[22] Morally, it leads to greater and greater permissiveness; and Plato's description of a permissive society in Book VIII (562b ff.) has a particularly sharp-edged vividness.[23]

There remains tyranny. Plato describes it as arising out of the chaos and dissension into which democracy degenerates; and though he would probably not have wished to maintain that this was an invariable rule, yet some tyrants, ancient and modern, have certainly started as popular leaders, and extreme social disunity may by reaction produce an extreme authoritarianism. Of Plato's treatment of tyranny three things may be said. (1) For him tyranny is essentially a personal rule. The tyrant needs followers, of course, and at a fairly early stage in his career he secures a 'personal bodyguard', a private army bound to him by ties of common interest and guilt. But the basis of his power is a personal one; he is the Leader, and his rule is essentially the exercise of his own personal preferences, the arbitrary rule of an individual. (2) Tyranny has a peculiar self-destructiveness. The tyrant can brook no rival, which means

that prominent personalities among his followers must be elim-
inated; anyone who can or will stand up to him will be swept
away. And he needs constant wars, external crises, to distract
attention from his internal misrule; which is another source of
strain. (3) The tyrant is essentially what we should call a criminal
type: the beginning of Book IX (571a) is an analysis of the
similarity of the tyrant and the criminal, who are said to combine
the characteristics of drunkard, sex-maniac, and madman. The
tyrant, with his 'master passion', is barely sane, and his life is
one of criminal indulgence. Fielding had the same thought in
Jonathan Wild.

There is little need to comment on this analysis. The domi-
nance of a dictator's personality, his private army, the purges
among his followers are familiar. We might comment that his
private life need not always be as wildly dissolute as Plato
suggests; he is more formidable, though not necessarily less
criminal or violent if it is not. But we still associate autocracy
with repression and violence.

The purpose of this section has been to show, by reviewing
Plato's analysis of contemporary forms of society, what he
thought the major social evils of his time were; for it was to
combat those evils that his own proposals were put forward.
We may summarize as follows. In timarchy (Sparta) Plato saw
two major evils. The evil of a split community in which one
section exploits and holds down the remainder by force; and
the evil of lack of intelligence – the Spartan might have many
good qualities but he simply had not the intellectual capacity to
know what he was doing; indeed he mistrusted the intellect and
everything to do with it. In oligarchy the cardinal fault is desire
for wealth (a fault which was already apparent in timarchy).
Wealth as a social motive is to be mistrusted, and a ruling class
which is devoted to its wealth, and which owes its position and
power to wealth, will substitute exploitation for government.
In democracy there is a radical lack of cohesion, because there
is no proper respect for authority, moral or political. Democratic
government is weak government, which plays on the weaknesses
of the common man instead of giving him the leadership he
needs; and it is liable to degenerate into a bitter class-struggle

between haves and have-nots. Finally, in tyranny we see the danger that the violent and criminal instincts, normally kept under control, will get out of hand. The criminal is present in all societies (certainly in oligarchy and democracy); but in tyranny he has come into his own, and society is run by its criminal elements with the arch-criminal in charge. We may briefly sum up by saying that disunity, incompetence and violence, which he had seen at Athens and at Syracuse, were the main dangers against which Plato thought society must be protected.

3. THE MAIN IDEAS OF THE *REPUBLIC*

The title *Republic* is doubly misleading to a modern reader. In the first place it suggests that Plato might be writing about a 'republic' in the modern sense, that is, about a particular form of government. In fact the title in Greek can mean indifferently 'constitution', 'state', or 'society'; the Latin translation is *respublica*, a word bearing originally the same sort of meanings, and only coming later to bear the narrower meaning of a particular *kind* of constitution, the meaning it now bears in the English transliteration. Plato, in fact, was writing about society or the state, and that is what his title means. The mistranslation is now hallowed by time, and it would be pedantic to change it; but explanation is required.

But when that explanation has been given, the modern reader may still find something rather different from what it leads him to expect. He will expect, in a work on politics, some references to ethics or education; they are topics which recur constantly both in political practice and theory. But he will also expect a great deal of discussion of constitutional and legal matters. What is to be the sovereign body? How is its sovereignty to be exercised? What are to be the relations of legislature, executive and judiciary? How is executive power to be exercised? What subordinate bodies or organizations are there to be, and what powers are they to have? These are the sort of questions which he will expect to find examined. In fact, when he turns to the *Republic*, he will hardly find them mentioned at all. There is of

course a good deal of discussion of social and political matters;
for example the discussion of contemporary forms of society
with which section 2 of this Introduction has been concerned,
and which occupies most of Books VIII and IX (Part IX). And
Parts II, IV and VI deal largely with political and social topics.
But even in these parts of the book Plato is more interested in
principles than in details, and we find moral considerations
constantly coming in. And the rest of the work is largely devoted
to what we should regard as ethics (Parts I and V), education
(Parts III and VIII), theory of knowledge (Part VII), art (Part X),
and religion (Part XI). For this there are several reasons. The
Greek city-state, as we have seen, was a comparatively simple
affair; there was less constitutional machinery to talk about.
And just because the political community was smaller and more
intimate the Greeks distinguished less sharply than we do
between ethics and politics. We tend to think that there is a
sphere of private conduct where the state is not concerned,
where, as we should say, it is a matter for the individual conscience; but, on the whole, that way of thinking is foreign to the
Greeks. The 'ancient Greek view' was 'that the law of the state
is the source of all standards of human life, and that the virtue
of the individual is the same as the virtue of the citizen.[24] That
is perhaps an overstatement; but it serves to bring out the
difference of the Greek approach, an approach which did not
prevent the Greeks from being violently individualistic in practice, but which did make them link politics and ethics more
closely than we do. But there are further more particular reasons.
The *Republic*, as we have seen, was written in the years after
the founding of the Academy: the Academy's aim was to train
philosopher statesmen, and the *Republic*, as a statement of that
aim, was bound to deal at length with education. Plato had
decided that the world's ills would not be cured till philosophers
ruled; the education of philosophers therefore becomes the most
important of political activities. If they can be educated rightly,
and given power, the details of administration can safely be left
in their hands – this Plato explicitly says.[25] For all these reasons
the *Republic* was bound to deal at length with education, and
with the moral principles underlying the organization of society,

as well as with the general lines on which it should, ideally, be organized; which leaves little room for more practical details, much as we should often like to have them. We have therefore a book which is as much about ethics and education and philosophy as about politics in the strict sense. To some of Plato's ideas in these fields we now turn.

(1) Ethics

The *Republic* starts with a moral and political question: what is justice? The Greek word *dikaiosunē* is a wide one and covers both individual and social morality, and from the start therefore the inquiry is concerned with both individual and community, both ethics and politics. It soon becomes clear that the question that is being asked is: What is the basis of social and moral obligation? Why should I be either law-abiding or moral if I don't feel like it? More simply still: Why should I be good? The problem is stated in three stages. First Socrates shows that the conventional view that justice is 'giving a man his due' is inadequate. Then Thrasymachus comes in with what is, in effect, a flat denial of the conventional view. He is, as we have seen, a typical Sophist and is meant to stand as the representative of a line of thought, not uncommon at the end of the fifth century, which rejected conventional morality as a sham, and substituted self-interest. This section of the argument is often rather complicated (see the section headings). Its purpose is to advance the argument a stage by showing that though conventional morality may often be muddled and inadequate, it is equally unsatisfactory to reject it as a sham. After Thrasymachus has been reduced to silence, Glaucon and Adeimantus, who remain the chief respondents throughout the rest of the dialogue, say that they are still unsatisfied and that they are going to restate his case for him. And what they in effect ask Socrates to do is to show them that morality is more than a matter of social approval. Glaucon puts the case that morality is a matter of expediency, an agreement made for mutual convenience, that we are only moral because it pays us or it is our part of a bargain, but that given the chance we should all behave extremely badly (358e–359 and note 46): Adeimantus reinforces him by stressing the comparatively mercenary motives normally advanced for good behaviour. The problem they put to Socrates is to show that, quite apart from motives of reward or social approval, morality is preferable in itself to immorality, right to wrong.

Socrates' immediate reply is to say that the problem is too difficult to solve in the individual; he must look at it 'in larger letters' in society. And so there follows in Parts II, III, and IV the first sketch of the ideal society. But when he returns to the individual in Part V he tries to answer the question in the way that he has been asked; he tries, that is, to show, by an analysis of the elements in the human mind, that its well-being, full development and happiness are to be secured by doing right and not by doing wrong, to prove thereby that virtue is its *own* reward. And though other rewards, including rewards and punishments in the life after death, are brought in in Book X, they are a merely secondary consideration.

The elements in the mind which the moralist has to take into account are according to Plato threefold (see opening note to Part V, section 2); and it has been suggested that this threefold division is a more or less arbitrary reflection into the individual of the three classes into which his state is organized. The matter is hardly as simple as that. The three elements in the mind and the three classes in society may have a common source in the Orphic–Pythagorean tradition; but one is unlikely to have produced the other directly. But the criticism, though an oversimplification, does bring out a feature of Plato's thought – his tendency to argue from the state or community to the individual rather than vice versa. He is inclined to decide first what he thinks would socially be desirable, and then to cut the individual to fit it, rather than to think of the individual first and then consider how his needs can be met. Though, therefore, it is unlikely that the three elements in the mind were invented to fit the three classes in the state, the movement of thought, from society to individual, is significant.

That the threefold division is not, however, without foundation in experience is suggested in the headnote to Part V, section 2. But it must be regarded as an attempt to classify the elements involved in moral conflict and decision, and not as a full account of human psychology. There are large parts of human experience (such as sensation and perception) which it does not attempt to touch, and it is better treated as a classification of motives for action, as which it has some merits, than as an exhaustive or scientific analysis of the mind, which it certainly is not. The main criticism that can be made of it from this point of view is that it omits any consideration of what we call the will. But we are often extremely hazy about what we mean by the will; it is, to the ordinary man, little more than a label for the fact that we often have to make an *effort* to make ourselves do things. And Plato would probably claim to have sufficiently recognized that fact in his element of Reason, which clearly includes not only the faculty of deliberation, but also the ability to decide and to act on our decisions however much effort that calls for. We all know the difference between acting from deliberate choice, acting from a generous impulse, and acting on animal appetite; and that is the difference which Plato is trying to express.

His answer to the question 'What is justice?' is that, in the individual, it consists in keeping a proper balance between the three elements; each will then be 'doing its own job' (cf. 433*d*). True morality consists, in fact, in giving due satisfaction to the different elements in us, and preventing any of them dominating at the expense of the others. Physical desire, ambition and intellect must all have their due and proper fulfilment, and find their proper place in the good life.

That, in short, is Plato's solution of the problem of individual morality. And there are two questions, at any rate, which it may prompt us to ask. (1) Is the threefold classification of impulses really adequate? It has been suggested that it is not without foundation, and that the criticism that it ignores the will can to some extent be met. But how adequate and how useful is it all the same? How far does it do justice to the complexities of moral choice? (2) The formula as it stands, though it tells us a great deal, leaves a good many blanks. What is the 'proper' place of intellect and appetite? What is the satisfaction 'due' to each? How is the balance to be struck? Plato's own answer the reader must glean from the text. But one is left with the impression that it would be a good deal more ascetic than the ordinary man would find comfortable. The Guardians' life is austere, to say the least of it; and little as we know of the life of the third class, what we do know does not suggest that it will be luxurious (cf. 421d–e, 422a). Clearly we can fill in the formula in different ways; but Plato, though he has no wish to eradicate physical appetite, took, on the whole, a low view of physical pleasures (cf. 580e ff.), and his own interpretation would have been an austere one. He was always something of a Puritan and never seems to have looked very kindly on the ordinary man's pleasures.

Of the nature of justice in society as opposed to the individual little need be said. Justice is defined as 'minding your own business', that is, fulfilling your proper function in society. When all are doing that there is no room for the most dreaded of all evils, disunity. And there are few who would quarrel in general terms with the view that social justice has been achieved when each class and element in society is fulfilling its proper function. But again the formula leaves many blanks. What are the different classes or elements in society? What is their proper function, and what is their due? Does not Plato lay himself open to Sir Karl Popper's charge that, under this formula, 'The criterion of morality is the interest of the state. Morality is nothing but political hygiene'?[26] But these are questions that are largely political, and the discussion of Plato's answers to them must for the moment be postponed.

(2) Education

Plato's views of education can largely be left to speak for themselves. He thought it of paramount importance, and, since commentaries on him have nearly all been written by dons or schoolmasters, he has been much praised for so thinking. Without in any way questioning the importance of education, one may perhaps ask whether it really has quite the power to transform society that Plato and others have thought. There are so many other influences that determine both society and the individual; and anyone engaged in the business of teaching who keeps his sense of proportion will perhaps view his work with a little greater scepticism and a little more saving humility.

But there are one or two other points, besides the conviction of its importance, which are noteworthy in what Plato has to say on the subject.

He was the first person to formulate what we should today call a university course. For that is what his course of further education is (Part VIII), even though it is spread out over a far longer period; and the Academy, though it may have had a rival in the school of Isocrates and predecessors in the Sophists, was the first university in Europe. The literary education which precedes it (Part III) is the equivalent of our secondary, and the earlier stage of learning to read and write which that implies the equivalent of our primary education. So that we may say that our three stages are all, explicitly or implicitly, already recognized in the *Republic*.

As far as its curriculum is concerned, we may say that after the primary stage, in which reading and writing are the important elements, the main subjects studied in school are literary and humanistic. The Greek boy who studied Homer and the other poets, and the citizen of the *Republic* who studied Plato's specially prepared books, was studying the literature and history of his country, and the equivalent of our Bible. And in the course of that study he would expect to learn something of the culture, history and traditions of his own and of neighbouring peoples, as well as the accepted moral and religious beliefs. At the university stage Plato's Guardians transferred their attention to mathematics, science and philosophy. For that is what is meant in modern terms by the study of mathematics and 'dialectic' which Plato outlines. The natural sciences were little developed in his day, and though what he says about astronomy (528*e*, 529*a*) reads oddly today, it was the insistence in the Academy on the application of mathematical methods to astronomy which created it as a science; and the exact sciences[27] would almost certainly feature in Plato's curriculum if he were drawing it up today. While 'dialectic' simply means philosophy.

So much for intellectual content. But Plato was as concerned to train the character as the mind, and throughout the account of the secondary stage of education he is insistent that its object is moral training as much as intellectual; the section on physical education ends (411e–412a) with an emphatic assertion that physical and intellectual education are not concerned to deal one with the mind and one with the body, but are jointly directed to the training of character. And in so far as the training of character has been a distinctive feature in English education, Plato would approve and perhaps claim to have had some influence on it.

But in all he does the educator should remember that his aim is not to 'put into the mind knowledge that was not there before' – though he may do that within limits – but to turn the mind's eye to the light so that it can see for itself (518a–e); his business, in other words, is not to stick thoughts into his pupils' heads but to make them think for themselves. This is perhaps the best-known passage on education in the *Republic*, because of the importance and truth of the principle which it states.

We turn to the actual provision of education. It must be provided exclusively by the state. Anything of such crucial importance cannot be left to private initiative. And because of its crucial importance in forming the minds of the young, the curriculum must also be controlled and defined by the State. Plato thought, for reasons which he explains at length in Part III, that most current Greek literature was highly unsuitable as a medium of education. He therefore proposed a rigid control which should apply not only to school text-books, but to all art and literature.[28] There is to be no expression of opinion other than what the State allows; the arts must be the servant of what social order requires. That is what the long sections on literature and art amount to.

That the arts have their place in education, and so far, by implication, a social function we should agree. But our own habit of thought regards freedom of expression as an essential liberty, and freedom to teach what one chooses as no less essential. We should agree with Plato that it is for the State to provide education; but provision need not imply detailed control, and few would wish it to censor text-books and determine the content of the curriculum. The classic arguments for liberty of thought and expression were stated by J. S. Mill.[29] It is enough to point the contrast.

But we may note two things. First, that the degree of central control of the curriculum today varies in different parts of the world, and that whatever we think that degree of control should be, we are left with many questions to answer. What should the content of teaching be, and what its objectives for society and for the individual? Plato can at least claim to have started the debate.

Second, that Plato himself, with his strong poetic sense, was obviously uneasy about his treatment of the poets, and adds in Book x a kind of justificatory appendix. There is no space here to discuss the aesthetic theory he puts forward. In the *Laws* (Book II, 654 ff., Book VII) the arts are still subordinated to social purposes; but elsewhere, notably in the *Ion, Symposium* and *Phaedrus*, the approach is different. There Plato speaks of artistic and other creation as something that cannot be reduced to rule; it is a form of madness, but a 'madness' that is god-given (*Phaedrus* 244a). That madness he must have experienced in himself, and known that it cannot be simply subjected to sober social purposes; the very power of the arts makes them dangerous. The tension is resolved in the *Republic* and *Laws* in favour of social order. But Plato knew very well that beside Apollo, the god of order, there stood Dionysus; and that even Apollo's priestess at Delphi spoke under the influence of divine madness.

(3) Philosophy and Religion

Because the ideal state is to be governed by philosophers, philosophy inevitably plays a large part in the *Republic*; it is the central theme of Parts VII and VIII. But the treatment of it is always rather allusive. Plato is concerned rather with the place of philosophy in the educational curriculum, the kind of studies which lead to it, its usefulness and its effects on the character, than with a detailed exposition of his philosophic beliefs. Their relevant features are brought out in a series of similes – the Sun, the Divided Line and the Cave; but the *Republic* does not attempt to expound the Platonic philosophy in detail.

The most important feature of that philosophy, for the purpose of the *Republic*, is the belief in two realms or levels of
reality: the realm of change and appearance, the everyday, physical world in which we live; and the realm of the forms, a realm
of externals and absolutes. For further explanation the reader
must be referred to the sections in question (especially Part VII,
section 5, 6, 7, and Part VIII, section 3) and the introductory
headings to them. But the following more general comments
may be made.

Though the training described in Part VIII is one of rigorous
intellectual discipline, a training, as we might say, in the technique of exact thinking, the object at which it is aimed is a
matter of personal experience. The teacher, as we have seen,
turns the pupil's eye to the light; the pupil is not a passive
recipient of knowledge, but must grasp the truth for himself.
This applies particularly to the truths of philosophy, about
which Plato writes in the Seventh Letter: 'the truths of philosophy are not expressible as are those of other subjects; after
long study and discussion under the guidance of an experienced
teacher, a spark may suddenly leap, as it were, from mind to
mind, and the light of understanding so kindled will then feed
itself.'[30]

This is partly the expression of an educational truth and
an educational method. But it goes further. For the ultimate
objective of the philosophic training is religious, and the language of the Seventh Letter and of the *Republic* is the language
of religious experience. The vision of the form of the good is
not entirely dissimilar to what others have called the vision of
God. That is not to say that the Form of the Good and God are
to be identified; they probably should not be, though scholars
have disputed the point. But the experience is religious; it has
the characteristics that William James noted in all mystical
experience,[31] it is a state of knowledge and yet incommunicable
in ordinary language. And it is therefore appropriate that the
Republic should end with a religious myth. For whatever Plato
may have thought about the details of the myth, it is clear that
it is intended to express in pictorial and poetic form the general
philosophic and religious conviction of the *Republic* that the

temporal is only the shadow of the eternal, and that the human soul is responsible not simply to itself but to God.

(4) Society and Politics

What Plato has to say on these topics can conveniently be considered under three headings: the Class System, Property and the Family, and the Philosopher Ruler.

The Class System. Plato arrives at this from the principle that in any society men will group themselves according to their occupations. In the economic sphere you will get producers, merchants, traders and so on. The economic structure of the society of which he was thinking, and in which he lived, is elementary; and he is thinking of occupations and not income-groups. But the principle is clear enough. He goes on to apply it in the sphere of war and government. The armies of Greece in the fifth century were citizen-armies; but the fourth century saw the rise of the professional soldier, and that may, in part, have suggested to Plato that his Guardians, who first appear as a military group, should be specialists in war. But it soon appears that they are to perform the functions not only of soldiering but also of government, and they are sub-divided into Rulers proper and Auxiliaries, who correspond, roughly, to Government and Army–Executive–Police (opening note to Part IV, section 1), as opposed to the rest of the population, who make up the third class. Plato's three classes in fact are not so much three as two, one of which is further sub-divided.

Many object at once to this division of society into three distinct classes, with a definite order of subordination between them. The words 'hierarchic society' or 'caste system' are used to describe it disapprovingly. Plato might reply that the quarrel is to some extent about words. Any society, he might say, is bound to show economic groupings; few societies can do without their professional army; and in all societies someone has to give orders and someone obey, which means that in practice there will be a minority of people issuing orders or seeing they are obeyed (the government) and a majority obeying them (the rest). What people differ about is whether and to what extent these primary groupings should be complicated by further class-divisions based on birth or wealth, and how the governmental minority should in fact be chosen. To Plato's views on these last two topics, which are what the objectors really dislike, we shall return. Meanwhile it is important to see just what his three classes and their mutual relations are.

About his third class he does not tell us a great deal. They are not in any sense a proletariat or working class. They comprise all those engaged in economic activities – farmers, manufacturers, traders, rich or poor (for they are allowed to own property). Their function is to provide for the material and economic needs of the community. Their virtue is obedience, and it is pretty clear that they will be under strict control. The Guardians will see that there is no excessive wealth and poverty among them (422*a*), and will presumably direct and control all their activities. For they are the body of the governed whom the governing minority administers.

The governing minority, the Guardians, discharge between them, primarily, the functions of government and army. But that is, as already indicated, too narrowly imprecise a description. The function of the Rulers is to govern, that is to say, to take all those decisions of policy which it is the business of government to take. The Auxiliaries' function is 'to assist the Rulers in the execution of their decisions', or 'to enforce the decisions of the Rulers' (414*b*). We must think of them as combining the functions of civil service, military and police; as being, that is, charged with the execution and implementation (if necessary by force) of government decisions. And if we think of a society in which there is a government by full-time, trained experts, who are precluded by law from any other function, and who have a body of trained civil servants, together with the necessary police and military forces to assist them, we get some idea in modern terms of this part of Plato's proposals.

The two top classes are, as we have seen, really sub-divisions of a single class. They share the same way of life, and are put through the same elaborate system of training and promotion outlined in Part VII. There are a large number of promotion bars to be passed, quite enough to grade the Auxiliaries for their various functions, while leaving a small homogeneous Ruler class to emerge at the top; but all have started with equal opportunities. The third class have no say in matters of government; but Plato constantly emphasizes that the Rulers have their interests at heart (the difference between timarchy and the ideal is that in timarchy oppression has replaced benevolent government) and the Rulers govern with the willing consent of the governed (431e). This relationship is set out in the Foundation Myth (415a–c).

Two further criticisms may be considered here. First, Aristotle's criticism that we are not in fact told nearly enough about the third class. And though Plato is deliberate in his avoidance of detail, it is difficult not to agree that the criticism is just. There are too many essential questions left unanswered. The second criticism is that Plato's Guardians are a 'hereditary caste'. The critic, of course, assumes that this, if true, is itself a condemnation. But his interpretation is wrong. Plato emphatically asserts (415c) that promotion from the third class is not only possible but an important feature of his scheme, just as demotion from the two upper classes is also; and in Book VIII we are told that it is failure in this matter that leads to the change to timarchy. It is, of course, extremely hard to see how the scheme is to work, as Aristotle again remarks. Cornford[32] suggests that all classes must share a common education up to the age of eighteen, in order that the Rulers can promote and demote; certainly the choice would have to be made by then, and this would be one way of making it, and would be in tune with Plato's views on the importance of education. But there is nothing in the text to suggest it, and we cannot speak with certainty. There is, however, no reason to doubt that Plato means what he says about promotion and demotion (see note on promotion, demotion and infanticide in Part VI, section 2). The real point is that what he wants is an aristocracy of talent. He thinks, as we shall see, that he can get this largely by breeding, as one breeds race-horses; but the breeding process is not infallible, and so there must be provision for both promotion and demotion, there must be both snakes and ladders, even though we don't know exactly what the rules are to be. Belief in an aristocracy of talent may be wicked; but it is not the same as belief in a hereditary caste.

Property and the Family. This brings us to Plato's views on property and the family. And the provisions he makes under this head apply only to the two upper classes, the Guardians. The third class, we presume, live under the normal arrangements. But among the Guardians both private property and the family are to be abolished. Plato's dislike of both has one main cause. He thought that private interests and private affections distracted a man from his duties to the community; and both are centred in the family. As far as the abolition of private property is concerned, we have seen already how deeply he distrusted the desire for wealth as a social motive. He thought that it led to nothing but disunity, that pursuit of riches corrupted government and disrupted society, and that as a criterion of suitability for political power they were worthless. He accordingly proposed to limit the differences of wealth in his third class very strictly, and by abolishing property altogether in his Guardian class to eliminate the profit-motive from political influence.

On the abolition of private property among the Guardians Aristotle[33] made comments that have become classic. You do not, he pointed out, necessarily get rid of evils by changing institutions; the fault may lie in human nature and not in the system of private property. The instinct to possess is natural, and, provided it does not degenerate into selfishness, a source of proper pleasure; property which is common is apt to be treated not with the care given to something which is our own but with the carelessness so often shown to what is other people's. The argument is on a simple level, but anticipates modern controversy between individualism and collectivism.[34]

Plato's reasons for abolishing the family are slightly more complex. He dislikes the distraction of family affections, but he has other reasons as well. He starts from the principle of the equality of the sexes. By this he means that, though men and women have different functions in the process of reproduction, they should, apart from that difference, follow the same careers, share the same education and have the same opportunities. Women may not always be able to do quite such heavy or energetic work as men, as for example in war; but within the limitations imposed by their physique equality is to be absolute.

It follows logically that they must be exempted so far as possible from family responsibilities. For under the family system what stands in the way of the kind of sex equality which Plato wants is the domestic responsibility for running a household and bringing up a family. With complete logic therefore he removes that responsibility by abolishing the family and substituting for it a system of state nurseries. This has the further advantage that it makes possible the breeding of Guardians on scientific lines. The production of children is a matter of such vital importance to the state that it is clearly undesirable to leave it to the unregulated operation of private enterprise and individual affection (this point of view comes out in the *Laws* too); Plato therefore arranges for sexual intercourse to be strictly regulated, and confined to certain regular 'marriage festivals', when suitable partners will be mated, with a view to producing the best type of Guardian, just as one breeds dogs or race-horses.[35]

The details of Plato's arrangements may seem to us quite impracticable. Perhaps the best way to get them into proper perspective is to refer to the scheme to be found in Aldous Huxley's *Brave New World*. There child-bearing has been abolished entirely, and babies are produced in laboratories, where they are fitted by heredity and subsequent conditioning for the different types of occupation required by the community. The physical relationship between men and women is reduced to a matter of private pleasure and shorn of its emotional implications. These arrangements would have seemed to Plato admirable. Under them the whole business of the production and education of citizens becomes a matter of exact control and knowledge; men and women can be put on a footing of complete equality, with the necessity for periodic child-bearing, which still remained in the *Republic*, finally removed, and with the tiresome business of the physical relationship reduced to a minimum of importance.

For Plato's attitude to the physical relationship seems to have been one of indifference tempered by dislike. He knew the instinct as an unruly one; but he always ranked physical pleasures low and believed that unruly instincts were there to be restrained, though he recognized that the sex instinct, like others, must have its outlet. And his experience of emotional attachments between people appears to have been confined to friendships between men. Of love between the sexes, so far as we know, he had no experience, nor would he have valued it highly. In that he was, to some extent, no doubt, influenced by the lower status which women held in Greek society. This has been much exaggerated, and Professor Kitto has written on the subject with refreshing good sense,[36] nor need we suppose that the kind of attachment between husband and wife to which Aristotle's will bears evidence was uncommon. Plato's attitude was more personal than typically Greek. Nevertheless, his desire for equality between the sexes was no doubt in part a protest against the very limited scope women were given in contemporary Athenian society.[37] So far most modern opinion would agree with him, and it may be said that his scheme looks forward to the greater freedom women enjoy in our own day, and perhaps anticipates the objectives of the Women's Liberation movement. Yet one may doubt the desirability or possibility of the exact similarity of role which Plato demanded. To sweep aside the physiological differences as unimportant, and ignore the psychological differences they entail, is to be in danger of ignoring women's special excellences. To free women, to any extent, from family ties is to free them to do other things; but if you merely expect them to do the same things as men, they are likely, as Plato in effect said, to end up as inferior men.[38] Is it not better to recognize the difference rather that pretend it does not exist?

From the more strictly eugenic standpoint, neither Plato's nor Aldous Huxley's proposals are very much like practical politics. But Plato might well point to our increasing knowledge of heredity as an indication that he was on the right lines, and look forward to the day when greater knowledge would give us greater control. How that control was exercised he would not much care, provided that it was used to breed better citizens, but he would certainly be interested by, and perhaps quote in his own justification, any evidence that there is a hereditary element in talent. In practice, however, he would have to agree that the family is not likely to disappear, and he retains it, under strict supervision, in the *Laws*.

But he is open to another more general criticism. He assumes that family affections and loyalties can only be a source of weakness: that the good family man must be a worse citizen. Family loyalties can, of course, be distracting. But the assumption is an absurd one, though typical of Plato's love of uniformity. He could not see that the greater loyalty draws strength and force from the lesser which it contains, or that his attempt to diffuse family and other loyalties and affections through the community (463c–e) could only lead, as Aristotle pointed out, to their dilution and weakening. He was unable, as Aristotle again said, to distinguish between unity and uniformity.[39]

The Philosopher Ruler. The Philosopher Ruler is the central theme of the *Republic*; it is the aim of its whole educational curriculum to produce him, and much that has already been said has dealt with him directly or by implication. At the end of the long course of training there is left a small class (how large we are not told) of those who have survived all tests and mastered the whole curriculum; they are the Philosopher Rulers. They represent the highest talent, are given the highest training and are put at the disposal of the state. They do not serve the state because they want to, they are philosophers who have seen the supreme vision and would prefer to spend their time in philosophy. But they have a duty to their fellow-men, and that they discharge by doing the work of government for which their training has fitted them; they are a dedicated minority ruling in the interests of all.

There is a perennial attraction in this conception of the highest talent put at the disposal of the community, of the ruler whose heart is in heaven dedicating himself to the service of society. We should respect Plato's vision, but not forget its dangers. We may ask first, on the plane of a humdrum realism, whether the long course of abstract studies which Plato proposes is really the best training for dealing with men and affairs; and whether the method of selection he proposes, based largely on proficiency in abstract subjects – examinations in mathematics, science and philosophy up to the age of thirty-five – is a sensible one. Is not this one of the fallacies to which educators are prone – the belief that people who do well in their courses will do well at everything, and that the longer they spend on them the better they will do? Is not a wider curriculum and a lot more practical experience more likely to produce a better ruler?

More important is the objection that government by a self-perpetuating minority of experts is in any case undesirable, and in particular 'undemocratic'. We have seen that recruits for the course which begins at the age of twenty are drawn from all the classes, though the vast majority of them come from the top two, because they are bred for the job. They are chosen by the Rulers on their merits: there is no question of democratic election, because, as we have seen, Plato thought that as bad a way of choosing rulers as choosing them by their wealth. And before we dismiss Plato's scheme out of hand, we should remember the methods we use today for picking people for administrative and managerial training, the tests of character and ability applied by the Civil Service Commissioners, for example, and reflect that those are the modern parallels to what he proposes. He is concerned to pick people for their competence for the job, and not for characteristics, such as wealth or persuasiveness, that have no necessary connection with that competence. Indeed he might well, at this point, put some questions to us. He would remind us that society today is infinitely more complicated than it was in his day. He would ask us how we think this increasingly complicated structure is to be administered if not by men and women who have the character and competence needed. He could then point out that the amount of ability available in any community is limited, and perhaps quote modern statistics in support of this. And if men are not equal in talent and abilities, surely no society can afford to work on the assumption that they are, least of all modern society. Must we not do our best to ensure that the available talent is most profitably employed, that differences of talent are recognized and the highest talent put to the best use? 'Which brings you back,' he might conclude, 'to the philosopher ruler.' For, as we have seen, what Plato wanted was an aristocracy of talent, and we must see the principles behind his detail. And if we want a modern brief description of his kind of society, 'Managerial Meritocracy' is perhaps the nearest we can get; it emphasizes the need for qualifications and competence in government, though it leaves out many of the other elements in the Platonic solution.

More fatal is the objection that the conception of a philosopher ruler encourages us to look for a degree of knowledge and integrity which are in fact not to be found. The knowledge of all human beings is limited, and for any group of them to think that they have the key to all human problems is presumptuous and absurd. But that is what the philosopher ruler is supposed to have; and certain types of doctrinaire are liable to a similar illusion. Yet to put the government of human affairs into the hands of any class of supposed experts is to ask from them more than they can possibly give. And quite apart from limitations of knowledge, there is the moral problem. Power is a corrupting influence, a corruption which few can resist; and on the whole political leaders are not men of more than average moral integrity – we are perhaps lucky if they are as good as that. It is better to act on that assumption, and to limit power lest it should be abused, than to look for the perfect ruler who needs no such limitation. The argument against Plato's system, in fact, is not that it trusts the common man too little but that it trusts his rulers too much.

4. FINAL ASSESSMENT

Any final assessment of the *Republic* is very difficult. The older generations of commentators were perhaps too apt to idealize Plato; they partly ignored and partly excused anything with which they disagreed, and it is sometimes not easy to discover from them that Plato was not a good nineteenth-century liberal. Hardly a note of criticism will be found, for example, in such an admirable standard commentary as A. E. Taylor's *Plato*. Commentators during the last fifty years have become more critical. Professor Fite, in *The Platonic Legend*, deprecates earlier idealization, and finds Plato to be an aristocrat, something of a snob, and the advocate of a restrictively organized society. With the growth of totalitarian regimes, criticism became sharper, but often, because of contemporary anxieties, less balanced. Mr Crossman, trying in his *Plato Today* to assess how Plato would have looked at our contemporary world, sums him up as a reactionary who encouraged in practice the 'dictatorship of the Virtuous Right' and who advocated the unscrupulous use of propaganda.[40] Sir Karl Popper's criticisms are even more formidable, both because of their weight of detail and their wide currency.[41] Plato is a totalitarian opposed to all liberal or humanitarian ideas.[42] He is a Utopian, in the sense that his method of approach to political problems is to prepare in advance a 'blue-print of the society at which we aim'[43] and then be ruthless in putting it into effect; he similarly supposes that politics can be reduced to an exact science,[44] a view for which he is also criticized by Mr Weldon and Professor Fite who speak of his 'illusion of geometrical method' and 'scientific prepossession'.[45] And Sir Karl has further charges. Plato advocates the use by his Rulers of the unscrupulous lie, is a 'historicist' and a 'racialist'.[46]

These charges are, of course, not entirely groundless. But it is important to distinguish those which have some basis from those which are due to misunderstanding or which reflect contemporary modern anxieties rather than what Plato said or meant. Thus the charge of countenancing the unscrupulous use of propaganda rests partly on the mistranslation of the Greek *gennaion pseudos* as 'noble lie' (see opening note to Part IV, section 1).[47] The Foundation Myth is clearly intended to express in fictional form (cf. Part III, note 2) essential truths about the new society, just as the myths on which we bring up children express – or should express (cf. Part III) – truths about God and human behaviour. It is not a piece of propaganda in any proper sense of the word. Plato is of course aware that in some circumstances it may not be desirable to tell the exact truth; there are 'medicinal lies', which Rulers may on occasion use, as ordinary people use them. But the only use actually recommended in the *Republic* is to deceive those who are 'unlucky' in the eugenically rigged lots at the marriage festivals – and here there is perhaps a certain irony. The charge of racism is even more questionable. Racism is an emotive issue today, and it is important first to state clearly what it entails. A racist must assume that birth into a particular racial group in itself confers superiority, he must despise other racial groups to a greater or lesser extent, and be ready to persecute them or ill-treat them. How far are these attitudes to be found among the Greeks generally and in Plato in particular? The Greeks were certainly conscious of their difference from other peoples, whom they called collectively 'barbarians'. But as Professor Kitto has pointed out[48] the term 'barbarian' was not one of 'loathing or contempt': it was simply a general term for those who did not speak Greek, but made odd 'bar-bar' noises. The Greeks knew very well that this included both comparatively primitive peoples, and peoples such as the Persians and Egyptians who had established civilizations which many of them admired. Not unnaturally they preferred their own way of life and culture, and after the Persian wars they were conscious of a certain enmity between themselves and the 'barbarian' world. But it is extremely doubtful whether the term 'racism' can be used with any propriety of this general attitude. It is an attitude which Plato seems largely to have shared. 'Barbarians' are foreigners in a sense that fellow-Greeks are not, and if Greeks do fight each other, they should exercise greater restraint than they would in wars with foreigners. But the purpose of this passage (469b–471c) is to inhibit some of the more brutal practices of ancient warfare when waged between Greeks, who are naturally akin, rather than to advocate their use against barbarians. Indeed, though Plato to a great extent shared the ordinary Greek attitude, he expresses admiration in the *Laws* for the Egyptians, he can express in the *Theaetetus*[49] a contemptuous opinion of the advantages of birth, and allow the possibility of his ideal state being realized among 'barbarians' (Part VII, note 38). And there is one point at which Sir Karl's anxiety to press home the charge of racism leads him to positive mis-statement. Having described the Foundation Myth, in emotive and misleading terms, as the Myth of Blood and Soil,[50] he proceeds to treat the 'metals' as 'racial characteristics'. This (to be blunt) is sheer nonsense.

Plato's citizens are all Greeks – the section on warfare emphatically describes them as such (469e–470e); and the qualities symbolized by the metals are therefore not racial at all.[51] Plato was, as has so often been observed, temperamentally an aristocrat. And he believed that the qualities needed in his rulers were, in general, hereditary, and that given knowledge and opportunity you could deliberately breed for them. But belief in a hereditary class of rulers, though it may be mistaken or even, if you will, wicked, is not a form of racism, any more than was the concern in the past of so many English parents that their children should marry into 'good families'. And as we have seen, Plato is emphatic that exceptions occur and that promotion and demotion are a necessary part of his scheme. The charge of racism hardly sticks. Nor, if we consider the Greek background, does the charge of 'historicism', by which Sir Karl means a belief in historical inevitability, the doctrine that there are predictable regularities in the course of human history which the historical and social sciences can discover. It is true that Plato in Book VIII (540a ff.) speaks as if there were an inevitable process of degeneration in human society; and that in the *Timaeus* and *Laws* he speaks of recurrent natural catastrophes after which the arts and sciences have painfully to be relearned. But a belief in decline from a golden age and a belief in recurrent cycles were not uncommon in antiquity, and it is doubtful how far, even in Plato, they reached the level of serious philosophical doctrine. Most peoples have views about the past, expressed in stories; but these hardly rank with the theories of Hegel and Marx.[52]

In other charges there is more substance. Plato had little sympathy with democracy as he had seen it in Athens (pp. xxv ff. and Part IX, section 6), nor would he have had much sympathy with any regime in which popular approval was an important factor in selecting those who are to direct the workings of society. If government is, as it must be, operated by a chosen minority, then the people's choice is liable to be a bad choice because the people are so easily deceived. This may show an aristocratic bias; but Plato's basic preference was not for an aristocracy in the common sense, but for trained expertise. It is true that he thinks this is likely to be provided by heredity guided by eugenics; but expertise and trained ability are the guiding criteria. Mr Crossman thinks that the result would be a dictatorship of the Virtuous Right. But Plato, as Sir Karl rightly points out, is a Utopian and a planner; and that approach is more characteristic of the Virtuous Left, as perhaps Bertrand Russell[53] and Professor Fite[54] were suggesting when they pointed to Soviet Russia as the state most nearly run on Platonic principles. Was Plato then a totalitarian – Sir Karl's main charge? If by a 'totalitarian' we mean one for whom the state is everything, the individual nothing, then, great as is his interest in people and personalities in much of what he wrote, when he turned explicitly to society and politics the individual seems to count for very little. There seem to be two approaches to the consideration of social and political issues. One, remembering the importance of order and coherence in society, stresses the need for planning and central authority. The other, remembering the diversity of human beings, stresses the need for a variety of institutions and a diversity of pattern. We may call them the centralist and the pluralist views. One will tend to overstress authority and order, the other to degenerate in practice into chaos. Plato was a centralist, partly because he was also a Utopian and thought, as his critics charge, that politics could be a much more exact study than it is. He wanted a plan, he wanted power to order society according to it, and he had, perhaps, a touch of the ruthlessness which this kind of approach often engenders. You only have to be determined enough to realize heaven on earth to be sure of raising hell.[55]

The *Republic*, in fact, is a long book, covering many topics, and the impression it makes on us depends to some extent on the eyes with which we look at it. Let us be critical: Plato would have wished it. But let us keep a sense of proportion and not ride our own political hobby-horses too hard. Let us remember that a great deal of the *Republic* is not about politics at all. A large part of it is about education, and has been a continued source of stimulus to educational thinking; there is a great deal about individual morality – the balance of impulses under the control of reason, the passionate desire for truth, the underlying religious seriousness. There is literary criticism, there is

philosophy, there is a wealth of incidental comment on many
things. When we do come to politics we find that Plato has little
sympathy with the kind of outlook we should call 'democratic'.
He had seen democracy at work in Athens, and was too deeply
critical of its faults to regard it as a desirable form of government
(though he was equally critical of other forms). And if we
disagree with him, we should start by trying to understand
his criticisms and the problems he was trying to solve. The
Philosopher Ruler is a mirage, a product of the kind of idealism
which asks too much of human nature and is then disappointed
by what it finds; but he does stand for a set of problems which
are real, and to which every society must find its answer.

5. FORM AND STYLE

The *Republic* is traditionally divided into ten books, but this
division, as has often been pointed out, was dictated rather by
the technicalities of book-production in the ancient world, the
amount that would go on to a papyrus roll, than by the sequence
of the argument. The division into parts and sections in this
translation attempts to represent the structure of the argument
more nearly. The traditional division into books and the
Stephanus numbers and letters are given in the margin for
purpose of reference.

The *Republic* is in dialogue form and its style is conversational. The dialogue form was used by some of Plato's contemporaries, Xenophon, for example, as well as by Plato himself;
and many have used it since his day. But in the hands of his
successors and imitators it is often more formal than dramatic,
more a device for stating different points of view than the
representation of a discussion between people. Cicero's dialogues, for example, though they may have their conversational
interludes, are in the main speeches explaining different philosophical doctrines; and Berkeley's dialogues have little of the air
of a real discussion about them. This is partly because of the
particular conditions under which Plato wrote. The Athenians
loved an argument; their political life was one of constant

discussion in Assembly and law court, and they spent most of their spare time in the public places of Athens gossiping, debating, discussing or listening to others. The activity of Socrates fitted naturally into this context, and though a discussion with him must surely have been, in reality as well as in Plato's representation, a rather one-sided affair, yet those who took part in it undoubtedly felt that they had taken part in a genuine argument. Socrates was a conversationalist, not a lecturer.

It is this conversational atmosphere that Plato reproduces in his dialogues. Their style, of course, varies with the turns of the argument; it can be light-hearted or serious, philosophical or descriptive or dramatic according to the context. And in a work of the length of the *Republic* the dramatic and conversational element can vary; in much of the argument there is very little of it. But none the less the general impression left is that of a conversation, and the style at which the translator must aim is that of an intelligent discussion; he must use the kind of language that people really do use when they are talking about the sort of topics with which the *Republic* deals.

In addition to this problem of preserving the conversational atmosphere of the original dialogue, the translator is faced with the difficulty of terminology. This difficulty faces every translator because no two languages exactly correspond and he is constantly compelled to make choices with which others may disagree; but moral and abstract terms of the kind that occur constantly throughout the *Republic* are notoriously difficult, and Plato is the least technical of writers and has no precisely specialized vocabulary. Faced with these difficulties, translators of his dialogues have in general taken one of two alternative courses, which may be called the faithful or the free. The faithful translator tries to transfer as much detail as possible from one language to another. The approach has its advantages because it is clearly desirable to lose as little as possible in the transfer. But there are many authors, Plato among them, who cannot properly be translated word for word. The result is too often 'tedious, or grotesque, or silly, or pompous and verbose'. The words are Cornford's,[56] and his criticism of Shorey's Loeb version of the *Republic* which follows is very much to the point;

Shorey is a great help to those who know Greek, but of limited use to those who do not. The other alternative is the one adopted by Cornford himself, which is to produce a version in natural and readable English, but to be fairly free in rendering the Greek, and to cut and compress if the original seems tedious. It is of course true that Plato, one of the most readable of authors, ought not to be represented in English by a version which has the defects which Cornford censures. But his method has its disadvantages too. It can lapse into paraphrase and lose the give and take of the original dialogue form, tiresome as this may sometimes seem to the English reader. The first edition of this translation, as its critics have pointed out, erred on the side of freedom and lapsed too often into paraphrase. In the present version, an attempt has been made to keep the English closer to the Greek without falling into the worst faults of a literal version. I hope that readers will continue to find this second version readable, and that those in particular who use it for teaching will find it closer to the original and so better suited to their purposes than its predecessor.

NOTES

1. Book II, 48. See Thucydides: *The Peloponnesian War*, trans. Rex Warner (Penguin Classics).
2. Thucydides, II, 65.
3. See 338c ff.
4. Thucydides and Aristotle thought it the best Athens ever had.
5. *Cambridge Ancient History*, vol. V, ch. XII. p. 349.
6. Socrates was himself also, in spite of his political detachment, critical of some aspects of Athenian democracy: cf. W. K. C. Guthrie, *History of Greek Philosophy*, III, pp. 409 ff.
7. See H. Tredennick, *The Last Days of Socrates* (Penguin Classics), for Plato's account of Socrates' trial and death.
8. F. M. Cornford, *The Republic of Plato* (Oxford University Press), p. xxiv.
9. Cf. 337d.
10. Cf. M. L. Clarke, *Higher Education in the Ancient World*.
11. For Dion's constitutional intentions the ancient source is Plutarch's

Life of Dion, ch. 53. He may have drawn on Plato's Seventh and Eighth *Letters* which deal with Sicilian affairs, but had other sources (cf. W. H. Porter, *Plutarch: Life of Dion* (Hodges, Figgis, 1952); Plato: *Phaedrus and Letters VII and VIII*, trans. W. Hamilton (Penguin, 1973)). Mary Renault's *Mask of Apollo* (Longmans, Green, 1966) gives a fictional reconstruction of these events in Sicily.

12. D. E. W. Wormell, *Literary Tradition concerning Hermias of Atarneus*: Yale Classical Studies, vol. V, 1935.

13. There seems to be no evidence for R. H. S. Crossman's statement (*Plato Today*, p. 182) that Plato at the end of his life 'knew he had failed'. See H. I. Marrou, *History of Education in Antiquity*, pp. 99–100, for a list of others whom he influenced.

14. Plato: *The Laws* (translated by T. J. Saunders, Penguin), pp. 27–8, and Appendix, pp. 543–5.

15. I. Crombie, *Examination of Plato's Doctrines*, I, p. 76.

16. J. B. Bury, *A History of Greece* (Macmillan), p. 132; on Spartan education see Marrou, op. cit., Part I, ch. II.

17. Bury, op. cit., p. 133.

18. Thucydides, III, 82.

19. Figures are conjectural; cf. V. Ehrenberg, *The Greek State* (Norton), p. 30; A. H. M. Jones, *Athenian Democracy* (Blackwell, 1957), pp. 8–11.

20. See p. xi.

21. Book II, 65.

22. Crossman, *Plato Today*, p. 106.

23. Those who advocate government by mass meetings and 'participatory democracy' would do well to study Plato's account.

24. W. Jaeger, *Paideia*, vol. II, p. 157.

25. See 425c ff.

26. K. R. Popper, *The Open Society*, I, p. 107.

27. But the joke in the comic poet Epicrates about pupils in the Academy trying to decide whether a pumpkin should be classified as a grass is evidence for an interest in classification (logic) rather than botany.

28. Cf. 398a–b and the opening of Book X, from which it is clear that the same principles apply not only to literature used in school but to literature and art generally.

29. *On Liberty*, ch. II. See also his opposition to state-controlled education in ch. V.

30. *Seventh Epistle*, 341c.

31. William James, *Varieties of Religious Experience* (Longmans, Green), ch. XVI.

32. Op. cit., p. 62.

33. *Politics*, Book II, chs. 1 and 2.

34. Aristotle might today be in sympathy with the statement of the case against collectivism in Hayek's *Road to Serfdom*.

35. On the animal analogy see Rankin, *Plato and the Individual*, pp. 51 ff.

36. H. D. F. Kitto, *The Greeks* (Penguin, 1951), p. 219 f.

37. Cf. *Laws*, VII, 805, where he remarks that 'almost every state, under present conditions, is only half a state' because women have so circumscribed a role.

38. Cf. Crossman, *Plato Today*, p. 136.

39. *Politics*, Book II, chs. 1 and 2.

40. Pp. 32, 96.

41. *The Open Society*, vol. I: *The Spell of Plato*; fifth edition, 1966.

42. Op. cit., pp. 106 ff.

43. Op. cit., p. 157.

44. Op. cit., pp. 29 ff.

45. T. D. Weldon, *The Vocabulary of Politics*, pp. 33 ff.; W. Fite, *The Platonic Legend* (Scribner's Sons, 1934), ch. x.

46. Op. cit., pp. 3 ff., 140 ff.

47. Crossman, op. cit., p. 91; Popper, op. cit., pp. 140 ff.; Popper's translation is 'lordly lie'. Cf. also p. 118 below.

48. *The Greeks*, p. 1.

49. *Theaetetus*, 174d–175b.

50. Op. cit., p. 140.

51. Cf. the Foundation Myth (415a–c): all citizens are of the 'same stock'.

52. Those interested in pursuing further what Sir Karl means more generally by 'historicism' should consult his *Poverty of Historicism*.

53. *Practice and Theory of Bolshevism*, p. 30.

54. Op. cit., p. 218.

55. The treatment of Sir Karl Popper in the foregoing paragraphs is inevitably, because of limitation of space, sketchy and inadequate. With his general approach to political and social matters I find myself largely in sympathy; my disagreement is with much of his interpretation of Plato.

56. *Republic of Plato*, Preface, p. v.

Further Reading

Compiled by Rachana Kamtekar

TEXT, EDITIONS, COMMENTARIES

Plato, vol. IV of the Oxford Classical Texts, ed. J. Burnet (Oxford, 1902).

J. Adam, *The* Republic *of Plato*, 2nd edn (Cambridge: Cambridge University Press, 1963), 2 vols., with critical notes, commentary and appendices; introduction by D. A. Rees.

COMPANIONS

Of the many introductions and companions to Plato's *Republic*, the best remains J. Annas, *An Introduction to Plato's* Republic (Oxford: Clarendon Press, 1981). Each chapter concludes with suggestions for further readings.

Other companions to the *Republic* that are of interest:

N. P. White, *A Companion to Plato's* Republic (Indianapolis: Hackett, 1979) is the closest to a traditional commentary, offering a summary and comments on each piece of Plato's text. Students puzzling over a particular passage can find here a starting point for interpretation and references to other related passages. White argues against the view (held by a number of the commentators mentioned below) that Plato's concern with justice is of reconciling duty versus interest.

R. Nettleship, *Lectures on the* Republic *of Plato*, 2nd edn (London: Macmillan, 1958), reconstructed from lecture notes by Nettleship's Oxford students in 1885 and 1887–8, approaches the *Republic* as a discussion of the role of morality in the good human life.

R. C. Cross and A. D. Woozley, *Plato's* Republic: *A Philosophical Commentary* (London: Macmillan, 1964) discusses the *Republic* using the tools of linguistic philosophy; this commentary often refers to the Lee translation (Penguin, 1955).

N. R. Murphy, *The Interpretation of Plato's* Republic (Oxford: Clarendon Press, 1951) is addressed to students of philosophy with at least some knowledge of Greek and helpfully compares positions taken in the *Republic* and in other works in the history of philosophy.

B. Bosanquet, *A Companion to Plato's* Republic *for English Readers* (London: Rivingtons, 1906) is a line-by-line commentary on the 1866 English translation of the *Republic* by J. L. Davies and D. J. Vaughan (New York: A. L. Burt); it gives an interpretation of Plato on Hegelian lines. The introduction quotes long excerpts from other Greek thinkers for comparison and contrast.

Of the introductions produced since Annas's, one that is particularly interesting on political topics is S. Sayers, *Plato's* Republic: *An Introduction* (Edinburgh: Edinburgh University Press, 1999).

In a class by itself is C. D. C. Reeve, *Philosopher-Kings: the argument of Plato's* Republic (Princeton: Princeton University Press, 1988), a book-length philosophical discussion which is neither introduction nor companion, but still manages to stay close to the text while providing a unified, bold and original interpretation of the *Republic*.

HISTORICAL BACKGROUND

D. M. Lewis, J. Boardman, S. Hornblower and M. Ostwald (eds.), *The Cambridge Ancient History* (2nd edn), *Vol. VI: The Fourth Century* (Cambridge: Cambridge University Press, 1995) is a tremendous resource; the essays most relevant to Plato's immediate context are by M. M. Austin on society and economy, P. J. Rhodes on political arrangements, M. Ostwald and J. P.

Lynch on the rise of programmes of higher education, and H. D. Westlake on Plato's political involvement with Dion in Sicily. Since Plato stages his dialogues in an earlier generation, the essays in *Vol. V: The Fifth Century* (1992) provide important background as well.

Alternatively, M. I. Finley, *The Ancient Greeks* (Penguin, 1963) provides a concise introduction that can be held in one hand.

GENERAL WORKS ON PLATO

There are a number of good philosophical introductions to Plato's work as a whole. W. K. C. Guthrie's very readable *A History of Greek Philosophy to Plato* (Cambridge: Cambridge University Press, 1962) treats Plato's early and middle period works in vol. 4 and his later works and the Academy in vol. 5.

A reliable, readily available, and concise topical introduction to Plato is G. M. A. Grube, *Plato's Thought* (Indianapolis: Hackett, 1980).

Much more dense, but very valuable, is I. Crombie, *An Examination of Plato's Doctrines* (2 vols., published simultaneously in London by Routledge & Kegan Paul and in New York by Humanities Press, 1962, 1963).

By a sociologist rather than a philosopher, A. W. Gouldner's *Enter Plato* (New York: Basic Books, 1965) takes a fresh and illuminating approach by focusing on Plato's contributions to social theory.

COLLECTIONS OF CRITICAL ESSAYS

R. Kraut (ed.), *Plato's* Republic: *Critical Essays* (Lanham: Rowman & Littlefield, 1997) is an excellent collection, including most of the individual pieces recommended below.

G. Fine (ed.), *Plato* (2 vols.), in the Oxford Readings in Philosophy series (Oxford: Oxford University Press, 1999), is a collection of philosophical essays, many on or pertinent to the

Republic, which have become classics. Especially useful for a student of the *Republic* are the articles by J. Cooper and B. Williams on psychology; J. Annas, M. F. Burnyeat, R. Kraut, and C. C. W. Taylor on politics; T. Irwin and A. Nehamas on the theory of the Forms; G. Fine on knowledge and belief.

R. Kraut (ed.), *The Cambridge Companion to Plato* (Cambridge: Cambridge University Press, 1992) has excellent topical essays to orient readers of Plato; particularly relevant to the *Republic* are the articles by R. Kraut (on the goodness of justice), I. Mueller (on the place of mathematics in education), and N. White (on the Forms). The volume also has an extensive bibliography.

G. Vlastos (ed.), *Plato: A collection of critical essays* (2 vols.) (New York: Doubleday, 1971) contains classics by an earlier generation. The most influential of these are D. Sachs's challenge to the success of the central argument of the *Republic*, 'A Fallacy in Plato's *Republic*', and responses by R. Demos, J. D. Mabbott, and G. Vlastos. The volumes present alternative viewpoints on other topics as well.

O. Hoffe (ed.), *Platon, Politeia* (Berlin: Akademie Verlag, 1997) is a volume of commissioned essays each on one substantial portion of the *Republic*; although prepared for German students, this volume has a number of important essays in English.

N. D. Smith (ed.), *Plato: Critical Assessments* (London: Routledge, 1998), in four volumes, is a (pricey) collection of influential pieces of Anglo-American Platonic scholarship of the second half of the twentieth century. Vol. 1 is on methods of interpretation; the three subsequent volumes are devoted, respectively, to early, middle and late dialogues.

ON PARTICULAR TOPICS IN
THE *REPUBLIC*

(NB: These topics overlap a great deal in the *Republic* and in discussions of it.)

(i) Ethics

Two excellent overviews of the ethics of fifth- and fourth-century BC Greece to contextualize the *Republic* are:
A. W. H. Adkins, *Merit and Responsibility: A Study in Greek Values* (Oxford: Clarendon Press, 1960) and
K. J. Dover, *Greek Popular Morality in the Time of Plato and Aristotle* (Oxford: Basil Blackwell, 1974, and Indianapolis: Hackett, 1994).

The best direct discussion of the variety of ethical topics in the *Republic* is T. Irwin, *Plato's Ethics* (Oxford: Oxford University Press, 1995), which devotes nearly half its chapters to the *Republic*.

(ii) Psychology

Useful for background are:
D. B. Claus, *Towards the Soul* (New Haven, Conn.: Yale University Press, 1981; Yale Classical Monographs Series 2) and
J. Bremmer, *The Early Greek Concept of the Soul* (Princeton: Princeton University Press, 1983).

An excellent article for explaining the mechanics and the point of the *Republic*'s account of the tri-partite soul is J. Cooper, 'Plato's Theory of Human Motivation' in *History of Philosophy Quarterly*; 1(1), pp. 3–21. (reprinted in G. Fine (1999), vol. 2).

C. Kahn, 'Plato's theory of desire', *Review of Metaphysics* 41 (1987), pp. 77–103, brings out important differences between Plato's psychology and contemporary belief-desire psychology.

Three very fine works on Plato's city–soul analogy are:
B. Williams, 'The Analogy of City and Soul in Plato's *Republic*' in E. N. Lee, A. P. D. Mourelatos and R. M. Rorty (eds.), *Exegesis and Argument: Studies in Greek Philosophy Presented to Gregory Vlastos*, pp. 196–206 (Assen, Netherlands: van Gorcum & Co., 1973). This essay is reprinted in G. Fine (1999), vol. 2;

J. Lear, 'Inside and Outside the *Republic*', *Phronesis* 38 (1992),
    pp. 184–215; and
G. R. F. Ferrari, *City and Soul in Plato's* Republic [Lecturae
    Platonis, 3] (Sankt Augustin: Academia Verlag, 2002).

Any student of Plato will want to consult C. Bobonich, *Plato's
Utopia Recast: His Later Ethics and Politics* (Oxford, 2002),
which explains the development of Plato's moral psychology
and political philosophy from the *Republic* to the *Laws*; chapter
1 makes a compelling case for the view that the *Republic*'s
moral psychology makes it impossible for ordinary citizens to
be genuinely virtuous or happy.

(iii) Metaphysics and Epistemology

The best beginning for the *Republic*'s compressed and incomplete account of the theory of Forms is N. White, *Plato
on Knowledge and Reality* (Indianapolis: Hackett, 1976),
chapter 4.

Two more difficult, but also richly rewarding, studies are:
R. Patterson, *Image and Reality in Plato's Metaphysics*
    (Indianapolis: Hackett, 1985) and
T. Penner, *The Ascent from Nominalism: Some Existence
    Arguments in Plato's Middle Dialogues* (Dordrecht: Reidel,
    1987).

An explanation of Plato's (notorious) belief that Forms are
superior to sensibles is given in A. Nehamas, 'Plato on the
Imperfection of the Sensible World', *American Philosophical
Quarterly* 12 (1975), pp. 105–17, reprinted in his *Virtues of
Authenticity* (Princeton: Princeton University Press, 1999),
pp. 138–58.
    J. Moline, *Plato's Theory of Understanding* (Madison: Uni-
versity of Wisconsin Press, 1981) has an especially illuminating
discussion of the relationship between the epistemology and
psychology of the *Republic* (in chapter 3).

(iv) Politics

For background, M. Gagarin and P. Woodruff (tr.), *Early Greek Political Thought from Homer to the Sophists* (Cambridge Texts in the History of Political Thought, Cambridge, 1995) has an excellent selection of early political texts.

D. Dawson, *Cities of the Gods: Communist Utopias in Greek Thought* (Oxford: Oxford University Press, 1992) discusses the *Republic* in the tradition of Greek depictions of imaginary ideal societies from Hesiod to the Stoics.

Two books by classical historians that describe and explain the political specificities of the democratic Athens in which the *Republic* was written are:

W. R. Connor, *New Politicians of Fifth-Century Athens* (Princeton: Princeton University Press, 1971) and

J. Ober, *Mass and Elite in Democratic Athens: Rhetoric, Ideology, and the Power of the People* (Princeton: Princeton University Press, 1989).

Ober's later *Political Dissent in Democratic Athens: Intellectual Critics of Popular Rule* (Princeton: Princeton University Press, 1999) discusses Plato in great detail.

A useful overview of political topics in Plato's dialogues is provided in G. Klosko, *The Development of Plato's Political Thought* (New York: Methuen, 1986).

The work that has most influenced twentieth-century opinion about the politics of the *Republic* is K. R. Popper's passionate attack on Plato, *The Open Society and Its Enemies*, vol. I: *The Spell of Plato* (Routledge & Kegan Paul, 5th edn, 1966).

Highlights of the debate around Popper's Plato are collected in R. Bambrough, *Plato, Popper, and Politics* (Cambridge: Heffer, 1967).

A sober discussion of the issues in this debate is to be found in C. C. W. Taylor, 'Plato's Totalitarianism', *Polis* 5 (1986), pp. 4–29, reprinted in G. Fine (1999), vol. 2, pp. 280–96.

Moving away from the debate generated by Popper, there are a number of articles that can help to deepen one's understanding of the political thought of the *Republic*.

M. Schofield's collected papers on ancient political thought, *Saving the City* (London: Routledge, 1999), includes an essay, 'Plato on the Economy', which shows the importance the *Republic* places on economic activity, both for the city and for justice and injustice.

On social justice, see G. Vlastos's pieces, 'The Theory of Social Justice in the Polis in Plato's *Republic*' in H. North (ed.), *Interpretations of Plato: A Swarthmore Symposium* (Mnemosyne Bibliotheca Classica Batava Supplementum, Leiden: E. J. Brill, 1977), pp. 1–40 and 'The Rights of Persons in Plato's Conception of the Foundations of Justice' in H. Tristram Englehardt Jr. and Daniel Callahan (eds.), *Morals, Science and Society* (Hastings-on-Hudson, NY: The Hastings Center, 1978), pp. 172–201. For an alternative to Vlastos that brings out the utilitarian features of the *Republic*'s conception of social justice, see R. Kamtekar, 'Social Justice and Happiness in the *Republic*: Plato's Two Principles', *History of Political Thought* (vol. 22, 2001).

The *Republic*'s proposals for reforming the social roles of women and the family have received a great deal of attention since the 1970s. Excellent discussions include:

D. Wender, 'Plato: Misogynist, Paedophile, and Feminist' in *Arethusa* 6, no. 1 (1973), pp. 75–90;

J. Annas, 'Plato's *Republic* and Feminism', *Philosophy* 51, (1976), pp. 307–21, reprinted in Ward (ed.), *Feminism and Ancient Philosophy* (New York and London, 1996), pp. 3–12, as well as in G. Fine (1999), vol. 2, pp. 265–79;

E. Spelman, 'Hairy Cobblers and Philosopher-Queens' in her *Inessential Woman: Problems of Exclusion in Feminist Thought* (Boston: Beacon Press, 1988), pp. 19–36. Reprinted in N. Tuana (ed.), *Feminist Interpretations of Plato* (Pennsylvania State University Press, 1994), pp. 87–107;

S. M. Okin, 'Philosopher Queens and Private Wives: Plato on Women and the Family', *Philosophy and Public Affairs* 6 (1977), pp. 345–69;

H. Lesser, 'Plato's Feminism' in *Philosophy* 54 (1979), pp. 113–
   17; and
G. Vlastos, 'Was Plato a Feminist?', *Times Literary Supplement*
   issue 4485 (17–23 March 1989), pp. 276, 288–9, reprinted
   in N. Tuana (ed.), *Feminist Interpretations of Plato* (Pennsylvania State University Press, 1994), pp. 11–23.

There is a question taken by many commentators to be crucial
for an internal evaluation of the *Republic*'s political philosophy:
why should those whom Plato believes to be qualified to rule –
the philosophers – agree to rule? A compelling response to this
question is to be found in R. Kraut, 'Return to the Cave: *Republic* 519–521' in *Proceedings of the Boston Area Colloquium in
Ancient Philosophy*, vol. 7 (1991), reprinted in G. Fine (1999),
vol. 2.
   Finally, the question of whether the *Republic* presents political proposals that Plato intended to be put into practice, or
whether he only intended to put forward a psychological ideal,
is discussed in M. F. Burnyeat, 'Utopia and fantasy: the practicability of Plato's ideally just city' in J. Hopkins and A. Savile
(eds.), *Psychoanalysis, Mind and Art* (Oxford: Blackwell Pub-
lishers, 1992); this is reprinted in G. Fine (1999), vol. 2.

(v) Education, Culture, Art

For background, H. I. Marrou, *The History of Education in
Antiquity* (tr. G. Lamb, New York: Sheed and Ward, 1956) is
useful.
   Brilliantly linking together the themes of education, culture
and art across the *Republic* is M. F. Burnyeat, 'Culture and
Society in Plato's *Republic*', *The Tanner Lectures in Human
Values*, 20 (1999), pp. 215–324.

Further articles on the education of the Guardians are:
C. Gill, 'Plato and the Education of Character', in *Archiv für
   Geschichte der Philosophie* 67 (1985), pp. 1–26 and
R. Kamtekar, 'Imperfect Virtue', *Ancient Philosophy* 18 (Fall
   1998), pp. 315–37, which explains how, given the Guardians'
   distinctive moral-psychological capacities, their education

results in their possessing a type of virtue that is imperfect but genuine.

There is a small but useful collection of essays on Plato on topics in the arts in J. Moravcsik (ed.), *Plato on Beauty, Wisdom and the Arts* (a publication of the *American Philosophical Quarterly*, Totowa, New Jersey: Rowman and Littlefield, 1982).

Also of interest is A. Nehamas, 'Plato and the Mass Media', *Monist* 71 (1988), pp. 214–34, reprinted in his *Virtues of Authenticity* (Princeton: Princeton University Press, 1999), pp. 279–99.

I. Murdoch, *The Fire and the Sun: Why Plato Banished the Artists* (Oxford: Clarendon Press, 1977) is a beautifully written book by a novelist and philosopher grappling with Plato's attitude towards the arts.

(vi) Higher education

On the role of mathematics in higher education, the best place to begin is I. Mueller, 'Mathematical Method and Philosophic Truth' in *The Cambridge Companion to Plato*, pp. 170–99.

Also well worth reading is M. F. Burnyeat, 'Plato on Why Mathematics is Good for the Soul' in T. Smiley (ed.), *Mathematics and Necessity in the History of Philosophy* (Oxford: Oxford University Press, 2000).

T. Heath, *A History of Greek Mathematics*, in vol. 1 (Thales to Euclid), chapter 9, looks at all the mathematical passages and comments about mathematics in the *Republic*.

R. Robinson, *Plato's Earlier Dialectic* (Oxford: Clarendon Press, 1953) is an important discussion of philosophical method in Plato, including Socratic cross-examination, definition, hypothesis, analogy; three chapters are devoted to the *Republic*.

(vii) Alternative Interpretive Approaches

The readings suggested above are largely by scholars trained in the Anglo-American 'analytic' tradition. Readings in a 'Straussian' tradition include:

L. Strauss, *The City and the Man* (Chicago, Ill.: University of Chicago Press, 1964), chapter 2, pp. 50–138;

A. Bloom, *The Republic of Plato* (New York: Basic Books, 1968), which contains an interpretive essay;

S. Bernadete, *Socrates' Second Sailing* (Chicago, Ill.: University of Chicago Press, 1989), which has a commentary;

and from the 'Tubingen School', T. Szlezak, *Reading Plato* (London: Routledge, 1999).

Note on the Translation

The translation is made from the Oxford text, except when noted. I have constantly consulted Adam's edition (*The Republic of Plato*, CUP, second edition, 1965).

It is customary to refer to Plato's works by reference to the pages of an early edition (that of Stephanus, 1578), each page being subdivided into approximately equal segments, designated a–e. These numbers and letters are printed in the margin of this translation, and in the Table of Contents the first number occurring in each Part is printed in brackets after the title.

This revision of the Penguin *Republic* owes much to the readers and critics of the previous version. To its readers who have bought enough copies to require a resetting of the type; to its critics for suggesting the lines which the revision should follow. Criticism can be summed up in the comment of a student who said to me – in effect, but she did not use the words – 'I can't use it as a crib'. It was not, of course, intended to be so used. Dr Rieu's instructions to me were to aim at the 'general reader'. Though this is not a very definite description, it clearly relegates to the background any use for more strictly academic purposes. As things have turned out, however, many of the readers of the translation have been students or others engaged in academic work, and for them the earlier version, with its many abbreviations and its lapses into paraphrase, was not entirely suitable. In this revision I have tried to bring the English more severely close to the Greek, though still aiming to produce what one critic called 'a swift, natural version'; I have also tried to give the reader further help by expanding and revising notes and section headings. I cannot hope to have succeeded completely, and perhaps the main impression which the revision has left on me is that of the extreme difficulty of transferring the thought of even so lucid a writer as Plato from one language to another without some damage in the process. All too often I have been conscious of the alternatives open, and unsure whether I have chosen the most suitable.

The Republic

CHARACTERS IN THE DIALOGUE

SOCRATES, narrator.

GLAUCON and ADEIMANTUS, sole respondents in the dialogue after Book 1. Elder brothers of Plato.

POLEMARCHUS, a resident in Piraeus, the port of Athens: the dialogue takes place at his house.

CEPHALUS, a Syracusan by birth, Polemarchus' father and apparently resident with him. Respondent in the early part of the dialogue until his place is taken by Polemarchus.

THRASYMACHUS OF CHALCEDON, sophist and orator, the main respondent in Book 1.

LYSIAS and EUTHYDEMUS, Polemarchus' brothers. Lysias became an orator and speech-writer, noted for the purity of his style; a number of his speeches are still extant (e.g. 'Against Eratosthenes' in *Greek Political Oratory*, trans. A. N. W. Saunders: Penguin, 1970). NICERATUS, son of Nicias the Athenian statesman and general. CHARMANTIDES and CLEITOPHON, of whom we otherwise know nothing. The only one of this last group to speak in the dialogue is Cleitophon, and his is the briefest interjection (340).

The dramatic date of the dialogue is commonly supposed to be just before 420 BC, when Socrates would be about fifty.

PART I

INTRODUCTION

1. Prelude

The scene set and the characters introduced. The subject of the BK I *dialogue, justice or right conduct[1] is introduced in a preliminary discussion with Cephalus who, in effect, describes it as telling the truth and paying one's debts.*

I went down yesterday to the Piraeus with Glaucon, son of   327 a
Ariston. I wanted to say a prayer to the goddess and also to see
what they would make of the festival,[2] as this was the first time
they were holding it. I must say that I thought that the local
contribution to the procession was splendid, though the Thracian contingent seemed to show up just as well. We had said
our prayers and seen the show and were on our way back to
town when Polemarchus, son of Cephalus, noticed us in the   b
distance making our way home and sent his slave running on
ahead to tell us to wait for him. The slave caught hold of my
coat from behind and said 'Polemarchus says you are to wait.'
I turned and asked where his master was. 'He's coming along
behind you,' he said. 'Do wait.' 'We will,' said Glaucon, and
soon afterwards Polemarchus came up; with him were Adeimantus, Glaucon's brother, Niceratus, son of Nicias, and others   c
who had all apparently been to the procession. 'Socrates,' said
Polemarchus, 'I believe you are starting off on your way back
to town.' 'You are quite right,' I replied. 'Do you see how many
of us there are?' he asked. 'I do.' 'Well, you will either have to
get the better of us or stay here.' 'Oh, but there's another

alternative,' said I. 'We might persuade you that you ought to let us go.' 'You can't persuade people who won't listen,' he replied. 'No,' said Glaucon, 'you certainly can't.' 'Well, you

328 a can assume we shan't listen.' 'And don't you know,' added Adeimantus, 'that there is going to be a torch race in the evening on horseback, in honour of the goddess?' 'On horseback?' said I; 'that's a novelty. Do you mean a relay race, in which they carry torches on horseback and hand them on to each other?' 'Yes,' answered Polemarchus, 'and there's to be an all-night carnival as well, which will be worth seeing. We will go out

b after dinner and watch it; we shall meet a lot of young men there to talk to. So please do stay.' To which Glaucon replied, 'It looks as if we shall have to.' 'Well, if you think so,' I said, 'stay we must.'

So we went to Polemarchus' house, where we found his brothers Lysias and Euthydemus, and besides them Thrasymachus of Chalcedon, Charmantides of Paeania and Cleitophon, son of Aristonymus. Polemarchus' father, Cephalus, was

c there too; a very old man he seemed to me, for it was a long time since I had seen him last. He was sitting garlanded on some sort of an easy chair, as he had just been sacrificing in the courtyard. There were some chairs standing round about, so we sat down beside him. As soon as he saw me Cephalus welcomed me and said, 'You don't come down to the Piraeus to see us, Socrates, as often as you should. If I were still strong enough to

d make the journey to town easily, there would be no reason for you to come here; I would visit you. As it is, you ought to come here more frequently: for I myself find that as age blunts one's enjoyment of physical pleasures, one's desire for rational conversation and one's enjoyment of it increase correspondingly. So don't refuse me, but come and talk to the young men here and visit us as if we were old friends.' 'As a matter of fact, Cephalus,' I said, 'I enjoy talking to very old men, for they have

e gone before us, as it were, on a road that we too may have to tread, and it seems to me that we should find out from them what it is like and whether it is rough and difficult or broad and easy. You are now at an age when you are, as the poets say, about to cross the threshold,[3] and I would like to find out how it strikes you and what you have to tell us. Is it a difficult time of life, or not?'

'I'll certainly tell you how it strikes me, Socrates,' he said. 'For some of us old men often meet together, like the proverbial birds of a feather. And when we do meet, most of them are full of woes; they hanker for the pleasures of their youth, remembering how they used to make love and drink and go to parties and the like, and thinking it a great deprivation that they can't do so any more. Life was good then, they think, whereas now they can hardly be said to live at all. And some of them grumble that their families show no respect for their age, and proceed to harp on the miseries old age brings. But in my opinion, Socrates, they are putting the blame in the wrong place. For if old age were to blame, my experience would be the same as theirs, and so would that of all other old men. But in fact I have met many whose feelings are quite different. For example, I was once present when someone was asking the poet Sophocles about sex, and whether he was still able to make love to a woman; to which he replied, "Don't talk about that; I am glad to have left it behind me and escaped from a fierce and frenzied master." A good reply I thought then, and still do. For in old age you become quite free of feelings of this sort and they leave you in peace; and when your desires lose their intensity and relax, you get what Sophocles was talking about, a release from a lot of mad masters. In all this, and in the lack of respect their families show them, there is only one thing to blame; and that is not their old age, Socrates, but their character. For if men are sensible and good-tempered, old age is easy enough to bear: if not, youth as well as age is a burden.'

I was delighted by what he said, and tried to lead him on to say more by replying, 'I'm afraid that most people don't agree with what you say, Cephalus, but think that you carry your years lightly not because of your character but because of your wealth. For they say that the rich have many consolations.'

'Of course they don't agree with me,' he said, 'and there's something in what they say, though not as much as they think. The story about Themistocles is very much to the point. A Seriphian was abusing him and saying that his reputation was

329 a

b

c

d

e

330 a

due not to his personal merits but to his being an Athenian, and Themistocles answered, "I certainly should not have been famous if I had been a Seriphian, but nor would you if you had been an Athenian." The same remark applies to those who are not rich and find old age a burden: a good man may not find old age easy to bear if he's poor, but a bad man won't be at peace with himself even if he is rich.'

'Did you inherit most of your fortune,' I asked Cephalus, 'or did you make it yourself?'

b   'Did I make my fortune, Socrates?' he said. 'As a business man I rank somewhere between my grandfather and my father. For my grandfather, after whom I am named, inherited about as much as I now have and multiplied it several times over, while my father Lysanias reduced it to less than what it is now: for myself, I shall be pleased enough if I leave these boys of mine a little more than I inherited.'

'The reason why I asked,' I said, 'was that you did not seem
c   to me over-fond of money. And this is the way in general with those who have not made it themselves, while those who have are twice as fond of it as anyone else. For just as poets are fond of their own poems, and fathers of their own children, so money-makers become devoted to money, not only because, like other people, they find it useful, but because it's their own creation. So they are tiresome company, as they have a good word for nothing but money.'

'That's true,' he said.

d   'It is indeed,' said I. 'But I have another question. What do you think is the greatest advantage you have gained from being so rich?'

'One,' he replied, 'which many will perhaps not credit. For you know, Socrates, when a man faces the thought of death there come into his mind anxieties that did not trouble him before. The stories about another world, and about punishment
e   in a future life for wrongs done in this, at which he once used to laugh, begin to torment his mind with the fear that they may be true. And either because of the weakness of old age or because, as he approaches the other world, he has some clearer perception of it, he is filled with doubts and fears and begins to

reckon up and see if there is anyone he has wronged. The man
who finds that in the course of his life he has done a lot of wrong
often wakes up at night in terror, like a child with a nightmare,
and his life is full of foreboding: but the man who is conscious   331 *a*
of no wrongdoing is filled with cheerfulness and with hope, "the
comfort of old age" as Pindar calls it. For I love that passage
where he says of the man who has lived a just and godfearing
life,

> sweet hope,
> Who guides men's wandering purpose,
> Treads at his side, gladdens his heart,
> And comforts his old age.

Wonderful lines! Now it is chiefly for this that I think wealth is
valuable, not perhaps to everyone but to good and sensible men.
For wealth contributes very greatly to one's ability to avoid   *b*
both unintentional cheating or lying and the fear that one has
left some sacrifice to God unmade or some debt to man unpaid
before one dies. Money has many other uses, but taking one
thing with another I reckon that for a reasonable man this is by
no means its least.'

'That's fair enough, Cephalus,' I said. 'But are we really to   *c*
say that doing right[4], consists simply and solely in truthfulness
and returning anything we have borrowed? Are those not
actions that can be sometimes right and sometimes wrong?
For instance, if one borrowed a weapon from a friend who
subsequently went out of his mind and then asked for it back,
surely it would be generally agreed that one ought not to return
it, and that it would not be right to do so, nor to consent to tell
the strict truth to a madman?'

'That is true,' he replied.   *d*

'Well then,' I said, 'telling the truth and returning what we
have borrowed is not the definition of doing right.'

'Oh yes it is,' said Polemarchus, interrupting, 'at any rate if
we are to believe Simonides.'[5]

'Well,' said Cephalus, 'I bequeath the argument to the two of
you, for I must go and see about the sacrifice.'

'While I take over from you?' asked Polemarchus.

'You do,' said Cephalus with a smile, and left for his sacrifice.

2. The Conventional View of Justice Developed

Polemarchus takes up the argument and maintains that justice is giving a man his due. Socrates draws a series of unacceptable conclusions in order to demonstrate the inadequacy of this conventional view.

e   'Well then,' said I, 'as heir to this argument, tell me, what is this saying of Simonides that you think tells us the truth about doing right?'

'That it is right to give every man his due,' he replied; 'in that, I think, he puts the matter fairly enough.'

'It is indeed difficult to disagree with Simonides,' I said; 'he had the poet's wisdom and inspiration; but though you may know what he meant by what he said, I'm afraid I don't. For he clearly does not mean what we were talking about just now,

332 a that we should return anything entrusted to us even though the person asking for it has gone mad. Yet what one has entrusted to another is surely due to one, isn't it?'

'Yes.'

'Yet in no circumstances should one return it to a madman.'

'True.'

'So Simonides must mean something different from this when he says that it is right to give every man his due.'

'He certainly must,' he replied; 'for his thought is that one friend owes it as a due to another to do him good, not harm.'

'I see,' I said; 'then as between two friends one is not giving the other his due when he returns a sum of money the other has

b   entrusted to him if the return is going to cause harm – is this what Simonides means?'

'Certainly.'

'Well then, ought we to give our enemies too whatever is due to them?'

'Certainly,' he said, 'what is due to them; and that is, I

assume, what is appropriate between enemies, an injury of some sort.'

'It looks,' said I, 'as if Simonides was talking about what is right with a poet's ambiguity. For it appears that he meant that it is right to give everyone what is appropriate to him, but he called this his "due".' *c*

'Of course.'

'Yes, but look here,' I said, 'suppose someone asked him "How then does medical skill[6] get its name, Simonides? What does it supply that is due and appropriate and to whom?' How do you suppose he would reply?'

'Obviously that it is the skill that supplies the body with remedies and with food and drink.'

'And if he were asked the same question about cookery?'

'That it is the skill that supplies the flavour to our food.' *d*

'Then what does the skill we call justice supply and to whom?'

'If we are to be consistent, Socrates, it must be the skill that enables us to help and injure one's friends and enemies.'

'So Simonides says that justice is to benefit one's friends and harm one's enemies?'

'I think so.'

'Who then is best able to benefit his friends and harm his enemies in matters of health?'

'A doctor.'

'And in the risks of a sea voyage?' *e*

'A navigator.'

'And what about the just man? In what activity or occupation will he best be able to help his friends and harm his enemies?'

'In war: he will fight against his enemies and for his friends.'

'Good. Yet people who are healthy have no use for a physician, have they, Polemarchus?'

'True.'

'Nor those that stay on land of a navigator?'

'No.'

'Do you then maintain that those who are not at war have no use for a just man?'

'No, I certainly don't.'

'So justice is useful in peacetime?'

333 a   'It is.'

'So too is agriculture?'

'Yes.'

'For providing crops?'

'Yes.'

'And shoemaking?'

'Yes.'

'Presumably for supplying shoes.'

'Yes.'

'Well then, what is the use of justice in peacetime, and what do we get out of it?'

'It's useful in business.'

'And by that you mean some form of transaction between people?'

'Yes.'

b   'Well, if our transaction is a game of chess, is a just man a good and useful partner, or a chess player?'

'A chess player.'

'And if it's a matter of bricks and mortar, is the just man a better and more useful partner than a bricklayer?'

'No.'

'Well, for what kind of transaction is the just man a better partner than the bricklayer or the musician? Where does he excel the musician as the musician excels him in music?'

'Where money is involved, I suppose.'

'Except perhaps,' said I, 'when it's a question of buying or selling; if, for example, we are buying or selling a horse, a trainer would be a better partner, would he not?'

c   'I suppose so.'

'Or if it's a ship, a shipbuilder or sailor?'

'Presumably.'

'Then in what financial transactions is the just man a better partner than others?'

'When we want to put our money on deposit, Socrates.'

'In fact when we don't want to make use of it at all, but lay it by?'

'Yes.'

'So when we aren't making any use of our money, we find   *d*
justice useful?'

'It looks rather like it.'

'And so when you want to store a pruning-knife, justice is
useful both to the community and to the individual; but if you
want to use it then you turn to the vine dresser.'

'Apparently.'

'And if you want to keep your shield or your lyre safe you
need the just man, but if you want to use it the soldier or
musician?'

'That must follow.'

'And so in all spheres justice is useless when you are using
things, and useful when you are not?'

'Maybe.'

'Justice, then, can't be a very serious thing,' I said, 'if it's only   *e*
useful when things aren't used. But there's a further point. In
boxing and other kinds of fighting, skill in attack goes with skill
in defence, does it not?'

'Of course.'

'So, too, does not the ability to save from disease imply the
ability to produce it undetected?'   334 *a*

'I agree.'

'While ability to bring an army safely through a campaign
goes with ability to rob the enemy of his secrets and steal a
march on him in action.'

'I certainly think so.'

'So a man who's good at keeping a thing will be good at
stealing it?'

'I suppose so.'

'So if the just man is good at keeping money safe he will be
good at stealing it too.'

'That at any rate is the conclusion the argument indicates.'

'So the just man turns out to be a kind of thief, a view
you have perhaps learned from Homer. For he approves of   *b*
Odysseus' grandfather Autolycus[7] who, he says, surpassed all
men in stealing and lying. Justice, in fact, according to you and
Homer and Simonides, is a kind of stealing, though it must be
done to help a friend or harm an enemy. Is that your meaning?'

'It certainly isn't,' he replied, 'but I don't really know what I did mean. Yet I still think that justice is to help your friends and harm your enemies.'

c 'But which do you reckon are a man's friends or enemies? Those he thinks good, honest men and the reverse, or those who really are even though he may not think so?'

'One would expect a man's likes and dislikes to depend on what he thinks.'

'But don't men often make mistakes, and think a man honest when he is not, and vice versa?'

'Yes, they do.'

'In that case their enemies are good and their friends bad.'

'Certainly.'

'Then it's only right that they should help the bad and harm
d the good.'

'I suppose so.'

'Yet good men are just and not likely to do wrong.'

'True.'

'So that by your reckoning it is right to injure those who do no wrong.'

'Oh no, Socrates; it looks as if my reckoning was wrong.'

'Well then,' I said, 'it must be right to harm wrongdoers and help those who do right.'[8]

'That seems more reasonable.'

'So when men are mistaken in their judgements, Polemarchus,
e it will often be right for them to injure their friends, who in their eyes are bad, and help their enemies, who are good. Which is the very opposite of what we said Simonides meant.'

'That is the conclusion that follows, certainly,' he said. 'But let us put the matter differently. For our definitions of friend and enemy were perhaps wrong.'

'How wrong?'

'When we said a friend was one who *seemed* a good, honest man.'

'And how are we to change that?'

'By defining a friend as one who both *seems* and *is* an honest
335 a man: while the man who seems, but is not, an honest man seems a friend, but really is not. And similarly for an enemy.'

'On this reckoning the good man is a friend and the bad man an enemy.'

'Yes.'

'And you want us to add to our previous definition of justice (that justice was to do good to a friend and harm to an enemy) by saying that it is just to do good to one's friend if he is good, and to harm one's enemy if he is evil.'

'Yes,' he said, 'that puts it very fairly.'   *b*

'But does a just man do harm to anyone?'[9]

'Oh yes,' he replied: 'one *ought* to harm bad men who are our enemies.'

'If we harm a horse do we make it better or worse?'

'Worse.'

'Worse, that is, by the standard of excellence[10] by which we judge horses, not dogs?'

'Yes.'

'And a dog if harmed becomes a worse dog by the standard of excellence by which we judge dogs, not horses?'

'Surely.'

'But must we not then say of a man that if harmed he becomes   *c*
worse by the standards of human excellence?'

'Certainly.'

'But is not justice human excellence?'

'It surely must be.'

'So men if harmed must become more unjust.'

'So it would seem.'

'Well, musicians will hardly use their skill to make their pupils unmusical, or riding masters to make their pupils bad horsemen.'

'Hardly.'

'Then will just men use their justice to make others unjust? Or, in short, will good men use their goodness[11] to make others   *d*
bad?'

'That cannot be so.'

'For it is not the function of heat to cool things, but of its opposite.'

'Yes.'

'Nor the function of dryness to wet things, but of its opposite.'

'True.'

'Well then, it is not the function of the good man to do harm but of his opposite.'

'Clearly.'

'But is not the just man good?'

'Of course.'

'Then, Polemarchus, it is not the function of the just man to harm either his friends or anyone else, but of his opposite, the unjust man.'

'What you say seems perfectly true, Socrates.'

e   'So it wasn't a wise man who said that justice is to give every man his due, if what he meant by it was that the just man should harm his enemies and help his friends. This simply is not true: for as we have seen, it is never right to harm anyone at any time.'

'I agree.'

'So you and I,' said I, 'will both quarrel with anyone who says that this view was put forward by either Simonides or Bias or Pittacus or any of the canonical sages.'[12]

'For myself,' he replied, 'I am quite ready to join your side of the quarrel.'

336 *a*   'Do you know whose I think this saying is that tells us it is right to help one's friends and harm one's enemies? I think it must be due to Periander or Perdiccas or Xerxes or Ismenias of Thebes,[13] or someone else of wealth and arrogance.'

'Very likely,' he replied.

'Well, well,' said I; 'now we have seen that this is not what justice or right is, will anyone suggest what else it is?'

It will be noticed that throughout the foregoing argument Socrates continually draws analogies from various human occupations, from cookery to horse-breeding. To describe all such occupations the Greeks had a single word, Technē, for which there is no equivalent in English that will bring out the variety of its meaning. It includes both the fine arts (music) and the practical arts (cookery); all forms of skilled craftsmanship (ship-building) and various professional activities (navigation and soldiering); besides activities calling for scientific skill (medicine). It may thus be said to cover any skilled activity with its rules of operation, the knowledge of which is acquired by training. But it is a very elusive word to translate, varying between art, craft, professional skill, and science according to the emphasis of the context. The principle followed in this translation is to give the meaning that seems best to suit the context rather than retain a single word throughout; but behind the group of words used (which are sufficiently indicated by what has been said) there lies only the one word Technē in the Greek. Whether or how far the analogy from skilled activity of this kind, from craft or profession or science, to morals and politics is a sound one, is one of the fundamental questions which the reader of Plato must constantly be asking himself.

3. Thrasymachus and the Rejection of Conventional Morality

1. First Statement and Criticisms

Socrates has shown that there are confusions in conventional morality: Thrasymachus rejects it altogether and maintains that human behaviour is and should be guided by self-interest. He represents a type of view that was not uncommon in the fifth century, among the Sophists in particular, and which has indeed always had advocates. The precise interpretation of Thrasymachus' presentation of it is a matter of controversy (cf. Cross and Woozley, ch. 2) and Plato's treatment of him is unsympathetic, making him noisy and offensive. He starts, after some introductory argumentative sparring with Socrates, by saying that Right is the 'Interest of the Stronger'; and explains this to mean that the ruling class in any state will forcibly exact a certain type of behaviour from its subjects to suit its own interests. Morality is nothing more or less than the code of behaviour so exacted. Socrates first asks how this is affected by the fact that rulers may often be mistaken about their own interests; and then, when Thrasymachus replies that rulers, qua rulers, are never mistaken, uses the technē-analogy to show that rulers

don't pursue their own interests. Much of the detail of the
argument is of questionable validity, but Socrates' main point
is, briefly, that the exercise of any skill is, as such, disinterested.[14]

b   While we had been talking Thrasymachus had often tried to
interrupt, but had been prevented by those sitting near him,
who wanted to hear the argument concluded; but when we
paused and I asked my question, he was no longer able to keep
quiet but gathered himself together and sprang on us like a wild
beast, as if he wanted to tear us in pieces. Polemarchus and I
were panic-stricken, as Thrasymachus burst out and said, 'What
c   is all this nonsense, Socrates? Why do you go on in this childish
way being so polite about each other's opinions? If you really
want to know what justice is, stop asking questions and then
playing to the gallery by refuting anyone who answers you. You
know perfectly well that it's easier to ask questions than to
answer them. Give us an answer yourself, and tell us what you
d   think justice is. And don't tell me that it's duty, or expediency,
or advantage, or profit, or interest. I won't put up with nonsense
of that sort; give me a clear and precise definition.'
     I was staggered by his attack and looked at him in dismay. If
I had not seen him first I believe I should have been struck
dumb; but I had noticed him when our argument first began
e   to exasperate him, and so I managed to answer him, saying
diffidently: 'Don't be hard on us, Thrasymachus. If we have
made any mistake in our consideration of the argument, I assure
you we have not done so on purpose. For if we were looking for
gold, you can't suppose that we would willingly let mutual
politeness hinder our search and prevent our finding it. Justice
is much more valuable than gold, and you must not think we
shall slacken our efforts to find it out of any idiotic deference to
each other. I assure you we are doing our best. It's the ability
that we lack, and clever chaps like you ought to be sorry for us
337 a   and not get annoyed with us.'
     Thrasymachus laughed sarcastically, and replied, 'There you
go with your old affection, Socrates. I knew it, and I told the
others that you would never let yourself be questioned, but go

on shamming ignorance and do anything rather than give a straight answer.

'That's because you're so clever, Thrasymachus,' I replied, 'and you know it. You ask someone for a definition of twelve, and add "And I don't want to be told that it's twice six, or three times four, or six times two, or four times three; that sort of nonsense won't do." You know perfectly well that no one would answer you on those terms. He would reply "What do you mean, Thrasymachus; am I to give none of the answers you mention? If one of them happens to be true, do you want me to give a false one?" And how would you answer him?'

'That's not a fair parallel,' he replied.

'I don't see why not,' I said: 'but even if it is not, we shan't stop anyone else answering like that if he thinks it fair, whether we like it or not.'

'So I suppose that is what you are going to do,' he said; 'you're going to give one of the answers I barred.'

'I would not be surprised,' said I, 'if it seemed to me on reflection to be the right one.'

'What if I give you a quite different and far better reply about justice? What do you think should be your penalty then?'

'The proper penalty of ignorance, which is of course that those who don't know should learn from those who do; which is the course I propose.'[15]

'You must have your joke,' said he, 'but you must pay the fee for learning as well.'

'I will when I have any cash.'

'The money's all right,' said Glaucon; 'we'll pay up for Socrates.[16] So give us your answer, Thrasymachus.'

'I know,' he replied, 'so that Socrates can play his usual tricks, never giving his own views and when others give theirs criticizing and refuting them.'

'But, my dear man, what am I to do?' I asked. 'I neither know nor profess to know anything about the subject, and even if I did I've been forbidden to say what I think by no mean antagonist. It's much more reasonable for you to say something, because you say you know, and really have something to say. Do please therefore do me a favour and give me an answer, and don't grudge your instruction to Glaucon and the others here.'

Glaucon and the others backed up my request, and it was obvious that Thrasymachus was anxious to get the credit for the striking answer he thought he could give; but he went on pretending he wanted to win his point and make me reply. In *b* the end, however, he gave in, remarking, 'So this is the wisdom of Socrates: he won't teach anyone anything, but goes round learning from others and is not even grateful.'

To which I replied, 'It's quite true, Thrasymachus, to say I learn from others, but it's not true to say I show no gratitude. I am generous with my praise – the only return I can give, as I have no money. You'll see in a moment how ready I am to praise a good answer, for I'm sure the one you're going to give me will be good.'

c   'Listen then,' he replied. 'I say that justice or right[17] is simply what is in the interest of the stronger party. Now where is your praise? I can see you're going to refuse it.'

'You shall have it when I understand what you mean, which at present I don't. You say that what is in the interest of the stronger party is right; but what do you mean by interest? For instance, Polydamas the athlete is *stronger* than us, and it's in his *interest* to eat beef to keep fit; we are *weaker* than him, but *d* you can't mean that the same diet is in our *interest* and so *right* for us.'

'You're being tiresome, Socrates,' he returned, 'and taking my definition in the sense most likely to damage it.'

'I assure you I'm not,' I said; 'you must explain your meaning more clearly.'

'Well then, you know that some of our city-states are tyrannies, some democracies, some aristocracies?'

'True enough.'

'And that in each city power is in the hands of the ruling class?'

'Yes.'

e   'Each type of government enacts laws that are in its own interest, a democracy democratic laws, a tyranny tyrannical ones and so on; and in enacting these laws they make it quite plain that what is "right" for their subjects is what is in the interest of themselves, the rulers, and if anyone deviates from this he is punished as a lawbreaker and "wrongdoer". That is *339 a* what I mean when I say that "right" is the same thing in all states, namely the interest of the established government; and government is the strongest element in each state, and so if we argue correctly we see that "right" is always the same, the interest of the stronger party.'

'Now,' I said, 'I understand your meaning, and we must try to find out whether you are right or not. Your answer is that "right" is "interest" (though incidentally this is an answer which you forbade me to give), but you add the qualification "of the stronger party".'

'An insignificant qualification, I suppose you will say.'   *b*

'Its significance is not yet clear; what is clear is that we must consider whether what you say is true. For I quite agree that what is right is an "interest"; but you add that it is the interest "of the stronger party", and that's what I don't know about and what we must consider.'

'Go on,' he said.

'Very well,' said I. 'You say, do you not, that obedience to the ruling power is *right*?'[18]

'I do.'

'And are those in power in the various states infallible or not?'   *c*

'They are, of course, liable to make mistakes,' he replied.

'When they proceed to make laws, then, they may do the job well or badly.'

'I suppose so.'

'And if they do it well the laws will be in their interest, and if they do it badly they won't, I take it.'

'I agree.'

'But their subjects must act according to the laws they make, for that is what *right* is.'

'Of course.'

'Then according to your argument it is *right* not only to do   *d* what is in the interest of the stronger party but also the opposite.'

'What do you mean?' he asked.

'My meaning is the same as yours, I think. Let us look at it more closely. Did we not agree that when the ruling powers order their subjects to do something they are sometimes mistaken about their own best interest, and yet that it is *right* for the subject to do what his ruler enjoins?'

'I suppose we did.'

e   'Then you must admit that it is *right* to do things that are *not* in the interest of the rulers, who are the *stronger* party; that is, when the rulers mistakenly give orders that will harm them and yet (so you say) it is right for their subjects to obey those orders. For surely, my dear Thrasymachus, in those circumstances it must follow that it is "right" to do the opposite of what you say is right, in that the weaker are *ordered* to do what is against the interest of the stronger.'

340 *a*   'A clear enough conclusion,' exclaimed Polemarchus.

'No doubt,' interrupted Cleitophon, 'if we are to take *your* word for it.'

'It's not a question of *my* word,' replied Polemarchus; 'Thrasymachus himself agrees that rulers sometimes give orders harmful to themselves, and that it is right for their subjects to obey them.'

'Yes, Polemarchus, that was because he asserted that it was right to obey the orders of the rulers.'

b   '*And* that the interest of the stronger was right, Cleitophon. But having made both these assumptions he went on to admit that the stronger sometimes give orders which are not in their interest and which their weaker subjects obey. From which admission it follows that what is in the interest of the stronger is no more right than the reverse.'

'But,' objected Cleitophon, 'what Thrasymachus meant by the interest of the stronger was what the stronger *thinks* to be in his interest; this is what the subject must do, and this was the position Thrasymachus took up about what is right.'

'Well, it was not what he said,' replied Polemarchus.

c   'It does not matter, Polemarchus,' I said. 'If this is Thrasymachus' meaning let us accept it. Tell me, Thrasymachus, was this how you meant to define what is right, that it is that which *seems* to the stronger to be his interest, whether it really is or not? Is this how we are to take what you said?'

'Certainly not,' he replied; 'do you think that I call someone who is making a mistake "stronger" just when he is making his mistake?'

'I thought,' I said, 'that that was what you meant when you agreed that rulers are not infallible but sometimes make mistakes.'

'That's because you're so malicious in argument, Socrates. *d* Do you, for instance, call a man who has made a mistaken diagnosis a doctor by virtue of his mistake? Or when a mathematician makes a mistake in his calculations do you call him a mathematician by virtue of his mistake and when he makes it? We use this form of words, of course, and talk of a doctor or a mathematician or a teacher "making a mistake"; but in fact, I think, each of them, in so far as he is what we call him, is *e* infallible. And so to be precise (and precision is what you aim at) no skilled craftsman ever makes a mistake. For he makes his mistake because his knowledge fails him, and he is then no longer a skilled craftsman. So no craftsman or scientist ever makes a mistake, nor does a ruler so long as he is a ruler; though it's true that in common parlance one may *talk* about the doctor or ruler making a mistake, and that's how you should take the answer I gave you just now. To be really precise one must say that the ruler, in so far as he is a ruler, makes no mistake, and so infallibly enacts what is best for himself, which his subjects 341 *a* must perform. And so, as I said to begin with, "right" means the interest of the stronger party.'

'Well,' said I, 'so you think I'm malicious, do you, Thrasymachus?'

'I certainly do.'

'You think my questions were deliberately framed to distort your argument?'

'I know perfectly well they were. But they won't get you anywhere; you can't fool me, and if you don't you won't be able *b* to crush me in argument.'

'My dear chap, I wouldn't dream of trying,' I said. 'But to stop this sort of thing happening again, will you make this point clear; when you speak of the ruler and stronger party whose interest it is right that the weaker should serve, do you use the words in their more general sense or in the precise sense which you have just defined?'

'I mean ruler in the precisest sense,' he replied. 'Try your low tricks on that if you can – I ask no mercy. But you are not likely to succeed.'

c   'Surely,' I said, 'you don't think I'm foolish enough to try to beard the lion and trick Thrasymachus?'

'You tried just now,' he answered, 'but nothing came of it.'

'Well, let us leave it at that,' I said; 'but tell me, this doctor in the precise sense you have just been talking about, is he a businessman or a medical practitioner? I mean the man who really is a doctor.'

'A medical practitioner.'

'And a ship's captain? Is he a member of the crew or in command of it?'

'In command.'

d   'For it would, I take it, be wrong to take account of his mere presence on board to call him a member of the crew. For he is not captain by virtue of being on board, but because of his professional skill and command of the crew.'

'True.'

'And each one of these[19] has his own particular interest.'

'Yes.'

'And in each case the purpose of the professional skill[20] concerned is to further and provide for that interest?'

'That is its object.'

'Then has any form of professional skill any interest at which it aims over and above its own perfection?'

e   'What do you mean by that?'

'Suppose, for example,' I replied, 'that you were to ask me whether the body were self-sufficient, with no needs beyond itself, I should answer "It certainly has needs. That is the reason why medicine has been discovered, because the body has its defects and is not self-sufficient; medical skill was, in fact, developed to look after the interests of the body." Would that be a correct answer, do you think?'

'It would.'

342 a   'Then is the science or art of medicine itself defective? Does it

or any other skilled activity[21] need anything further to perfect[22] it? I mean as the eyes need sight and the ears hearing, so they also need an art to look to their interests and provide them with what they need in this respect. But is it a characteristic of skilled activity as such to be defective, so that each activity needs another to look after its interests, and this one another, and so *ad infinitum*? Or does each look after its own interest? Is it not rather true that each has no need either of its own or another's supervision to check its faults and watch its interests? For there is no fault or flaw in any science or art, nor is it its business to seek the interest of anything but its subject matter; each is faultless and flawless and right, so long as it is entirely and precisely what it is. Now consider, in your precise sense am I right or not?'

'You are right,' he said.

'Medicine therefore looks to the interest not of medicine but of the body.'

'Yes.'

'And training to the interest of the horse and not its owner. Nor does any form of skill[23] seek its own interest (it needs nothing) but that of its subject-matter.'

'It looks like it.'

'Yet surely,' I said, 'all forms of skill rule and control their subject-matter.'

Thrasymachus only agreed to this very reluctantly.

'Then no science[24] studies or enforces the interest of the controlling or stronger party, but rather that of the weaker party subjected to it.'

He agreed to this, too, in the end, though he tried to make a fight of it. Having secured his agreement I proceeded, 'Then it follows that the doctor *qua* doctor prescribes with a view not to his own interest but that of his patient. For we agreed that a doctor in the precise sense controlled the body and was not in business for profit, did we not?'

He assented.

'And did we not also agree that a ship's captain in the precise sense controlled the crew but was not one of them?'

He agreed.

'So that a captain in this sense is in control, but will not give his orders with his own interest in view, but that of the crew which he controls.'

He agreed reluctantly.

'And therefore, my dear Thrasymachus,' I concluded, 'no ruler of any kind, *qua* ruler, exercises his authority, whatever its sphere, with his own interest in view, but that of the subject of his skill. It is his subject and his subject's proper interest to which he looks in all he says and does.'

2. Second Statement and Final Refutation

To avoid a formal defeat in the argument Thrasymachus interrupts it with a restatement of his main position. What he says may be divided into two parts. First, he reiterates his opening contention (338c–e) that political power is merely the exploitation of one class by another. And (since Socrates has used the analogy from technē*) he illustrates his view by comparing the shepherd who fattens his flock for his own and his master's benefit. Ordinary morality is simply the behaviour imposed by exploiter on exploited, and is thus 'someone else's interest'. But, second, in addition to this political argument, he also maintains that, on the level of ordinary day-to-day behaviour, the pursuit of self-interest, in its narrowest and most obvious form, is both natural and right, and the course which pays the individual best.*

Socrates deals first with the more strictly political part of Thrasymachus' thesis, and argues that government, like any other form of professional skill, has its own standard of achievement, and is not merely a matter of profit-making or exploitation. The argument that 'money-making' or 'profit-making' is a separate activity may seem artificial to modern minds, for do we not exercise our profession to make our living? But what Plato is trying to say is that government is a job or profession like others, with specific tasks to perform, which it may perform well or ill, and that what the individual 'makes out of it' (as we should say) is to that extent irrelevant. This reinforces and extends the latter part of the argument of the preceding section.

At this stage of the argument it was obvious to everyone that 343 *a*
his definition of justice had been reversed, and Thrasymachus,
instead of replying, remarked, 'Tell me, Socrates, have you a
nurse?'

'What do you mean?' I returned. 'Why not answer my question, instead of asking that sort of thing?'

'Well, she lets you go drivelling round and doesn't wipe your
nose, and you can't even tell her the difference between sheep
and shepherd.'

'And why exactly should you say that?' I asked.

'Because you suppose that shepherds and herdsmen study the   *b*
good of their flocks and herds and fatten and take care of them
with some other object in view than the good of their masters
and themselves; and don't realize that the rulers of states, if they
are truly such, feel towards their subjects as one might towards
sheep, and think about nothing day and night but how they can
make a profit out of them. Your view of right and wrong, just   *c*
and unjust, is indeed wide of the mark. You are not aware that
justice or right is really what is good for someone else, namely
the interest of the stronger party or ruler, imposed at the expense
of the subject who obeys him. Injustice or wrong is just the
opposite of this, and rules those who are really simple and just,
while they serve their ruler's interests because he is stronger
than they, and as his subjects promote his happiness to the
complete exclusion of their own. I'm afraid you're very simple-   *d*
minded, Socrates; but you ought to consider how the just man
always comes off worse than the unjust. For instance, in any
business relations between them, you won't find the just man
better off at the end of the deal than the unjust. Again, in their
relations with the state, when there are taxes to be paid the
unjust man will pay less on the same income, and when there's
anything to be got he'll get a lot, the just man nothing. Thus if
it's a question of office, if the just man loses nothing else he will   *e*
suffer from neglecting his private affairs; his honesty will prevent
him appropriating public funds, and his relations and friends
will detest him because his principles will not allow him to do
them a service if it's not right. But quite the reverse is true of the
unjust man. I'm thinking of the man I referred to just now who

can further his own advantage in a big way: he's the man to
344 a   study if you want to find how much more private gain there is
in wrongdoing than in right. You can see it most easily if you
take the extreme of injustice and wrongdoing, which brings the
highest happiness to its practitioners and plunges its victims and
their honesty in misery – I mean, of course, tyranny. Tyranny is
not a matter of minor theft and violence, but of wholesale
b   plunder, sacred or profane, private or public. If you are caught
committing such crimes in detail you are punished and dis-
graced: sacrilege, kidnapping, burglary, fraud, theft are the
names we give to such petty forms of wrongdoing. But when a
man succeeds in robbing the whole body of citizens and reducing
c   them to slavery, they forget these ugly names and call him happy
and fortunate, as do all others who hear of his unmitigated
wrongdoing. For, of course, those who abuse wrongdoing and
injustice do so because they are afraid of suffering from it, not
of doing it. So we see that injustice, given scope, has greater
strength and freedom and power than justice; which proves
what I started by saying, that justice is the interest of the stronger
party, injustice the interest and profit of oneself.'

d   After deluging our ears with this shower of words, Thrasymachus intended to leave; the others, however, would not let
him, but insisted he should stay and answer for[25] what he had
said. I supported their pleas, saying, 'My dear Thrasymachus,
you can't mean to throw a theory like that at us and then leave
e   us without explaining it or examining its truth. Surely it's no
small matter to define the course we must follow if we're to live
our lives to the best advantage?'

    'I never supposed it was,' he countered.

    'You seemed to,' I replied; 'or perhaps it is that you have no
consideration for us, and don't care what sort of lives our
ignorance of what you claim to know makes us lead. Come on,
let us know your secret – it won't be a bad investment to give
345 a   so many of us the benefit of your knowledge. For as far as I am
concerned, you have not convinced me, and I don't think that
injustice pays better than justice even if it has a clear field to do
what it wants. No, my dear Thrasymachus; I grant you your
unjust man and I grant him the ability to continue his wrongdo-

ing by fraud or force, yet he still does not persuade me that   *b*
injustice pays better than justice. And there may be others who
feel the same as I do. It is for you, therefore, to persuade us that
we are wrong in valuing justice more highly than injustice.'

'And how am I to persuade you?' he retorted. 'If you don't
believe what I have just said, what more can I do? Do you want
ideas spoon-fed to you?'

'Not by you at any rate,' I replied. 'But to begin with, do stick
to what you say, or if you modify it, do so openly and above
board. For instance, to look at what you have just been saying,   *c*
you started by defining what a true doctor is: yet when you came
to the true shepherd you abandoned your former precision, and
now suppose that the shepherd's business is to fatten his flock,
not with a view to its own good, but in the hope either of a good
meal, like a prospective guest at a feast, or of making a sale, as
if he were a businessman, not a shepherd. Yet the shepherd's   *d*
skill is devoted solely to the welfare of the flock of which he is
in charge; and so long as it succeeds in discharging its function,
its own welfare is adequately provided for.[26] And so I thought
just now that we agreed that it followed that any kind of
authority, public or private, pursued only the welfare of the
subjects under its care. But tell me, do you think that the rulers   *e*
of states (rulers in the true sense, that is) really want to rule?'

'I don't think it, I know it,' he replied.

'Very well, Thrasymachus,' I said; 'but have you not noticed
that no one really wants to exercise other forms of authority?
At any rate, they expect to be paid for them, which shows that
they don't expect any benefit for themselves but only for their
subjects. For tell me, don't we differentiate between one art or   346 *a*
profession[27] and another by their different functions? And please
tell me what you really think, so that we can get somewhere.'

'That is how we differentiate them,' he replied.

'And so each one benefits us in a distinct and particular way;
medicine brings us health, navigation a safe voyage, and so on.'

'Certainly.'

'So wage-earning brings us wages; for that is its function. For   *b*
you don't identify medicine and navigation, do you? Nor, if you
are going to use words precisely, as you proposed, do you call

navigation medicine just because a ship's captain recovers his
health on a voyage because the sea suits him.'

'No.'

'Nor do you call wage-earning medicine if someone recovers
his health while earning money.'

c   'No.'

'Well then, can you call medicine wage-earning, if a doctor
earns a fee when he is curing his patient?'

'No,' he said.

'We are agreed then that each professional skill[28] brings its
own peculiar benefit?'

'I grant that.'

'Any common benefit, therefore, that all their practitioners
enjoy, must clearly be procured by the exercise of some
additional activity common to all.'

'It looks like it.'

'And further, if they earn wages it is a benefit they get from
exercising the profession of wage-earning in addition to their
own.'

He agreed reluctantly.

d   'This benefit of receiving wages does not therefore come to a
man as a result of the exercise of his own particular profession; if
we are to be precise, medicine produces health and wage-earning
wages, and building produces a house while wage-earning, following in its train, produces wages. Similarly all other arts and
professions each operate to the benefit of the subject which falls
to their particular charge; and no man will benefit from his
profession, unless he is paid as well.'

'It seems not,' he said.

e   'But if he works for nothing, does he still confer no benefit?'

'He surely does.'

'In fact it is clear enough, Thrasymachus, that no profession
or art or authority provides for its own benefit but, as we said
before, provides and orders what benefits the subject of which
it is in charge, thus studying the interest of the weaker party and
not the stronger. That was why I said just now that no one really
wants authority and with it the job of righting other people's
wrongs, unless he is paid for it; because in the exercise of his

professional skill, if he does his job properly, he never does or   347 a
orders what is best for himself but only what is best for his
subject. That is why, if a man is to consent to exercise authority,
you must pay him, either in cash or honours, or alternatively by
punishing him if he refuses.'

'What's that, Socrates?' said Glaucon; 'I recognize your two
kinds of reward, but I don't know what the punishment is or in
what sense you speak of it as pay.'

'Then you don't understand how the best men must be paid
if they are to be willing to govern. You know that to be over-   b
ambitious or mercenary is reckoned, and indeed is, something
discreditable?'

'Yes.'

'So good men will not consent to govern for cash or honours.
They do not want to be called mercenary for exacting a cash
payment for the work of government, or thieves for making
money on the side; and they will not work for honours, for they
aren't ambitious. We must therefore bring compulsion to bear
and punish them if they refuse – perhaps that's why it's com-   c
monly considered improper to accept authority except with
reluctance or under pressure; and the worst penalty for refusal
is to be governed by someone worse than themselves. That is
what, I believe, frightens honest men into accepting power, and
they approach it not as if it were something desirable out of
which they were going to do well, but as if it were something
unavoidable, which they cannot find anyone better or equally   d
qualified to undertake. For in a city of good men there might
well be as much competition to avoid power as there now is to
get it, and it would be quite clear that the true ruler pursues his
subjects' interest and not his own; consequently all wise men
would prefer the benefit of this service at the hands of others
rather than the labour of affording it to others themselves.'

*Socrates now turns to the other part of Thrasymachus' argu-
ment, that the pursuit of self-interest or injustice pays better
than that of justice. He deals with it in three stages.*

*(A) In the first there are ambiguities in the Greek which it is
difficult to render in English, and this section of the argument*

has been called 'embarrassingly bad'.[29] *The basis of the argument is again the* Technē *analogy. No two craftsmen or professional men are in disagreement about the standards of correctness in their own particular craft or profession, and in that sense are not in competition with each other; and since just men also do not compete with each other either, they are analogous to the skilled craftsman, and so the just man is 'wise and good', words which in Greek imply that he has both the knowledge and the effectiveness to lead the best kind of life, whatever that may be.*

e   'You see, then, that I entirely disagree with Thrasymachus' view that justice is the interest of the stronger; but the point is one that we can examine again later, and far more important is his recent statement[30] that the unjust man has a superior life to the just. Which side are you on, Glaucon? And which of us seems to be nearer the truth?'

'I think the just man's life pays the better.'

348 a   'Did you hear the list of good things in the unjust man's life which Thrasymachus has just gone through?' I asked.

'I heard them,' he replied, 'but I'm not persuaded.'

'Shall we then try and persuade him, if we can find any flaw in his argument?'

'By all means,' he said.

'We might, then, answer his speech by a rival one of our own, setting out the advantages of justice, to which he would make a rejoinder, to which we again would reply; but we shall then

b   have to count and measure up the advantages put forward by either side, and shall soon be wanting a jury to decide between them. But if we proceed by mutual agreement, as we have done so far, we can ourselves be both counsel and jury.'

'We can.'

'Which course, then, do you prefer?'

'The latter,' he replied.

'Well then,' said I, turning to Thrasymachus, 'let us begin again at the beginning. You say that perfect injustice pays better than perfect justice.'

c   'That's what I say,' he replied, 'and I've given you my reasons.'

'Then what do you say about this: is one of them an excellence[31] and one a fault?'[32]

'Of course.'

'Justice an excellence, I suppose, and injustice a fault?'

'My dear man,' he replied, 'is that likely? When I am telling you that injustice pays and justice doesn't.'

'Then what do you think?'

'The opposite,' he answered.

'You mean that justice is a fault?'

'No; it's merely supreme simplicity.'

'And so injustice is duplicity, I suppose.'   *d*

'No; it's common sense.'

'So you think that the unjust are good sensible men?'

'If they can win political power over states and peoples, and their wrongdoings have full scope. You perhaps think I'm talking of bag-snatching; even things like that pay,' he said, 'if you aren't found out, but they are quite trivial by comparison.'

'I see what you mean about that,' I said; 'but what surprised   *e* me was that you should rank injustice with wisdom and excellence, and justice with their opposites.'

'Yet that is just what I do.'

'That is a much tougher proposition,' I answered, 'and it's not easy to know what to say to it. For if you were maintaining that injustice pays, but were prepared to admit that it is a fault and discreditable quality, we could base our argument on generally accepted grounds. As it is, having boldly ranked injustice with wisdom and excellence, you will obviously attribute to it all the strength of character that we normally attribute   349 *a* to justice.'

'You've guessed my meaning correctly,' he said.

'Still, there must be no shirking,' I rejoined, 'and I must pursue the argument as long as I'm sure you are saying what you think. For I think you are really in earnest now, Thrasymachus, and saying what you think to be the truth.'

'What's it matter what I think?' he retorted. 'Stick to the argument.'

'It doesn't matter at all,' was my reply; 'but see if you can   *b* answer me this further question. Will one just man want to get the better[33] of another?'

'Certainly not; otherwise he would not be the simple, agreeable man we've just seen him to be.'

'And will he think it right and proper to do better than the unjust man or not?'

'He'll think it right and proper enough, but he'll not be able to.'

'That's not what I'm asking,' I said, 'but whether one just
c man thinks it improper to compete with another and refuses to do so, but will compete with an unjust man?'

'Yes, that is so,' he replied.

'Then what about the unjust man? Will he compete with the just and want more than his share in an act of justice?'

'Of course he will; he wants more than his share in everything.'

'Will one unjust man, then, compete with another in an unjust action and fight to get the largest share in everything?'

'Yes.'

'Then let us put it this way,' I said. 'The just man does not compete with his like, but only his unlike, while the unjust man
d competes with both like and unlike.'

'That puts it very well.'

'And the unjust man is a good sensible man, the just man not?'

'Well said again.'

'And so the unjust man is like the good sensible man, while the just man is not?'

'Of course, being the kind of person he is, the unjust man must be *like* others of his kind, and the just man unlike them.'

'Good. So each of them is of the same sort as those he is like.'

'Well, what next?'

'So far, so good, Thrasymachus. Do you recognize the distinc-
e tion between being musical and unmusical?'

'Yes.'

'And which of the two involves intelligence?'

'Being musical; and being unmusical does not.'

'And intelligence is good, lack of it bad.'

'Yes.'

'And the same argument applies to medicine.'

'It does.'

'Then does one musician who is tuning a lyre try to do better than another, or think that he ought to outdo him in tightening or loosening the strings?'

'I think not.'

'But he does try to do better than an unmusical layman?'

'He must try to do that.'

'What about a doctor then? In prescribing a diet is he trying 350 a to outdo other doctors and get the better of them in medical practice?'

'No.'

'But he tries to do better than the layman?'

'Yes.'

'Then do you think that over the whole range of professional knowledge[34] anyone who has such knowledge aims at anything more in word or deed than anyone with similar knowledge? Don't they both aim at the same result in similar circumstances?'

'I suppose there's no denying that.'

'But the man who has no knowledge will try to compete both with the man who has and with the man who has not.'   b

'Maybe.'

'And the man with professional knowledge is wise?'

'I agree.'

'And the wise man is good?'

'I agree.'

'So the good man, who has knowledge, will not try to compete with his like, but only with his opposite.'

'So it seems.'

'While the bad and ignorant man will try to compete both with his like and with his opposite.'

'So it appears.'

'But it was surely the unjust man, Thrasymachus, who, we found, competes both with his like and his unlike? That was what you said, wasn't it?'

'It was,' he admitted.

'While the just man will not compete with his like, but with   c his unlike.'

'True.'

'The just man, then,' I said, 'resembles the good man who has knowledge, the unjust the man who is ignorant and bad.'

'That may be.'

'But we agreed that each of them is of the same kind as the one he is like.'

'We did.'

'Then,' I concluded, 'we have shown that the just man is wise and good and the unjust bad and ignorant.'

d Thrasymachus' agreement to all these points did not come as easily as I have described, but had to be dragged from him with difficulty, and with a great deal of sweat – for it was a hot day. And I saw something then I had never seen before, Thrasymachus blushing. So when we had agreed that justice was goodness[35] and knowledge and injustice their opposites, I said, 'Well, we have settled that point, Thrasymachus; but you will remember that we also said that injustice was strength.'

'I remember well enough,' he replied; 'but I still don't accept your last arguments, and have more to say about them. Yet if I were to say it, I know you would accuse me of making speeches. e Either therefore let me say all I have to say, or else, if you prefer it, continue your cross-questioning; and I will answer "Very good", "Yes", and "No", like someone listening to old wives' tales.'

'But don't answer contrary to your real opinion,' I replied.

'Yes, I will, to please you,' he said, 'since you won't let me speak freely. What more can you ask?'[36]

'Nothing at all,' said I. 'Do as you suggest, and I will ask the questions.'

'Ask away then.'

(B) Thrasymachus had claimed that injustice is a source of strength. On the contrary, says Socrates, it is a source of disunity and therefore of weakness. There must be cooperation among thieves if they are to achieve any common action.

'Well then, to proceed with the argument, I return to my 351 a question about the relation of justice and injustice. We said,[37] I think, that injustice was stronger and more effective than justice, whereas if, as we have now agreed, justice implies excellence[38] and knowledge it will not, I think, be difficult to show that it is stronger than injustice, which, as must by now be obvious to anyone, involves[39] ignorance. But I don't want to argue in general terms like this, Thrasymachus, but rather as follows. *b* Would you say that a state might be unjust and wrongly try to reduce others to subjection, and having succeeded in so doing continue to hold them in subjection?'

'Of course,' he replied. 'And the most efficient state, whose injustice is most complete, will be the most likely to do so.'

'I understood that that was your argument,' said I. 'But do you think that the more powerful state needs justice to exercise this power over its neighbour or not?'

'If you are right and justice involves[40] knowledge, it will need *c* justice; but if I am right, injustice.'

'I am delighted that you are not just saying "yes" and "no", but are giving me a fair answer, Thrasymachus.'

'I'm doing it to please you.'

'Thank you,' said I. 'Then will you be kind enough to tell me too whether you think that any group of men, be it a state or an army or a set of gangsters or thieves, can undertake any sort of wrongdoing together if they wrong each other?'

'No.' *d*

'Their prospect of success is greater if they don't wrong each other?'

'Yes, it is.'

'Because, of course, if they wrong each other that will breed hatred and dissension among them; but if they treat each other justly, there will be unity of purpose and friendly feeling among them.'

'Yes – I won't contradict you.'

'That's very good of you,' I said. 'Now tell me this. If it is a function of injustice to produce hatred wherever it is, won't it cause men to hate each other and quarrel and be incapable of any joint undertaking whether they are free men or slaves?' *e*

'It will.'

'And so with any two individuals. Injustice will make them

quarrel and hate each other, and they will be at enmity with themselves and with just men as well.'

'They will.'

'And in a single individual it will not lose its power, will it, but retain it just the same?'

'Let us assume it will retain it.'

'Injustice, then, seems to have the following results, whether it occurs in a state or family or army or in anything else: it renders it incapable of any common action because of factions 352 *a* and quarrels, and sets it at variance with itself and with its opponents and with whatever is just.'

'Yes.'

'And it will produce its natural effects also in the individual. It renders him incapable of action because of internal conflicts and division of purpose, and sets him at variance with himself and with all who are just.'

'Yes.'

'And the gods, of course, are just.'

'Granted.'

b 'So the unjust man is an enemy of the gods, and the just man their friend.'

'Go on, enjoy your argument,' he retorted. 'I won't annoy the company by contradicting you.'

'If you will go on answering my questions as you are at present,' I replied, 'you will complete my entertainment. We have shown that just men are more intelligent and more truly effective in action, and that unjust men are incapable of any *c* joint action at all. Indeed, when we presumed to speak of unjust men carrying out any effective joint action between them, we were quite wrong. For had they been completely unjust they would never have kept their hands off each other, and there must have been some element of justice among them which prevented them wronging each other as well as their victims, and brought them what success they had; they were in fact only half corrupted when they set about their misdeeds, for had their corruption been complete, their complete injustice would have made them incapable of achieving anything. All this seems to *d* me to be established against your original contention.'

(C) Finally, Socrates shows that the just man is happier than the unjust. Using the idea of 'function', he argues that a man needs justice to enable him to perform his own particular function and so to achieve happiness. Justice, however, remains undefined. 'Happiness depends on conformity to our nature as active beings. What active principles that nature comprises, and how they are organized into a system we learn in the immediately following books' (A. E. Taylor, The Mind of Plato *(University of Michigan), p. 270).*

'We must now proceed to the further question which we set ourselves, whether the just live better and happier lives than the unjust. It is, in fact, already clear, I think, from what we have said, that they do; but we must look at the question more closely. For it is not a trivial one; it is our whole way of life that is at issue.'

'Proceed,' he said.

'I will,' I replied. 'So tell me, do you think a horse has a function?'

'Yes.'

e

'And would you define the function of a horse, or of anything else, as something one can only do, or does best, with the thing in question?'

'I don't understand.'

'Look at it this way. Can you see with anything but eyes?'

'No.'

'Again, can you hear with anything but ears?'

'Certainly not.'

'So we can rightly call these the functions of eye and ear.'

'Yes.'

'So again, could you cut off a vine-shoot with a carving-knife or a chisel or other tool?'

353 a

'You could.'

'But you would do the job best if you used a pruning-knife made for the purpose.'

'True.'

'Shall we then call this its "function"?'

'Yes, let us.'

'And I think you may see now what I meant by asking if the "function" of a thing was not that which only it can do or that which it does best.'

'Yes, I understand,' he replied, 'and I think that is what we
b   mean by a thing's function.'

'Good,' said I. 'And has not everything which has a function its own particular excellence?[41] Let me take the same examples again. The eyes have a function, have they not?'

'They have.'

'Have they also their own particular excellence?'

'They have their excellence also.'

'Then have the ears a function?'

'Yes.'

'And an excellence?'

'And an excellence.'

'And is not the same true of everything else?'

'Yes, it is.'

c   'Come, then; could the eyes properly perform their function if instead of their own peculiar excellence they had the corresponding defect?'

'How could they? For you mean, I suppose, blindness instead of sight?'

'I mean whatever their excellence may be. For I am not concerned with that yet, but only to find out whether a thing's characteristic excellence enables it to perform its function well, while its characteristic defect makes it perform it badly.'

'Yes, that is certainly true,' he replied.

'So we can say that the ears, if deprived of their own peculiar excellence, perform their function badly.'

'Certainly.'

d   'Then may we assume that the same argument applies in all other cases?'

'I agree.'

'Then the next point is this. Is there any function that it is impossible to perform with anything except the mind?[42] For example, paying attention, controlling, deliberating, and so on: can we attribute any of these to anything but the mind, of which we should say they were particular characteristics?'

'No.'

'And what about life? Is not that a function of mind?'

'Very much so,' he said.

'And the mind will surely have its peculiar excellence?'

'It will.'

'And if deprived of its peculiar excellence will it perform its   e
function well, or will it be incapable of so doing?'

'Quite incapable.'

'It follows therefore that a good mind will perform the functions of control and attention well, a bad mind badly.'

'It follows.'

'And we agreed,[43] did we not, that justice was the peculiar
excellence of the mind and injustice its defect?'

'We did.'

'So the just mind and the just man will have a good life, and
the unjust a bad life?'

'So it appears from your argument.'

'But the man who has a good life is prosperous and happy,
and his opposite the reverse?'

'Of course.'   354 a

'So the just man is happy, and the unjust man miserable?'

'So be it.'

'But it never pays to be miserable, but to be happy.'

'Of course.'

'And so, my dear Thrasymachus, injustice never pays better
than justice.'

'This is your holiday treat,' he replied, 'so enjoy it, Socrates.'

'If I do enjoy it, it's thanks to you, Thrasymachus,' I replied,
'for you have been most agreeable since you stopped being cross
with me. But I'm not enjoying it all the same; and it's my own   b
fault, not yours. I'm like a greedy guest who grabs a taste of the
next course before he has properly finished the last. For we
started off to inquire what justice is, but gave up before we had
found the answer, and went on to ask whether it was excellence
and knowledge or their opposites, and then when we stumbled
on the view that injustice pays better than justice, instead of
letting it alone off we went in pursuit, so that I still know
nothing[44] after all our discussion. For so long as I don't know

what justice is I'm hardly likely to find out whether it is an excellence or not, or whether it makes a man happy or unhappy.'

This section claims to prove that the just man is happier than the unjust. Similarly at 361d Glaucon asks Socrates to answer the question whether the just or unjust man is happier; and the theme of happiness will recur throughout the dialogue, as e.g. on 419–421c. The common Greek word for 'happy' (eudaimōn) has overtones rather different from those of the English word. It implies less an immediate state of mind or feeling ('I feel happy today') than a more permanent condition of life or disposition of character, something between prosperity and integration of personality, though of course feeling is involved too.

BK II   4. Adeimantus and Glaucon Restate the
                                        Case for Injustice

There has been a touch of broad caricature about the picture of Thrasymachus, and Plato evidently thinks that the view which he represents needs a clearer statement and fairer treatment. Accordingly, Glaucon says that he is not content with the way in which Socrates has dealt with Thrasymachus and proceeds to restate his argument in a different form; he is followed by Adeimantus, who supplements what he has said.

1. Glaucon argues that justice, or morality, is merely a matter of convenience. It is natural for men to pursue their own interests regardless of others; but it would be impossible to run an orderly society on that basis, and the system of morality is arrived at as a compromise. But it is only a compromise and has no other authority, as can be seen easily enough by considering how a man would behave if its sanctions were removed. And a contrast between the perfectly 'just' and perfectly 'unjust' man shows conclusively that 'injustice' is the more paying proposition.

357a   I thought, when I said this, that the argument was over; but in fact, as it turned out, we had only had its prelude. For

Glaucon, with his customary pertinacity, characteristically would not accept Thrasymachus' withdrawal, but asked: 'Do *b* you want our conviction that right action is in all circumstances better than wrong to be genuine or merely apparent?'

'If I were given the choice,' I replied, 'I should want it to be genuine.'

'Well then, you are not making much progress,' he returned. 'Tell me, do you agree that there is one kind of good which we want to have not with a view to its consequences but because we welcome it for its own sake? For example, enjoyment or pleasure, so long as pleasure brings no harm and its only result is the enjoyment it brings.'

'Yes, that is one kind of good.'

'And is there not another kind of good which we desire, both *c* for itself and its consequences? Wisdom and sight and health, for example, we welcome on both grounds.'

'We do,' I said.

'And there is a third category of good, which includes exercise and medical treatment and earning one's living as a doctor or otherwise. All these we should regard as painful but beneficial; we should not choose them for their own sakes but for the wages and other benefits we get from them.' *d*

'There is this third category. But what is your point?'

'In which category do you place justice and right?'

'In the highest category, which anyone who is to be happy *358 a* welcomes both for its own sake and for its consequences.'

'That is not the common opinion,' Glaucon replied. 'It is normally put into the painful category, of goods which we pursue for the rewards they bring and in the hope of a good reputation, but which in themselves are to be avoided as unpleasant.'

'I know that is the common opinion,' I answered; 'which is why Thrasymachus has been criticizing it and praising injustice. But it seems I'm slow to learn.'

'Listen to me then, and see if I can get you to agree,' he *b* said. 'For you seem to have fascinated Thrasymachus into a premature submission, like a snake charmer; but I am not satisfied yet about justice and injustice. I want to be told what exactly

each of them is and what effects it has as such on the mind of
its possessor, leaving aside any question of rewards or consequences. So what I propose to do, if you agree, is this. I shall
c revive Thrasymachus' argument under three heads: first, I shall
state the common opinion on the nature and origin of justice;
second, I shall show that those who practise it do so under
compulsion and not because they think it a good; third, I shall
argue that this conduct is reasonable because the unjust man
has, by common reckoning, a better life than the just man. I
don't believe all this myself, Socrates, but Thrasymachus and
hundreds of others have dinned it into my ears till I don't know
what to think; and I've never heard the case for the superiority
d of justice to injustice argued to my satisfaction, that is, I've never
heard the praises of justice sung simply for its own sake. That
is what I expect to hear from you. I therefore propose to state,
forcibly, the argument in praise of injustice, and thus give you
a model which I want you to follow when your turn comes to
speak in praise of justice and censure injustice. Do you like this
suggestion?'

e   'Nothing could please me better,' I replied, 'for it's a subject
which all sensible men should be glad to discuss.'

'Splendid,' said Glaucon. 'And now for my first heading, the
nature and origin of justice. What they say is that it is according
to nature a good thing to inflict wrong or injury,[45] and a bad
thing to suffer it, but that the disadvantages of suffering it exceed
the advantages of inflicting it; after a taste of both, therefore,
359 *a* men decide that, as they can't evade the one and achieve the
other, it will pay to make a compact with each other by which
they forgo both. They accordingly proceed to make laws and
mutual agreements, and what the law lays down they call lawful
and right. This is the origin and nature of justice. It lies between
what is most desirable, to do wrong and avoid punishment, and
what is most undesirable, to suffer wrong without being able to
get redress; justice lies between these two and is accepted not as
being good in itself, but as having a relative value due to our
b inability to do wrong. For anyone who had the power to do
wrong and was a real man would never make any such agreement with anyone – he would be mad if he did.[46]

'This then is the account they give of the nature and the origins of justice; the next point is that men practise it against their will and only because they are unable to do wrong. This we can most easily see if we imagine that a just man and an unjust man have each been given liberty to do what they like,   c
and then follow them and see where their inclinations lead them. We shall catch the just man red-handed in exactly the same pursuits as the unjust, led on by self-interest, the motive which all men naturally follow if they are not forcibly restrained by the law and made to respect each other's claims.

'The best illustration of the liberty I am talking about would be if we supposed them both to be possessed of the power which Gyges, the ancestor of Gyges the Lydian, had in the story. He   d
was a shepherd in the service of the then king of Lydia, and one day there was a great storm and an earthquake in the district where he was pasturing his flock and a chasm opened in the earth. He was amazed at the sight, and descended into the chasm and saw many astonishing things there, among them, so the story goes, a bronze horse, which was hollow and fitted with doors, through which he peeped and saw a corpse which seemed to be of more than human size. He took nothing from it save a gold ring it had on its finger, and then made his way out. He   e
was wearing this ring when he attended the usual meeting of shepherds which reported monthly to the king on the state of his flocks; and as he was sitting there with the others he happened to twist the bezel of the ring towards the inside of his hand.   360 a
Thereupon he became invisible to his companions, and they began to refer to him as if he had left them. He was astonished, and began fingering the ring again, and turned the bezel outwards; whereupon he became visible again. When he saw this he started experimenting with the ring to see if it really had this power, and found that every time he turned the bezel inwards he became invisible, and when he turned it outwards he became visible. Having made his discovery he managed to get himself included in the party that was to report to the king, and when he arrived seduced the queen, and with her help attacked and   b
murdered the king and seized the throne.

'Imagine now that two such rings existed and the just man

put on one, the unjust the other. There is no one, it would commonly be supposed, who would have such iron strength of will as to stick to what is right and keep his hands from taking other people's property. For he would be able to steal from the market whatever he wanted without fear of detection, to go into
c any man's house and seduce anyone he liked, to murder or to release from prison anyone he felt inclined, and generally behave as if he had supernatural powers. And in all this the just man would differ in no way from the unjust, but both would follow the same course. This, it would be claimed, is strong evidence that no man is just of his own free will, but only under compulsion, and that no man thinks justice pays him personally, since he will always do wrong when he gets the chance. Indeed, the
d supporter of this view will continue, men are right in thinking that injustice pays the individual better than justice; and if anyone who had the liberty of which we have been speaking neither wronged nor robbed his neighbour, men would think him a most miserable idiot, though of course they would pretend to admire him in public because of their own fear of being wronged.

e   'So much for that. Finally, we come to the decision between the two lives, and we shall only be able to make this decision if we contrast extreme examples of just and unjust men. By that I mean if we make each of them perfect in his own line, and do not in any way mitigate the injustice of the one or the justice of the other. To begin with the unjust man. He must operate like a skilled professional – for example, a top-class pilot or doctor, who know just what they can or can't do, never attempt the
361 a impossible, and are able to retrieve any errors they make. The unjust man must, similarly, if he is to be thoroughly unjust, be able to avoid detection in his wrongdoing; for the man who is found out must be reckoned a poor specimen, and the most accomplished form of injustice is to seem just when you are not. So our perfectly unjust man must be perfect in his wickedness; he must be able to commit the greatest crimes[47] perfectly and at
b the same time get himself a reputation for the highest probity,[48] while, if he makes a mistake he must be able to retrieve it, and, if any of his wrongdoing comes to light, be ready with a

convincing defence, or when force is needed be prepared to use force, relying on his own courage and energy or making use of his friends or his wealth.

'Beside our picture of the unjust man let us set one of the just man, the man of true simplicity of character who, as Aeschylus says, wants "to be and not to seem good".[49] We must, indeed, not allow him to seem good, for if he does he will have all the rewards and honours paid to the man who has a reputation for justice, and we shall not be able to tell whether his motive is love of justice or love of the rewards and honours. No, we must strip him of everything except his justice, and our picture of him must be drawn in a way diametrically opposite to that of the unjust man. Our just man must have the worst of reputations for wrongdoing even though he has done no wrong, so that we can test his justice and see if it weakens in the face of unpopularity and all that goes with it; we shall give him an undeserved and life-long reputation for wickedness, and make him stick to his chosen course until death. In this way, when we have pushed the life of justice and of injustice each to its extreme, we shall be able to judge which of the two is the happier.'

'I say, Glaucon,' I put in, 'you're putting the finishing touches to your two pictures as vigorously as if you were getting them ready for an exhibition.'

'I'm doing my best,' he said. 'And these being our two characters, it is not, I think, difficult to describe the sort of life that awaits each. And if the description is somewhat brutal, remember that it's not I that am responsible for it, Socrates, but those who praise injustice more highly than justice. It is their account that I must now repeat.

'They will say that the just man, as we have pictured him, will be scourged, tortured, and imprisoned, his eyes will be put out, and after enduring every humiliation he will be crucified, and learn at last that one should want not to be, but to seem just. And so that remark which I quoted from Aeschylus could be more appropriately applied to the unjust man; for he, because he deals with realities and does not live by appearances, really wants not to *seem* but to *be* unjust. He

Reaps thought's deep furrow, for therefrom
b   Spring goodly schemes[50]

– schemes which bring him respectability and office, and which
enable him to marry into any family he likes, to make desirable
matches for his children, and to pick his partners in business
transactions, while all the time, because he has no scruples
about committing injustice, he is on the make. In all kinds of
competition public or private he always comes off best and does
c down his rivals, and so becomes rich and can do good to his
friends and harm his enemies. His sacrifices and votive offerings
to the gods are on a suitably magnificent scale, and his services
to the gods, and to any man he wishes to serve, are far better
than those of the just man, so that it is reasonable to suppose
that the gods care more for him than for the just man. And so
they conclude, Socrates, that a better life is provided for the
unjust man than for the just by both gods and men.'

2. Adeimantus, *supplementing what Glaucon has said, stresses
the unworthy motives commonly given for right conduct. Men
only do right for what they can get out of it, in this life and the
next. They much prefer to do wrong, because in general it pays
better; and they are encouraged to do wrong by contemporary
religious beliefs which tell them that they can avoid punishment
in this world if they sacrifice to the gods lavishly enough, and in
the next if they go through the appropriate initiation ceremonies.
Adeimantus and Glaucon ask Socrates to show that just or right
conduct is preferable in itself and without reference to any
external rewards or punishments.*

d   When Glaucon had finished speaking I had it in mind again
to make some reply to him, but his brother Adeimantus fore-
stalled me, saying, 'You don't suppose that is a complete statement of the argument, do you, Socrates?'
'Well, isn't it?' I replied.
'The most essential point has not been stated.'
'Well,' said I, 'they say blood is thicker than water;[51] so if
your brother has left anything out, lend him a hand. Though as

far as I am concerned, he has said quite enough to floor me and make me quite incapable of coming to the rescue of justice.'

'That's nonsense,' he answered. 'But listen to what I have to say. In order to make clearer what I take to be Glaucon's meaning, we ought to examine the converse of the view he stated, that is, the arguments normally used in favour of justice and against injustice. For fathers tell their sons, and pastors and masters of all kinds urge their charges to be just not because they value justice for itself, but for the good reputation it brings; they want them to secure by a show of justice the power and family connections and other things which Glaucon enumerated, all of which are procured for the just man by a good reputation. And they go on to enlarge on the importance of reputation, and add that if a man stands well with heaven there is a whole list of benefits available for the pious, citing the authority of Hesiod and Homer. For Hesiod[52] says that for the just the gods make the oaks bear "acorns at the top, bees in the middle", while his "wool-bearing sheep are weighed down by their fleeces". And Homer[53] speaks in similar terms of "some perfect king, ruling with the fear of god in his heart, and upholding the right, so that the dark soil yields its wheat and barley, the trees are laden with ripe fruit, the sheep never fail to bring forth their lambs, nor the sea to provide its fish".

'The rewards which Musaeus and his son[54] give for the just are still more exciting. After they have got them to the other world they sit them down to a banquet of the Blest and leave them garlanded and drinking for all time, as if they thought that the supreme reward of virtue was to be drunk for eternity. And some extend the rewards of heaven still further and say that the pious and honest leave children's children and a long posterity to follow them. That is the sort of recommendation they produce for justice. The unjust and the irreligious they plunge into some sort of mud in the underworld or make them carry water in sieves, while in this world they give them a bad reputation and inflict on them all the punishments which Glaucon described as falling on the just man who seemed to be wicked – they can think of no others.

'So much for the way in which justice is recommended and

injustice blamed. But there is another line of argument about them which one meets in the poets as well as in ordinary conversation. People are unanimous in hymning the worth of self-control or justice, but think they are difficult to practise and call for hard work, while self-indulgence and injustice are easy enough to acquire, and regarded as disgraceful only by convention; wrong on the whole pays better than right, they say, and they are ready enough to call a bad man happy and respect him both in public and private provided he is rich and powerful, while they have no respect for the poor and powerless, and despise him, even though they agree that he is the better man. But most surprising of all are the stories about the gods and virtue, which tell how they often allot misfortune and a hard life to the good and the reverse to the wicked. There are itinerant evangelists and prophets who knock at the door of the rich man's house, and persuade him that by sacrifices and spells they have accumulated some kind of divine power, and that any wrong that either he or his ancestors have done can be expiated by means of charms and sacrifices and the pleasures of the accompanying feasts; while if he has any enemy he wants to injure they can for a small fee damage him (whether he is a good man or not) with their spells and incantations, by which they profess to be able to persuade the gods to do their will. In support of all this they cite the evidence of the poets. Some, in support of the easiness of vice, quote Hesiod:[55] "Evil can men attain easily and in companies: the road is smooth and her dwelling near. But the gods have decreed much sweat before a man reaches virtue" and a road that is long and hard and steep. Others quote Homer[56] on turning aside the gods –

The very gods are capable of being swayed. Even they are turned from their course by sacrifice and humble prayers, libations and burnt offerings, when the miscreant and sinner bend the knee to them in supplication.

Or they produce a whole collection of books of ritual instructions written by Musaeus and Orpheus, whom they call descendants of the Moon and the Muses; and they persuade not only

individuals but whole communities that, both for living and
dead, remission and absolution of sins may be had by sacrifices
and pleasant trivialities, which they are pleased to call   365 a
initiations, and which they allege deliver us from all ills in the
next world, where terrible things await those who have failed
to sacrifice.

'Now what do you think, Socrates, is likely to be the effect of
all this sort of talk about virtue and vice, and how far gods and
men think them worth while, on the minds of young men who
have enough natural intelligence to gather the implications of
what they hear for their own lives and how best to lead them,
the sort of person they ought to be and the sort of ends they   b
ought to pursue? Such a young man may well ask himself, in
Pindar's[57] words,

Shall I by justice reach the higher stronghold, or by deceit,

and there live entrenched securely? For it is clear from what
they tell me that if I am just, it will bring me no advantage but
only trouble and loss, unless I also have a reputation for justice;
whereas if I am unjust, but can contrive to get a reputation for
justice, I shall have a marvellous time. Well then, since the sages   c
tell me that "appearance has more force than reality" and
determines our happiness, I had better devote myself entirely to
appearances; I must put up a façade that gives the illusory
appearance of virtue, but I must always have at my back the
"cunning, wily fox" of which Archilochus[58] so shrewdly speaks.
You may object that it is not easy to be wicked and never be
found out; I reply, that nothing worth while is easy, and that all
we have been told points to this as the road to happiness. To
help us avoid being found out we shall form clubs and secret   d
societies, and there are always those who will teach us the art
of persuasion, political or forensic; and so we shall get our way
by persuasion or force and avoid the penalty for doing our
neighbour down. "Yet neither deceit nor force is effective
against the gods." But if there are no gods or if they care nothing
for human affairs, why should we bother to deceive them? And
if there are gods and they do care, our only knowledge of them   e

is derived from tradition and the poets who have written their
genealogies, and they tell us that they can be persuaded to
change their minds by sacrifices and "humble prayers" and
offerings. We must believe them in both types of testimony or
neither; and if we believe them then the thing to do is to sin first
and sacrifice afterwards from the proceeds. For if we do right
366 a we shall merely avoid the wrath of heaven, but lose the profits
of wrongdoing; but if we do wrong we shall get the profits and,
provided that we accompany our sins and wickednesses with
prayer, be able to persuade the gods to let us go unpunished.
"But we shall pay in the next world for the sins we commit
in this, either ourselves or our descendants." To which the
calculating answer is that initiation and the gods who give
absolution are very powerful, as we are told both by the most
b important among human societies, and by children of the gods
who have become poets and prophets with a divine message
and have revealed that these things are so.

'What argument, then, remains for preferring justice to the
worst injustice, when both common men and great men agree
that, provided it has a veneer of respectability, injustice will
enable us, in this world and the next, to do as we like with gods
c and men? And how can anyone, when he has heard all we have
said, possibly value justice and avoid laughing when he hears it
being praised, if he has any force of character at all, any advantages of person, wealth, or rank? For indeed if there is anyone
capable of disproving what we have said, and assuring himself
of the superiority of justice, his feeling for the wicked will be
forgiveness rather than anger; he will know that unless a man is
born with some heaven-sent aversion to wrongdoing, or unless
d he acquires the knowledge to refrain from it, he will never do
right of his own free will, but will censure wrongdoing only if
cowardice or age or weakness make him powerless to practise
it himself. That is all too obvious: once give him the power, and
he will be the first to use it as fully as he can.

'The root of the whole matter is the assertion from which this
whole discussion between the three of us started, Socrates, and
which we may put as follows. "All you professed partisans of
e justice, from the heroes of old whose tales have survived to our

own contemporaries, have never blamed injustice or praised justice except for the reputation and honours and rewards they bring; no one, poet or layman, has ever sufficiently inquired what the effect of each is on the mind[59] of the individual (an effect that may be unobserved by either gods or men), or explained how it is that injustice has the worst possible effect on the mind and justice the reverse. Had you adopted that method from the beginning and set about convincing us when we were young, there would be no need to protect ourselves against our neighbours wronging us; each man would be his own best protector, because he would be afraid that by doing wrong he was doing himself a grave and lasting injury."

'This, and indeed a good deal more than this, is what Thrasymachus and others would say about justice and injustice. It is, in my opinion, a gross distortion of their real effect; but (to be candid) I have stated it as forcibly as I can because I want to hear you argue against it. What we want from you is not only a demonstration that justice is superior to injustice, but a description of the essential effects, harmful or otherwise, which each produces on its possessor. And follow Glaucon's instructions and leave out the common estimation in which they are held. Indeed, if you do not assign to each the reputation the other bears, we shall consider that you are concerned to praise or blame the appearance and not the reality, and that your advice is that we should do wrong and avoid being found out, and that you agree with Thrasymachus that justice is what is good for someone else, the interest of the stronger party, while injustice is what is to one's own interest and advantage, and pursued at the expense of the weaker party. You have agreed that justice falls into the highest category of goods, of goods, that is, which are worth choosing not only for their consequences but also, and far more, for themselves, such things as sight, hearing, intelligence, health, and all other qualities which bring us a real and not merely an apparent benefit. Let us therefore hear you commending justice for the real benefits it brings its possessor, compared with the damage injustice does him, and leave it to others to dwell on rewards and reputation. I am prepared to listen to other people commending or condemning justice and

367 a

b

c

d

injustice in this way by an assessment of rewards and reputation; but you have spent your life studying the question, and from

e you, if I may say so, we expect something better. Prove to us therefore, not only that justice is superior to injustice, but that, irrespective of whether gods or men know it or not, one is good and the other evil because of its inherent effects on its possessor.'

PART II
PRELIMINARIES

1. First Principles of Social Organization

So far the discussion has been about justice (or right conduct or morality) in the individual. But Socrates now says that it is easier to study things on a large scale than on a small, and proposes accordingly to discuss justice in the state or community first, and then see how the conclusions so reached apply to the individual. This method of argument from the state or community to the individual, runs throughout the dialogue.

Socrates starts by asking how society is made up. His account is historical in form. But the Greeks knew little archaeology or prehistory, and the historical form should not be taken too seriously. Socrates is concerned to find out what are the underlying principles of any society, even the simplest. He finds them to be two. First, mutual need. Men are not self-sufficient, they need to live together in society. Second, difference of aptitude. Different people are good at different things, and it is best for all that each should concentrate on developing his particular aptitudes. In this sense, society, with its regulations, is a 'natural' growth.

Starting from these two principles Socrates deals first with what we should call the economic structure of society, though in a very simple form. He finds five main economic classes or functions: (1) Producers, agricultural or industrial, (2) Merchants, (3) Sailors and Shipowners, etc., (4) Retail traders, (5) Wage-earners or manual labourers. (Slaves are not mentioned, but their existence, it is clear from elsewhere (e.g. 469c, 471a), is assumed.[1] Plato would regard them as appendages to the classes he has defined rather than a separate class on their own.)

Socrates finally sketches the life that the simplest form of society, organized on these lines, would lead. Though he professes (372e) to regard this primitive society as the ideal, the description has sometimes been regarded as an ironic parody of the 'simple life' theories of Plato's day. It is perhaps better taken as a statement of the minimum conditions which must be fulfilled if society is to exist at all.

Much as I had always admired the talents of Glaucon and 368 a   Adeimantus, I was absolutely delighted by what they had said. 'Glaucon's admirer was right,' I began in reply, 'to open his poem on your achievements at the battle of Megara² with the words,

> Sons of Ariston, pair divine
> Sprung from a famous sire.

The words are apt; you must indeed have something divine about you, if you can put the case for injustice so strongly, and yet still believe that justice is better than injustice. And I am sure that you genuinely believe it; I can tell from your general b   character – though the speeches you have made would have left me in doubt about you. But the surer I feel the more doubtful I am what to do. I don't see how I'm to help you; I don't think I've got the ability – witness my failure to convince you just now, when I thought I had demonstrated the superiority of justice in my discussion with Thrasymachus. Yet I don't see how I can refuse; for I am afraid it would be wicked, while I've life and voice in me, to hear justice slandered as I have done and c   then refuse to come to the rescue. So I must do my best to help her.'

Glaucon and the rest of them all begged me to come to the rescue and not let the argument drop, but try to find out what justice and injustice are and what their real advantages. So I began by saying, quite frankly, 'This is a very obscure subject d   we're inquiring into, and I think it needs very keen sight. We aren't very clever, and so I think we had better proceed as follows. Let us suppose we are rather short-sighted men and are set to read some small letters at a distance; one of us then discovers the same letters elsewhere on a larger scale and larger surface: won't it be a godsend to us to be able to read the larger letters first and then compare them with the smaller, to see if they are the same?'

'Certainly,' replied Adeimantus; 'but what bearing has this on our inquiry about what is just?'   *e*

'I will tell you. Justice can be a characteristic of an individual or of a community,[3] can it not?'

'Yes.'

'And a community is larger than an individual?'

'It is.'

'We may therefore find justice on a larger scale in the larger entity, and so easier to recognize. I accordingly propose that we start our inquiry with the community, and then proceed to the   369 *a* individual and see if we can find in the conformation of the smaller entity anything similar to what we have found in the larger.'

'That seems a good suggestion,' he agreed.

'Well then,' said I, 'if we were to look at a community coming into existence, we might be able to see how justice and injustice originate in it.'

'We might.'

'This would, we may hope, make it easier to find what we are looking for.'

'Much easier.'   *b*

'Do you think, then, that we should attempt such a survey? For it is, I assure you, too big a task to undertake without thought.'

'We know what we are in for,' returned Adeimantus; 'go on.'

'Society originates, then,' said I, 'so far as I can see, because the individual is not self-sufficient, but has many needs which he can't supply himself. Or can you suggest any other origin for it?'

'No, I can't,' he said.

'And when we have got hold of enough people to satisfy our   *c*

many varied needs, we have assembled quite a large number of
partners and helpers together to live in one place; and we give
the resultant settlement the name of a community or state?'

'Yes, I agree.'

'And in the community all mutual exchanges are made on the
assumption that the parties to them stand to gain?'

'Certainly.'

'Come then,' I said, 'let us make an imaginary sketch of the
origin of the state. It originates, as we have seen, from our
needs.'

'Yes.'

d   'And our first and greatest need is clearly the provision of
food to keep us alive.'

'Clearly.'

'Our second need is shelter, and our third clothing of various
kinds.'

'Yes.'

'Well then, how will our state supply these needs? It will need
a farmer, a builder, and a weaver, and also, I think, a shoemaker
and one or two others to provide for our bodily needs.'

'True.'

'So that the minimum state would consist of four or five
men.'

e   'Evidently.'

'Then should each of these men contribute the product of his
labour for common use? For instance, should the farmer provide
enough food for all four of them, and devote enough time and
labour to food production to provide for the needs of all four?
Or, alternatively, should he disregard the others, and devote a
quarter of his time to producing a quarter the amount of food,
370 a   and the other three quarters one to building himself a house,
one to making clothes, and another to making shoes? Should
he, in other words, avoid the trouble of sharing with others and
devote himself to providing for his own needs only?'

To which Adeimantus replied, 'The first alternative is perhaps
the simpler.'

'Nor need that surprise us,' I rejoined. 'For as you were
speaking, it occurred to me that, in the first place, no two of us

are born exactly alike. We have different natural aptitudes,   *b*
which fit us for different jobs.'

'We have indeed.'

'So do we do better to exercise one skill[4] or to try to practise
several?'

'To stick to one,' he said.

'And there is a further point. It is fatal in any job to miss the
right moment for action.'

'Clearly.'

'The workman must be a professional at the call of his job;
his job will not wait till he has leisure to spare for it.'   *c*

'That is inevitable.'

'Quantity and quality are therefore more easily produced
when a man specializes appropriately on a single job for which
he is naturally fitted, and neglects all others.'

'That's certainly true.'

'We shall need more than four citizens, then, Adeimantus, to
supply the needs we mentioned. For the farmer, it seems, will
not make his own plough or hoe, or any of his other agricultural
implements, if they are to be well made. The same is true of the
builder and the many tools he needs, and of the weaver and   *d*
shoemaker.'

'True.'

'And so smiths and other craftsmen must share the work and
swell the numbers of our little community.'

'They must.'

'And it will still not be unduly large if we add cowherds and
shepherds and stockmen of various kinds, to provide oxen for
the plough and draught-animals for builder and farmer, as well   *e*
as hides and wool for shoemaker and weaver.'

'No,' he answered; 'but it will no longer be so very small.'

'What is more, it is almost impossible to found a state in a
place where it will not need imports.'

'Quite impossible.'

'So we shall need another class in our community to fetch for
it what it needs from abroad.'

'Yes.'

'And if our agent goes empty-handed, and takes with him

371 *a* nothing of which those from whom he is to get what we want
        are in need, he will return empty-handed, will he not?'

        'So I should think.'

        'So we must produce at home not only enough for our own
        needs but also enough goods of the right kind for the foreigners
        who supply us.'

        'We must.'

        'Which means an increase in the number of farmers and other
        workers in our state.'

        'Yes, there will be an increase.'

        'And it will of course include agents to handle the export and
        import of goods, that is to say, merchants. We shall need them
        too.'

        'We shall.'

        'And if our trade is to be overseas, we shall need a whole lot
b   of experts on ships and seafaring.'

        'Yes, a whole lot of them.'

        'Then within our state, how are its citizens to exchange the
        products of their labour? For such mutual exchange was the
        reason for its foundation.'

        'Obviously they will buy and sell.'

        'And that will require a market, and a currency as the medium
        of exchange.'

        'Certainly.'

c   'And if a farmer or any other producer brings his goods to
        market at a time when no one who wants to exchange with him
        is there, will he sit about in the market and neglect his own job?'

        'Certainly not,' he replied. 'There is a class who see here a
        chance of doing a service. It consists, in a well-run community,
        of those who are least fit physically, and unsuitable for other
        work. For their job ties them to the market place, where they
d   buy goods from those who want to sell and sell goods to those
        who want to buy.'

        'And so this requirement produces a class of retailers in our
        state. For that is what we call those who serve the public by
        buying and selling in the home market, as opposed to merchants
        who travel abroad.'

        'Agreed.'

'There is another class whose services we need – those who   *e*
have no great powers of mind to contribute, but whose physical
strength makes them suitable for manual labour. They market
their strength and call the return they get for it their wages, and
in consequence are usually called wage-earners.'

'That is so.'

'And with wage-earners our complement of citizens seems to
be complete.'

'Yes, I think so.'

'Then, Adeimantus, can we now say that our state is full
grown?'

'Perhaps we can.'

'If so, where are we to find justice and injustice in it? With
the introduction of which of the elements we have examined do
they originate?'

'I don't know, Socrates,' he replied, 'unless they arise some-   372 *a*
where in the mutual relationship of these elements.'

'You may be right,' said I; 'we must press on with our inquiry.
So let us first consider how our citizens, so equipped, will live.
They will produce corn, wine, clothes, and shoes, and will build
themselves houses. In the summer they will for the most part
work unclothed and unshod, in the winter they will be clothed
and shod suitably. For food they will prepare wheat-meal or   *b*
barley-meal for baking or kneading. They will serve splendid
cakes and loaves on rushes or fresh leaves, and will sit down to
feast with their children on couches of myrtle and bryony; and
they will have wine to drink too, and pray to the gods with
garlands on their heads, and enjoy each other's company. And
fear of poverty and war will make them keep the numbers of   *c*
their families within their means.'

'I say,' interrupted Glaucon, 'that's pretty plain fare for a
feast, isn't it?'

'You're quite right,' said I. 'I had forgotten; they will have a
few luxuries. Salt, of course, and olive oil and cheese, and
different kinds of vegetables from which to make various
country dishes. And we must give them some dessert, figs and
peas and beans, and myrtle-berries and acorns to roast at the
fire as they sip their wine. So they will lead a peaceful and   *d*

healthy life, and probably die at a ripe old age, bequeathing a similar way of life to their children.'

2. Civilized Society

Glaucon protests at the uncivilized nature of the life of this primitive society. Socrates proceeds to add to it the refinements of civilization, and so to multiply the number of trades and occupations and increase the population. The increase in wealth and population will lead to war, which means that we shall need a new class of soldiers to fight for us (the principle of specialization demands that they should be a separate class). These soldiers or 'Guardians' Plato will develop into the ruling class of his state: they retain their military function but their function as governors soon overshadows it.

The society described in this section would have seemed quite normal to the ordinary Athenian. Plato's profession to regard it as 'luxurious' and 'fevered', in contrast to that described in the previous section, which is 'true' and 'healthy', may be, as we have seen (heading to section 1), partly ironic. But he did regard contemporary society (which is what he is here in effect describing) as in need of reform; and the rest of the Republic *contains the basis of the reforms which he thought necessary to reduce it to health (cf. 399e).*

'Really, Socrates,' Glaucon commented, 'that's just the fodder you would provide if you were founding a community of pigs!'

'But how would you do it, Glaucon?' I asked.

'Give them the ordinary comforts,' he replied. 'Let them recline in comfort on couches[5] and eat off tables, and have the sort of food we have today.'

e   'All right,' I said, 'I understand. We are to study not only the origins of society, but also society when it enjoys the luxuries of civilization. Not a bad idea, perhaps, for in the process we may discover how justice and injustice are bred in a community. For though the society we have described seems to me to be the true one, like a man in health, there's nothing to prevent us, if you

wish, studying one in a fever. Such a society will not be satisfied
with the standard of living we have described. It will want   373 a
couches and tables and other furniture, and a variety of deli-
cacies, scents, perfumes, call-girls and confectionery. And we
must no longer confine ourselves to the bare necessities of our
earlier description, houses, clothing, and shoes, but must add
the fine arts of painting and embroidery, and introduce materials
like gold and ivory. Do you agree?'

'Yes,' he said.   b

'We shall have to enlarge our state again. Our healthy state is
no longer big enough; its size must be enlarged to make room
for a multitude of occupations none of which is concerned with
necessaries. There will be hunters and fishermen, and there will
be artists, sculptors, painters and musicians; there will be poets
with their following of reciters, actors, chorus-trainers, and
producers; there will be manufacturers of domestic equipment
of all sorts, especially those concerned with women's dress   c
and make-up. And we shall need a lot more servants – tutors,
wet-nurses, nannies, cosmeticians, barbers, butchers and cooks.
And we shall need swineherds too: there were none in our
former state, as we had no need of them, but now we need pigs,
and cattle in quantities too, if we are to eat meat. Agreed?'

'There's no denying it.'

'With our new luxuries we shall need doctors too, far more   d
than we did before.'

'We certainly shall.'

'And the territory which was formerly enough to support us
will now be too small.'

'That is undeniable.'

'If we are to have enough for pasture and plough, we shall
have to cut a slice off our neighbours' territory. And if they
too are no longer confining themselves to necessities and have
embarked on the pursuit of unlimited material possessions, they
will want a slice of ours too.'

'The consequence is inevitable.'   e

'And that will lead to war, Glaucon, will it not?'

'It will.'

'For the moment,' I said, 'we are not concerned with the

effects of war, good or bad; let us merely go on to note that we have found its origin to be the same as that of most evil, individual or social.'[6]

'Yes, I agree.'

374 a   'But it means a considerable addition to our state, the addition of an army, which will go out and defend the property and possessions we have just described against all comers.'

'But can't the citizens fight for themselves?'

'Not if the principle, on which we all, yourself included, agreed when we started constructing our state, is sound. And that was, if you remember, that one man could not do more than one job or profession[7] well.'

b   'Yes, that is true.'

'Well, soldiering is a profession, is it not?'

'Very much so.'

'And is it of any less consequence to us than shoemaking?'

'Certainly not.'

'Well, we forbade our shoemaker to try his hand at farming or weaving or building and told him to stick to his last, in order that our shoemaking should be well done. Similarly with other trades, we assigned each man to the one for which he was

c   naturally suited, and which he was to practise throughout his life to the exclusion of all others, and so become good at his job and never miss the right moment for action. Now it is surely of the greatest importance that the business of war should be efficiently run. For soldiering is not so easy a job that a man can be a soldier at the same time as he is a farmer or shoemaker or follows some other profession; why, you can't even become a competent draughts or dice player if you don't practise seriously from childhood, but only do it in your spare time. Does a man

d   become competent as an infantryman, or in any other branch of military service, the moment he picks up a shield or any of the other tools of the soldier's trade? Merely to pick up the tools of any other trade does not turn a man into a craftsman or games-player: the tool is useful only to the man who knows how to use it and has had enough practice in the use of it.'

'True; otherwise tools would indeed be precious.'

'And so the business of our defence force, just because it is the most important of all, requires a correspondingly complete freedom from other affairs and a correspondingly high degree of skill and practice.'

e

'I suppose it does,' he said.

'It will need also natural aptitude.'

'Of course.'

'And so we should make it our business, if we can, to choose men with suitable natural aptitudes for the defence of our state.'

'We should.'

'And let me say,' I added, 'that it's no mean task to undertake. Still, we must not shrink from it, but do it to the best of our ability.'

'We must.'

375 a

3. Qualities Required in the Guardians

The need for a defence force or Guardian class (the Greek word, phulakes, occurs for the first time at the end of the last section) having been thus established, the other classes (producers, merchants, etc.) fall into the background and are hardly mentioned again. Plato's main concern is with the production of Philosopher Rulers, and the rest of the Republic *is largely devoted to the educational and other measures needed to turn the Guardians into Philosophers.*

The Guardians are now compared to watchdogs, and shown to need physical strength, courage, and a philosophic temperament. Courage requires 'high spirits'. The Greek word (thūmos) which this phrase translates is used by Plato to cover a group of characteristics such as pugnacity, enterprise, ambition, indignation, which he will later regard as one of the three main elements of the mind or personality. In traditional English 'mettle' or 'spirit' (as e.g. in 'a man of mettle', 'a man of spirit') is a fair translation, and the slang term 'guts' and the politer 'vitality' have a somewhat similar meaning; compare also the distinction made in common parlance between qualities of the 'heart' and 'head', and see below, opening note to Part v, section 2.

'Don't you think,' I asked, 'that the natural qualities needed in a well-bred watch-dog have a certain similarity to those which a good[8] young man needs for Guardian-duty?'

'What similarity?'

'I mean that each must have keen perceptions and speed in pursuit of his quarry, and also strength to fight if need be when he catches it.'

'Yes, he will need all these qualities.'

'And also courage, if he is to fight well.'

'Of course.'

'And no horse or dog or any other creature can be courageous if it has no spirit. For have you not noticed what an irresistible and unbeatable thing high spirits are, giving their possessor
b a character quite fearless and indomitable in the face of all dangers?'

'I have indeed.'

'We know therefore what the physical qualities of our Guardians must be.'

'Yes.'

'And also that in character[9] they must be high-spirited.'

'Yes.'

'But if they have these qualities, Glaucon,' I said, 'won't they be aggressive in their behaviour to each other and to the rest of the community?'

'It won't be easy to prevent it.'

c 'And yet they ought to be gentle towards their fellow-citizens, and dangerous only to their enemies; otherwise they will destroy each other before others can destroy them.'

'True.'

'What are we to do, then?' I said. 'Where are we to find a disposition at once gentle and full of spirit? For gentleness and high spirits are natural opposites.'

'They seem to be.'

d 'But yet if we deprive them of either quality, they won't make good Guardians; we seem to be asking the impossible, and if so a good Guardian is an impossibility.'

'I am afraid so,' he agreed.

I felt myself in a difficulty, but I thought over what we had

just been saying, and then exclaimed: 'You know, we really
deserve to be in a difficulty. For we have failed to press our
analogy far enough.'

'In what way?'

'We have not noticed that there are natures which combine
the qualities we thought incompatible.'

'And where are they to be found?'

'In different kinds of animal, but particularly in the watch-dog
to which we have compared our Guardian. For you must have
noticed that it is a natural characteristic of a well-bred dog to   *e*
behave with the utmost gentleness to those it is used to and
knows, but to be savage to strangers?'

'Yes, I've noticed that.'

'The kind of character we were looking for in our Guardian
is therefore quite a possibility and not at all unnatural.'

'So it appears.'

'Would you agree then that our prospective Guardian needs,
in addition to his high spirits, the disposition of a philosopher?'

'I don't understand what you mean,' he said.   376 *a*

'You will find it in the dog, and a remarkable quality it is.'

'What sort of quality?'

'It is annoyed when it sees a stranger, even though he has
done it no harm: but it welcomes anyone it knows, even though
it has never had a kindness from him. Haven't you ever thought
how remarkable this is?'

'I can't say I ever thought about it before,' he replied. 'But of
course it's what a dog does.'

'And yet it is a trait that shows discrimination and a truly
philosophic nature,' I said.

'How so?'

'Because,' I replied, 'the dog distinguishes the sight of friend
and foe simply by knowing one and not knowing the other.   *b*
And a creature that distinguishes between the familiar and the
unfamiliar on the grounds of knowledge or ignorance must
surely be gifted with a real love of knowledge.'

'There is no denying it,' he said.

'But is not philosophy the same thing as the love of
knowledge?'[10]

'It is.'

'And so for man too we may venture to lay it down that gentleness towards his own fellows and neighbours requires a
c   philosophic disposition and a love of learning.'

'We may,' he said.

'And so our properly good Guardian will have the following characteristics: a philosophic disposition, high spirits, speed, and strength.'

'I entirely agree.'

PART III
EDUCATION:
THE FIRST STAGE

In reading what follows it is important to have in mind one or two of the main features of Greek education in Plato's day. It was, normally, a matter for the private individual: and in making it the concern of the state, Plato was doing something that to the Athenian (though not to the Spartan; and Plato was to some extent influenced by Sparta) was an innovation. Education had three principal subdivisions: reading and writing, physical education, and what we may call secondary or literary education. This last consisted mainly in a study of the works of the poets, which were learnt to be recited and, where necessary, sung to the lyre, so that it included a knowledge of music; it corresponded, broadly, to the secondary stage of our own system, and was followed by two years' military training which began at eighteen. It must also be remembered that the Greeks had no Bible, and what the Bible has been to us as a source of theology and morals, the poets were to the Greeks. And if Plato seems very preoccupied with the moral and theological aspect of the poets it is because it was from them that the ordinary Greek was expected to acquire his moral and theological notions.

1. Secondary or Literary Education

Since the minds of the young are very impressionable we must, if we are to educate them properly, make sure that the poetry on which they are brought up is suitable for the purpose. Most existing poetry is unsuitable: (a) theologically, because it misrepresents God. God is perfectly good, and therefore change-less and incapable of deceit, and must never be otherwise represented.

[376] 'That then would be our Guardians' basic character. But how are they to be brought up and educated? If we try to answer this question, I wonder whether it will help us at all in our main
d inquiry into the origin of justice and injustice in society? We do not want to leave out anything relevant, but we don't want to embark on too long a discussion.'

To which Adeimantus replied, 'I expect the discussion will help our inquiry all right.'

'Then, my dear Adeimantus, we must certainly pursue the question,' I rejoined, 'even though it proves a long business.'

'We must.'

'So let us tell the tale of the education of our imaginary Guardians as if we had all the leisure of the traditional story-teller.'

e 'Let us by all means.'

'What kind of education shall we give them then? We shall find it difficult to improve on the time-honoured distinction between the physical training we give to the body and the education[1] we give to the mind and character.'

'True.'

'And we shall begin by educating mind and character, shall we not?'

'Of course.'

'In this education you would include stories, would you not?'

'Yes.'

377 a 'These are of two kinds, true stories and fiction.[2] Our education must use both, and start with fiction.'

'I don't know what you mean.'

'But you know that we begin by telling children stories. These are, in general, fiction, though they contain some truth. And we tell children stories before we start them on physical training.'

'That is so.'

'That is what I meant by saying that we must start to educate the mind before training the body.'

'You are right,' he said.

'And the first step, as you know, is always what matters most,[3] particularly when we are dealing with those who are young and tender. That is the time when they are easily moulded and *b* when any impression we choose to make leaves a permanent mark.'

'That is certainly true.'

'Shall we therefore readily allow our children to listen to any stories made up by anyone, and to form opinions that are for the most part the opposite of those we think they should have when they grow up?'

'We certainly shall not.'

'Then it seems that our first business is to supervise the production of stories, and choose only those we think suitable, and *c* reject the rest. We shall persuade mothers and nurses to tell our chosen stories to their children, and by means of them to mould their minds and characters which are more important than their bodies.[4] The greater part of the stories current today we shall have to reject.'

'Which are you thinking of?'

'We can take some of the major legends as typical. For all, whether major or minor, should be cast in the same mould and *d* have the same effect. Do you agree?'

'Yes: but I'm not sure which you refer to as major.'

'The stories in Homer and Hesiod and the poets. For it is the poets who have always made up fictions and stories to tell to men.'

'What sort of stories do you mean and what fault do you find in them?'

'The worst fault possible,' I replied, 'especially if the fiction is an ugly one.'

'And what is that?'

'Misrepresenting the nature of gods and heroes, like a portrait *e* painter whose portraits bear no resemblance to their originals.'

'That is a fault which certainly deserves censure. But give me more details.'

'Well, on the most important of subjects, there is first and foremost the foul story about Ouranos[5] and the things Hesiod

378 a says he did, and the revenge Cronos took on him. While the
story of what Cronos did, and what he suffered at the hands of
his son, is not fit as it is to be lightly repeated to the young and
foolish, even if it were true; it would be best to say nothing
about it, or if it must be told, tell it to a select few under oath of
secrecy, at a rite which required, to restrict it still further, the
sacrifice not of a mere pig but of something large and difficult
to get.'

'These certainly are awkward stories.'

b 'And they shall not be repeated in our state, Adeimantus,' I
said. 'Nor shall any young audience be told that anyone who
commits horrible crimes, or punishes his father unmercifully, is
doing nothing out of the ordinary but merely what the first and
greatest of the gods have done before.'

'I entirely agree,' said Adeimantus, 'that these stories are
unsuitable.'

'Nor can we permit stories of wars and plots and battles
c among the gods; they are quite untrue, and if we want our
prospective guardians to believe that quarrelsomeness is one of
the worst of evils, we must certainly not let them be told the
story of the Battle of the Giants or embroider it on robes,[6] or
tell them other tales about many and various quarrels between
gods and heroes and their friends and relations. On the contrary,
if we are to persuade them that no citizen has ever quarrelled
with any other, because it is sinful, our old men and women
d must tell children stories with this end in view from the first,
and we must compel our poets to tell them similar stories when
they grow up. But we can admit to our state no stories about
Hera being tied up by her son,[7] or Hephaestus being flung out
of Heaven by his father for trying to help his mother when she
was getting a beating,[8] nor any of Homer's Battles of the Gods,[9]
whether their intention is allegorical or not. Children cannot
distinguish between what is allegory and what isn't, and
opinions formed at that age are usually difficult to eradicate or
change; we should therefore surely regard it as of the utmost
e importance that the first stories they hear shall aim at encouraging the highest excellence of character.'

'Your case is a good one,' he agreed, 'but if someone wanted details, and asked what stories we were thinking of, what should we say?'

To which I replied, 'My dear Adeimantus, you and I are not engaged on writing stories but on founding a state. And the founders of a state, though they must know the type of story   379 a the poet must produce, and reject any that do not conform to that type, need not write them themselves.'

'True: but what are the lines on which our poets must work when they deal with the gods?'[10]

'Roughly as follows,' I said. 'God must surely always be represented as he really is, whether the poet is writing epic, lyric, or tragedy.'

'He must.'

'And in reality of course god is good, and he must be so   b described.'

'Certainly.'

'But nothing good is harmful, is it?'[11]

'I think not.'

'Then can anything that is not harmful do harm?'

'No.'

'And can what does no harm do evil?'

'No again.'

'And can what does no evil be the cause of any evil?'

'How could it?'

'Well then; is the good beneficial?'

'Yes.'

'So it must be the cause of well-being.'

'Yes.'

'So the good is not the cause of everything, but only of states of well-being and not of evil.'

'Most certainly,' he agreed.   c

'Then god, being good, cannot be responsible for everything, as is commonly said, but only for a small part of human life, for the greater part of which he has no responsibility. For we have a far smaller share of good than of evil, and while god must be held to be sole cause of good, we must look for some factors other than god as cause of the evil.'

'I think that's very true,' he said.

'So we cannot allow Homer or any other poet to make such
d a stupid mistake about the gods, as when he says that

Zeus has two jars standing on the floor of his palace, full of fates, good
in one and evil in the other;

and that the man to whom Zeus allots a mixture of both has
"varying fortunes sometimes good and sometimes bad", while
the man to whom he allots unmixed evil is "chased by ravening
e despair over the face of the earth".[12] Nor can we allow references
to Zeus as "dispenser of good and evil".[13] And we cannot
approve if it is said that Athene and Zeus prompted the breach
of solemn treaty and oath by Pandarus, or that the strife and
380 *a* contentions of the gods were due to Themis and Zeus.[14] Nor
again can we let our children hear from Aeschylus that

God implants a fault in man, when he wishes to destroy a house
utterly.[15]

No: we must forbid anyone who writes a play about the
sufferings of Niobe (the subject of the play from which these
last lines are quoted), or the house of Pelops, or the Trojan war,
or any similar topic, to say they are acts of god; or if he does he
must produce the sort of interpretation we are now demanding,
b and say that god's acts were good and just, and that the sufferers
were benefited by being punished. What the poet must not be
allowed to say is that those who were punished were made
wretched through god's action. He may refer to the wicked as
wretched because they needed punishment, provided he makes
it clear that in punishing them god did them good. But if a state
c is to be run on the right lines, every possible step must be taken
to prevent anyone, young or old, either saying or being told,
whether in poetry or prose, that god, being good, can cause
harm or evil to any man. To say so would be sinful, inexpedient,
and inconsistent.'

'I should approve of a law for this purpose and you have my
vote for it,' he said.

'Then of our laws laying down the principles which those

who write or speak about the gods must follow, one would be this: *God is the cause, not of all things, but only of good.*'

'I am quite content with that,' he said.

'And what about our second law? Do you think god is a kind   *d*
of magician who can appear at will in different forms at different times, sometimes turning into them himself and appearing in many different shapes, at other times misleading us into the belief that he has done so? Or is he without deceit and least likely of all things to change his proper form?'

'I can't answer that off-hand,' he replied.

'Well, if anything does change its proper form, must not the change be due either to itself or to something else?'   *e*

'It must.'

'And are not things in the best condition least liable to change or alteration by something else? For instance, the healthiest and strongest physiques are least liable to change owing to diet and exercise, and the healthiest and strongest plants owing to sun   381 *a*
and wind and the like.'

'That is so.'

'And are not characters[16] which have most courage and sense least liable to be upset and changed by external influences?'

'Yes.'

'And similarly any composite object, a piece of furniture or a house or a garment, is least subject to wear and tear if it is well made and in good condition.'

'That is true.'   *b*

'So, in general, whether a thing is natural or artificial or both, it is least subject to change from outside if its condition is good.'

'So it seems.'

'But god and the things of god are entirely perfect.'

'That is undeniable.'

'On this argument, then, god is not in the least likely to take on many forms.'

'Not in the least.'

'Then will god change or alter himself of his own will?'

'If he changes at all,' he replied, 'that must be how he does.'

'Will the change increase or decrease his goodness and beauty?'

c   'Any change must be for the worse. For god's beauty and goodness are perfect.'

'You are absolutely right,' I said. 'And, that being so, do you think that anyone, man or god, would deliberately make himself worse in any respect?'

'Impossible,' he said.

'Then it must also be impossible,' I replied, 'for a god to wish to change himself. Every god is perfect in beauty and goodness, and remains in his own form without variation for ever.'

'The conclusion is unavoidable.'

d   'So we cannot have any poet saying that the gods "disguise themselves as strangers from abroad, and wander round our towns in every kind of shape";[17] we cannot have stories told about the transformations of Proteus[18] and Thetis,[19] or poets bringing Hera on the stage disguised as a priestess begging alms
e   for "the lifegiving children of Inachus, river of Argos".[20] We must stop all stories of this kind, and stop mothers being misled by them and scaring their children with harmful myths by telling tales about a host of gods that prowl about at night in a strange variety of shapes. So we shall prevent them blaspheming the gods and making cowards of their children.'

'None of these things should be allowed.'

'Then if the gods are themselves incapable of change, will they deceive us and bewitch us into thinking that they appear in all sorts of disguises?'

'They might, I suppose.'

382 *a*   'Come,' said I, 'can god want to disguise himself and lie to us, either in word or action?'

'I don't know,' he replied.

'But,' I asked, 'don't you know that gods and men all detest true falsehood, if I may so describe it?'

'What do you mean?'

'I mean that no man wants to be deceived in the most important part of him and about the most important things; that is when he is most terrified of falsehood.'

'I still don't understand.'

b   'Because you think I'm talking about something mysterious,' I answered. 'But all I'm talking about is being deceived *in one's own mind* about realities, and so being the victim of falsehood and ignorance; that is where men are least ready to put up with the presence of falsehood and particularly detest it.'

'Yes, I agree with that.'

'But surely when a man is deceived in his own mind we can fairly call his ignorance of the truth "true falsehood". For a false statement is merely some kind of representation of a state of mind, an expression consequent on it, and not the original *c* unadulterated falsehood. Don't you agree?'

'Yes.'

'So real falsehood is detested by gods and men.'

'I agree.'

'But what about spoken falsehood? Is it not sometimes and on some occasions useful, and not then detestable? We can use it, for example, as a kind of preventive medicine against our enemies, or when anyone we call our friend tries to do something wrong from madness or folly. And we can make use of it in the *d* myths we are engaged in discussing; we don't know the truth about the past but we can invent a fiction[21] as like it as may be.'

'That's perfectly true.'

'In which of these ways is falsehood of use to god? Does he need to make up fictions because he does not know the past?'

'It would be absurd to suppose so.'

'So god is not the author of poetic fictions.'

'No.'

'Does he tell lies because he is afraid of his enemies, then?'

'Certainly not.'   *e*

'Or because of the folly or madness of any of his friends?'

'God loves neither the foolish nor the mad,' he replied.

'God has, then, no reason to tell lies.'

'None.'

'So we conclude that there is no falsehood at all in the realm of the spiritual and divine?'

'Most certainly.'

'God is therefore without deceit or falsehood in action or word, he does not change himself, nor deceive others, awake or dreaming, with visions or words or special signs.'

'I agree entirely with what you say.'   383 *a*

'Do you agree then that the second principle to be followed in all that is said or written about the gods is that they shall not be represented as using magic to disguise themselves nor as playing us false in word or deed?'

'I agree.'

'And so among the many things we admire in Homer we shall not include the dream Zeus sent to Agamemnon.[22] Nor shall we admire Aeschylus[23] when he makes Thetis say that Apollo sang

b at her wedding in praise of her child

> Promising him long life, from sickness free,
> And every blessing: his triumphant praise
> Rejoiced my heart. Those lips, I thought, divine,
> Flowing with prophecy, must God's promise speak.
> Yet he the singer, he our wedding guest,
> Phoebus Apollo, prophet, slew my son.

If a poet says this sort of thing about the gods we shall be angry and refuse to let him produce his play; nor shall we allow it to be used to educate our children – that is if our Guardians are to grow up godfearing and holy, so far as that is humanly possible.'

'I agree entirely with your principles,' he said, 'and we can treat them as law.'

(b) Morally, most existing poetry is unsuitable because in its representations of gods and heroes it describes, and so encourages, various forms of moral weaknesses.

BK III 'As far as the gods are concerned, then, we have now outlined the sort of stories which men ought and ought not to hear from
386 *a* their earliest childhood, if they are to honour the gods and their parents, and know how important it is to love one another.'

'And I think we are quite right,' he said.

'But what if they are to be brave? Must we not extend our range to include something that will give them the least possible
b fear of death? Will anyone who in his heart fears death ever be brave?'

'Certainly not.'

'And will anyone who believes in terrors in the after-life be without fear of death, and prefer death in battle to defeat and slavery?'

'No.'

'It looks, then, as if we shall have to control story-tellers on this topic too. We must ask the poets to stop giving their present gloomy account of the after-life, which is both untrue and unsuitable to produce a fighting spirit, and make them speak *c* more favourably of it.'

'I agree,' he said.

'We must begin, then,' I said, 'by cutting out all passages such as the following –

I would rather be a serf in the house of some landless man, with little enough for himself to live on, than king of all dead men that have done with life;[24]

and this

and expose to mortal and immortal eyes the hateful chambers of decay *d* that fill the gods themselves with horror;[25]

and

Ah then, it is true that something of us does survive even in the Halls of Hades, but with no intellect at all, only the ghost and semblance of a man;[26]

and this

he alone has a mind to reason with: the rest are mere shadows flitting to and fro;[27]

and

his disembodied soul took wing for the House of Hades, bewailing its lot and the youth and manhood that it left;[28]

387 a   and this

> the spirit vanished like a wisp of smoke and went gibbering under
> ground;[29]

and

> gibbering like bats that squeak and flutter in the depths of some
> mysterious cave when one of them has fallen from the rocky roof,
> losing his hold on his clustered friends, with shrill discord the company
> set out.[30]

b   We must ask Homer and the other poets to excuse us if we
delete all passages of this kind. It is not that they are bad poetry
or are not popular; indeed the better they are as poetry the more
unsuitable they are for the ears of children or men who are to
be free and fear slavery more than death.'
    'I absolutely agree.'
    'We must get rid, too, of all those horrifying and frightening
names in the underworld – the Rivers of Wailing and Gloom,
c   and the ghosts and corpses, and all other things of this kind
whose very names are enough to make everyone who hears
them shudder. They may do well enough for other purposes;
but we are afraid that the thrill of terror they cause will make
our Guardians more nervous and less tough than they should
be.'
    'And our anxiety is justified.'
    'Shall we get rid of them then?'
    'Yes.'
    'And require writers and poets to proceed on the opposite
principle?'
    'Clearly.'
d   'We must also, I suppose, cut out pitiful laments by famous
men.'
    'We must,' he replied, 'if we are to be consistent.'
    'Let us see if the excision will be justified. We agree, surely,
that one good man does not think death holds any terror for
another who is a friend of his.'

'We do.'

'And so he would hardly mourn for him as if he had suffered something terrible.'

'That is true.'

'And what is more, we reckon that such a man is in himself most self-sufficient in what is needed for a good life and of all men least dependent on others.'   *e*

'True.'

'So the loss of son or brother, or of property, or anything else of the kind, will hold the least terrors for the good man.'

'He will be least affected by them.'

'So when any catastrophe of the kind overtakes him, he will lament it less and bear it more calmly than others.'

'He will.'

'Then we should be quite right to cut out from our poetry lamentations by famous men. We can give them to the less   388 *a* reputable women characters or to the bad men, so that those whom we say we are bringing up as Guardians of our state will be ashamed to imitate them.'

'You are quite right.'

'We shall therefore again request Homer and the poets not to describe Achilles, the son of a goddess, as

sometimes lying on his side, sometimes on his back, and then again on his face,

and then standing up and

wandering distraught along the shore of the unharvested sea,[31]

or   *b*

picking up the dark dust in both hands and pouring it on his head,[32]

with all the weeping and lamenting the poet describes. Nor can we allow a Priam, who was closely related to the gods, in his entreaties to grovel in the dung and implore them all, calling on each man by his name.[33]

Still more emphatically shall we request the poets not to represent the gods lamenting with words like

c   Ah misery me, the unhappy mother of the bravest of men.[34]

And least of all can we have them presuming to misrepresent the greatest of all gods by making him say

I have a warm place in my heart for this man who is being chased before my eyes round the walls of Troy.[35]

and

Fate is unkind to me – Sarpedon whom I dearly love is destined to be
d   killed by Patroclus son of Menoetius.[36]

For, my dear Adeimantus, if our young men listen to passages like these seriously and don't laugh at them as unworthy, they are hardly likely to think this sort of conduct unworthy of them as men, or to resist the temptation to similar words and actions. They will feel no shame and show no endurance, but break into complaints and laments at the slightest provocation.'
e   'That is quite true.'
    'But that is not the behaviour our argument has just required; and we must trust it till someone produces a better one.'
    'Yes, we must.'
    'And surely we don't want our guardians to be too fond of laughter either. Indulgence in violent laughter commonly invites a violent reaction.'
    'I have noticed that,' he said.
389 a   'We must not therefore allow descriptions of reputable characters being overcome by laughter. And similar descriptions of gods are far less allowable.'
    'Far less, I agree.'
    'So we can't have Homer saying of the gods

and a fit of helpless laughter seized the happy gods as they watched Hephaestus bustling up and down the hall.[37]

Your argument won't allow that.'

'Call it my argument if you like,' he replied; 'in any event we   *b* can't allow it.'

'And surely we must value truthfulness highly. For if we were right when we said just now[38] that falsehood is no use to the gods and only useful to men as a kind of medicine, it's clearly a kind of medicine that should be entrusted to doctors and not to laymen.'

'Clearly.'

'It will be for the rulers of our city, then, if anyone, to use falsehood in dealing with citizen or enemy for the good of the State; no one else must do so. And if any citizen lies to our   *c* rulers, we shall regard it as a still graver offence than it is for a patient to lie to his doctor, or for an athlete to lie to his trainer about his physical condition, or for a sailor to misrepresent to his captain any matter concerning the ship or crew, or the state of himself or his fellow-sailors.'

'Very true.'

'And so if anyone else is found in our state telling lies,   *d* "whether he be craftsman, prophet, physician or shipwright",[39] he will be punished for introducing a practice likely to capsize and wreck the ship of state.'

'We must punish him if we are to be as good as our word.'

'Then again we shall want our young men to be self-controlled.'

'Of course.'

'And for the mass of men does not self-control largely consist in obedience to their rulers, and ruling their own desire for the   *e* pleasures of eating, drinking, and sex?'

'I agree.'

'We shall approve, therefore, the sort of thing that Homer makes Diomede say,

Be quiet, man, and take your cue from me;[40]

and verses like those which follow it,

The Achaeans moved forward, breathing valour, in silent obedience to
their officers.[41]

And there are other similar passages.'
    'They deserve approval.'
    'But what about

You drunken sot, with the eyes of a dog and the courage of a doe,[42]

390 a and the lines that follow? Can we approve of them and other
impertinences of the rank and file against those in authority, in
prose or verse?'
    'We cannot.'
    'For they are hardly suitable to encourage the young to self-
control, though we need not be surprised if they give pleasure
in other ways. What do you think?'
    'I agree.'
    'Then is it likely to encourage self-restraint if the poet rep-
resents the wisest of men saying that he thinks the best moment
b of all is when

the tables are laden with bread and meat, and a steward carries round
the wine he has drawn from the bowl and fills their cups?[43]

And what about lines like

death by starvation is the most miserable end that one can meet?[44]

And then there is the story of how Zeus stayed awake, when all
the other gods and men were asleep, with some plan in mind,
c but forgot it easily enough when his desire for sex was roused;
he was indeed so struck by Hera's appearance that he wanted
to make love to her on the spot, without going indoors, saying
that he had never desired her so much since the days when they
first used to make love "without their parents' knowledge".[45]
And there's the story of Hephaestus trapping Ares and Aphro-
dite because of similar goings-on.'[46]

'All these are in my view most unsuitable,' he commented emphatically.

'But when a poet tells or a dramatist presents tales of endur-   *d*
ance against odds by famous men, then we must give him an audience. For instance, when Homer makes Odysseus strike himself on the chest, and "call his heart to order", saying,

Patience my heart! You have put up with fouler than this.'[47]

'We must certainly listen to him then.'
'But we must not let him make his characters mercenary or grasping.'
'Certainly not.'   *e*
'We cannot let a poet say,

The gods can be won with gifts, and so can the king's majesty.[48]

We cannot agree that Achilles' tutor Phoenix gave him proper advice when he told him not to desist from his "wrath" and help the Achaeans unless they brought him presents. Nor can we consent to regard Achilles as so grasping that he took Aga-memnon's presents, or refused to give up Hector's body unless he was paid a ransom.'[49]   391 *a*

'It would be quite wrong,' he said, 'to commend things of this sort.'

'I say it with hesitation, because of Homer's authority,' I went on, 'but it is positively wicked to say these things about Achilles or believe them when we hear them said. There are other examples. Achilles says to Apollo,

You have made a fool of me, Archer-king, and are the most mischievous of gods: how much I should like to pay you out if I had the power.[50]

He refuses to obey the River Scamander, who is a god, and is   *b*
ready to fight him, and he sends the lock of his hair dedicated to the River Spercheius as a gift to 'the Lord Patroclus', who was already dead.[51] We can believe none of this, and we shall

regard as untrue also the whole story of the dragging of the
body of Hector round the tomb of Patroclus and the slaughter
c of prisoners at his pyre.[52] We cannot, in fact, have our citizens
believe that Achilles, whose mother was a goddess, and whose
father, Peleus, was a man of the utmost self-control and a
grandson of Zeus, and who had in Chiron the wisest of schoolmasters, was in such a state of inner confusion that he combined
in himself the two contrary maladies of ungenerous meanness
about money and excessive arrogance to gods and men.'

'You are right,' he said.

'We must therefore neither believe nor allow the story of the
dreadful rapes attempted by Theseus, son of Poseidon, and
d Peirithous, son of Zeus,[53] or any of the other lies now told about
the terrible and wicked things which other sons of gods and
heroes are said to have dared to do. We must compel our poets
to say either that they never did these things or that they are not
the sons of gods; we cannot allow them to assert both. And they
must not try to persuade our young men that the gods are the
source of evil, and that heroes are no better than ordinary
e mortals; that, as we have said, is a wicked lie, for we have
proved that no evil can originate with the gods.'

'Of course.'

'Moreover such lies are positively harmful. For those who
hear them will be lenient towards their own shortcomings if
they believe that this sort of thing is and was always done by
the relatives of the gods,

> close kin of Zeus, to whom
> the ancestral altar high in heaven
> on Ida's mount belongs,

and in whose veins

> still runs the blood of gods.[54]

We must therefore put a stop to stories of this kind before they
392 a breed in our young men an undue tolerance of wickedness.'

'We certainly must.'

So far the argument has been confined to the poets' treatment of gods and heroes: similar rules cannot be laid down for the treatment of men until justice has been defined.

'What kind of literature remains, then, for us to deal with in our definition of what can and cannot be allowed? For we have now described the kind of things that should and should not be said about gods and demi-gods, heroes and the life after death.'

'Yes, we have dealt fully with them.'

'What is left would seem to be literature dealing with men.'

'Obviously.'

'But we cannot deal with that topic at present.'

'Why not?'

'Because I am afraid that we shall find that poets and story-tellers are in error in matters of the greatest human importance.   *b* They have said that unjust men are often happy, and just men wretched, that wrongdoing pays if you can avoid being found out, and that justice is what is good for someone else but is to your own disadvantage. We must forbid them to say this sort of thing, and require their poems and stories to have quite the opposite moral. Do you agree?'

'I'm quite sure you're right,' he replied.

'But if you agree I am right there, can I not already claim your agreement about the subject we are discussing at such length?'

'Yes, you are quite right.'

'We must not agree, therefore, about the kind of thing that   *c* ought to be said about human life, until we have defined justice, and the advantages it naturally[55] brings to its possessor irrespective of appearances.'

'Quite true.'

(c) Formal requirements

Plato turns from content to form. He classes poetry according to the degree to which it employs what we should call 'direct speech' as opposed to indirect speech and narrative. Direct speech involves what he calls 'representation',[56] that is, it requires the poet or narrator to put himself in the position of the character speaking, think his thoughts, and feel his feelings.

Plato objects to this on the grounds that he does not want his
Guardians to deviate from their own character by representing
other characters, especially bad characters. If the discussion
seems at times, to us, academic, we should remember that the
Greek schoolboy, when reciting Homer, was 'expected to throw
himself into the story and deliver the speeches with the tones
and gestures of an actor', and that it is to such 'imaginative
identification',[57] *and therefore to any use of the drama in edu-*
cation that Plato, rightly or wrongly, objects.

'So much then for the subject-matter of literature. We must
next deal with its style of presentation, and so cover both *what*
is to be said and *how* it is to be said.'

To this Adeimantus replied that he did not understand what
d I meant. 'Then I must explain,' I said; 'perhaps you will see if I
put it this way. Any story or poem narrates things past, present,
or future, does it not?'

'There is no alternative.'

'And for the purpose it employs either simple narrative or
representation, or a mixture of both.'

'I'm still not quite clear what you mean.'

'I'm afraid I'm being ridiculously obscure,' I said. 'So let me
e try to explain my meaning by confining myself to a particular
example, like an incompetent lecturer. You know the beginning
of the *Iliad*, where the poet says that Chryses begs Agamemnon
393 a to release his daughter; and when Agamemnon gets angry and
refuses, Chryses calls down the wrath of the god[58] on the
Greeks?'

'Yes.'

'Well, up to the words

He appealed to the whole Achaean army, and most of all to its two
commanders, the sons of Atreus,[59]

the poet is speaking in his own person, and does not attempt to
persuade us that the speaker is anyone but himself. But after-
b wards he speaks in the person of Chryses, and does his best to
make us think that it is not Homer but an aged priest who is

talking. This is the way in which he constructs almost all his
narrative of the Trojan war and of what happened in Ithaca and
in the *Odyssey* generally.'

'That is true enough,' he said.

'So his narrative consists of both speeches and of passages
between speeches, does it not?'

'It does.'

'And when he makes a speech in the person of someone else,   c
shall we not say that he assimilates his manner of speech as
nearly as he can to that of the character concerned?'

'We shall; why do you ask?'

'Is not to assimilate oneself to another person in speech or
manner to "*represent*" the person to whom one is assimilating
oneself?'

'It is.'

'This then is the sort of way in which Homer and the other
poets use representation in the course of their narrative.'

'Yes, I understand.'

'If, of course, the poet never concealed his own personality
his poetic narrative would be wholly devoid of representation.   d
But to prevent any possibility of further misunderstanding, I
will explain how this could be done. Suppose that Homer, after
telling how Chryses came with his daughter's ransom to beg her
back from the Achaeans, and in particular from their kings, had
gone on not as if it were Chryses speaking but Homer, there
would have been no representation but only narrative. The
passage would have run as follows (I'm not a poet, so I shall
give it in prose) – The priest came and prayed that the gods   e
would allow the Achaeans to capture Troy and return in safety,
and begged the Achaeans to show their respect for the god by
releasing his daughter in exchange for the ransom. The others
respected his request and agreed, but Agamemnon was angry
and told him to go away now and never return; otherwise his
sceptre and priestly garlands might afford him no protection.
Agamemnon added that he would not release his daughter
before she grew old with him in Argos, and that if the old man
wanted to get home safely he had better go, and not provoke   394 a
him any more. The old man was afraid when he heard what

Agamemnon said, and departed without a word, but when he had left the camp he prayed earnestly to Apollo, calling on him by all his titles and reminding him of the services he had rendered him in building temples and offering sacrifices; and he begged Apollo in his prayer that, in return, he would avenge his tears

b on the Achaeans with his arrows. That,' I concluded, 'is how the passage would run in simple narrative without representation.'

'I understand,' he replied.

'And so you will also understand,' I went on, 'that the opposite of this is when one omits the poet's words between the speeches and leaves only dialogue.'

'Yes, I understand,' he answered; 'that is what happens in tragedy, for example.'

'You have taken my meaning exactly,' I said. 'And I think I have now made clear what I failed to explain before, that poetry

c and fiction fall into three classes. First, that which employs representation only, tragedy and comedy, as you say. Secondly, that in which the poet speaks in his own person; the best example is lyric poetry. Thirdly, that which employs both methods, epic and various other kinds of poetry. Is that clear?'

'Yes: I understand now what you were trying to say,' he said.

'And you will remember that just before that I said that we had settled the question of subject-matter and must now deal with that of form.'

'Yes, I remember.'

d 'What I meant, then,' I said, 'was that we must decide whether we should allow our poets to use representation freely in their narrative, and if not when they should and should not use it and how, or whether we should forbid it entirely.'

'I suspect,' he replied, 'that you are wondering whether we should allow tragedy and comedy in our state or not.'

'Maybe,' I replied, 'or maybe the question is more far-reaching. I don't know yet; we must go wherever the wind of the argument carries us.'

'Fair enough,' he said.

e 'Do you think, then, Adeimantus, that we want our guardians to be capable of playing many parts[60] or not? Does it not follow, from the principles we adopted earlier, that one man does only one job well, and that if he tries to take on a number of jobs, the division of effort will mean that he will fail to make his mark at any of them?'

'The conclusion follows.'

'And it will also apply to representation; a man cannot play many parts[61] as well as he can one.'

'He cannot.'

'It is unlikely therefore that anyone engaged on any worthwhile occupation will be able to give a variety of representations.[62] For the same writers are incapable of equally good work even in two such closely allied forms of representation as comedy and tragedy. You did say these were both forms of representation, did you not?' 395 a

'Yes; and it's true that a man can't write both.'

'Nor can the same people be reciters[63] and actors, or actors in tragedy and comedy. All these are forms of representation, are they not?' b

'They are.'

'And human nature seems to be more finely subdivided than this, which makes it impossible to play many roles well, whether in real life or in representations of it on the stage.'

'That's very true.'

'So we argued originally that our Guardians were to be freed from all forms of manual work; their function was to be the expert provision of freedom for our state, and that and nothing else not relevant to it was to be their sole business. They must neither do nor represent actions of any other kind. If they do take part in dramatic or other representations, they must from their earliest years act the part only of characters suitable to them – men of courage, self-control, piety, freedom of spirit and similar qualities. They should neither do a mean action, nor be clever at acting a mean or otherwise disgraceful part on the stage for fear of catching the infection in real life. For have you not noticed how dramatic and similar representations, if indulgence in them is prolonged into adult life, establish habits of physical poise, intonation and thought which become second nature?'[64] d

'Indeed I have,' he replied.

'Since then we care for our Guardians, and want them to be
men of worth,' I said, 'we will not allow them to take the parts
of women, young or old (for they are men), nor to represent
e   them abusing their husbands or quarrelling with heaven and
boasting of their supposed good fortune, or mourning and
lamenting in misfortune. Far less can we permit representation
of women in sickness or love or childbirth.'

'We must forbid this sort of thing entirely.'

'And the same is true of representations of slaves – male or
female – when they are doing the work of slaves.'

'Agreed.'

'And of bad men who are cowards and whose behaviour is
just the opposite of what we have just described. Such characters
396 a   indulge in comic abuse and use foul language, drunk or sober,
and say and do other typical things that are an offence against
themselves and their neighbours. Nor, I suppose, ought they to
get into the habit of imitating actions or words of madmen. Our
Guardians must recognize that there are men and women who
are mad and bad, but they must not represent them in poetry or
drama.'

'You are quite right,' he said.

'Then can we tolerate representations of smiths or craftsmen
b   at work, or men rowing triremes or in command of them, or
anything else of the kind?'

'No: because none of these are occupations to which our
Guardians are allowed to pay any attention.'

'And what about horses neighing and bulls bellowing, and
rivers splashing and the sea roaring, and thunder rolling, and so
on?'

'We have already forbidden madness and the imitation of
madmen,' he replied.

'What you mean, if I understand you rightly, is that there is
one style of narrative which the man of really good character
will employ when he has anything to say, and another style in
c   which the man of opposite character and upbringing will always
choose to express himself.'

'Describe them,' he said.

'I think,' I replied, 'that the decent man, when he comes in

the course of a narrative to a speech or action by a man of good
character will be willing to impersonate him and feel no shame
at this kind of representation. This will be especially true if he
is representing the good man behaving with steadiness and
determination, and only failing in a few respects and to a limited   *d*
degree, owing to illness or love or drink or some other misfortune. But if he comes across an unworthy character, he will be
ashamed to copy seriously a man worse than himself, except
perhaps for his short periods of good behaviour, and will not
consent to do so. He has no practice in such representation, and
will refuse with disgust to model himself on characters which   *e*
his judgement despises as lower than his own and put himself
in their place, except perhaps for the purpose of amusement.'
'Very likely.'
'He will, in fact, make use of the form of narrative which we
mentioned when we were talking of Homer's epics a few minutes
ago, and will combine both representation and narrative, but
the proportion of representation will be small. Or am I wrong?'
'No, that's just the kind of principle on which he will express
himself.'
'And other types of man will be all the readier to widen their   397 *a*
range the worse they are, and will think nothing beneath them.
They will seriously try to represent in public all the things we
were talking about. We shall have the noises of thunder and
wind and hail, and of axles and wheels, the notes of trumpets,
pipes, flutes, and every possible instrument, the barking of dogs,   *b*
the baaing of sheep, and twittering of birds. And so this style of
expression will depend largely on representation by sound and
gesture, and narrative will play but a small part.'
'That follows too.'
'These then are the two styles of expression to which I
referred,' I said.
'Yes, I see,' he replied.
'And of these two styles, one is pretty uniform, given music
of appropriate mode and rhythm to accompany it. In fact if one
handles it rightly one and the same mode and harmony can be
employed throughout, because of the uniformity of the style,   *c*
and something similar is true of rhythm.'

'That is certainly true,' he said.

'The other style, on the other hand, will have the opposite requirements. It will need every kind of mode, and every kind of rhythm, if it is to find suitable expression, as its variety of change is unlimited.'

'Very much so.'

'But must not all poets and speakers go in for one or other of these two styles or some combination of them?'

'They must.'

d   'Then what are we to do?' I asked. 'Are we to admit all three into our city, or pick on one of the unmixed styles or the combination of the two?'

'My own vote,' he replied, 'would go to the unmixed style which represents the good man.'

'And yet, Adeimantus,' I reminded him, 'the combination of the two styles is very pleasant, and the opposite style to the one you have chosen gives most pleasure of all to children and nurses and the general public.'

'Yes, it gives most pleasure.'

e   'But perhaps you will say that it is unsuitable for our state, because there one man does one job and does not play two or a multiplicity of roles.'

'It certainly is unsuitable.'

'And so ours is the only state in which we shall find (for example) the shoemaker sticking to his shoemaking and not turning pilot as well, the farmer sticking to his farming and not taking on court work into the bargain, and the soldier sticking to his soldiering and not running a business as well, and so on?'

'Yes.'

398 a   'So if we are visited in our state by someone who has the skill to transform himself into all sorts of characters and represent all sorts of things, and he wants to show off himself and his poems to us, we shall treat him with all the reverence due to a priest and giver of rare pleasure, but shall tell him that he and his kind have no place in our city, their presence being forbidden by our code, and send him elsewhere, after anointing him with myrrh and crowning him with fillets of wool. For ourselves, we

b   shall for our own good employ story-tellers and poets who are severe rather than amusing, who portray[65] the style of the good man and in their works abide by the principles we laid down for them when we started out on this attempt to educate our military class.'[66]

'That undoubtedly is what we should do,' he said, 'if we had the choice.'

'And I think,' said I, 'that that probably completes our survey of the literature and stories to be employed in our education. We have dealt both with subject-matter and with form.'

'I agree,' he replied.

(d) Musical requirements

Music is dealt with on a similar basis. Greek music was employed largely as an accompaniment to song, and what this section is concerned to say is that, having laid down rules governing the content and form of poetry, we must now require their musical accompaniment to be appropriate. As appears from the text, the Greeks recognized several types or styles of music, and were inclined to associate them with different types of feeling and character, an association made by both Plato and Aristotle. So particular varieties of the Lydian style were regarded as mournful, the Ionian scale as relaxing, the Dorian and Phrygian as expressing courage and self-control. But the technicalities of Greek music are not easy to understand: see the Oxford Classical Dictionary, *under* Music.

'Then we are left with the varieties of song and music to *c* discuss,' I went on.

'That's pretty obvious.'

'And I suppose that it would be pretty easy for anyone to discover what sort of requirements we must make about them, if we are to be consistent.'

Glaucon laughed. 'I'm afraid I'm not included in your "any-one",' he said; 'for at the moment I can't really suggest what we ought to say – though I'm not without my suspicions.'

'Well at any rate you can agree easily enough that song consists of three elements, words, mode, and rhythm.' *d*

'Yes, I agree to that.'

'As far as the words are concerned, then, the same principles will apply as those we have just laid down for words not set to music, both for their content and form.'[67]

'True.'

'And surely the mode and rhythm should suit the words.'

'Certainly.'

'But we agreed as far as the words are concerned to dispense with dirges and laments, did we not?'

'We did.'

e   'Tell me then – you are a musician – which are the modes suitable for dirges?'

'The Mixed Lydian and the Extreme Lydian and similar modes.'

'Then we can reject them,' I said: 'even women, if they are respectable, have no use for them, let alone men.'

'Quite right.'

'But drunkenness, softness, or idleness are also qualities most unsuitable in a Guardian?'

'Of course.'

'What, then, are the relaxing modes and the ones we use for drinking songs?'

'The Ionian and certain Lydian modes, commonly described as "languid".'

399 a   'Will they then,' I asked, 'be of any use for training soldiers?'

'None at all,' he replied. 'You seem to be left with the Dorian and Phrygian.'

'I'm no expert on modes,' said I; 'but leave me one that will represent appropriately the voice and accent of a brave man on military service or any dangerous undertaking, who faces misfortune, be it injury or death, or any other calamity, with

b   the same steadfast endurance. And I want another mode to represent him in the voluntary non-violent occupations of peacetime: for instance, persuading someone to grant a request, praying to God or instructing or admonishing his neighbour, or again submitting himself to the requests or instruction or persuasion of others and acting as he decides, and in all showing no conceit,

c   but moderation and common sense and willingness to accept the outcome. Give me these two modes, one stern, one pleasant, which will best represent sound courage and moderation in good fortune or in bad.'

'The two modes you are asking for,' he rejoined, 'are the two I have just mentioned.'

'And so,' I went on, 'we shan't need for our music and song a multiplicity of strings or a wide harmonic range.'   *d*

'Apparently not.'

'We shan't therefore keep craftsmen to make instruments of many strings or wide range, like harps and zithers.'

'I suppose not.'

'Then will you allow flutes and flute-makers in our city? Has not the flute the widest range of all, being in fact the original which other instruments of wide range imitate?'

'That's plain enough,' he said.

'We are left, then, with the lyre and the cithara for use in our city. Though the shepherds in the country might have some sort of pipe.'

'That seems to be the conclusion of our argument.'

'We aren't really doing anything revolutionary, you know,   *e* my dear Glaucon,' I said, 'in preferring Apollo and his instruments to Marsyas[68] and his.'

'Good God, no,' he replied.

'And in the dog's name,'[69] I rejoined, 'we have, without noticing it, been purging our state of the luxury from which we said it suffered.'

'And very sensible too,' he replied.

'Well, let us continue the purge,' said I. 'After mode we should presumably deal next with rhythm. We shan't want very elaborate or varied combinations, but merely need to find which rhythms suit a life of courage and discipline. We shall then adapt the beat and tune to the appropriate words, and not the words   400 *a* to the beat and tune. But it's your business to say what these rhythms are, as you did with the modes.'

'I'm afraid I really can't do that,' he replied. 'There are three basic types of rhythm, from which the various rhythmic combinations are built up, just as in sound there are four elements which go to build up the modes. So much I know and can tell

you. But which are suited to represent which kind of life, I
cannot say.'

b   'Well, we'll consult Damon[70] about it,' I said, 'and ask him
what combinations are suitable to express meanness, insolence,
madness, and other evil characteristics, and which rhythms we
must keep to express their opposites. I seem to remember hearing him talking rather obscurely about "composite march
rhythms", "dactyls", and "heroics", arranging them in various
mysterious ways and marking longs and shorts; he talked also,
I think, about "iambics and trochees", and assigned them quan-
c   tities of different lengths. And I believe that he praised or blamed
the composition of the foot as well as the rhythm as a whole,
or perhaps it was the combination of the two: I really can't
remember. In any case, as I said, we can refer to Damon. For it
would need a lot of argument to settle the details, don't you
think?'

'Heavens, yes!'

Summary

*Plato proceeds to sum up the general purpose of this stage of
education – to train both character and moral and aesthetic
judgement, these last two being closely allied. The influence of
environment on growing minds is again emphasized: it is
because of this that so rigid a control of the music and poetry
to be used in education is required. Mathematical and (so far as
it then existed) scientific training is reserved for a later stage of
the Guardians' education: see Part VIII. But a reference there
to introducing 'arithmetic and geometry' in childhood shows
that though no reference is made to them here some mathematics
is to be studied at this earlier stage (536d).*

'But there is one thing you can decide at once, that beauty
and ugliness result from good rhythm and bad.'

'That is undeniable.'

d   'And good rhythm is the consequence of music adapted to a
good style of expression,[71] bad rhythm of the opposite; and the
same is true of mode, good and bad, if, as we said a moment

ago, both the rhythm and mode should be suited to the words and not vice versa.'

'The words must of course determine the music,' he said.

'But what about the style and diction?' I asked. 'Don't they depend on character?'

'They must.'

'And the rest on style?'

'Yes.'

'Good literature, therefore, and good music, beauty of form and good rhythm all depend on goodness of character;[72] I don't mean that lack of awareness of the world which we politely call   *e* "goodness", but a mind and character truly well and fairly formed.'

'I quite agree.'

'And are not these things which our young men must pursue, if they are to perform their function in life properly?'

'They must.'

'The graphic arts are full of the same qualities and so are the   401*a* related crafts, weaving and embroidery, architecture and the manufacture of furniture of all kinds; and the same is true of living things, animals and plants. For in all of them we find beauty and ugliness. And ugliness of form and bad rhythm and disharmony are akin to poor-quality expression and character, and their opposites are akin to and represent good character and discipline.'

'That is perfectly true.'

'It is not only to the poets therefore that we must issue orders   *b* requiring them to portray good character in their poems or not to write at all; we must issue similar orders to all artists and craftsmen, and prevent them portraying bad character, ill-discipline, meanness, or ugliness in pictures of living things, in sculpture, architecture, or any work of art, and if they are unable to comply they must be forbidden to practise their art among us. We shall thus prevent our guardians being brought up among representations of what is evil, and so day by day and little   *c* by little, by grazing widely as it were in an unhealthy pasture, insensibly doing themselves a cumulative psychological[73]

damage that is very serious. We must look for artists and craftsmen capable of perceiving the real nature of what is beautiful,
and then our young men, living as it were in a healthy climate,
will benefit because all the works of art they see and hear
influence them for good, like the breezes from some healthy
d country, insensibly leading them from earliest childhood into
close sympathy and conformity with beauty and reason.'

'That would indeed be the best way to bring them up.'

'And that, my dear Glaucon,' I said, 'is why this stage of
education is crucial. For rhythm and harmony penetrate deeply
into the mind and take a most powerful hold on it, and, if
education is good, bring and impart grace and beauty, if it is
e bad, the reverse. And moreover the proper training we propose
to give will make a man quick to perceive the shortcomings of
works of art or nature, whose ugliness he will rightly dislike;
anything beautiful he will welcome gladly, will make it his own
402 a and so grow in true goodness of character; anything ugly he will
rightly condemn and dislike, even when he is still young and
cannot understand the reason for so doing, while when reason
comes he will recognize and welcome her as a familiar friend
because of his upbringing.'

'In my view,' he said, 'that is the purpose of this stage of
education.'

'Well then,' I went on, 'when we were learning to read we
were not satisfied until we could recognize the limited number
of letters of the alphabet in all the various words in which they
occurred; we did not think them beneath our notice in large
b words or small, but tried to recognize them everywhere on the
grounds that we should not be literate till we could.'

'That is true.'

'And we can't recognize reflections of the letters in water or
in a mirror till we know the letters themselves. The same skill
and training are needed to recognize both.'

'Yes, they are.'

'Then I must surely be right in saying that we shall not be
c properly educated ourselves, nor will the Guardians whom we
are training, until we can recognize the qualities of discipline,
courage, generosity, greatness of mind, and others akin to them,

as well as their opposites, in all their many manifestations. We must be able to perceive both the qualities themselves wherever they occur and representations of them, and must not despise instances great or small, but reckon that the same skill and training are needed to recognize both.'[74]

'You are most certainly right,' he agreed.

'And is not the fairest sight of all,' I asked, 'for him who has   *d*
eyes to see it, the combination in the same bodily form of beauty of character and looks to match and harmonize with it?'

'It is indeed.'

'And what is very beautiful will also be very attractive, will it not?'

'Certainly.'

'It is, then, with people of this sort that the educated man will fall in love; where the harmony is imperfect he will not be attracted.'

'Not if the defect is one of character,' he replied; 'if it's a physical defect, he will not let it be a bar to his affection.'   *e*

'I know,' I said; 'you've got, or once had, a boy friend like that. And I agree with you. But tell me: does excessive pleasure go with self-control and moderation?'

'Certainly not; excessive pleasure breaks down one's control just as much as excessive pain.'

'Does it go with other kinds of goodness?'

'No.'

'Then does it go with violence and indiscipline?'   403 *a*

'Certainly.'

'And is there any greater or keener pleasure than that of sex?'

'No: nor any more frenzied.'

'But to love rightly is to love what is orderly and beautiful in an educated and disciplined way.'

'I entirely agree.'

'Then can true love have any contact with frenzy or excess of any kind?'

'It can have none.'

'It can therefore have no contact with this sexual pleasure,   *b*
and lovers whose mutual love is true must neither of them indulge in it.'

'They certainly must not, Socrates,' he replied emphatically.

'And so I suppose that you will lay down laws in the state we are founding which will allow a lover to associate with his boy friend and kiss him and touch him, if he permits it, as a father does his son, if his motives are good; but require that his association with anyone he's fond of must never give rise to suspicion
c   of anything beyond this, otherwise he will be thought a man of no taste or education.'

'That is how I should legislate.'

'And that, I think,' said I, 'concludes what we have to say about this stage of education, and a very appropriate conclusion too – for the object of education is to teach us to love what is beautiful.'

'I agree.'

2. Physical Education

Plato does not go into detail but makes it clear that he is thinking of a military as much as of an athletic training: which is why, perhaps, he tends to regard it, as appears later, as a stage of education, lasting approximately from the eighteenth to the twentieth year, rather than as something which accompanies the secondary education which he has just finished describing. Young men at Athens in the fourth century spent two years, from eighteen to twenty, doing a course of compulsory military training, and it is of military training as much as of physical education in our sense that Plato is thinking.

The passage proceeds to criticize certain developments of contemporary medicine of which Plato disapproved (criticisms which read harshly to us, though they indicate that Plato is thinking of health education in general as much as physical education in the narrower sense), and more briefly, to condemn litigiousness (Plato undoubtedly has contemporary Athens in mind); it ends by emphasizing that physical, as much as literary, education is aimed primarily at the development of character.

'The next stage in the training of our young men will be physical education.'

'Of course.'

'And here again they must be carefully trained from childhood onwards. My own opinions about this are as follows: let me see *d* if you agree. In my view physical excellence does not of itself produce a good mind and character: on the other hand, excellence of mind and character *will* make the best of the physique it is given. What do you think?'

'I agree.'

'If the mind therefore has been adequately trained, we should do well then to leave to it the minutiae of physical training: all we need do, for brevity's sake, is to give a rough outline.' *e*

'Yes.'

'We have already forbidden drunkenness.[75] A Guardian is the last person in the world to get drunk and not know where he is.'

'It would be absurd,' he replied, 'for a Guardian to need someone to look after him.'

'What about diet? Our Guardians, you will agree, are competing in the most important of all contests.'

'Yes.'

'Is the ordinary athlete's physical condition appropriate for *404 a* them?'

'Perhaps so.'

'But the athlete in training is a sleepy creature and his health delicately balanced. Haven't you noticed how they sleep most of their time, and how the smallest deviation from their routine leads to serious illness?'

'Yes, I've noticed that.'

'So we shall need a more sophisticated form of training for our soldier athletes. They must be as wakeful as watchdogs, their sight and hearing must be of the keenest, and their health must not be too delicate to endure the many changes in the water they drink and in the rest of their diet and the varieties of temperature that campaigning entails.' *b*

'I agree.'

'And do you not also agree that the best form of physical

training would be one akin to the simple education we have just been describing?'

'What do you mean?'

'I mean a physical training that is simple and flexible, particularly in its training for war.'

'In what way?'

'Even Homer can tell you that,' I replied. 'For you know that when his heroes are on campaign he does not feast them on fish,

c although they are on the shore of the Hellespont, nor on boiled meat, but only roast. That is what suits soldiers best, because it is, generally speaking, easier to cook something direct on the fire than carry round pots and pans for the purpose.'

'Much easier.'

'And Homer, I think, never mentions seasonings. Indeed, even the ordinary athlete knows that if he is to be fit he must keep off everything of that sort.'

'And he is quite right to act on the knowledge.'

d 'If that's your view I assume that you don't approve of the luxury of Syracusan and Sicilian cooking.'

'I should think not.'

'And what about Corinthian girl-friends? Do you disapprove of them for men who want to keep fit?'

'I certainly do.'

'You would disapprove too of the supposed delights of Attic confectionery?'

'Inevitably.'

'We might, I think, with justice compare these luxurious ways of living and eating with the music and song which used a wide

e range of mode and rhythm.'

'Quite so.'

'Elaborate music, we found, produces indiscipline, and elaborate food produces disease. But simplicity in music produces discipline of character, and simplicity in physical education health of body.'

'Very true.'

405 a 'And the prevalence of indiscipline and disease in a community leads, does it not, to the opening of law courts and surgeries in large numbers, and law and medicine begin to

give themselves airs, especially when they are taken with great seriousness even by free men.'

'That is bound to happen.'

'And when not only the lower classes and manual workers, but also those who have some pretensions to a liberal education, need skilled doctors and lawyers, that is a pretty conclusive proof that the education in a state is disgracefully bad. For is it not a strikingly disgraceful sign of a bad education if one has to seek justice at the hands of others as one's masters and judges *b* because one lacks it in oneself?'

'I can't think of anything more disgraceful,' he said.

'Yet it's still more disgraceful, don't you think,' I replied, 'when a man not only spends most of his life in court as plaintiff or defendant, but is even vulgar enough to be proud of it – proud that he is an expert law-breaker, up to all the dodges, and that he knows all the holes to wriggle through to avoid a *c* conviction? And all this for mean and unworthy ends, without any idea how far better it is to arrange one's life so that one has no need of a jury dozing on the bench.'

'Yes,' he agreed, 'that's still more disgraceful.'

'And it's disgraceful too to need a doctor not only for injury or regular disease, but because by leading the kind of idle life *d* we have described we have filled our bodies with gases and fluids, like a stagnant pool, and driven the medical profession to invent names for our diseases, like flatulence and catarrh. Don't you agree?'

'I do indeed,' he replied, 'these new-fangled names for diseases are very far-fetched.'

'And I don't think you would have found them in the days of Asclepius,'[76] I added. 'Or so I should judge from the fact that *e* when Eurypylus was wounded at Troy, and given Pramnian wine sprinkled with barley-meal and grated cheese to drink – a mixture you would have thought would have given him a fever 406 *a* – the sons of Asclepius had no fault to find with the women who gave him the drink, or with Patroclus who was treating him.'

'And yet it was an odd prescription for a wounded man,' he said.

'Not,' I replied, 'if you reflect that it was not till the days of

Herodicus, so they say, that doctors made use in their treatment of modern methods of cosseting disease. Herodicus was an athletic trainer, whose health failed, and he proceeded to make
b first and foremost himself, and then many others after him, miserable by a combination of medicine and physical training.'

'How did he do that?'

'By dying a lingering death. His whole attention was devoted to his disease which was mortal; he could not cure himself of it, but spent the rest of his life too busy to do anything but doctor himself and being made wretched by any departure from his routine treatment. And his skill prolonged the struggle against death till he was an old man.'

'What a reward for skill!'

c 'And quite a suitable one for a man who did not know that it was not from ignorance or lack of experience of it that Asclepius did not reveal this method of treatment to his successors, but because he knew that when things are well run each man has a job in society which he must do, and has no time to spend his life being ill and undergoing cures. We see that this applies to the working class, and it is absurd not to see that it also applies to the wealthy and privileged, as we think them.'

'Explain,' he said.

d 'If a carpenter is ill,' I replied, 'and goes to a doctor, he expects to be given an emetic and be cured, or to get rid of the trouble by purge or cautery or operation. If he is ordered to undergo a long cure, wrapping his head up and all that sort of thing, he will probably say that he's no time to be ill and that a life in which one must give all one's attention to one's ailments and none to one's proper job simply is not worth living. Then he
e will dismiss the doctor who has given the advice, go back to his normal routine, and either regain his health and get on with his job, or, if his constitution won't stand it, die and be rid of his troubles.'

'That's the right way for that sort of man to treat medical advice,' he agreed.

'The reason being,' I said, 'that he has a job to do, and if he
407 *a* does not do it, life is not worth while.'

'Yes, clearly.'

'But hasn't the rich man his proper job to do, which will make his life not worth living if he is prevented from doing it?'

'He isn't usually reckoned to have.'

'You haven't listened to Phocylides,'[77] was my reply, 'who said that when a man no longer has to work for his living, he should "practise excellence".'

'I should have thought he might start even earlier,' he said.

'Don't let's quarrel with him about that,' I returned, 'but let us inform ourselves whether the rich man should make this his job, and whether his life is worth living if he can't carry on with it. If valetudinarianism prevents a man giving his attention to carpentry and similar occupations, isn't it also a hindrance to obeying Phocylides' orders?'

'It certainly is a hindrance. There's nothing worse than this fussiness about one's health, in excess of normal physical training. It's tiresome in the home, as well as in the army or in a sedentary civilian office.'

'Worst of all, it makes any kind of study or thought or private meditation difficult. If you are always wondering if you've got a headache or are feeling giddy, and blaming your philosophical studies for it, you will always be prevented from exercising and proving your talents. You'll always think you're ill, and never stop worrying about your health.'

'That's what's likely to happen.'

'Let us say, then, that Asclepius too knew all this, and therefore introduced medical treatment for those who have a good constitution and lead a healthy life. If they get some specific disease, he gets rid of it by drugs or surgery, but tells them to go on leading their normal life so as not to make them less useful to the community. But he makes no attempt to cure those whose constitution is basically diseased by treating them with a series of evacuations and doses which can only lead to an unhappy prolongation of life, and the production of children as unhealthy as themselves. No, he thought that no treatment should be given to the man who cannot survive the routine of his ordinary job, and who is therefore of no use either to himself or society.'

'You talk as if Asclepius was a real statesman!'

'Of course he was,' said I, 'and because he was we find that

408 *a* his sons are good soldiers at Troy, and doctor people in the way
I am describing. You will remember how, when Menelaus was
wounded by Pandarus, they "sucked out the blood and skilfully
applied soothing ointments".[78] But they gave him no further
orders about diet, any more than they did to Eurypylus; for they
thought that "ointments" were enough to cure a man who had
previously lived a regular and healthy life, whatever mixture he
drank after treatment. The life of a man whose constitution was

b bad and undermined by loose living was, they thought, of no
use to them or to anyone else; it was not their business to use
their skill on such cases or cure them, even if they were richer
than Midas.'

'Discerning men, these sons of Asclepius.'

'Which is as it should be,' I said. 'But Pindar and the tragedians[79] don't believe us, and say that Asclepius was a son of
Apollo, that he was bribed by a large fee to cure a rich man

c who was at death's door, and blasted by a thunderbolt in
consequence. But we cannot, if we are to be consistent, agree
with them on both counts: if he was son of a god he was not out
for profit, and if he was out for profit he was not son of a god.'

'All that is very true. But tell me, Socrates,' he asked, 'surely
we shall need good doctors in our state? And good doctors are
likely to be those who have the widest experience in treating

d patients both in health and sickness, just as good judges[80] are
likely to be those who have mixed with all sorts of people.'

'We certainly need good doctors and judges,' I answered, 'but
do you know what I mean by good?'

'I shall if you tell me.'

'I will try. But your question puts together dissimilar
things.'

'What do you mean?'

'The best way for a doctor to acquire skill is to have, in
addition to his knowledge of medical science, as wide and as
early an acquaintance as possible with serious illness; in addition
he should have experienced all kinds of disease in his own person

e and not be of an altogether healthy constitution. For doctors
don't use their bodies to cure other people's bodies – if so, they
could not allow their health to be or become bad – they use their

minds; and if their mental powers are or become bad their treatment can't be good.'

'True.'

'But with a judge it's a matter of mind controlling mind. And the mind must not be brought up from its youth to associate with wickedness, or to run through a whole range of crimes in order to get first-hand experience on which to be able to judge them quickly in other people, as the doctor does with diseases of the body: on the contrary, the mind must, while it is still young, remain quite without experience of or contact with bad characters, if its condition is to be truly good and its judgements just. That is why people of good character seem simple[81] when they are young, and are easily taken in by dishonesty – because they have nothing corresponding in themselves to give them a sympathetic understanding of wickedness.'

'That is commonly their experience,' he agreed.

'Which is why a good judge must not be a young man,' I replied, 'but an old one to whom knowledge of wickedness has come late in life, not as a feature he perceives in his own character, but as an evil whose nature he has learned after long practice to discern in other people, something about which he has knowledge but of which he has no personal experience.'

'A man like that would be a real judge indeed.'

'And a good one, which is what you asked,' I pointed out; 'for he has the qualities of mind to make him a good one.[82] But your wily, suspicious type, who has done many wrongs and thinks himself super-smart, looks pretty formidable so long as he is dealing with men like himself, against whom his own bad principles put him on his guard; but when he comes up against men of experience and good character he looks very silly with his untimely suspicions and the unawareness of what honesty is which he owes to his own lack of good principle. But he meets more rogues than honest men, and so appears a clever fellow and not a silly one, both to himself and others.'

'That's perfectly true,' he said.

'We must not look to this type, then, for our good and wise judge, but to the other. Wickedness can never know either itself or excellence, but excellence, when education is added to natural

endowment, can in course of time acquire knowledge of wicked-
e ness as well as of itself. It is the good man, therefore, and not
the bad man who will, in my opinion, make our wise judge.'

'I agree with you.'

'This then is the kind of medical and judicial provision for
which you will legislate in your state. It will provide treatment
410*a* for those of your citizens whose physical and psychological
constitution is good; as for the others, it will leave the unhealthy
to die, and those whose psychological constitution is incurably
corrupt it will put to death.'

'That seems to be the best thing both for the individual sufferer
and for society.'

'And so,' I said, 'your young men, so long as they maintain
their simple form of education, which, as we have said, breeds
self-control, will take care not to need judicial treatment.'

'True.'

b 'And if being so educated they follow on the same track in
their physical training, they will, if they choose, succeed in never
needing a doctor except in real necessity.'

'I agree.'

'It is, of course, to stimulate their energy and initiative[83] that
they undergo these strenuous exercises in their physical training,
not merely to make themselves tough, which is the object of the
diet and exercises of the ordinary athlete.'

'You are quite right.'

'And that, my dear Glaucon,' I went on, 'is why I say that the
c purpose of the two established types of education (mental[84] and
physical) is not, as some suppose, to deal one with the mind and
the other with the body.'

'What is it then?' he asked.

'I think that perhaps the main aim of both is to train the
mind.'

'And how do they do that?'

'Have you noticed,' I asked, 'how a lifelong devotion to
physical exercise, to the exclusion of anything else, produces a
certain type of mind? Just as a neglect of it produces another
type?'

'What do you mean?'

'One type tends to be uncivilized and tough, the other soft   *d*
and over-sensitive, and . . .'

'Yes, I have noticed that,' he broke in; 'excessive emphasis on
athletics produces an excessively uncivilized type, while a purely
literary training leaves men indecently soft.'

'It is the energy and initiative in their nature that may make
them uncivilized,' I said; 'if you treat it properly it should make
them brave, but if you overstrain it it turns them tough and
uncouth, as you would expect.'

'I agree,' he said.

'The philosophic temperament, on the other hand, is gentle;   *e*
too much relaxation may produce an excessive softness, but if
it is treated properly the result should be humane and civilized.'

'That is so.'

'Now we agreed that our Guardians must have both these
elements in their nature, did we not?'

'Yes.'

'And must not these two elements be harmoniously adjusted?'   411 *a*

'Of course.'

'And will proper adjustment produce a character that is self-
controlled and brave?'

'Certainly.'

'And maladjustment one that is cowardly and crude?'

'Very much so.'

'So when a man surrenders to the sound of music and lets its
sweet, soft, mournful strains, which we have just described, be
funnelled into his soul through his ears, and gives up all his time
to the glamorous moanings of song, the effect at first on his
energy and initiative of mind, if he has any, is to soften it as iron
is softened in a furnace, and made workable instead of hard
and unworkable: but if he persists and does not break the   *b*
enchantment, the next stage is that it melts and runs, till the
spirit has quite run out of him and his mental sinews (if I may
so put it) are cut, and he has become what Homer calls "a feeble
fighter".'

'That is all very true.'

'This result is one that follows quickly if he is naturally
spiritless in the first place. But if he is a man of spirit, the effect

is, by weakening his spirit, to make him unstable, a man who flies into a rage at a trifle and calms down as quickly. His energy

c has degenerated into peevishness and ill temper and he is subject to constant irritability.'

'Exactly.'

'On the other hand, there is the man who takes a lot of strenuous physical exercise and lives well, but has little acquaintance with literature or philosophy. The physical health that results from such a course first fills him with confidence and energy, and increases his courage.'

'It certainly does.'

'But what happens if he devotes himself exclusively to it, and

d has no intelligent interests? Any latent love he may have for learning is weakened by being starved of instruction or inquiry and by never taking part in any discussion or educated activity,[85] and becomes deaf and blind because its perceptions are never cleared and it is never roused or fed.'

'That is what happens.'

'And so he becomes an unintelligent philistine, with no use for reasoned discussion, and an animal addiction to settle every-

e thing by brute force. His life is one of clumsy ignorance, unrelieved by grace or beauty.'

'That describes him exactly.'

'What I should say therefore is that these two branches of education seem to have been given by some god to men to train these two parts of us – the one to train our philosophic part, the other our energy and initiative.[86] They are not intended the one to train body, the other mind, except incidentally, but to

412 *a* ensure a proper harmony between energy and initiative on the one hand and reason on the other, by tuning each to the right pitch.'

'Yes, so it seems.'

'And so we may venture to assert that anyone who can produce the perfect blend of the physical and intellectual[87] sides of education and apply them to the training of character, is producing music and harmony of far more importance than any mere musician tuning strings.'

'A very reasonable assertion, Socrates.'

'We must therefore ensure, my dear Glaucon,' I said, 'that there is always someone like this in charge of education in our state, if its constitution is to be preserved.'

'We most certainly must.'

PART IV
GUARDIANS AND
AUXILIARIES

1. The Three Classes and Their Mutual Relations

The Guardian class is subdivided into Guardians proper, or Rulers, and Auxiliaries. The Rulers exercise supreme authority in the state and are selected by exacting tests (the educational aspect of these is dealt with later, Part VIII). The Auxiliaries (I retain the traditional translation: there is no single term which describes their function completely) discharge Military, Police, and Executive duties under the orders of the Rulers. Everything which the Rulers do is done for the good of the community. Plato sketches a Foundation Myth and stringently requires that children are to be moved from class to class according to merit and capability; he does not give details, which might have been difficult to work out, but there is no reason to doubt his seriousness.

Plato has been criticized for his Foundation Myth as if it were a calculated lie. That is partly because the phrase here translated 'magnificent myth' (see 414b) has been conventionally mistranslated 'noble lie'; and this has been used to support the charge that Plato countenances manipulation by propaganda. But the myth is accepted by all three classes, Guardians included. It is meant to replace the national traditions which any community has, which are intended to express the kind of community it is, or wishes to be, its ideals, rather than to state matters of fact. And one of Plato's own criticisms of democracy was that its politicians constantly mislead it, governing by propaganda rather than reason (cf. 488a–d, 493a–d).

'That, then, is an outline of the way in which we should educate [412] and bring up our Guardians. For we need not go into detail *b* about their choral performances, hunting and field sports, athletic competitions and horse-races. The details follow naturally from what we have said, and should give no particular difficulty.'

'Yes, I dare say they won't be particularly difficult,' he agreed.

'Well,' I continued, 'what comes next? We shall have to decide, I suppose, which of our Guardians are to govern, and which to be governed.'

'I suppose so.'   *c*

'Well, it is obvious that the elder must govern, and the younger be governed.'

'That is obvious.'

'And again that those who govern must be the best of them.'

'That's equally obvious.'

'And the best farmers are those who have the greatest skill at farming, are they not?'

'Yes.'

'And so if we want to pick the best Guardians, we must pick those who have the greatest skill in watching over the community.'[1]

'Yes.'

'For that shan't we need men who, besides being intelligent and capable, really care for the community?'

'True.'   *d*

'But we care most for what we love.'

'Inevitably.'

'And the deepest affection is based on identity of interest, when we feel that our own good and ill fortune is completely bound up with that of something else.'

'That is so.'

'So we must choose from among our Guardians those who appear to us on observation to be most likely to devote their lives to doing what they judge to be in the interest of the *e* community, and who are never prepared to act against it.'

'They are the men for our purpose.'

'A close watch must be kept on them, then, at all ages, to see if they stick to this principle, and do not forget or jettison, under the influence of force or witchcraft,[2] the conviction that they must always do what is best for the community.'

'What do you mean by jettison?' he asked.

'I will explain,' I said. 'It seems to me that when any belief leaves our minds, the loss is either voluntary or involuntary. Voluntary when the belief is false and we learn better, involuntary whenever the belief is true.'

413 *a*

'I understand what you mean by a voluntary loss, but not by an involuntary one.'

'But why? Surely you agree that men are always unwilling to lose a good thing, but willing enough to be rid of a bad one. And isn't it a bad thing to be deceived about the truth, and a good thing to possess the truth? For I assume that by possessing the truth you mean believing that things are as they really are.'

'Yes, you are quite right,' he conceded, 'and I agree that men are unwilling to lose a belief that is true.'

b   'So when it happens it must be due to theft or witchcraft or force.'

'Now I don't understand again,' he said.

'I'm afraid I'm talking too theatrically,' I answered. 'By "theft" I simply mean the insensible process by which people are persuaded to relinquish their beliefs by argument, or else simply forget them in course of time. Now perhaps you understand.'

'Yes.'

'By "force" I mean what happens when men change their opinions under the influence of pain or suffering.'

'This too I understand,' he said. 'You are right.'

c   'And I think that you too would call it "witchcraft"[3] when people change their opinions under the spell of pleasure or impulse of panic.'

'Yes, such delusions always seem to act like witchcraft.'

'To go back to what I was saying, then,' I continued, 'we must look for the Guardians who will stick most firmly to the principle that they must always do what they think best for the community. We must watch them closely from their earliest years,

and set them tasks in doing which they are most likely to forget
or be led astray from this principle; and we must choose only   *d*
those who don't forget and are not easily misled. Do you agree?'
    'Yes.'
    'And with the same end in view we must see how they stand
up to hard work and pain and competitive trials.'
    'We must.'
    'We must also watch their reactions to the third kind of test,
witchcraft. If we want to find out if a colt is nervous we expose
him to alarming noises: so we must introduce our Guardians
when they are young to fear and, by contrast, give them opportunities for pleasure, proving them far more rigorously than we   *e*
prove gold in the furnace. If they bear themselves well and are
not easily bewitched, if they show themselves able to maintain
in all circumstances both their own integrity and the principles
of balance and harmony they learned in their education, then
they may be expected to be of the greatest service to the community as well as to themselves. And any Guardian who survives
these continuous trials in childhood, youth, and manhood
unscathed, shall be given authority in our state; he shall be   414 *a*
honoured during his lifetime and when he is dead shall have the
tribute of a public funeral and appropriate memorial. Anyone
who fails to survive them we must reject.
    'That in brief, and without going into details,' I concluded,
'is the way in which I would select and appoint our Rulers and
Guardians.'
    'And that's the way I think it should be done,' he replied.
    'Strictly speaking, then, it is for them that we should reserve   *b*
the term Guardian in its fullest sense, their function being to see
that friends at home shall not wish, nor foes abroad be able, to
harm our state: while the young men whom we have been
describing as Guardians should more strictly be called Auxiliaries, their function being to assist the Rulers in the execution
of their decisions.'[4]
    'I agree,' he said.
    'Now I wonder if we could contrive one of those convenient
stories we were talking about a few minutes ago,[5] I asked, 'some
magnificent myth that would in itself carry conviction to our

c whole community, including, if possible, the Guardians themselves?'

'What sort of story?'

'Nothing new – a fairy story like those the poets tell and have
persuaded people to believe about the sort of thing that often
happened "once upon a time", but never does now and is not
likely to: indeed it would need a lot of persuasion to get people
to believe it.'

'You seem to be hesitating to tell us more,' he said.

'And when I do you will understand my hesitation,' I assured
him.

'Never mind,' he replied, 'tell us.'

d 'I will,' I said, 'though I don't know how I'm to find the
courage or the words to do so. I shall try to persuade first the
Rulers and Soldiers,[6] and then the rest of the community, that the
upbringing and education we have given them was all something
that happened to them only in a dream. In reality they were
fashioned and reared, and their arms and equipment manufac-
e tured, in the depths of the earth, and Earth herself, their mother,
brought them up, when they were complete, into the light of
day; so now they must think of the land in which they live as
their mother and protect her if she is attacked, while their
fellow-citizens they must regard as brothers born of the same
mother earth.'

'No wonder you were ashamed to tell your story,' he com-
415 a mented. I agreed that it was indeed no wonder, but asked him
to listen to the rest of the story.

'We shall,' I said, 'tell our citizens the following tale:[7]

"You are, all of you in this community,[8] brothers. But when
god fashioned you, he added gold in the composition of those
of you who are qualified to be Rulers (which is why their prestige
is greatest); he put silver in the Auxiliaries, and iron and bronze
in the farmers and other workers. Now since you are all of the
same stock, though your children will commonly resemble their
b parents, occasionally a silver child will be born of golden parents,
or a golden child of silver parents, and so on. Therefore the first
and most important of god's commandments to the Rulers is

that in the exercise of their function as Guardians their principal care must be to watch the mixture of metals in the characters of their children. If one of their own children has traces of bronze or iron in its make-up, they must harden their hearts, assign it its proper value, and degrade it to the ranks of the industrial *c* and agricultural class where it properly belongs: similarly, if a child of this class is born with gold or silver in its nature, they will promote it appropriately to be a Guardian or an Auxiliary. And this they must do because there is a prophecy that the State will be ruined when it has Guardians of silver or bronze."[9]

That is the story. Do you know of any way of making them believe it?'

'Not in the first generation,' he said, 'but you might succeed *d* with the second and later generations.'

'Even so it should serve to increase their loyalty to the state and to each other. For I think I understand what you mean.'

2. The Rulers' and Auxiliaries' Way of Life

The Rulers and Auxiliaries are to live a life of austere simplicity, without private property or (as will appear more clearly later, in the opening note to Part VI, section 2) family life; for private property was, Plato thought, the chief temptation that led men to sacrifice public to personal interests (cf. 464c). The happiness of both will lie in their service to the community; for it is the happiness of the community as a whole, and not of any particular class, that is the objective.

'But let us leave that to popular tradition to decide, and arm our earthborn citizens and conduct them to their city, under the leadership of the Rulers. On arrival the Rulers[10] must pick a site for a camp which will best enable them to control any internal disaffection or to repel any attack by an external enemy, descending like a wolf on the fold. When they have made their *e* camp, they will sacrifice to the appropriate gods, and then arrange sleeping quarters. Do you agree?'

'Yes.'

'And these quarters must provide adequate shelter both in summer and winter, mustn't they?'

'Yes; for I take it you mean them to live there.'

'I do; but as soldiers and not as men of means.'

'What is the difference?'

416 a 'I will try to explain. It would be the most dreadful disgrace for a shepherd to keep sheep-dogs so badly bred and trained, that disobedience or hunger or some bad trait or other led them to worry the sheep and behave more like wolves than dogs.'

'It would of course be dreadful.'

b 'We must therefore take every possible precaution to prevent our Auxiliaries treating our citizens like that because of their superior strength, and behaving more like savage tyrants than partners and friends.'

'We must certainly try to prevent that.'

'And the greatest possible precaution will have been taken, will it not, if they have been properly educated?'

'As in fact they have been,' he said.

To which I replied, 'We oughtn't to be too positive about that, my dear Glaucon; what we can be positive about is what c we have just said, namely that they must be given the right education, whatever that may be, as the surest way to make them behave humanely to each other and the subjects in their charge.'

'That is true.'

'It would therefore be reasonable to say that, besides being so educated, they should be housed and their material needs provided for in a way that will not prevent them being excellent d Guardians, yet will not tempt them to prey upon the rest of the community.'

'That is very true.'

'Well then,' I said, 'if they are to have these characteristics, I suggest that they should live and be housed as follows. First, they shall have no private property beyond the barest essentials. Second, none of them shall possess a dwelling-house or storehouse to which all have not the right of entry. Next, their food shall be provided by the other citizens as an agreed wage for the duties they perform as Guardians; it shall be suitable for brave men living under military training and discipline, and in quantity *e* enough to ensure that there is neither a surplus nor a deficit over the year. They shall eat together in messes and live together like soldiers in camp. They must be told that they have no need of mortal and material gold and silver, because they have in their hearts the heavenly gold and silver given them by the gods as a permanent possession, and it would be wicked to pollute the heavenly gold in their possession by mixing it with earthly, for theirs is without impurity, while that in currency among men is 417 *a* a common source of wickedness. They alone, therefore, of all the citizens are forbidden to touch or handle silver or gold; they must not come under the same roof as them, nor wear them as ornaments, nor drink from vessels made of them. Upon this their safety and that of the state depends. If they acquire private property in land, houses, or money, they will become farmers and men of business instead of Guardians, and harsh tyrants *b* instead of partners in their dealings with their fellow citizens, with whom they will live on terms of mutual hatred and suspicion; they will be more afraid of internal revolt than external attack, and be heading fast for destruction that will overwhelm themselves and the whole community.

'For all these reasons we should provide for the housing and other material needs of the Guardians in the way I have described. So shall we legislate accordingly?'

'Let us do so by all means,' answered Glaucon.

'But look here, Socrates,' interrupted Adeimantus, 'how BK IV would you answer the objection that you aren't making your Guardians particularly happy? It's their own fault, of course, 419 because the state is in their control, but they don't seem to get any good out of it. Other rulers possess lands and build themselves fine large houses and furnish them magnificently; they offer their own private sacrifices to the gods, they entertain visitors, and acquire the gold and silver you were just talking about, and everything else which is commonly thought to make a man happy. But one might almost describe your Guardians as a set of hired mercenaries quartered in the city with nothing to 420 *a* do but perpetual guard-duty.'

'Yes,' I replied, 'and what is more, they do it for their keep only, and get no pay over and above it like other men, so that they can't go for a holiday abroad on their own if they want to; they have nothing to spend on women or on all those other things on which those who are commonly reckoned well off spend their money. And there are a whole lot of other charges you have omitted.'

'Let us take them as read then,' he said.

b   'And you want to know how we should reply?'

'Yes.'

'I think,' I said, 'that we shall find our reply if we stick to the path we have been pursuing, and say that, though it would not in fact be in the least surprising if our Guardians were very happy indeed, our purpose in founding our state was not to promote the particular happiness of a single class, but, so far as possible, of the whole community. Our idea was that we were most likely to find justice in such a community, and similarly

c   injustice in a really badly run community, and in light of our findings be able to decide the question we are trying to answer. We are therefore at the moment trying to construct what we think is a happy community by securing the happiness not of a select minority, but of the whole. The opposite kind of community we will examine presently.[11] Now if we were painting a statue, and were met with the criticism that we were not using the most beautiful colours for the most beautiful parts of the body – for we had not coloured the eyes, the body's most precious feature, purple, but black – we could, I think, reason-

d   ably reply as follows: "It is absurd to expect us to represent the beauty of the eye in a way which does not make it look like an eye at all, and the same is true of the other parts of the body; you should look rather to see whether we have made the whole beautiful by giving each part its proper colour. So, in the present case," we might go on, "don't make us give our Guardians the

e   kind of happiness that will make them anything but Guardians." We could perfectly well clothe our farmers in robes of state and put crowns on their heads and tell them to cultivate the land at their pleasure, and we could make our potters lie on couches round the fire, and let them drink and enjoy themselves, putting their wheel at their side for them to make pots only as they felt inclined; indeed, we could try to make the whole community happy by giving everyone else similarly blissful conditions. But you must not tell us to do so; for the result of such advice will be that our farmers are no longer farmers nor our potters potters, and that all the classes that make up our community lose their proper character. In other cases this does not matter much – the community suffers nothing very terrible if its cobblers are bad and become degenerate and pretentious; but if the Guardians of the laws and state, who alone have the opportunity to bring it good government and prosperity, become a mere sham, then clearly it is completely ruined. 421 a

'So if we are making genuine Guardians, who will be the last to harm the community, while our critic prefers idlers[12] happily enjoying themselves in something more like a fun-fair than a city, then he is not thinking of a community at all. We must therefore decide whether our object in setting up the Guardian class is to make it as happy as we can, or whether happiness is a thing we should look for in the community as a whole. If it is, our Guardians and Auxiliaries must be compelled to act accordingly and be persuaded, as indeed must everyone else, that it is their business to perfect themselves in their own particular job; then our state will be built on the right basis, and, as it grows, we can leave each class to enjoy the share of happiness its nature permits.' b

c

'That,' he said, 'seems to put it very fairly.'

3. Final Provisions for Unity

The Guardians must see that in the Third Class, which is alone allowed to possess property, extremes of wealth and poverty are excluded. Their military training will ensure success in war, but they must maintain unity by not allowing the state to grow too large, and by ensuring that the measures for promotion and demotion from one class to another are carried out. Above all they must maintain the educational system unchanged; for on education everything else depends, and it is an illusion to imagine that mere legislation without it can effect anything of consequence.

Religious arrangements are to be left to the Oracle at Delphi, 'which was normally consulted before the foundation of a new city'.[13]

'I wonder,' I asked, 'whether you will think a closely related view of mine as reasonable?'

'What exactly is it?'

d 'That there are two things that can ruin and corrupt the rest of our workers.'

'What are they?'

'Wealth and poverty,' I said.

'And how do they do it?'

'Well, do you think that a potter who has become rich will want to ply his trade any longer?'

'No.'

'He will become more idle and careless than he was, won't he?'

'Much more.'

'And so a worse potter.'

'Yes, much worse.'

'And again, if he is prevented by poverty from providing himself with tools and other necessities of his trade the quality

e of his work will deteriorate, and his sons and anyone else studying the trade under him will not be taught it so well.'

'Inevitably.'

'Both poverty and wealth, therefore, have a bad effect on the quality of the work and on the workman himself.'

'So it appears.'

'So we have found two further things,' I said, 'which our Guardians must at all costs prevent from slipping unobserved into our state.'

'What are they?'

422 a 'Wealth and poverty,' I answered. 'One produces luxury and idleness and a desire for novelty, the other meanness and bad workmanship and the desire for revolution as well.'

'I agree,' he replied. 'But here's another question. How do

you think our state will be able to fight a war, Socrates, if it has no wealth, especially if it is compelled to fight against an enemy that is both large and wealthy?'

'Obviously it would be more difficult to fight a single enemy of this sort than two,' I said.   *b*

'What do you mean?' he asked.

'In the first place,' I said, 'if they have to fight, our Guardians will fight as trained soldiers against their rich antagonists.'

'Yes, I grant that.'

'But come, Adeimantus,' I said, 'don't you think that one boxer in perfect training is easily a match for two men who are not boxers, but rich and fat?'

'Not if they both set on him at once, perhaps.'

'Not even if he is able to retreat a little, and then turn on the leader and hit him, and repeat the process often in the hot sun?   *c* Surely in this way he could get the better of more than two?'

'Yes, of course: there would be nothing surprising in that.'

'And don't you agree that rich men are likely to have more knowledge and experience of boxing than of war?'

'Yes.'

'Well then, it would appear that our trained soldiers should easily be a match for two or three times their number.'

'I will grant that,' he said; 'I think you are right.'

'So suppose we send envoys to one of the two states to say,   *d* truly enough, "Unlike you we have no use for silver or gold, which are forbidden us, though not to you. If therefore you will fight on our side you shall have all the other state has." Do you think that any state hearing these terms will prefer to fight against our tough and wiry watchdogs, rather than with them and against fat and tender sheep?'

'I should think not. But don't you think that our state might be in some danger because of its lack of wealth, if the others pooled all their resources?' he asked. To which I replied: 'You're lucky to be able to think of any community as worth the name   *e* of "state" which differs from the one we are building.'

'But what should I call the others?' he asked.

'We ought to find some grander name for them,' I replied. 'Each of them is, as the proverb says, not so much a single state

as a collection of states. For it always contains at least two
423 a states, the rich and the poor, at enmity with each other; each of
these in turn has many subdivisions, and it is a complete mistake
to treat them all as a unity. Treat them as a plurality, offer to
hand over the property or the power or the persons of one
section to another, and you will have allies in plenty and very
few enemies. As long as your state maintains the discipline we
have laid down, it will remain supreme, I don't mean in common
estimation, but in real truth, even though it has only a thousand
defenders. You won't easily find a single state so great anywhere
b among the Greeks or barbarians, though you'll find many,
many times its size, that are thought much greater. Or do you
disagree?'

'No, certainly not.'

'I suggest, therefore,' I said, 'that our Rulers might use this as
the best standard for determining the size of our state and the
amount of territory it needs and beyond which it should not
expand.'

'What standard?'

'The state should, I think,' I replied, 'be allowed to grow so
long as growth is compatible with unity, but no further.'

c 'A very fair limit,' he said.

'So we can add to the instructions we shall give our Guardians
one to the effect that they are to avoid at all costs either making
the state too small or relying on apparent size, but keep it
adequate in scale and a unity.'

'A nice easy job for them!' he remarked ironically.

'And here's an easier one,' I continued in the same vein; we
d mentioned it before when we said that if any child of a Guardian
is a poor specimen, it must be degraded to the other classes,
while any child in the other classes who is worth it must be
promoted to the rank of Guardian. By this it was implied that
all the other citizens ought individually to devote their full
energy to the one particular job for which they are naturally
suited. In that way the integrity and unity both of the individual
and of the state will be preserved'.[14]

'Yes, a still easier job!' he replied.

'But seriously, Adeimantus,' I said, 'we aren't asking a great deal of them, as might be supposed; it will all be quite easy, provided they take care of the really "big thing", as the proverb has it, though "sufficient condition" would be a better expression.'   e

'And what is that?'

'The system of education and upbringing. If they are well educated, and become reasonable men, they can easily see to all we have asked them to, and indeed a good many things we have for the moment omitted, such as the position of women, marriage, and the production of children, all of which ought so far as possible to be dealt with on the proverbial basis of "all things in common between friends".'[15]   424 a

'Yes, they can deal with all these problems.'

'And once we have given our system[16] a good start,' I pointed out, 'the process of improvement[17] will be cumulative. By maintaining a sound system of education and upbringing you produce citizens of good character; and citizens of sound character, with the advantage of a good education, produce in turn children better than themselves and better able to produce still better children in their turn, as can be seen with animals.'   b

'That is likely enough.'

'In a word therefore, those in charge of our state must stick to the system of education and see that no deterioration creeps in; they must maintain it as a first priority and avoid at all costs any innovation in the established physical or academic curriculum. When they hear someone saying that men pay most attention

to the latest song on the singer's lips,[18]

they must be afraid that people will think that the poet means not new songs, but a new *kind* of song, and that that is what he is recommending. But such innovation should not be recommended, nor should the poet be so understood. You should hesitate to change the style of your literature, because you risk everything if you do; the music and literature[19] of a country cannot be altered without major political and social changes – we have Damon's word for it and I believe him.'   c

'And you can set me down as a believer too,' said Adeimantus.

d   'And so it is here, in education, that our Guardians must build their main defences.'[20]

'It is in education that disorder[21] can most easily creep in unobserved,' he replied.

'Yes,' I agreed, 'because people treat it as child's-play,[22] and think no harm can come of it.'

'It only does harm,' he said, 'because it gradually makes itself at home and quietly undermines morals and manners; from them it issues with greater force and invades business dealings

e   generally, and then, Socrates, spreads into the laws and constitution with complete lack of restraint, until it has upset the whole of private and public life.'

'Is it really as bad as that?' I said.

'Yes, I think it is.'

'Then doesn't it follow, as we said to begin with, that the amusements in which our children take part must be better regulated; because once they and the children become disorderly, it becomes impossible to produce serious citizens with a respect for order?'

425 a   'Yes, it follows.'

'But if children play on the right lines from the beginning and learn orderly habits from their education, these produce quite the opposite results, following and fostering their growth and correcting any previous flaws there may have been in the society.'

'True enough.'

'And people so brought up discover rules which seem quite trivial, but which their predecessors had entirely neglected.'

b   'What sort of rules?'

'For example, that the young should observe a proper silence in the presence of their elders, give up their seats to them and stand, and look after their parents; besides the whole business of one's dress and bearing, keeping one's hair and clothes and shoes tidy, and so on. Do you agree?'

'Yes.'

'But I think it would be silly to legislate for such things. Written regulations won't either produce them or maintain them.'

'No, they won't.'

'No, Adeimantus,' I said; 'for it's the direction given by education that is likely to determine all that follows – like calls to like, doesn't it?'[23] *c*

'Yes, of course.'

'And we should expect the final consequence to be a grand result that is good or the opposite.'

'Inevitably,' he agreed.

'And that,' I concluded, 'is why I should not try to legislate for such minor matters.'

'And you are quite right,' he said.

'Then what about business transactions? For example, contracts made in the market and contracts for manufacture, questions of slander and assault, the lodging of legal actions and *d* empanelling of juries, exaction and payment of market or harbour dues, and the general business of regulating business and police and harbour-charges and other similar affairs. Are we to venture on legislation in these fields?'

'Good men need no orders,' he said. 'They will find out easily *e* enough what legislation is in general necessary.'

'They will,' I agreed, 'if god enables them to preserve the laws we have already described.'

'Otherwise,' he said, 'they will spend their whole time making and correcting detailed regulations of the sort you've described, always expecting to achieve perfection.'[24]

'You mean,' said I, 'that they will lead lives like invalids who lack the restraint to give up a vicious way of life.'

'Exactly.'

'And a very attractive life they lead! For all their cures and *426 a* medicines have no effect – except to make their ailments worse and more complicated – yet they live in hope that every new medicine they are recommended will restore them to health.'

'Exactly,' he said; 'that's just what happens to that sort of invalid.'

'Then,' I replied, 'is not another attractive trait their way of detesting anyone who tells them the truth – that until they put an end to their eating and drinking and womanizing and *b* idleness, they will get no good out of drugs or cautery or operations, or out of spells or charms or anything else of the kind?'[25]

'Not so very amusing,' he said; 'there's nothing attractive in resenting good advice.'

'It looks as if you don't approve of this sort of people.'

'I certainly don't.'

'And you won't approve if a whole city follows the course we have described, I suppose. For I think you will agree that this is what cities are doing which mismanage their affairs but forbid
c on pain of death any alteration in the established constitution; they will honour as a great and profoundly wise man anyone who leaves them to their mismanagement, but flatters them agreeably and gives them pleasure by running their errands, or is clever at anticipating and fulfilling their wishes.'

. 'I agree that that's what they're doing,' he said, 'and I don't approve in the least.'

d 'And what about those who are willing and eager to apply the flattery? Aren't you surprised at their boldness and irresponsibility?'

'Yes, except when they are deceived by popular applause into thinking that they really are statesmen.'

'Oh come,' I said, 'won't you forgive them? Surely a man who doesn't know how to use a foot-rule can hardly avoid thinking
e himself a six-footer if lots of people like himself tell him he is?'

'Hardly.'

'Then don't be hard on them. They are really very amusing. They legislate for all the affairs we described, and then improve on their own legislation, under the impression that they can put an end to breaches of contract and all the other things I was talking about, and not knowing that the operation's about as hopeful as cutting off a Hydra's head.'

427 a 'Yet that's all they're doing,' he said.

'I shouldn't have thought, therefore,' I concluded, 'that a real legislator ought to bother about making laws and institutions of this sort either in a bad state or a good one: in one because they are no use and nothing comes of them, in the other because they are partly obvious and partly the automatic result of earlier training.'

'Then what have we left to do in the way of legislation?' he   *b*
asked. I replied that there was nothing indeed for us to do
ourselves. 'But,' I said, 'there remain for Apollo and the Delphic
oracle laws of the highest importance and value to make.'

'What about?' he asked.

'The founding of temples and the institution of sacrifices, and
other services to the gods and spirits and heroes, besides the
arrangements for the burial of the dead and the rites we must
pay to the powers of the other world to secure their goodwill.
We know nothing about all these things ourselves, and when
we found our state we won't entrust them, if we have any sense,   *c*
to anyone but their traditional interpreter. And it is Apollo
who by tradition is the interpreter of such matters to all men,
delivering his interpretation from his seat at the earth's centre.'

'You are right; we must act accordingly.'

PART V
JUSTICE IN STATE
AND INDIVIDUAL

1. Justice in the State

The State which we have founded must possess the four 'cardinal virtues' of wisdom, courage, discipline, and justice. (Plato does not call them 'virtues', and the translation therefore uses the more neutral term 'qualities'.) It will have wisdom because of the knowledge possessed by the Rulers, courage because of the courage of the Auxiliaries, and self-discipline because of the harmony between all three Classes and their common agreement 'about who ought to rule'. Finally, justice is the principle which has in fact been followed throughout, the principle of one man one job, of 'minding one's own business', in the sense of doing the job for which one is naturally fitted and not interfering with other people.

[427] d 'Well, we seem to have got your city founded for you, Adeimantus,' I said. 'Now you must look at it and get your brother and Polemarchus and the rest of them to see if they can help you throw enough light on it for us to see where justice and injustice are to be found, how they differ from each other, and which of them anyone who is to be happy needs, irrespective of whether gods or men think he has it or not.'

'Nonsense, Socrates,' said Glaucon. 'You promised to deal with the problem yourself, because you said it would be wicked
e for you not to give justice all the support of which you were capable.[1]

'That's true,' I said; 'I remember. I must do as I said, but you must all help.'

'Yes, we will,' he said.

'I think we shall probably find what we want as follows. If we have founded it properly, our state is presumably perfect.'

'It must be.'

'Then it will obviously have the qualities of wisdom, courage, self-discipline, and justice.'[2]

'Obviously.'

'Then if we can identify some of these qualities in it, the ones that are left will be the ones we are still looking for.'

'Yes.'

428 a

'So suppose us to be looking first for one of any four things. If we find it, well and good. But if we find the other three before it, by so doing we have in effect identified the object of our search, which must obviously be the one left over.'

'That's true.'

'Should we not therefore follow this method in the present case, where again there are four things at issue?'

'Obviously.'

'The first of the four that I can see clearly is wisdom, and there is one odd feature about it.'

b

'What?' he asked.

'The state we have described seems to me to be genuinely wise. For its judgement is good, isn't it?'

'Yes.'

'And the quality of good judgement is clearly a form of knowledge, as it is because of knowledge and not because of ignorance that we judge well.'

'Clearly.'

'But there are many different kinds of knowledge in our city.'

'Of course there are.'

'And do we say it has wisdom and judgement because of the knowledge of its carpenters?'

'Certainly not – that merely makes it good at carpentry.'

c

'So it's not called wise because of its knowledge of woodwork and the excellence of its designs?'

'No.'

'The same is presumably true of bronze and other materials.'

'The same is true,' he said.

'And I expect you would agree that knowledge of farming merely makes it good at agriculture.'

'Yes.'

'Well then,' I said, 'is there any form of knowledge to be found among any of the citizens in the state we've just founded which is exercised not on behalf of any particular interest but on behalf of the city as a whole, in such a way as to benefit the *d*   state both in its internal and external relations?'

'There is.'

'What is it, and where shall we find it?' I asked.

'It is the Guardians' knowledge,' he answered, 'and is to be found with those we called Guardians in the full sense.'

'And how do you describe the state because of it?'

'I say it has good judgement and wisdom.'

'And do you think that there will be more metal-workers in *e*   our state or Guardians in this sense?'

'Many more metal-workers,' he said.

'Won't the Guardians, in fact, be far fewer in number than any other group with special knowledge and name?'

'Yes.'

'So the state founded on natural principles is wise as a whole in virtue of the knowledge inherent in its smallest constituent part or class, which exercises authority over the rest. And it appears further that the naturally smallest class is the one which *429 a*   is endowed with that form of knowledge which alone of all others deserves the title of wisdom.'

'That is all perfectly true,' he agreed.

'Well, then, we have somehow or other managed to find this one of our four qualities and its place in our society.'

'And as far as I'm concerned I'm quite satisfied with our findings,' he said.

'And it's not very difficult,' I went on, 'to see courage and the place of courage, which makes us call our state brave.'

'Tell me how.'

b   'We shall say it's brave or cowardly with sole reference to the part which defends it and campaigns for it.'

'That is all that we need refer to.'

'Because I don't think that members of other classes have the power, by being cowardly or brave, to make the state one or the other.'

'No, they haven't.'

'Our city is therefore brave too in virtue of a part of itself. That part retains in all circumstances the power to judge, on the basis laid down by our lawgiver in its education, what and what sort of things are to be feared. For that, I take it, is what you mean by courage.' *c*

'I didn't quite understand what you said,' he answered; 'say it again.'

'I say,' I replied, 'that courage is a sort of safe-keeping.'

'What sort?'

'The sort that will *safely keep* the opinion inculcated by the established education about what things and what kind of things are to be feared. And by retaining it in *all circumstances* I meant retaining it safely, without losing it in pleasure or pain, desire *d* or fear. If you like, I'll give you an analogy.'

'Yes, do.'

'Well, take dyeing,' I said. 'You know that, when they want to dye wool purple, they are very particular about the natural colour of the material, which must be white; they then subject it to an elaborate process in order to prepare it to take the dye before they actually dip it. And the colour of anything dyed by this process remains fast, and the dye won't come out if you wash the material, whether you use soap or not; but if they start *e* with wool of any other colour or don't give it this treatment – well, you know what happens to it.'

'Yes – the colour washes out and it looks silly,' he said.

'Assume, then,' I said, 'that this was the sort of result we were doing our best to achieve in choosing our soldier-class, and in educating them physically and mentally. Our whole object was 430*a* to steep them in the spirit of our laws like a dye, so that nature and nurture might combine to fix in them indelibly their convictions about what is dangerous, and about all other topics, and prevent them being washed out by those most powerful detergents, pleasure, so much more effective than soap and soda, and pain and fear and desire, the most effective of all. This kind *b* of ability to retain safely in all circumstances a judgement about what is to be feared, which is correct and in accord with law,[3] is what I propose to call courage, unless you have any alternative to suggest.'

'No,' he replied, 'I haven't. For I imagine that you would not regard mere uninstructed judgement, such as an animal or slave might have on these matters, as being in accordance with law, even if right, and that you would use some other name for it.'

c 'You are quite right,' I said.

'Then I accept your description of courage.'

'Accept it as a description of the ordinary citizen's courage, and you won't be far wrong,' I replied; 'we will go into it more fully later, if you like.[4] For the moment it's justice not courage we are looking for, and for this purpose I think the description's adequate.'

'That is fair enough.'

'Well, we are left with two qualities to look for in our state,' I *d* said, 'self-discipline and the real object of our whole inquiry, justice.'

'Yes, we are.'

'I wonder if we could find justice without having to bother further about self-discipline.'

'Personally,' he said, 'I don't know, and I shouldn't want to find it, if it meant we were to give up looking for self-discipline. What I should like you to do is to look for self-discipline first.'

e 'And it would be wrong to refuse you,' I said.

'Then carry on,' he said.

'I will,' I replied, 'At first sight, self-discipline looks more like some sort of harmony or concord than the other virtues did.'

'In what way?'

'Self-discipline,' I said, 'is surely a kind of order, a control of certain desires and appetites. So people use "being master of oneself" (whatever that means) and similar phrases as indications of it. Isn't that so?'

'Certainly.'

'But "master of oneself" is an absurd phrase. For if you're master *of* yourself you're presumably also subject *to* yourself,

and so *both* master *and* subject. For there is only one person in   431 *a*
question throughout.'

'Undoubtedly.'

'What the expression is intended to mean, I think, is that there
is a better and a worse element in the personality[5] of each
individual, and that when the naturally better element controls
the worse then the man is said to be "master of himself", as a
term of praise. But when (as a result of bad upbringing or
bad company) the smaller forces of one's better element are   *b*
overpowered by the numerical superiority of one's worse, then
one is adversely criticized and said not to be master of oneself
and to be in a state of indiscipline.'

'Which is quite reasonable.'

'Then look at our newly founded state,' I said, 'and you will
find the first of these descriptions applies to it. For you will
admit that it is right to call it master of itself, if we speak of
self-discipline and self-mastery where the better part rules the
worse.'

'Yes, I see; that's quite true.'

'And, what is more, the greatest number and variety of desires
and pleasures and pains is generally to be found in children   *c*
and women and slaves, and in the less respectable majority of
so-called free men.'

'Certainly.'

'While the simple and moderate desires, guided by reason and
right judgement and reflection, are to be found in a minority
who have the best natural gifts and best education.'

'True.'

'This feature too you can see in our state, where the desires
of the less respectable majority are controlled by the desires and   *d*
the wisdom of the superior minority.'

'Yes, I can see that.'

'And so if any city is to be said to be master of its pleasures
and desires, and of itself, ours must be.'

'That is certainly true.'

'Then on all these counts we can surely say it is self-
disciplined.'

'We can indeed,' he said.

e   'And of our state, if of any, it will be true that government and subjects will agree about who ought to rule. Or don't you think so?'

'I'm quite sure of it,' he said.

'In these circumstances, of which class do you think discipline is characteristic, rulers or subjects?'

'Of both, I suppose,' he replied.

'So you can see how right we were to guess just now that self-discipline was like a kind of concord.'

'Why?'

'Because, unlike courage and wisdom, which made our state
432 a brave and wise by being present in a particular part of it, self-discipline stretches across the whole scale. It produces a harmony between its strongest and weakest and middle elements, whether you measure by the standard of intelligence, or of strength, or of numbers or money or the like. And so we are quite justified in regarding self-discipline as this unanimity in which there is a natural concordance between higher and lower about which of them is to rule in state and individual.'

'I entirely agree.'

b   'Good,' said I; 'it looks as if we had spotted three of the qualities we are looking for in our state. What about the fourth of them, to which it will owe another form of excellence? It must obviously be justice.'

'Obviously.'

'Then we must stand like hunters round a covert and make sure that justice does not escape us and disappear from view. It
c must be somewhere about. Try and see if you can catch sight of it before I can, and tell me where it is.'

'I wish I could,' he said. 'All you can reasonably expect of me is to follow your lead and see things when you point them out.'

'Then follow me and hope for the best.'

'I will,' he said; 'lead on.'

'It looks to me,' I said, 'as if we were in a pretty impassable and obscure spot; it's certainly dark and difficult to find a way through. But we must push on all the same.'

d   'Yes, we must,' he agreed.

I cast about a bit and then cried, 'Tally ho, Glaucon! I think we are on the track, and our quarry won't altogether escape us.'

'That's good news.'

'We really are being a bit slow.'

'In what way?'

'Our quarry is lurking right under our feet all the time, and we haven't seen it but have been making perfect fools of ourselves. We are like people searching for something they have in their hands all the time; we're looking away into the distance   *e* instead of at the thing we want, which is probably why we haven't found it.'

'How do you mean?'

'I mean that it seems to me that we have failed to understand that we have in a sort of way been talking about it all through our discussion.'

'You are a long time leading up to what you've got to say; I'm getting impatient.'

'Well then, listen, and see if you think I'm talking sense. I   433 *a* believe justice is the requirement we laid down at the beginning as of universal application when we founded our state, or else some particular form of it. We laid down, if you remember, and have often repeated, that in our state one man was to do one job, the job he was naturally most suited for.'

'Yes, we did.'

'And further, we have often heard it said and often said ourselves that justice consists in minding your own business and   *b* not interfering with other people.'[6]

'Yes.'

'So perhaps justice is, in a certain sense, just this minding one's own business. Do you know my grounds for so thinking?'

'No; what are they?'

'Because I think that the quality left over, now that we have discussed discipline, courage and wisdom, must be what makes it possible for them to come into being in our state and preserves them by its continued presence[7] when they have done so. And we agreed that it would be justice that was left over if we found   *c* the other three.'

'It must be.'

'Now, if we were asked to judge which of these qualities by its presence contributed most to the goodness of our state, we should find it a difficult decision to make. Is it the agreement between rulers and subjects? Is it the retention by our soldiers of a law-abiding judgement about what is and is not to be feared? Is it the wisdom and watchfulness of our Guardians? Or is the greatest contribution to its excellence made by the quality which makes each individual – child or woman, slave, *d* free man or artisan, ruler or subject – get on with his own job and not interfere with other people?'

'A difficult decision, I agree.'

'At any rate, wisdom, discipline, courage, and the ability to mind one's own business are all rivals in this respect. And we can regard justice as making a contribution to the excellence of *e* our city that rivals that of the rest.'

'Yes, certainly.'

'Look at it again this way. I assume that you will make it the duty of our rulers to administer justice?'

'Of course.'

'And won't they try to follow the principle that men should not take other people's belongings or be deprived of their own?'

'Yes, they're bound to.'

'Their reason presumably being that it is *just*.'

'Yes.'

'So we reach again by another route the conclusion that justice *434 a* is keeping what is properly one's own and doing one's own job.'

'That is true.'

'There's another point on which I should like your agreement. Suppose a builder and a shoemaker tried to exchange jobs, or to take on the tools and the prestige of each other's trade, or suppose alternatively the same man tried to do both jobs, would this and other exchanges of the kind do great harm to the state?'

'Not much.'

'But if someone who belongs by nature to the class of artisans *b* and businessmen is puffed up by wealth or popular support or physical strength or any similar quality, and tries to enter our military class; or if one of our military Auxiliaries tries to get into the class of administering Guardians for which he is unfit, and they exchange tools and prestige; or if a single individual tries to do all these jobs at the same time – well, I think you'll agree that this sort of mutual interchange and interference spells destruction to our state.'

'Certainly.'

'Interference by the three classes with each other's jobs, and interchange of jobs between them, therefore, does the greatest *c* harm to our state, and we are entirely justified in calling it the worst of evils.'

'Absolutely justified.'

'But will you not agree that the worst of evils for one's own community is injustice?'

'Of course.'

'So that is what injustice is. And conversely, when each of our three classes (businessmen, Auxiliaries, and Guardians) does its own job and minds its own business, that, by contrast, is justice and makes our state just.'

'I entirely agree with what you say,' he said. *d*

'Don't let's be too emphatic about it yet,' I replied. 'If we find that the same pattern applies to the individual and is agreed to yield justice in him, we can finally accept it – there will be nothing to prevent us; if not, we shall have to think again. For the moment let us finish our investigation.'

2. The Elements in Mental Conflict

Plato starts by reasserting the parallel between state (society) and individual; 'since the qualities of a community are those of the component individuals, we may expect to find three corresponding elements in the individual soul. All three will be present in every soul; but the structure of society is based on the fact that they are developed to different degrees in different types of character' (Cornford, p. 126). After a warning that in what follows we must not expect too much philosophic precision, Plato proceeds to examine the conflict of motives in the individual, and concludes that we cannot, without contradiction, assume the existence of less than three types of motive or impulse in the mind. First there is reason, the faculty that calculates and decides: second there is desire or appetite, in the sense of bare physical and instinctive craving. There is also a third type of motive, covering, as noted above (opening note to Part II, section 3), such characteristics as pugnacity, enterprise, ambition, indignation, which are often found in conflict with unthinking impulse.

This is often referred to as Plato's doctrine of 'the three parts of the soul'. Two main questions arise in understanding it: (1) To what extent and in what sense does Plato think of separate 'parts' of the soul or mind? In the present passage the words he uses most commonly (eidos, genos) mean 'kinds', 'types', 'forms', though he does on occasion use the Greek word for part (meros); the words ('element', 'constituent') used in the translation are intended to be indeterminate. Elsewhere Plato sometimes speaks as if the soul or mind had three distinct parts, as in the Phaedrus and Timaeus, sometimes as if there were a single stream of mental energy manifesting itself in different activities, as in the Symposium. We perhaps do well, first, to remember that he has warned us that he is not speaking with scientific precision, but rather on the level of ordinary conversation; and, second, to bear in mind that he is concerned with morals and not with psychology, with a general classification of the main motives or impulses to action, rather than a scientific analysis of the mind. He is, in fact, probably always conscious that in speaking of 'parts' ('elements' or what not) of the soul he is using a metaphor. (2) What exactly are the three 'elements' that Plato describes? There is little difficulty with two of them. By 'appetite' Plato means the purely instinctive desires in their simplest form; it is easy enough, on a common-sense level, to recognize them. 'Reason' includes not only the ability to understand and to think before we act, the faculty of calculation and foresight, but also the ability to make up one's mind, the faculty of decision. The third element at first appears more miscellaneous, including, as we have seen, such qualities as indignation, courage, determination, spirit, and so on. Two illustrations may help us to understand it. First the distinction, still commonly made, between 'heart' and 'head'. When we make that distinction *we do not include under 'heart' the mere animal instincts; we perhaps include more of the 'feelings' than Plato, but our meaning is not far from his second 'part of the soul'. (In the* Timaeus *reason is located in the head, 'spirit' in the breast, i.e. heart, and appetite in the belly.) Second, when Butler analysed the motives of moral action he found them threefold. Conscience, a rational faculty capable of judgement and having authority; particular passions, like hunger and thirst; and 'self-love', or, as we might call it today, the 'self-regarding instinct', or perhaps the instinct of self-preservation and self-assertion.[8] Each of these two analyses recognizes a rational, controlling, authoritative part of the mind; each recognizes animal instinct; but each also recognizes a third element, one which is not easy to define, but which is perhaps most comprehensively described as self-regard, and which ranges from self-assertion, through self-respect, to our relations with others (Butler coupled 'self-love' and 'benevolence') and our concern for our reputation and good name.*

Plato uses two words, thumos *and* thumoeides, *for this element in the mind. Neither is easy to translate. I have used 'anger', 'indignation', 'spirit' as seemed to suit the context best.*

'We thought it would be easier to see justice in the individual if we looked for it first in some larger field which also contained it. We thought this larger field was the state, and so we set about founding an ideal state, being sure we should find justice in it because it was good. Let us therefore transfer our findings to the individual, and if they fit him, well and good; on the other hand, if we find justice in the individual is something different, we will return to the state and test our new definition. So by the friction of comparison we may strike a spark which will illuminate justice for us, and once we see it clearly we can fix it firmly in our own minds.'

'That is the right method; let us follow it,' he said.

'Then when we apply the same term to two things, one large and the other small, will they not be similar in respect of that to which the common term is applied?'

'Yes.'

b   'So there will be no difference between a just man and a just city, so far as the element of justice goes.'

'None.'

'But we agreed that a state was just when its three natural constituents were each doing their job, and that it was self-disciplined and brave and wise in virtue of certain other states and dispositions of those constituents.'

'That is so,' he said.

'Well, then, my dear Glaucon,' I continued, 'we shall expect to find that the individual has the same three elements in his personality[9] and to be justified in using the same language of

c   him because he is affected by the same conditions.'

'That must follow.'

'Another nice little inquiry we've tumbled into!' I exclaimed. 'Has the personality these three constituents or not?'

'I shouldn't call it a little inquiry,' he said; 'but it's probably true enough, Socrates, that, as the saying goes, anything that's worth while is difficult.'

'So it seems. And I must tell you that in my opinion we shall

d   never find an exact answer by the method of argument we are using in our present discussion – to get one we should have to go much further afield[10] but we can probably find one that will be satisfactory by the standards we have so far used in our inquiry.'

'That's good enough,' he replied; 'at any rate, it would suit me for the present.'

'And it will be quite enough for me.'

'Then press on with the investigation.'

e   'Well, we are bound to admit that the elements and traits that belong to a state must also exist in the individuals that compose it. There is nowhere else for them to come from. It would be absurd to suppose that the vigour and energy for which northern people like the Thracians and Scythians have a reputation aren't due to their individual citizens; and similarly with intelligence,

436 *a* which can be said to be the main attribute of our own part of the world, or with the commercial instinct which one connects particularly with the Phoenicians and Egyptians.'

'That's perfectly true.'

'Here, then, we have a fact which is not particularly difficult to recognize.'

'Not at all difficult.'

'What is difficult is to see whether we perform all these functions with the same part of us, or each with a different part. Do we learn with one part of us, feel angry with another, and desire the pleasures of eating and sex and the like with another? *b* Or do we employ our mind[11] as a whole when our energies are employed in any of these ways? These are questions it's difficult to answer satisfactorily.'

'I agree,' he said.

'Then let us try to decide whether the faculties concerned are the same or different.'

'How are we to do it?'

'Clearly one and the same thing cannot act or be affected in opposite ways at the same time in the same part of it and in relation to the same object; so if we find these contradictions, we shall know we are dealing with more than one faculty.' *c*

'Granted.'

'Then look here –'

'Yes – go on.'

'Can a thing be at rest and in motion at the same time and in the same part of itself?'

'No.'

'Let us be even more precise, to avoid ambiguities later on. If we were told that a man, who was standing still but moving his hands and his head, was simultaneously both at rest and in motion, we should not accept that as a proper statement of the case, but say that part of him was standing still and part of him in motion. Isn't that so?' *d*

'Yes.'

'We might have a still more ingenious case put to us. It might be argued as a further refinement that a top, spinning round a fixed axis, is both at rest and in motion as a whole, as indeed is any body in circular motion on the same spot. We should not agree, but argue that it is not the same *parts* of such bodies that are at rest and in motion; they have both an axis and a *e* circumference, and their axis, as it has no inclination in any direction, is at rest, but their circumference is in motion. And further, if their axis inclines in any direction, right or left, forward or back, while they are still spinning, then they are not at rest at all.'

'That is quite correct,' he agreed.

'We shan't, then, be shaken by objections of this kind into believing that the same thing can ever act or be affected in opposite ways, or bear opposite predicates, at the same time in 437 *a* the same part of itself and in relation to the same thing.'

'*I* certainly shan't.'

'Anyway,' I said, 'we don't want to have to examine all such objections and prove at length they aren't true, so let us proceed on the assumption we are right, it being understood that if we change our minds all the consequences of our assumption will fall to the ground.'

b   'Yes, that's the thing to do.'

'Then would you not class assent and dissent, impulse and aversion to something, attraction and repulsion and the like as *opposite* actions or states – no matter which?'

'Yes,' he said, 'I should.'

'And what about hunger and thirst and the desires generally,' I went on, 'or, again, willing and wishing, don't they all fall under one of the two classes of opposites just mentioned? When *c* a man's mind desires anything, don't you either say that he has an *impulse* to what he desires or speak of his trying to *attract* anything he wishes to get? And again, if he wants to get possession of anything, is it not as a result of *assent* given by his mind to an inward question prompted by his longing to get it?'

'I agree.'

'And what about disinclination, unwillingness and dislike? Shouldn't we put them in the opposite class, with repulsion and rejection?'

d   'Of course.'

'That being so, we can say that the desires form a class, of which those we call thirst and hunger are the clearest examples.'

'Yes.'

'And thirst is the desire for drink, hunger for food?'

'Yes.'

'Then is thirst, in so far as it is thirst, the desire in the mind for anything more than simply drink? Is it thirst for hot drink or cold, for a lot to drink or a little, or, in short, for any particular kind of drink at all? Isn't it rather that if heat is added to thirst it brings with it the desire for cold, while cold brings the desire for heat; and if the thirst is great because accompanied by magnitude you want a lot to drink, if it's small you only want a little?[12] Simple thirst, on the other hand, is the desire for its natural object, drink, without qualification: and the same is true of hunger and food.'

'In that case,' he said, 'each desire is directed simply towards its own natural object, and any qualification is an addition.'

'And we must beware,' I went on, 'of letting ourselves be taken off our guard and upset by the objection that no one simply desires drink, but drink that is good for him, and similarly food that is good for him. For – so runs the argument – all men desire what is good for them, and therefore, if thirst is a desire, it will be the desire for drink (or what not) that is good for one; and the same is true of the other desires.'[13]

'It's an argument which perhaps has some force,' he said.

'Yes,' I answered, 'but when two terms are correlative it seems that either both must be qualified or both unqualified.'

'I don't understand.'

'Well, you can understand that what is "greater" must always be greater than *something*.'

'Of course.'

'And that *something* is smaller.'

'Yes.'

'And what is *much* greater is *much* greater than something *much* smaller. Agreed?'

'Yes.'

'And the same is true of greater and smaller *in the past* or *in the future*.'

'Of course. What then?'

'And is not the same also true of more and less, double and half and the like, of heavier and lighter, quicker and slower, of hot and cold, and indeed of all similar correlative terms?'

'Yes, it is.'

'But what about the various branches of knowledge? Does not the same relationship hold? Knowledge unqualified is knowledge simply of something learned (or whatever we should call the object of knowledge); knowledge of a particular kind is knowledge of a particular kind of object. For example, when
d men discovered how to make houses, this was a form of knowledge differing from others, and was called building.'   ·

'Well?'

'And wasn't it so called because it is knowledge of a certain kind different from all other kinds of knowledge?'

'Yes.'

'And isn't it knowledge of a certain kind because it has a certain kind of object? And is not the same true of all forms of skill[14] and knowledge?'

'Yes, that is so.'

'I hope you can see now,' I said, 'that that is what I meant when I said that among correlative terms if the first is unqualified so is the second, if the first is qualified so again is the second. And I don't mean that you can transfer the epithet simply from
e one term to the other, saying for example that the knowledge of health and disease is healthy and diseased, or that the knowledge of good and evil is itself good and evil. What I mean is that when the object of knowledge is of a particular kind, for example health or disease, then the knowledge itself must also be of a particular kind, and is in consequence no longer called knowledge simply, but medical knowledge, by addition of a qualifying epithet.'

'I understand; and I think you are right.'

439 *a*   'To return to thirst then,' I said, 'is it not something which is what it is in relation to something else? It is, of course, thirst for –'

' – for drink; I agree,' he said.

'And for a particular *kind* of drink there will be a particular kind of thirst. But thirst in itself is the desire not for a lot or a little to drink, or for good drink or bad, or, in a word, for any *kind* of drink at all, but for drink pure and simple.'

'Exactly.'

'The mind of the thirsty man, therefore, in so far as he is

thirsty, simply wants to drink, and it is to that end that its *b*
energies are directed.'

'Clearly.'

'If therefore there is something in it that resists its thirst, it
must be something in it other than the thirsty impulse which is
dragging it like a wild animal to drink. For we have agreed that
the same thing cannot act in opposite ways with the same part
of itself towards the same object.'

'That is impossible.'

'For instance, it is not fair to say that an archer's hands are
pulling and pushing the bow at the same time, but that one hand
is pushing it, the other pulling.'

'Certainly.'   *c*

'Now, can we say that men are sometimes unwilling to drink
even though they are thirsty?'

'Oh yes; that is often true of many people,' he said.

'Then how are we to describe such cases?' I asked. 'Must we
not say that there is one element in their minds which bids them
drink, and a second which prevents them and masters the first?'

'So it seems.'

'And isn't the element of prevention, when present, due to
our reason, while the urges and impulses are due to our feelings *d*
and unhealthy cravings?'

'It looks like it.'

'Then we shan't be without justification if we recognize these
two elements as distinct. We can call the reflective element in
the mind the reason, and the element with which it feels hunger
and thirst, and the agitations of sex and other desires, the
element of irrational appetite – an element closely connected
with satisfaction and pleasure.'

'Yes, that is a reasonable view to take,' he agreed.   *e*

'Well, we've defined two elements in the mind, then,' I said.
'Now, is indignation,[15] and the part in which we feel it, a third
element, or is it of the same nature as one of the two we have
defined?'

'Maybe it's the same as appetite,' he said.

'I rely on a story I once heard,' I answered. 'It's about Leon-
tion, son of Aglaion, who was on his way up from the Piraeus,

under the outer side of the north wall, when he noticed some corpses lying on the ground with the executioner standing by them. He wanted to go and look at them, and yet at the same time held himself back in disgust. For a time he struggled with himself and covered his eyes, but at last his desire got the better of him and he ran up to the corpses, opening his eyes wide and saying to them, "There you are, curse you – a lovely sight! Have a real good look!"[16]

'I've heard the story too.'

'And it shows,' I said, 'that anger is different from desire and sometimes opposes it.'

'Yes, it does.'

'And don't we often see other instances of a man whose desires are trying to force him to do something his reason disapproves of, cursing himself and getting indignant at their violence? It's like a struggle between political factions, with indignation fighting on the side of reason. But I don't suppose you've ever observed indignation, either in yourself or in anyone else, taking the side of the desires and resisting the decision of reason.'

'No, certainly not.'

'And what about a man who feels he's in the wrong? The more honest he is, the less angry he feels at hunger or cold or any similar suffering which he thinks is inflicted on him with justification. As I say, his indignation simply refuses to be roused.'

'Quite true.'

'And what if he thinks he's being wronged? Then his indignation boils over and fights obstinately for what he thinks right, persevering and winning through hunger and cold and all similar trials. It won't give up the struggle till death or victory, or till reason calls it back to heel and calms it, like a shepherd calls his dog.'

'That describes it exactly,' he agreed; 'and,' he went on, 'in our state we said the Auxiliaries were to be like watchdogs obeying the Rulers, who were the shepherds of the community.'

'I see you quite understand what I mean. But there's another point to notice.'

'What?'   e

'That we've changed our mind about this third element in the mind. We were wondering if it was something like appetite; now we have gone to the other extreme and are saying that, when there's a conflict in the mind, it's more likely to take up arms for reason.'

'That's quite true.'

'Then is it different from reason? Or is it a form of reason, so that there are not three, but only two elements in the mind, reason and appetite? The state was made up of three classes,   441 a businessmen, auxiliaries, and governors; is the mind like it in having spirit as a third element, which, unless corrupted by bad upbringing, is reason's natural auxiliary?'

'There must be a third element.'

'Yes there must,' I said, 'if spirit can be shown to be distinct from reason, as it is from appetite.'

'But that's not difficult to prove,' he answered. 'You can see it in children, who are full of spirit as soon as they're born; but some never seem to acquire any degree of reason and most of them only at a late stage.'   b

'That puts it very well,' I agreed; 'and you can see the same thing happening in animals. There is further evidence in the passage from Homer we quoted before,[17] where Odysseus "strikes himself on the chest and calls his heart to order". It is clear enough that Homer here makes one element rebuke another, distinguishing the power to reflect about good and evil from unreasoning passion.'[18]   c

'You are absolutely right.'

3. Justice in the Individual

Justice in the individual is now defined analogously to justice in the state. The individual is wise and brave in virtue of his reason and 'spirit' respectively: he is disciplined when 'spirit' and appetite are in proper subordination to reason. He is just in virtue of the harmony which exists when all three elements of the mind perform their proper function and so achieve

*their proper fulfilment; he is unjust when no such harmony
exists.*

'Well, it's been a rough passage, but we have pretty well
reached agreement that there are the same three elements in the
personality of the individual as there are in the state.'

'True.'

'Must it not follow, then, that the individual is wise in the
same way and with the same part of himself as the state?'

'That is so.'

d   'And that the individual is brave with the same part and in
the same way as the state, and that there is the same correspondence in all the other constituents of excellence?'

'That must follow.'

'And so, my dear Glaucon,' I went on, 'we shall also say that
the individual man is just in the same way that the state is just.'

'That must inevitably follow too.'

'And I suppose we have not forgotten that the state was
just when the three elements within it each minded their own
business.'

'No, I don't think we've forgotten that.'

'Then we must remember that each of us will be just and
e   perform his proper function only if each part of him is performing its proper function.'[19]

'Yes, we must certainly remember that.'

'So the reason ought to rule, having the wisdom and foresight
to act for the whole, and the spirit ought to obey and support
it.'

'Certainly.'

'And this concord between them is effected, as we said, by a
combination of intellectual and physical training, which tunes
442 a up the reason by a training in rational argument and higher
studies, and tones down and soothes the element of "spirit" by
harmony and rhythm.'

'Certainly.'

'When these two elements have been so brought up, and
trained and educated to their proper function, they must be put
in charge of appetite, which forms the greater part of each man's

make-up and is naturally insatiable. They must prevent it taking its fill of the so-called physical pleasures, for otherwise it will get too large and strong to mind its own business and will try *b* to subject and control the other elements, which it has no right to do, and so wreck the life of all of them.'

'True.'

'At the same time,' I went on, 'won't these two elements be the best defence that mind and body have against external enemies? One of them will do the thinking, the other will fight under the orders of its superior and provide the courage to carry its decisions into effect.'

'Yes, I agree.'

'And we call an individual brave because of this part of him, I think, when he has a spirit which holds fast to the orders of *c* reason about what he ought or ought not to fear, in spite of pleasure and pain?'

'That is quite right.'

'And we call him wise in virtue of that small part of him which is in control and issues the orders, knowing as it does what is best for each of the three elements and for the whole made up of them.'

'Yes, I agree.'

'Then don't we call him self-disciplined when all these three elements are in friendly and harmonious agreement, when reason and its subordinates are all agreed that reason should rule and there is no civil war among them?' *d*

'That is exactly what we mean by self-control or discipline in a city or in an individual.'

'And a man will be just by following the principle we have stated so often.'

'That must be so.'

'Well, then,' I said, 'is our picture in any way indistinct? Does it look as if justice in the individual were different from what we found it to be in the state?'

'I can't see any difference,' he answered.

'If there are still any doubts in our minds,' I said, 'a few commonplace examples should finally convince us.' *e*

'What sort of examples?'

'Well, suppose for instance we were asked whether our state or a man of corresponding nature and training would embezzle money deposited with him. Do you think we should reckon him

443 a more likely to do it than other people?'

'He would be the last person to do such a thing.'

'And wouldn't it be out of the question for him to commit sacrilege or theft, or to betray his friends or his country?'

'Out of the question.'

'And he would never break a solemn promise or any other agreement.'

'Certainly not.'

'And he would be the last man to commit adultery, dishonour his parents, or be irreligious.'

'The last man,' he agreed.

b   'And is not the reason for all this that each element within him is performing its proper function, whether it is giving or obeying orders?'

'Yes, that is the reason.'

'Are you now convinced, then, that justice is what produces men and states of this character?'

'Yes, I am quite convinced,' he said.

'So our dream has come true, and, as we guessed,[20] we have

c   been lucky enough, with god's help, to run across a basic pattern of justice at the very beginning of the foundation of our state.'

'Yes, we have.'

'In fact, my dear Glaucon, the provision that the man naturally fitted to be a shoemaker, or carpenter, or anything else, should stick to his own trade has turned out to be a kind of adumbration of justice – hence its usefulness.'

'So it seems.'

'Justice, therefore, we may say, is a principle of this kind; its real concern is not with external actions, but with a man's

d   inward self, his true concern and interest. The just man will not allow the three elements which make up his inward self to trespass on each other's functions or interfere with each other, but, by keeping all three in tune, like the notes of a scale (high, middle, and low, and any others there be), will in the truest sense set his house to rights, attain self-mastery and order, and live on good terms with himself. When he has bound these elements into a disciplined and harmonious whole, and so become fully one instead of many, he will be ready for action of any kind, whether it concerns his personal or financial welfare, whether it is political or private; and he will reckon and call any of these actions just and honourable if it contributes to and helps to maintain this disposition of mind, and will call the knowledge which controls such action wisdom. Similarly, he will call unjust any action destructive of this disposition, and the opinions which control such action ignorance.'

'That is all absolutely true, Socrates.'

'Good,' I said. 'So we shan't be very far wrong if we claim to have discovered what the just man and the just state are, and in what their justice consists.'

'No, we shan't.'

'Shall we make the claim, then?'

'Yes.'

'So much for that,' I said. 'And next, I suppose, we ought to consider injustice.'

'Obviously.'

'It must be some kind of civil war between these same three elements, when they interfere with each other and trespass on each other's functions, or when one of them rebels against the whole to get control when it has no business to do so, because its natural role is to be a slave to the rightfully controlling element. This sort of situation, when the elements of the mind are confused and displaced, is what constitutes injustice, indiscipline, cowardice, ignorance and, in short, wickedness of all kinds.'

'Yes, that's so.'

'And if we know what injustice and justice are, it's clear enough, isn't it, what acting unjustly and doing wrong are or, again, what acting justly is?'

'How do you mean?'

'Well,' I said, 'there is an exact analogy between these states of mind and bodily health and sickness.'

'How?'

'Healthy activities produce health, and unhealthy activities produce sickness.'

'True.'

'Well, then, don't just actions produce justice, and unjust
d actions injustice?'

'They must.'

'And health is produced by establishing a natural relation of control and subordination among the constituents of the body, disease by establishing an unnatural relation.'

'True.'

'So justice is produced by establishing in the mind a similar natural relation of control and subordination among its constituents, and injustice by establishing an unnatural one.'

'Certainly.'

'It seems, then, that excellence is a kind of mental health or
e beauty or fitness, and defect a kind of illness or deformity or weakness.'[21]

'That is so.'

'And each is in turn the result of one's practice, good or bad.'

'They must be.'

4. Conclusion

The definition of justice has now been given; but Socrates has been asked (367b–e above) not only to define it, but to show that it pays better in all circumstances than injustice. This, says Glaucon, is now as self-evident as that health is preferable to disease. But Socrates objects that it cannot be fully seen until our study of the good state and the good man, now complete, is supplemented by a study of the different forms of bad state and corresponding bad character. Of these there are four, and Socrates is about to describe them, when he is interrupted. He does not return to the description until Book VIII (Part IX of this translation).

'We are left, then, I suppose, with the question whether it pays to act justly and behave honourably and be just irrespective

of appearances, or to do wrong and be unjust provided you 445 *a*
escape punishment and consequent improvement.'

'I think we have already shown the question to be an absurd
one, Socrates,' he replied. 'Men don't reckon that life is worth
living when their physical health breaks down, even though they
have all the food and drink and wealth and power in the world.
So we can hardly reckon it worth living when the natural principle by which we live breaks down in confusion, and a man of
his own choice avoids the one thing that will rid him of wicked- *b*
ness and injustice, the acquisition of justice and excellence, now
that they have been clearly shown to be as we have described
them.'

'Yes, it is an absurd question,' I agreed. 'But I don't think we
ought to give up just when we've got to a point from which we
can get a really clear view of the facts.'

'The last thing in the world we want to do is to give up,' he
returned.

'Follow me, then,' I said, 'and you will see how many different
forms of wickedness I think there are – a thing which, inciden- *c*
tally, is well worth seeing.'

'Go on. I'm waiting your lead.'

'You know, we seem to me to have climbed in our argument
to a kind of peak, from which we can see that there is only one
form of goodness, but an infinite variety of wickedness, though
there are four varieties in particular that are worth our
attention.'

'Explain.'

'We shall probably find that there are as many types of character as there are types and forms of political constitution.'

'And how many is that?'   *d*

'Five of each,' I replied.

'And what are they?'

'The first type of political constitution is the one we have been
describing. It can be called by either of two names. If there is a
single outstanding man among the Rulers, it is called a Mon-
archy; if not, it is called an Aristocracy.'

'True.'

'This, then, I regard as one of my five forms. For, whether

control is in the hands of a single man or of a larger number,
e they won't make any change of importance in the constitution
of our State so long as they have been brought up and educated
as we have described.'

'They aren't likely to,' he said.

BK V   'This, then, is the kind of state and constitution and the kind
of man I call good and true. And that being so, I call all other
449 *a* forms of social organization and conditions of individual
character bad or defective. We can classify their faults under
four headings.'

'What are they?' he asked.

PART VI
WOMEN AND THE
FAMILY

*The next three books, V–VII (Parts VI–VIII in this translation)
are in form a digression; but in fact Plato is dealing with two
features of his State which he can hardly pass over without
further explanation. (1) He has, for the Rulers and Auxiliaries,
abolished the family and private property (opening note to Part
IV, section 2ff.); he now deals more fully with the reasons for
and consequences of this, under two main headings, the Status
of Women and the Abolition of the Family. (2) He has also
(412c–414d) sub-divided Guardians into Rulers and Auxiliaries
and the long sections on the Philosopher Ruler and Further Education of the Guardians describe further how this is to be done.*

1. The Status of Women

*Socrates is interrupted and asked to explain in greater detail his
references to the 'community of wives and children'. He starts
by considering the position of women in society. His argument
is in principle a very simple one. He asks whether difference of
sex is, in itself, a proper basis for differentiation of occupation
and social function, and answers that it is not. The only difference between men and women is one of physical function – one
begets, the other bears children. Apart from that, both can and
both should follow the same range of occupations and perform
the same functions (though men will, on the whole, perform
them better); they should receive the same education to enable
them to do so. In this way society will get the best value from
both.*

Though Plato's ideas would have seemed revolutionary to
the ordinary Greek, the status of women had been a topic of
discussion before he wrote, and ideas similar to those which
he puts forward were in the air, and had been parodied by
Aristophanes.

[449]   I was going on to describe these forms of wickedness in order,
and to show how they seemed to me to derive from each other,
b   when Polemarchus, who was sitting a little way from Adeimantus, stretched out a hand and took hold of his coat at the
shoulder. He pulled him towards him and, leaning forward,
whispered something in his ear, of which I only caught the
words 'What shall we do? Shall we let it go?'

'Certainly not,' replied Adeimantus aloud; and when I asked
what it was they weren't going to let go, he answered, 'You.'
c   'And why me?' I said.

'We think you are being lazy,' he answered, 'and trying to
avoid dealing with a most important section of the argument.
You think you are going to get away with a passing reference to
it, as if it was perfectly obvious that the principle "all things in
common between friends" should apply to women and
children.'[1]

'But wasn't I quite right?' I asked.

'Yes, but here, as so often, what is right needs explanation.
What sort of holding "in common" do you mean? There are
d   many possibilities; so let us be told the one you mean. We have
been waiting for you to give us some idea of how the Guardians
are to produce children, and bring them up when they are born,
and how this whole business of community of wives and children
is to work; for it seems to us that this is a matter in which it is
vital to society that the right arrangements should be made. You
were just going on to other forms of constitution before dealing
adequately with it, but, as you heard just now, we resolved that
450a   we would not let you do so till you had discussed it as fully as
everything else.'

'This resolution has my vote too,' added Glaucon.

'In fact, Socrates,' said Thrasymachus, 'you can take it we're
unanimous.'

'What trouble you're causing by holding me up like this,' I said. 'It's an enormous subject, and you're really starting again from the beginning just as I was congratulating myself on having finished with our state, and was feeling glad that no one had questioned the description I had given. You don't know what a *b* hornet's nest you're stirring up by bringing up the subject. I deliberately avoided it before, because I saw all the trouble it would cause.'

'But what do you think we are here for?' asked Thrasymachus; 'idle speculation² or serious discussion?'

'But a discussion must have some limit,' I said.

'My dear Socrates,' said Glaucon, 'anyone with any sense knows there's no limit short of a lifetime when one's discussing this sort of thing. Don't worry about us and don't give up, but answer our questions. Tell us how you think our Guardians are *c* to have wives and children in common, and how the children are to be looked after between their birth and the beginning of their education, which everyone agrees is a most difficult stage. Do explain to us how it's all to be managed.'

'I can assure you it won't be easy to explain,' I said. 'There's so much that is doubtful, far more than there is in anything we've so far discussed. It may indeed be doubted whether what I describe is possible at all and, granted it's possible, it may well be doubted if it's for the best. Hence my hesitation in tackling the subject; I'm afraid, my dear Glaucon, you will think I'm *d* merely day-dreaming.'

'You really needn't hesitate. We're a sympathetic audience, and not unduly unreceptive or sceptical,' he said. To which I replied, 'It's good of you to say so; I suppose you are trying to encourage me.'

'I am,' he said.

'Well, you're having just the opposite effect,' said I. 'If I was sure I knew what I was talking about, encouragement would be in place; when one's talking among sensible friends about issues which touch them nearly, and knows one is telling the truth, one can speak with certainty and confidence. But when one is doing what I am doing now, and trying to discuss things about *e* which one is far from certain, it's a frightening and tricky

business; not because I may make a fool of myself – it would be childish to worry about that – but because if I slip up I shall
451a drag my friends down with me in my fall, just where it's most important to be sure of the truth. I only hope Fate won't punish me for what I am going to say. For, I believe, it's better in fact to be guilty of manslaughter than of fraud about what is fair and good and just. It's a risk better run with enemies than friends, and so your encouragement is cold comfort.'

b   Glaucon laughed. 'My dear Socrates,' he said, 'if we are led into error by this discussion, we'll acquit you of manslaughter, absolve you of fraud, and discharge you without a stain on your character. So cheer up, and say on.'

'Well,' I said, 'the law says that a discharge from the courts leaves one's character clean, and so I suppose the same holds good here.'

'Then proceed on that assumption,' he said.

'Well, then,' I began, 'we must go back and pick the subject up again. We ought perhaps to have discussed it in its proper place,
c but maybe it's a good plan to let the women come on the stage now, after the men have played their part, especially in view of your challenge. We can, I think, only make satisfactory arrangements for the possession and treatment of women and children by men born and educated as we have described, if we stick to the course on which we started; our object, you remember, was to make them like watchdogs guarding a flock.'[3]
d   'Yes.'

'Let us, then, proceed to arrange for their birth and upbringing accordingly. We can then see if it suits our purpose.'

'How do you mean?'

'What I mean is this. Ought female watchdogs to perform the same guard-duties as male, and watch and hunt and so on with them? Or ought they to stay at home on the grounds that the bearing and rearing of their puppies incapacitates them from other duties, so that the whole burden of the care of the flocks falls on the males?'
e   'They should share all duties, though we should treat the females as the weaker, the males as the stronger.'

'And can you use any animal for the same purpose as another,' I asked, 'unless you bring it up and train it in the same way?'

'No.'

'So if we are going to use men and women for the same purposes, we must teach them the same things.'

'Yes.'

'We educated the men both physically and mentally.'

'Yes.'

452a

'We shall have to train the women also, then, in both kinds of skill, and train them for war as well, and treat them in the same way as the men.'

'It seems to follow from what you said,' he agreed.

'I dare say,' I rejoined, 'that their novelty would make many of our proposals seem ridiculous if they were put into practice.'

'There's no doubt about that,' he said.

'And won't the most ridiculous thing of all be to see the women taking exercise naked[4] with the men in the gymnasium? It won't only be the young women; there will be elderly women too, just as there are old men who go on with their exercises when they are wrinkled and ugly to look at.'

b

'Lord!' he said, 'that's going to be a funny sight by present standards.'

'Still,' I said, 'now we've launched out on the subject we must not be afraid of the clever jokes that are bound to be made about all the changes that follow in the physical training and education of women, and above all about them being trained to carry arms and ride.'

c

'You are quite right.'

'So having started off, we must go on to legislate for the real difficulties. We will ask the critics[5] to drop their usual practice and to be serious for once, and remind them that it was not so long ago that the Greeks thought – as most of the barbarians still think – that it was shocking and ridiculous for men to be seen naked. When the Cretans, and later the Spartans, first began to take exercise naked, wasn't there plenty of material for the wit of the comedians of the day?'

'There was indeed.'

d

'But when experience showed them that it was better to strip than wrap themselves up, what reason had proved best lost its absurdity to the eye. Which shows how idle it is to think anything ridiculous except what is wrong. Indeed, anyone who tries to raise a laugh at the sight of anything but what is foolish and

e wrong will never, when he is serious again, make goodness the object of his admiration.'

'That is certainly true,' he said.

'The first thing we have to agree on, then, is whether these proposals are feasible or not. For, whether it's asked in joke or

453 a in earnest, we must allow people to ask the question, Is the female of the human species naturally capable of taking part in all the occupations of the male, or in none, or in some only? And if in some, is military service one of them? That's the best way to begin, and the way in which we are most likely to reach a fair conclusion.'

'Yes, I agree.'

'Then shall we ask ourselves the question on behalf of our imaginary critic, so that his position does not go undefended?'

b 'Go ahead.'

'Let us then suppose him to say: "My dear Socrates and Glaucon, there's really no need for others to criticize you. You have yourselves, at the beginning of the process of founding your state, agreed on the principle that each man was naturally fitted for a particular job of his own."'

'Yes, we must certainly admit that.'

'"Well," he will continue, "isn't there a very great natural difference between men and women?" And when we admit that too, he will ask us whether we ought not to give them different roles to match these natural differences. When we say yes, he

c will ask, "Then aren't you making a mistake and contradicting yourselves, when you go on to say that men and women should follow the same occupations, in spite of the great natural difference between them?" What about that? Are you clever enough to answer him?'

'It's not easy to answer on the spur of the moment,' he replied. 'I can only turn to you and ask you to explain our case in reply, whatever it is.'

'Now that's just what I was afraid of, Glaucon,' I protested;
'I saw all this coming – that's why I was so unwilling to start   *d*
legislating about the possession of wives and bringing up
children.'

'It certainly doesn't look an easy job,' he admitted.

'It isn't,' I replied. 'But the fact is that you've got to swim
whether you're thrown into a swimming bath or into the middle
of the sea.'

'True enough.'

'So we must swim on and try to keep our heads above water
in this argument, in the hope of being rescued by Arion's dolphin[6] or some other miracle.'

'Yes, I suppose we must.'   *e*

'Well, let's see if we can find a way out. We admit that
different natures ought to have different kinds of occupation,
and that men and women have different natures; and yet we go
on to maintain that these admittedly different natures ought to
follow the same occupations. That is the charge we have to
meet, isn't it?'

'That is it.'

'You know, Glaucon, it's extraordinary how powerful the   454 *a*
influence of debating technique[7] can be.'

'In what way?'

'I think a lot of people fall under it quite unconsciously, and
fail to see the difference between scoring points in debate and
arguing seriously. They are unable to draw the distinctions in
kind needed for the discussion of a subject, and so get side-
tracked into purely verbal contradiction; they aren't really arguing, but only scoring points.'

'That does often happen,' he agreed. 'But does it apply to us
now?'

'It certainly does. At any rate, I'm afraid we're unconsciously   *b*
starting to score debating points.'

'How?'

'We are sticking obstinately to the verbal debating point that
different natures should not be given the same occupations; but
we haven't considered what kind of sameness or difference of
nature we mean, and what our intention was when we laid

down the principle that different natures should have different jobs, similar natures similar jobs.'

'No, we've not taken that into consideration.'

c   'Yet we might just as well, on this principle, ask ourselves whether bald men and long-haired men are of the same or opposite natures, and, having agreed that they are opposite, allow bald men to be cobblers and forbid long-haired men to be, or vice versa.'

'That would be absurd.'

'But the reason why it is absurd,' I pointed out, 'is simply that we never meant that natures are the same or different in an unqualified sense, but only with reference to the kind of same-
d   ness or difference which is relevant to various employments. For instance, we should regard a man and a woman with medical ability as having the same nature. Do you agree?'

'Yes.'

'But a doctor and a carpenter we should reckon as having different natures.'

'Yes, entirely.'

'Then if men or women as a sex[8] appear to be qualified for different skills or occupations,' I said, 'we shall assign these to each accordingly; but if the only difference apparent between
e   them is that the female bears and the male begets, we shall not admit that this is a difference relevant for our purpose, but shall still maintain that our male and female Guardians ought to follow the same occupations.'

'And rightly so,' he agreed.

'Then let us proceed to ask our opponent to tell us for what
455 a   professions or occupations in the structure of society men and women are differently suited by nature.'

'A fair question.'

'But he may well reply, as you did just now, that it's not easy to answer on the spur of the moment, though there would be no great difficulty if he were given time to think.'

'He may.'

'So shall we ask anyone who makes this objection to follow
b   us and see if we can show him convincingly that there is no social function[9] peculiar to woman?'

'Go ahead.'

'Then let us ask him to answer this question. When you say a man has a natural capacity or incapacity for a subject, don't you mean that he learns it easily or finds it difficult; and that if his natural capacity is good he can pick it up himself after a little instruction, whereas if it is bad he can't remember what he's learnt even after long instruction and practice? And if he has natural capacity aren't his mind and body well coordinated, if he hasn't, uncoordinated?[10] Aren't these the sort of criteria by which you distinguish natural capacity or lack of it?' *c*

'No one will deny that.'

'Then is there any human activity at which men aren't far better in all these respects than women? We need not waste time over exceptions like weaving and various cooking operations, at which women are thought to be experts, and get badly laughed at if a man does them better.'

'It's quite true,' he replied, 'that in general the one sex is much better at everything than the other. A good many women, it is true, are better than a good many men at a good many things. But the general rule is as you stated it.' *d*

'There is therefore no administrative occupation[11] which is peculiar to woman as woman or man as man; natural capacities are similarly distributed in each sex, and it is natural for women to take part in all occupations as well as men, though in all women will be the weaker partners.'

'Agreed.' *e*

'Are we therefore to confine all occupations to men only?'

'How can we?'

'Obviously we can't; for we are agreed, I think, that one woman may have a natural ability for medicine or music, another not.'

'Yes.'

'And one may be good at athletics, another have no taste for them; one be good at soldiering, another not.' *456 a*

'I think so.'

'Then may a woman not be philosophic or unphilosophic, high-spirited or spiritless?'

'She may.'

'Then there will also be some women fitted to be Guardians: for these natural qualities, you will remember, were those for which we picked our men[12] Guardians.'

'Yes, they were.'

'So men and women have the same natural capacity for Guardianship, save in so far as woman is the weaker of the two.'

'That is clear.'

b   'We must therefore pick suitable women to share the life and duties of Guardian with men, since they are capable of it and the natures of men and women are akin.'

'Yes.'

'And the same natures should follow the same pursuits, shouldn't they?'

'Yes.'

'We come back again, then, to our former position, and agree that it is not unnatural that our Guardians' wives should share their intellectual and physical training.'

'There's no doubt about it.'

'So our proposed legislation was no impossible day-dream; c we were legislating in accordance with nature and it is our present contrary practice which now seems unnatural.'

'It looks like it.'

'We set out, didn't we, to discover whether our proposals were practicable, and whether they were the best that could be made?'

'We did.'

'We have now agreed that they are practicable.'

'Yes.'

'Then we must go on to settle whether they are the best.'

'Clearly.'

'Well then, to make a woman into a Guardian we presumably need the same education as we need to make a man into one, d especially as it will operate on the same nature in both.'

'True.'

'There's another point I'd like your opinion on.'

'What is it?'

'Do you suppose some men are better than others? Or are all equal?'

'They certainly aren't all equal!'

'Then in our imaginary state which will produce the better men – the education which we have prescribed for the Guardians or the training our shoemakers get?'

'It's absurd to ask.'

'All right. So the Guardians will be the best citizens?'

'Far the best.'

'Then won't the women Guardians be the best women?'

'Much the best again.'

'And is there anything better for a state than to produce men and women of the best possible kind?'

'No.'

'But that is the result of the education of body and mind which we have described.'

'Of course it is.'

'So the arrangements we proposed are not only possible but also the best our state could have.'

'Yes.'

'Our women Guardians must strip for exercise, then – their excellence[13] will be all the clothes they need. They must play their part in war and in all other duties of a Guardian, which will be their sole occupation; only, as they are the weaker sex, we must give them a lighter share of these duties than men. And any man who laughs at women who, for these excellent reasons, exercise themselves naked is, as Pindar says, "picking the unripe fruit of laughter"[14] – he does not know what he is laughing at or what he is doing. For it is and will always be the best of sayings that what benefits us is fair,[15] what harms us shameful.'[16]

'I agree entirely.'

2. Marriage and the Family

If men and women are to lead the same lives, the family must be abolished. But the sex instinct has to be satisfied and controlled, and new citizens produced. Plato therefore substitutes for the family a system of eugenic breeding analogous to that used in breeding domestic animals. There will be mating festivals

at which the Rulers will contrive that the couples from whom
they wish to breed shall mate; the children will be looked after
in state nurseries. The advantages of the system from Plato's
point of view are, first, that it makes it possible to breed good
citizens, and, second, that it gets rid of the distracting loyalties,
affections and interests of the family system, and diverts them
to the service of the community – the Guardians will become one
family. Here, again, the community overshadows the individual,
and the women Guardians 'bear children for the state' (460e).[17]

[457]   'Well, then, we've escaped one wave without drowning, and
dealt with the regulations about women. We have laid it down
that our men and women Guardians should both follow
c common occupations; and we've proved without inconsistency
that our proposals are both practical and advantageous.'

'Yes, and a pretty big wave it was.'

'You won't say that,' I said, 'when you see the next one.'

'Go on then; let me see it.'

'It follows from what we've said, and from our whole previous
argument –'

'What follows?'

' – that our men and women Guardians should be forbidden
d by law to live together in separate households, and all the
women should be common to all the men; similarly, children
should be held in common, and no parent should know its child,
or child its parent.'

'That's a much bigger wave,' he said. 'And we shall meet
much more scepticism about the possibility or advantages of
such a thing.'

'I don't think there can be much doubt about the advantages
of women and children being held in common, or about it being
the ideal arrangement, if it were possible,' I said; 'but about its
possibility there are likely to be grave doubts.'

e   'Both points will surely be disputed,' he answered.

'You mean I'm to be attacked on both issues,' I said. 'I had
hoped you would agree about the advantages of the proposal,
and that I should evade that issue and only have to discuss its
possibility.'

'I know,' he replied; 'but you failed to make your escape, and are charged on both counts.'

'I must stand my trial, then,' I said. 'But grant me one favour. Let me indulge my fancy like an idle day-dreamer out for a 458 *a* solitary walk. To save himself the trouble of thinking whether what he wants is possible, he gives up all thought of ways and means and imagines his wish fulfilled; he then goes on to amuse himself with a further detailed description of all he intends to do when his wishes are realized, thus encouraging his habit of mental laziness. I'm not feeling very strong myself, and I want *b* to put off any discussion of the possibility of my proposals till later, and assuming them, if I may for the moment, to be possible, to consider how the Guardians would put them into practice, and to show how they would in fact be to the best advantage both of the Guardians and of the state as a whole. I will try to go into these questions with you first, and leave the question of possibility till later, if you will allow it.'

'Yes, I will allow it. Continue.'

'Well, I suppose,' I began, 'that if our Rulers and their Auxili- *c* aries are each to be worthy of their name, the Auxiliaries must be willing to obey orders, and the Rulers to issue them, either in direct obedience to the laws, or in obedience to their spirit when we have left them discretion.'

'A reasonable supposition.'

'As law-giver, you have already picked your men Guardians. You must now pick women of as nearly similar natural cap- acities as possible to go with them. They will live and feed together, and have no private home or property. They will mix *d* freely in their physical exercises and the rest of their training, and their natural instincts will necessarily lead them to have sexual intercourse. Or do you think necessity is too strong a term?'

'The necessity will be sexual and not mathematical,' he said; 'but sex is perhaps more effective than mathematics when it comes to persuading or driving the common man to do anything.'

'Much more,' I agreed. 'But to continue – it would be a sin either for mating or for anything else in a truly happy society to take place without regulation. Our Rulers would not allow it.' *e*

'No, it wouldn't be right.'

'It follows that we must arrange for marriage, and make it as sacred an affair as we can. And a sacred marriage is one that produces the most beneficial results.'

'Yes, certainly.'

459 a   'How, then, are we to get the most beneficial results? Tell me,' I said to Glaucon, 'haven't I seen a lot of hunting dogs and game birds at your house? And there's something about their breeding and mating you must have noticed.'

'What?'

'In the first place, though they are all well bred, don't some of them prove superior to the rest?'

'Yes.'

'Then do you breed from all indifferently? Or do you take care to breed so far as possible from the best of them?'

'From the best of them.'

b   'And does that mean from the youngest, or the oldest, or those in their prime?'

'Those in their prime.'

'Otherwise, don't you reckon that your breeds of birds and dogs would degenerate badly?'

'I do.'

'What about horses and other animals? Does the same apply to them?'

'It would be surprising if it didn't.'

'My goodness,' I exclaimed, 'what outstanding Rulers we shall need, if the same thing is true of human beings!'

c   'That's true enough,' he replied. 'But why exactly?'

'Because it will be necessary for them to use a lot of medicines; and we commonly consider that a comparatively low-grade doctor can treat patients who are prepared to submit to a diet and do not need medicine, but that when medicine is required someone rather higher-powered is called for.'

'That's true; but what is its bearing?'

'This – that our Rulers will have to employ a great deal of fiction and deceit for the benefit of their subjects; and you will

d   remember that we agreed that they might be used as a kind of medicine.'[18]

'It is the right way to use them.'

'And there will be considerable scope for this "right use" in marriage and procreation.'

'How?'

'We must, if we are to be consistent, and if we're to have a real pedigree herd,[19] mate the best of our men with the best of   *e* our women as often as possible, and the inferior men with the inferior women as seldom as possible, and bring up only the offspring of the best.[20] And no one but the Rulers must know what is happening, if we are to avoid dissension in our Guardian herd.'

'That is very true.'

'So we must arrange statutory festivals in which our brides and bridegrooms will be brought together. There will be religious sacrifices and our poets will write songs suitable to the   460 *a* occasion. The number of unions we will leave to the Rulers to settle. Their aim will be to keep numbers[21] constant, allowing for wastage by war and disease and the like, and, so far as they can, to prevent our state becoming too large or too small.'

'Quite right.'

'And we shall have to devise an ingenious system of drawing lots, so that our inferior Guardians can, at each mating festival, blame the lot and not the Rulers.'

'That will certainly be necessary.'

'And among the other honours and rewards our young men   *b* can win for distinguished service in war and in other activities, will be more frequent opportunities to sleep with women;[22] this will give us a pretext for ensuring that most of our children are born of that kind of parent.'

'Quite right.'

'Each generation of children will be taken by officers appointed for the purpose, who may be men or women or both – for men and women will of course be equally eligible for office –'

'Yes, of course.'

'These officers will take the children of the better Guardians   *c* to a nursery and put them in charge of nurses living in a separate part of the city: the children of the inferior Guardians, and any defective offspring of the others, will be quietly and secretly disposed of.'[23]

'They must be if we are to keep our Guardian stock pure,' he agreed.

'They will arrange for the suckling of the children by bringing their mothers to the nursery when their breasts are still full,

d taking every precaution to see that no mother recognizes her child; if the mothers have not enough milk they will provide wet-nurses. They will see that the mothers do not suckle children for more than a reasonable length of time, and will hand over all the sitting up at night and hard work to nurses and attendants.'

'Child-bearing will be an easy job for the Guardians' wives on those conditions,' he commented.

'Which is as it should be,' I replied. 'But to continue with our proposals. We said that one should breed from creatures in their prime.'

'That's true.'

e 'Would you agree that a woman is in her prime for about twenty, a man for about thirty years?'

'Which twenty and which thirty?'

'A woman,' I replied, 'should bear children for the state from her twentieth to her fortieth year; a man should beget them for the state from the time he passes his prime as a runner[24] until he is fifty-five.'

461 *a* 'That is the period of their prime, both physically and mentally.'

'If any man or woman above or below these ages takes a hand in the begetting of children for the community, we shall regard it as a sin and a crime. If they escape detection, the child they beget will be begotten in secrecy and fear and incontinence, without the sacrifices and prayers made by priests and priestesses and by the whole state at each marriage festival, and without the prayers they offer that the children may be better and more

b useful citizens than the parents.'

'That is true.'

'The same rule will apply if any man still in his mating years lays hands on a woman of child-bearing age without the Rulers' sanction; we shall regard him as putting upon the state a child that is a bastard on both civil and religious grounds.'

'Quite rightly.'

'But when our men and women get past the age for breeding, then we can leave them free to mate as they please, provided that no man mates with his daughter or granddaughter, or with his mother or any of her forebears, and no woman with her son or father or their descendants or forebears. But we shall first order them to make every effort to prevent any conception which takes place in these unions from seeing the light at all, and if they fail to prevent its birth, to dispose of it as a creature that must not be reared.'[25]

'That is all quite reasonable. But how,' he asked, 'can they distinguish fathers and daughters and the other relations you mentioned just now?'

'They can't,' I answered. 'But a man will call all males born in the tenth or the seventh month[26] after he has been a bridegroom sons and all females daughters, and they will call him father; similarly, he will call their children grandchildren, and they will in turn call his marriage-group grandfathers and grandmothers, while all who are born during the period when their mothers and fathers were producing children will call each other brothers and sisters. This will enable them to observe the prohibitions we mentioned. There will be no rule to prevent brothers and sisters cohabiting, if the lot so falls out and Delphi approves.'[27]

'I quite agree.'

Promotion, Demotion and Infanticide

The passage 459e–461e has been interpreted by Adam in his edition (p. 357, Appendix IV) and by Popper, The Open Society, Vol. I, p. 51, as implying that Plato sanctioned infanticide. A more balanced discussion than Popper's can be found in R. B. Levinson, In Defence of Plato, p. 185, and H. D. Rankin, Plato and the Individual, Ch. III. With this passage should also be considered what Plato says about movement between classes (415a–b, 423c). Briefly the position seems to be as follows:

(1) There would be nothing very shocking to Greek sentiment in the suggestion of infanticide. It was practised at Sparta, where weak or deformed children were exposed, after examination by public authority. The extent to which it was practised at Athens is a matter of dispute, but there seems no doubt that it was practised, even if only to a limited extent, with unwanted (e.g. illegitimate) or defective children. And the custom seems to have been widespread in the Greek world in general (Levinson, p. 196; Barclay, Educational Ideals in the Ancient World, Appendix A).

(2) The most important piece of evidence is supplied by Plato himself. In the opening pages of the Timaeus *he gives what is generally recognized as a summary of the social and political provisions of the* Republic. *What he says about promotion and demotion runs as follows: 'You will remember too that we said that the children of the good were to be brought up, and those of the bad distributed secretly among the rest of the community; and the Rulers were to keep an eye on the children as they grew up and promote any who deserved it, and degrade into the places of the promoted any in their own ranks who seemed unworthy of their position.' The 'secret distribution' of the* Timaeus *is very similar to the 'quiet and secret disposal' of the* Republic *(460c). Thus it appears that Plato's own interpretation of what he said in the* Republic *was that children of inferior Guardians (and perhaps (415b–d) children of any Guardian who were below standard) would be distributed among the third class. Such distribution would, obviously, have to be done unobtrusively and without general knowledge. Where Plato is open to criticism in this part of his proposals is that he never gives any particulars of the provisions that would be needed to effect the promotion, demotion and distribution which he so emphatically states to be necessary (cf. Levinson, p. 540; Rankin, pp. 72–3).*

(3) But in addition to the 'children of inferior Guardians' (and sub-standard children generally) there are three other groups of children (or perhaps four) mentioned by Plato in this passage:

(a) defective children,

(b) children of Guardians within the breeding ages begotten without sanction outside the Mating Festivals,

(c) children of the over-age,

and perhaps *(d) children of any man or woman outside the breeding age 'who takes a hand in the begetting of children for the community' (461a). It is not easy to see exactly what Plato means by this last group; unions between those above the prescribed age are covered under (c), and the other possibilities appear to be unions between those below the prescribed age and between those above or below the prescribed age and those within it. These must be subject to a similar disapproval to that attaching to those in group (b), in that both are without religious or official legal sanction, children in group (b) being in addition explicitly characterized as illegitimate. From Plato's point of view children in both groups, being the product of unions that were against the law, would be illegitimate.*

As to infanticide – *it seems likely enough in view of Greek practice that Plato would have favoured the exposure of children in group (a) (though they are only referred to in a passing phrase). And if, as has been argued above, illegitimate children were commonly exposed, the same would be true of groups (b) and (d). His language is most explicit about group (c) and, as note 25 suggests, the natural interpretation of it is that it gives a choice of abortion and infanticide. If this interpretation is correct, it seems reasonable to suppose that Plato would have favoured infanticide in the other cases. To sum up: Plato seems to have sanctioned infanticide (1) of defective children (the grounds here would be eugenic), (2) of children born to over-age Guardians (eugenic grounds again no doubt), (3) of children in any sense illegitimate (i.e. conceived in contravention of the laws regulating the relation of the sexes). In this last instance he seems, as Rankin says, to have regarded the child as having a hereditary taint due to the moral weakness of the parents. As for children of 'inferior' Guardians, or sub-standard children of any Guardians ('mixed-metal' children, 415b), Plato's own emphatic statements in the* Republic *and his equally unambiguous restatement in the* Timaeus *can only mean that the normal*

procedure is to relegate them to the third class. But their inferi-
ority can hardly have been judged at birth, and Plato is at fault
in giving no indication of how relegation and promotion are to
be decided (cf. Rankin, p. 55). In addition, his language in this
passage is often obscure and minatory. This may, as Rankin
suggests, be due to a basic dislike of killing, which he tries to
avoid by the analogy of breeding animals which permeates the
whole passage.

'Well, that completes the description of how women and
children are to be held in common among the Guardians in your
state, Glaucon. And the next business of our argument,' I went
on, 'is, I take it, to establish that it fits into our general plan and
462 a   is indeed much the best arrangement.'

'Yes, certainly.'

'The best way to reach agreement about that will be to ask
ourselves what we regard as the greatest social good, the objective of the law-giver's activity, and what as the greatest
social evil; and then to consider whether the proposals we
have just outlined bear the imprint of the good and not of the
evil.'

'Yes, that is the way.'

b   'Is there anything worse for a state than to be split and
fragmented, or anything better than cohesion and unity?'

'No.'

'And is not cohesion the result of the common feelings of
pleasure and pain which you get when all members of a society
are glad or sorry at the same successes and failures?'

'Certainly.'

'But cohesion is dissolved when feelings differ between individuals, and the same events, whether of public or individual
c   concern, delight some and dismay others.'

'Of course.'

'And doesn't this happen when the members of society no
longer agree in their use of the words "mine" and "not mine",
"somebody else's" and "not somebody else's"?'

'That is very true.'

'So the best-ordered state is one in which as many people as possible use the words "mine" and "not mine" in the same sense of the same things.'

'Much the best.'

'What is more, such a state most nearly resembles an individual. For example, when one of us hurts his finger, the whole partnership of body and soul, constituting a single organism under a ruling principle, perceives it and is aware as a whole of the pain suffered by the part, and so we say that the man in question has a pain in *his* finger. And the same holds good of any other part in which a man suffers pain or enjoys pleasure.'   *d*

'Yes,' he agreed, 'and, as you said, the same thing is most nearly true of the best-run communities.'

'That is because such a community will regard the individual who experiences gain or loss as a part of itself, and be glad or sorry as a whole accordingly.'   *e*

'That's bound to be so in a well-regulated society.'

'It's time for us to return to our own state and see whether it has these features we've agreed on, or whether we must look elsewhere for them.'

'Let us do so.'

'Well, our state, like others, contains both rulers and common people.'   463 *a*

'It does.'

'And they will all call each other fellow-citizens.'

'True.'

'And in states other than our own, what do the common people call their rulers, in addition to calling them fellow-citizens?'

'In most states they call them masters;[28] in a democracy they call them simply the rulers.'[29]

'But what will the common people say the rulers in our state are besides fellow-citizens?'

'Protectors and defenders.'   *b*

'And what will the rulers say about the common people?'

'That they provide their pay and livelihood.'

'And what do the rulers in other states call the common people?'

'Slaves.'

'And what do they call each other?'

'Fellow-rulers.'

'And in our state?'

'Fellow-Guardians.'

'And tell me, in other states, do not some of these fellow-rulers call each other friends and others not?'

'Yes, that's quite common.'

'And don't they think and speak of their friends as "one of
c us", and of others as "not one of us"?'

'Yes.'

'And what about our Guardians? Could any of them seriously think or say he had nothing to do with his fellows?'

'Certainly not,' he replied. 'For he's bound to regard any of them he meets as related to him, as brother or sister, father or mother, son or daughter, grandparent or grandchild.'

'You are quite right. And here is a further point. They won't be allowed to treat these legally defined relationships as merely
d nominal, but will be required to behave accordingly, to show their fathers all the customary honour and love, and to obey their parents; any other behaviour will be considered impious and wrong, and subject both to divine and human disapproval. Isn't this the sort of traditional strain you'll expect your citizens to chant in the ears of the children about their conduct towards those they are to call their fathers and other relations?'

e 'Yes. It would be absurd for them merely to use the words without the appropriate actions.'

'In our society of all societies, then, the citizens will agree in their use of that phrase we were talking about just now, and will refer to the successes and misfortunes of an individual fellow-citizen as "*my* success" or "*my* misfortune".'

'That is very true,' he agreed.

'And didn't we say that this way of thinking and talking leads
464 a to common feelings of pain and pleasure?'

'Yes, and we were quite right.'

'Our citizens, then, are devoted to a common interest, which they call *my own*; and in consequence entirely share each other's feelings of joy and sorrow.'

'Yes.'

'And the element in our constitution to which this is especially due is the community of women and children in the Guardian class.'

'Yes, that is the chief reason for it.'

'But we agreed that this unanimity was the greatest good a *b* society can enjoy – we compared, you remember, a well-run society to the human body, in which the whole is aware of the pleasure and pain of the part.'

'And we were quite right,' he said.

'And so we may say that the community of women and children among its protectors confers the greatest of all benefits on our state.'

'Yes, we may.'

'And what is more, we are being quite consistent, because we said earlier that our Guardians, if they were to do their job properly, should have no houses or land or any other possessions *c* of their own, but get their daily bread from others in payment for their services, and consume it together in common.'

'Yes, we said that.'

'Then don't you agree that, as I say, these further arrangements will make them even truer Guardians than before? They will prevent the dissension that starts when different people call different things their own, when each carts off to his own private *d* house anything he can lay hands on for himself, and when each has his own wife and children, his own private joys and sorrows; for our citizens, whose interests are identical and whose efforts are all directed so far as is possible towards the same end, feel all their joys and sorrows together.'

'Yes, I entirely agree.'

'And besides, since they have no private property except their own persons (everything else being common), won't litigation virtually disappear? There won't in fact be any of the quarrels *e* which are caused by having money or children or family.'

'They will inevitably be rid of all that sort of thing.'

'And there will be no justification for actions of violence and assault; for we shall decree that it is both fair and right for one man to defend himself against another of the same age. This will make them keep themselves fit.'

'Which will be an advantage.'

'And the regulation is one that has the additional advantage
465 *a* that if one man is angry with another, he can take it out of him
on the spot, and will be less likely to pursue the quarrel further.'

'True enough.'

'But we shall lay it down that older men are to have authority
over all younger men, and power to punish them.'

'Obviously.'

'And that, as is only right, no younger man shall attempt to
do violence to or strike his elders, unless ordered to do so by the
Rulers. Indeed I don't think that the young will behave badly to
their elders in any way, because they will be prevented by two
effective safeguards, fear and respect. Respect will stop them
laying hands on their parents, and they will fear the assistance
b the victim would get from those who count themselves his sons
and brothers and parents.'

'Yes, that follows.'

'Our laws in fact will mean that the Guardians will live at
complete peace with each other.'

'Complete peace.'

'And if they don't quarrel among themselves, there will be no
danger of rebellion or of faction in the rest of the community.'

'None whatever.'

'There are other minor evils they will get rid of, which are
c really so insignificant that I hesitate to mention them. The poor
won't have to flatter the rich, and there will be none of the
difficulties and anxieties of raising a family and earning what is
necessary to feed a household of servants – borrowing, not
paying one's debts, and scraping enough together somehow for
one's wife and servants to spend. All these and similar vexations
are, I think you will agree, too obvious and too sordid to be
worth talking about.'

d 'They're obvious even to a blind man.'

'Well, they will be rid of them all, and will lead a far more
blissful life than any Olympic victor.'

'How?'

'They have far more to make them really happy. Their victory
is more distinguished, and their maintenance by the public more

complete. Their victory brings security to the whole community, and their reward is that they and their children are maintained and have all their needs supplied at public cost, that they are held in honour by their fellow-citizens while they live, and given *e* a worthy burial when they die.'

'These are indeed great rewards.'

'And yet do you remember,' I asked, 'how earlier on someone or other objected that we weren't making our Guardians happy, because they were to have nothing of their own in spite of being in control of everything? And you will remember that *466 a* we answered that we would return to the question later, if convenient; but that for the moment we were concerned to make our Guardians into guardians and to ensure the highest degree of happiness for the community as a whole without concentrating attention on the happiness of any particular section of it.'

'Yes, I remember.'

'Well, if the life our Guardians are to lead is better and more splendid than an Olympic victor's, we can't really compare it *b* with a cobbler's or farmer's or any other manual worker's.'

'I should think not.'

'None the less, it is only right to repeat again what I said then: if any Guardian looks for happiness in a way unworthy of his status, if he tires of the restraint and security of the ideal life we have drawn for him, and is impelled by some senseless and extravagant idea of happiness into using his power to appropriate the community's wealth – well, he will learn the wisdom of *c* Hesiod's saying that the half is more than the whole.'[30]

'My advice to him would be to stick to his own way of life.'

'Do you agree, then, that the best arrangement is for our men and women to share a common education, to bring up their children in common and to have a common responsibility, as Guardians, for their fellow-citizens, as we have described? That women should in fact, so far as possible, take part in all the same occupations as men, both in peace within the city and on *d* campaign in war, acting as Guardians and hunting with the men like hounds, that this is the best course for them and that there is nothing unwomanly[31] in this natural partnership of the sexes?'

'I agree,' he said.

3. The Rules of War

Socrates has promised to show next that his proposals are not only desirable but possible. But he digresses (perhaps because he has just mentioned the function of women in war and the subject is therefore in his mind) to discuss the conduct of war. He deals first with the familiarization of children with military operations, then with military rewards and punishments, and finally with the rules of warfare and treatment of enemies. He deprecates war between Greek states and lays down rules to regulate and humanize it. He clearly regards war as a permanent feature of human affairs; but, equally clearly, he hopes for a measure of Greek unity, and regards non-Greeks (barbarians) as in some measure natural enemies.

'It remains, then,' I said, 'to decide whether and how this sharing of functions is possible among human beings, as it is among animals.'

'You've taken the words out of my mouth,' he replied.

e 'I suppose the arrangements they will make for the conduct of war are fairly obvious?' I asked.

'What will they be?' he said.

'Men and women will serve together, and take the children
467 *a* to war with them when they are old enough, to let them see, as they do in other trades, the job they will have to do when they grow up. And besides seeing what goes on, they will fetch and carry and make themselves useful to their mothers and fathers during the campaign. Haven't you noticed how, in a craft like the potter's, children serve a long apprenticeship, watching how things are done, before they take a hand in the work themselves?'

'Yes, I have.'

'Oughtn't the Guardians to take just as much care, when they are training their children, to let them see what their duties are and get used to them?'

'It would be absurd if they didn't.'

'And besides, any animal fights better in the presence of its
b young.'

'That's true. But isn't there a considerable risk, Socrates, that if they are defeated, as may well happen in war, their children will be killed as well as themselves, and what is left of the state be unable to recover?'

'That's perfectly true,' I replied. 'But in the first place do you think they should avoid risks altogether?'

'No.'

'Then, if they are to take risks, ought they not to do so when they will really be the better for success?'

'Obviously.'

'But won't it make all the difference to children who are to be fighting men when they grow up if they see something of war when they are young? Isn't it a risk worth taking?'

'Yes, well worth it.'

'We must therefore act on that assumption and make it possible for our children to be spectators of war, but take measures to ensure their safety, and all will be well.'

'Yes.'

'Then, to begin with, their fathers will be as knowledgeable as men can be in these matters, and be able to tell whether a campaign is dangerous or not.'   *d*

'That seems likely,' he said.

'So they will take them on some campaigns, and avoid others.'

'True.'

'And they will put them in charge of really trustworthy officers, who are qualified both by age and experience to act as their leaders and look after them.'

'That is as it should be.'

'Yes, but things often turn out very differently from what we expect.'

'They do indeed.'

'So I think we ought to give our children wings as an additional precaution, so that they can fly away if necessary.'

'What do you mean?' he asked.   *e*

'I mean that we must put them on horseback as young as possible, and when they have learnt to ride take them to see the fighting, on horses that aren't too spirited or fiery, but fast and easy to manage. Then they will get the best view of their future job and be able to follow their more experienced leaders to safety quite easily, if need be.'

'That seems to me a good arrangement.'

468 a   'Then what about the actual fighting? What treatment will your soldiers expect for themselves or give their enemies? I wonder if I'm right about that.'

'Tell us what you think.'

'I think that any of them who deserts or throws away his arms or shows any similar signs of cowardice should be relegated to the artisans or farmers.'

'Certainly.'

'And any of them taken prisoner should be abandoned to his captors to deal with as they wish.'

b   'I entirely agree.'

'Then what about anyone who has distinguished himself for bravery? Do you agree that he should first be duly crowned, while the army is still in the field, by his fellow-campaigners, by young men[32] and children in turn?'

'Yes.

'And that they should shake his hand?'

'I agree again.'

'But I'm afraid you won't agree to what I'm going to say next.'

'What is it?'

'That he should exchange kisses with them.'

'I think it's the best idea of all,' said Glaucon. 'And what is
c   more, I should add to your law a clause that would forbid anyone to refuse his kisses for the rest of the campaign, as an encouragement to those in love with a boy or girl to be all the keener to win an award for bravery.'

'A very good clause,' I said. 'For we have already said that the better citizens are to be more frequently selected for marriage than others and have more free choice in such matters, so that they may have correspondingly more children.'

'So we said.'

'And we have Homer's authority for honouring bravery in the
d   young. For he tells how, when Ajax had distinguished himself in battle, he was "paid the honour" of a helping from the "long

chine of the beast"[33] as if it were a suitable honour for a brave
man in his prime, something which, in addition to the distinction
it brought, would increase his strength.'

'And how right Homer was.'

'Then we will follow his advice, this time at any rate. At
sacrifices and similar occasions we will reward excellence,
according to its degree, not only with song and the other privileges we mentioned, but "with the best seat at the table, the first
cut off the joint, and a never empty cup".[34] In this way we shall   *e*
honour the bravery of our men and women and improve their
physique.'

'An excellent suggestion.'

'Good. And then those who die bravely on active service we
shall reckon as men of gold –'

'They certainly deserve it.'

'– and believe with Hesiod that when they die they "become   469 *a*
holy, beneficent Guardian Spirits on earth, protectors to shield
mortal men from harm".'[35]

'Yes, we will believe him.'

'And we shall bury them with whatever special ceremonies
Delphi prescribes, in reply to our inquiry, for men of such divine
and heroic mould.'

'Of course we shall.'

'And for the rest of time treat their tombs with reverence and
worship them as Guardian Spirits.[36] And we shall pay the same   *b*
honour to all those who are judged to have lived a life of special
distinction and who die of old age or other cause.'

'Very right.'

'And how will our soldiers treat their enemies?'

'In what respect?'

'First, over slavery. Do you think it is right for Greek states
to sell Greeks into slavery, or to allow others to do so, so far as
they can prevent it? Ought they not rather to make it their
custom to spare their fellows, for fear of falling under barbarian   *c*
domination?'

'It would be infinitely better to spare them.'

'There will then be no Greek slave in our state, and it will
advise other Greek states to follow suit.'[37]

'Certainly. That would encourage them to let each other alone and turn against the barbarian.'

'Then is it a good thing to strip the dead, after a victory, of anything but their arms? It gives the cowards an excuse not to
d pursue the enemy who are still capable of fight, if they can pretend they are doing their duty by poking about among the dead. Indeed, many an army has been lost before now by this habit of plunder.'

'It surely has.'

'And don't you think there's something low and mean about plundering a corpse, and a kind of feminine small-mindedness in treating the dead body as an enemy when the fighting spirit
e which fought in it has left it and flown? It's rather like the dog's habit of snarling at the stones thrown at it, but keeping clear of the person who's throwing them.'

'Yes, it's very like that.'

'So we'll have no stripping of corpses and no refusal to allow burial.'[38]

'I entirely agree,' he said.

'Nor shall we dedicate the arms of our enemies in our temples, particularly if they are the arms of fellow-Greeks and if we have
470 a any concern for friendship with them. On the contrary, we shall be afraid that we should desecrate a temple by offering them the arms of our own kin, unless indeed Apollo rules otherwise.'

'Quite right.'

'Then what about devastating the lands and burning the houses of Greek enemies? How will your soldiers treat their enemies over that?'

'I'd like to know what you think about it.'

'I don't think they ought to do either, but confine themselves
b to carrying off the year's harvest. Shall I tell you why?'

'Please do.'

'I think that the two terms "war" and "civil strife" reflect a real difference between two types of dispute. And the two types I mean are the one internal and domestic, the other external and foreign; and we call a domestic dispute "civil strife", and an external one "war".'

'What you say is very much to the point.'

'Then do you think it equally to the point if I say that all   *c*
relations between Greek and Greek are internal and domestic,
and all relations between Greek and barbarian foreign and
external?'

'Admirable.'

'Then when Greek fights barbarian or barbarian Greek we
shall say they are at war and are natural enemies, and that their
quarrel is properly called a "war"; but when Greek fights Greek
we shall say that they are naturally friends, but that Greece is
sick and torn by faction, and that the quarrel should be called
"civil strife".'   *d*

'I agree with your view.'

'Consider, then,' I went on, 'what happens in civil strife in its
normal sense, that is to say, when there is civil war in a single
state. If the two sides ravage each other's land and burn each
other's houses, we think it an outrage, and regard two parties
who dare to lay waste the country which bore and bred them as
lacking in all patriotism. But we think it reasonable, if the victors   *e*
merely carry off their opponents' crops, and remember that they
can't go on fighting for ever but must come to terms some time.'

'Yes, because the last frame of mind is the more civilized.'

'Well, then,' I said, 'your city will be Greek, won't it?'

'It must be.'

'And its people good and civilized?'

'Certainly.'

'Then they will love their fellow-Greeks, and think of Greece
as their own land, in whose common religion they share.'

'Yes, certainly.'

'And any dispute with Greeks they will regard as civil strife,   471 *a*
because it is with their own people, and so won't call it "war".'

'That's true.'

'So they will fight in the hope of coming to terms.'

'Yes, they will.'

'They will in fact correct them in a friendly way, rather than
punish them with enslavement and destruction; they will act in
a spirit of correction, not of enmity.'

'Exactly.'

'It follows that they will not, as Greeks, devastate Greek lands

or burn Greek dwellings; nor will they admit that the whole
people of a state – men, women, and children – are their enemies,
b but only the hostile minority who are responsible for the quarrel.
They will not therefore devastate the land or destroy the houses
of the friendly majority, but press their quarrel only until the
guilty minority are brought to justice by the innocent victims.'

'For myself,' he said, 'I agree that our citizens ought to behave
in this way to their enemies; though when they are fighting
barbarians they should treat them as the Greeks now treat each
other.'

'Then let us lay it down as a law for our Guardians, that they
c are neither to ravage land nor burn houses.'

'We will do so,' he agreed; 'it is a good rule, like all our
others.'

PART VII
THE PHILOSOPHER
RULER

1. The Ideal and the Actual

Socrates is again reminded of his promise to demonstrate the practicability of his State. He starts by distinguishing the ideal from the approximations to it which are the best that can be achieved in practice, and maintaining that even if the ideal he has sketched cannot be realized in every detail, it has still been worth describing as a standard to aim at. He then goes on to assert that the only hope of realizing it, even imperfectly, is for political power to be put in the hands of 'philosophers'.

'But it seems to me, Socrates, that if we let you go on like this [471] you will forget that you still have to show that the state we have described is a practical possibility, and if so how; all you've just been saying has merely been putting the question off. I'll admit that your state would be ideal if it existed, and I'll fill in the gaps in your description myself. I know that the mutual loyalty the citizens would feel because they know they can call each other brothers, fathers, and sons, would make them most formidable   d enemies; and that the presence of their women on campaign, whether they fought with them or acted as a reserve, would make them altogether invincible, because of the panic it would cause in their enemies and the support it would give in case of need. I can see also how many domestic advantages they would   e have that you have left unmentioned. I grant all this, and a thousand other things too, *if* our state existed, and I don't want to hear any more details. Let us forget them and concentrate now on the job of proving to ourselves *that* it can exist and *how* it can exist.'

472 a   'This is a very sudden attack,' I countered, 'and you've no mercy on my delays. I've just escaped two waves; but the third, which you are trying to bring on me now, is the biggest and the most difficult of the three, though you may not know it. When you have seen and heard it, you will forgive me and see how reasonable was the hesitation which made me afraid to put forward and examine such a paradoxical theory.'

   'The more of these excuses we hear,' he replied, 'the less likely
b we are to let you off explaining how this social system can be realized. Get on, and don't waste time.'

   'Well,' I said, 'perhaps I ought to remind you first of all that we started our discussion by trying to find out what justice and injustice are.'

   'Yes – what of it?' he asked.

   'I was only going to ask whether, when we find out what justice is, we shall require the just man to answer the description precisely, and be an exact counterpart of what justice is. Or
c shall we be content if he approximates to it very closely and has a bigger share[1] of it than other men?'

   'That will content us.'

   'Then it is an ideal pattern[1] we were looking for when we tried to say what justice and injustice are in themselves, and to describe what the perfectly just or perfectly unjust man would be like if he ever existed. By turning our eyes to *them* and seeing what measure of happiness or its opposite[2] they would enjoy, we would be forced to admit that the nearer we approximate to
d them the more nearly we share their lot. That was our purpose, rather than to show that the ideal could be realized in practice, was it not?'

   'That is quite true.'

   'If a painter, then, paints a picture of an ideally beautiful man, complete to the last detail, is he any the worse painter because he cannot show that such a man could really exist?'

   'No, certainly not.'

e   'But haven't we been painting a word-picture of an ideal state?'

'True.'

'Is our picture any the worse drawn, then, because we can't show how it can be realized in fact?'

'No.'

'That, then, is the truth of the matter. But if I'm to go on, to oblige you, and try to show how and under what conditions we can get nearest our ideal, I must ask you to admit that the same principles apply to my exposition.'

'What principles?'

'Does practice ever square with theory? Is it not in the nature   473 *a*
of things that, whatever people think, practice should come less close to truth than theory? Do you agree or not?'

'I agree.'

'Then don't insist on my showing that every detail of our description can be realized in practice, but grant that we shall have met your demand that its realization should be possible if we are able to find the conditions under which a state can most   *b*
closely approximate to it. Will you be content with that? I would.'

'And so will I.'

'The next thing, I suppose, is to try to show what fault it is in the constitutions of existing states that prevents them from being run like ours, and what is the least change that would bring them into conformity with it – a single change if possible, failing that two, or as few and as small as may be.'

'Certainly.'   *c*

'I think we can show that the transformation can be effected by a single change,' I said, 'but it's hardly a small or easy one, though it is possible.'

'Tell us what it is.'

'I'm now facing what we called the biggest wave,' I replied. 'I'll tell you what it is, even if it swamps me in a surge of laughter and I'm drowned in contempt; so listen to what I'm going to say.'

'Go on.'

'The society we have described can never grow into a reality or see the light of day, and there will be no end to the troubles   *d*
of states, or indeed, my dear Glaucon, of humanity itself,[3] till

philosophers become kings in this world, or till those we now
call kings and rulers really and truly become philosophers, and
political power and philosophy thus come into the same hands,

e   while the many natures now content to follow either to the
exclusion of the other are forcibly debarred from doing so. This
is what I have hesitated to say so long, knowing what a paradox
it would sound; for it is not easy to see that there is no other
road to real happiness[4] either for society or the individual.'

Glaucon's reply to this was to exclaim, 'My dear Socrates, if

474 *a*   you make pronouncements of that sort, you can't be surprised
if a large number of decent people take their coats off, pick up
the nearest weapon, and come after you in their shirt sleeves
to do something terrible to you. If you can't find an argument
to hold them off and escape, you'll learn to your cost what it
is to be laughed at.'

'But it's all your doing,' said I.

'And I've done very well too,' he retorted. 'But I won't desert
you, and will give you what help I can, though it won't amount
to more than goodwill and encouragement; and maybe I'm
better attuned to your questions than others. So you must try to

b   convince the sceptics of the truth of what you say with that
amount of help.'

'You're such a powerful ally that I must make the attempt,' I
replied.

2. Definition of the Philosopher

The word 'philosophos' *was by no means unambiguous in
Greek, and Plato proceeds to define what he means by it and
to explain the qualities of character he demands in his true
philosopher. The philosopher is the man who loves (Greek
*philein) *wisdom (sophia) in the widest sense, including especi-
ally learning, knowledge and truth. To explain this Plato has to
bring in his own philosophical beliefs, and in particular his theory
of 'forms'. The word 'form' is now the common rendering of
the Greek* eidos *or* idea. *The older rendering, 'idea', is avoided
because of its misleading suggestion of a purely subjective notion.*

Unfortunately Plato never gives in his dialogues a full or direct exposition of the theory; we have to reconstruct it from allusions and from the passages such as the present, where it is, in effect, assumed and used for the purpose of a particular argument. In places, indeed, it is difficult to be certain, because Plato never developed a set technical terminology, whether the forms are referred to or not (cf. Part III, note 74). Only the briefest explanation can be attempted here. It can well begin with a quotation from Cornford's translation (p. 176). Plato, he says, is concerned with knowledge of unchanging objects: 'in this respect the Forms resemble the laws of nature sought by modern natural science: a law is an unseen intelligible principle, a unit underlying an unlimited multiplicity of similar phenomena, and supposed to be unalterable. The Forms, however, are not laws of the sequence or co-existence of phenomena, but ideals or patterns, which have a real existence independent of our minds and of which the many individual things called by their names in the world of appearances are like images or reflections.' To this may be added the account given by Aristotle (himself a pupil and member of the Academy) of the origin and purpose of the theory (Metaphysics A, ch. 6). He tells us that Plato at an early stage fell under the influence of the doctrines of the Heracleitean school, who believed 'that all sensible things are in a state of flux and that there is no such thing as knowledge of them'. Plato was also, he says, influenced by Socrates, who was interested in ethical questions and not in the natural world, and who was concerned to find definitions of ethical terms. Plato generalized Socrates' procedure and supposed that definitions of the right kind in any field must, because they yielded knowledge in the full sense, refer to a level or realm of reality other than the sensible world of which such full knowledge was not possible. Another influence to which Aristotle refers elsewhere is that of mathematics; this comes in the main from the Pythagoreans. Mathematical propositions and theorems are in an important sense independent of the sensible world; the theorems of Euclid for instance are proved by reasoning, not by measuring lines and angles. (Such knowledge is often traditionally called a priori.) It is not surprising that Plato, reflecting on this, should have been reinforced in the view that there is a level of reality more ultimate than the senses show us, and a corresponding knowledge attainable only by reason.

To apply all this to the Republic: – *we have both in this section and in the similes of the Divided Line (Part VII, section 6) and Cave (Part VII, section 7) the contrast between two levels of reality. The unchanging forms, which are the objects of the philosopher's knowledge, are what is ultimately real. The world perceived by the senses, the world of change, though not* unreal, *has a lower status ontologically than the realm of forms. (The contrast between ultimate reality and the world as it* appears *to the senses is of course familiar in philosophy, and was already familiar in Plato's day. Parmenides had contrasted reality and appearance, and Plato's contemporary Democritus, from a very different point of view, regarded the world revealed by the senses as having only a secondary reality compared with the ultimate realities, atoms and void.) The difference between the two realms is marked, and indeed for Plato demonstrated, in this section and in the Line simile, by a difference in mode of apprehension. On the one hand there is 'knowledge' (epistēmē). The Greek word is used in a number of senses. It can mean knowledge, 'how to', professional skill and the organized body of knowledge which goes with it (cf. 350a where it bears this meaning); for Plato it came to mean knowledge in the full sense, thorough understanding, reached and accounted for by rational argument, as for example in mathematics (though it has an element, which appears in the Line, of direct intuitive perception). Contrasted with knowledge is 'opinion' or 'belief' (doxa). Neither word translates it adequately, because neither brings out the basic contrast between full knowledge and mere supposition, however confident. Doxa is cognate to the verb dokein which means 'to seem' and is used in phrases which we translate as 'I think so', 'it seems to me'. But however confident and correct the judgement so expressed, it still lacks authenticity because its foundations are inadequate.*

Though Plato as we have seen never developed a set terminology there are certain words and expressions which he is in the habit of using about the forms. We have already (note 1 above) seen him use the word paradeigma, *indicating that the form is a pattern or standard. The pattern–likeness relation recurs in the* Timaeus; *the particular instances of it are then 'images'* (eikones) *or 'likenesses'* (homoiomata). *The form as standard is important particularly in ethics and mathematics. More commonly in the* Republic *the form is called* the so-and-so, *or* so-and-so 'in itself' – *the beautiful, or beauty in itself (or simply beauty itself): sometimes, as on* 507b, *what beauty* [really] *is. This is sometimes translated as 'absolute beauty'; 'absolute', however, has later philosophical associations and is perhaps best avoided. But the two most characteristic words are those from which the theory takes its name,* idea *and* eidos, *which originally meant 'shape', 'appearance', and came to be used non-visually of any common characteristic and so to mean 'type', 'essential structure or nature', 'quality'. So we are told in Part* x (596a) *that there is a form for 'each set of particular things, to which we apply the same name'. The relation of forms to particulars is often said to be one of 'presence' in them* (parousia) *and particulars are said to 'share in' or 'partake of' the form* (metechein): 'just acts' *are 'just' because they share or partake in the form of justice, which gives them their common quality, though it is not to be identified with it (just acts are not perfectly just nor drawn circles perfectly circular).*

Briefly therefore we may say that the forms are objects of knowledge (as opposed to opinion), are what is ultimately real (as opposed to what appears or seems), are standards or patterns to which different but similar particulars approximate, though imperfectly (this meaning is particularly relevant in morals and mathematics), and are the common factor in virtue of which we give groups of particular things a common name.

1. The Philosopher and the Two Orders of Reality

The philosopher is in love with truth, that is, not with the changing world of sensation, which is the object of opinion, but with the unchanging reality which is the object of knowledge. (Plato seems to use epistēmē *and* gnōsis *interchangeably for 'knowledge', and both are so translated: cf. opening note for Part* VII, *section 6.)*

In much of this section the argument centres round the Greek word einai. *This has a wider range of meaning than the English 'to be', normally used to translate it. It may be used in the common predicative sense ('Socrates is wise'); it may assert or imply existence (there is no separate Greek verb for 'to exist'); it may be used to speak of what* really *is, what is ultimately and genuinely real, as opposed to what merely* appears *to be so; and in suitable contexts it can be used to refer to what is* true (*what is so, as opposed to what is not*). *Plato, his predecessors and contemporaries were much occupied with the consequent ambiguities, with many of which Plato dealt in his later dialogue, the* Sophist.

'If we are somehow to escape the attack which you say threatens us, we must define these philosophers who we dare to claim should be rulers. When they stand clearly revealed we shall be able to defend ourselves by showing that there are some who

c are naturally fitted for philosophy and political leadership, while the rest should follow their lead but let philosophy alone.'

'It's time for a definition,' he said.

'Then follow my lead,' I replied, 'and we will see if we can reach a satisfactory explanation somehow or other.'

'Lead on.'

'Well, I hardly need to remind you,' said I, 'that if a man can be properly said to love something, it must be clear that he feels affection for it as a whole, and does not love part of it to the exclusion of the rest.'

d 'I'm afraid I do need reminding,' he replied, 'because I'm not quite with you.'

'I hardly expected that answer from you, Glaucon,' I replied; 'anyone as susceptible as you should surely remember that those of your amorous temperament are always getting bitten with a passion for boys in the bloom of youth, and think they all deserve attention and affection. You know how it is. You

e praise a snub nose by calling it charming, a Roman nose you call commanding, and one between the two beautifully proportioned; a dark complexion is manly, a fair one divine. And who do you think invented the description "honey-pale" but some lover making fond excuses for pallor on the cheek of youth? In fact there's no pretext you won't make and nothing you won't say to avoid rejecting youth at its flower.'   475 *a*

'If you insist on attributing these habits of lovers to me, I'll agree for the sake of argument.'

'Well then,' I said, 'it's just the same with people who love wine. Haven't you noticed how with them any pretext is good enough to recommend any wine?'

'Yes indeed.'

'And I expect you've noticed too how those who love honour, if they can't get command of any army, will take a battalion, and if the more important people don't look up to them, are content if the smaller fry do, so passionately keen are they on   *b* prestige of any sort.'

'That's very true.'

'Then tell me this – when we say someone has a passion for something or other, don't we mean that he wants everything of that particular kind, and not some things only?'

'Yes.'

'And so a philosopher's passion is for wisdom of every kind without distinction?'

'True.'

'Then we shan't regard anyone as a lover of knowledge or wisdom who is fussy about what he studies, especially if he is   *c* young and has not yet the judgement to know what is good for him and what is not, just as we don't say that anyone who is fussy about his food has a good appetite or a passion for eating, but call him a poor eater and not a food-lover.'

'And we shall be quite right.'

'But the man who is ready to taste every branch of learning, is glad to learn and never satisfied – he's the man who deserves to be called a philosopher, isn't he?'

'That description covers a lot of peculiar people,' was   *d* Glaucon's reply to this. 'For those who love looking and listening enjoy learning about things, and so fall under your description; but they're a peculiar lot to class as philosophers, because nothing would induce them to spend time on any kind of serious argument. They run round the city and country Dionysia, never

missing a festival, as if they were under contract to listen to
every performance. Are we to call all those who share such
e   tastes, or are devotees of the minor arts, philosophers?'

'Certainly not, though there is some resemblance.'

'Then who are the true philosophers?' he asked.

'Those who love to see the truth.'

'That is clearly right; but what does it mean?'

'It would be difficult,' I said, 'to explain it to anyone else; but
you, I think, will agree with me on the following point.'

'What point?'

'That, since beauty and ugliness are opposites, they are *two*.'

476 *a*   'Of course.'

'And as they are *two*, each of them is single.'

'That is so.'

'The same is true of justice and injustice, good and evil, and
all qualities;[5] each of them is in itself single, but they seem to be
a multiplicity because they appear everywhere in combination
with actions and material bodies and with each other.'

'That is true.'

b   'I use this principle to distinguish your sight-lovers and art-
lovers and practical men from the philosophers in the true sense,
who are the subject of our discussion.'

'And how do you do it?'

'Those who love looking and listening are delighted by beautiful sounds and colours and shapes, and the works of art which
make use of them, but their minds are incapable of seeing and
delighting in the essential nature of beauty itself.'

'That is certainly so,' he agreed.

'And those who can reach beauty itself and see it as it is in
itself are likely to be few.'

c   'Very few indeed.'

'Then what about the man who recognizes the existence of
beautiful things, but does not believe in beauty itself, and is
incapable of following anyone who wants to lead him to a
knowledge of it? Is he awake, or merely dreaming? Look; isn't
dreaming simply the confusion between a resemblance and the
reality which it resembles, whether the dreamer be asleep or
awake?'

'I should certainly say that a man in that state of mind was dreaming.'

'Then what about the man who, contrariwise, believes in *d* beauty itself and can see both it and the particular things which share[6] in it, and does not confuse particular things and that in which they share? Do you think he is awake or dreaming?'

'He is very much awake.'

'And so, because he knows, we can rightly call his state of mind one of knowledge; and that of the other man, who holds opinions only, opinion.'

'Certainly.'

'And if the man who we say holds opinions but does not know is annoyed, and questions the truth of our statement, can we manage to soothe him and win him over gently, without *e* letting him know the extent of his disease?'

'We certainly must.'

'Let's think what to say to him. Shall we begin our inquiry by telling him that we don't in the least grudge him any knowledge he has, and are indeed delighted he knows anything; and then go on to ask him if he will answer this question, "Does a man who knows, know something or nothing?" You answer for him.'

'I shall answer that he knows something.'

'Something which is, or which is not?'[7]

'Something which is; how could he know something that was *477 a* not?'[8]

'Then are we satisfied that, whichever way we look at it, what fully *is* is fully knowable, what in no way *is* is entirely unknowable?'

'Quite satisfied.'

'Good. Then if there is anything whose condition is such that it both is and is not, would it not lie between what absolutely *is* and what altogether *is not*?'

'It would.'

'Then since knowledge is related to what *is*, and ignorance, necessarily, to what *is not*, we shall have to find out whether to what lies *between* them there corresponds something *between* ignorance and knowledge, if there is such a thing.'   *b*

'Yes.'

'Isn't there something we call opinion?'

'Of course.'

'Is it the same faculty[9] as knowledge or different?'

'Different.'

'So opinion and knowledge must have different correlates corresponding to their difference of faculty.'

'They must.'

'Then knowledge is related to what is, and knows[10] what is *as* it is. But there's a distinction I think I should make before I go on.'

'What is it?'

c   'Let us class together as "faculties" the powers in us, and in other things that enable us to perform all the various functions of which we are capable. Thus I call sight and hearing faculties – do you understand the type of thing I mean?'

'Yes, I understand.'

'Then let me tell you what I think about them. A faculty has neither colour, nor shape, nor any of the similar qualities by

d   observation of which I distinguish other things one from another; I can only identify a faculty by watching its field and its effects, and I call faculties the same if their field and effects are the same, different if these are different. What about you? What do you do?'

'The same as you.'

'Let us go back, then,' I said. 'Tell me, do you think knowledge is a faculty? Could you classify it otherwise?'

'No; it is the most powerful of all faculties.'

e   'And should opinion be classified as a faculty?'

'Yes, it is the power which enables us to hold opinions.'

'But a little while ago you agreed that knowledge and opinion were different.'

'Yes,' he replied, 'because no reasonable person would identify the infallible with the fallible.'

'Splendid,' I said; 'we are clearly agreed that opinion and

478 a   knowledge are different.'

'We are.'

'Each therefore has a different natural field and a different capacity.'

'That follows.'

'But, of course, knowledge is related to what is; it *knows*[11] what is *as* it is.'

'Yes.'

'While the characteristic of opinion is to form opinions, didn't we say?'

'Yes.'

'Is its subject-matter the same as that of knowledge? And are the fields of knowledge and opinion the same? Or is that impossible?'

'It's impossible on the principles we've agreed. If different faculties have different natural fields, and belief and knowledge are two separate faculties, as we maintain, then it follows that the fields of knowledge and opinion must be different.'   *b*

'Then if the field of knowledge is what is, the field of opinion must be something other than what is.'

'Yes.'

'Is it what is not? Or is it impossible even to hold an opinion about what is not? Consider. An opinion is surely related to something. Or is it possible to hold an opinion and yet grasp nothing?'[12]

'No, that's impossible.'

'So a man who holds an opinion grasps something.'

'Yes.'

'But what is not can hardly be called something – it is, properly speaking, nothing.'

'True.'

'Now, we were compelled to correlate ignorance with *what is not*, knowledge with *what is*.'[13]

'Quite right.'

'So a man who holds an opinion is concerned with neither?'

'Agreed.'

'So opinion is neither ignorance nor knowledge.'

'So it seems.'

'Then does it lie beyond them? Is it clearer than knowledge, or less clear than ignorance?'

'No.'

'Then in that case,' I asked, 'do you think it is darker than knowledge, but clearer than ignorance?'

'Very much so.'

d   'Does it lie between the two?'

'Yes.'

'Opinion is in fact intermediate between them.'

'Certainly.'

'Now we said before[14] that if there was anything that appeared both to be and not to be, it would be of a kind to lie between what fully *is* and what absolutely *is not*, and would be correlated neither with knowledge nor ignorance but with what appears to be between them.'

'True.'

'And we now see that what we call opinion occupies that intermediate position.'

'That is so.'

e   'It remains for us to discover something that has its share both of being and not-being, and cannot be said to have the characteristics of either without qualification; if we find it we can fairly say that it is the object of opinion, thus correlating extremes to extremes and intermediate to intermediate. Do you agree?'

'Yes.'

479 a   'Having established these principles, I shall return to our friend who denies that there is any beauty in itself or any eternally unchanging form of beauty, that lover of sights, who loves visible beauty but cannot bear to be told that beauty is really one, and justice one, and so on – I shall return to him and ask him, "Is there any of these many beautiful objects of yours that may not also seem ugly? Or of your just and righteous acts that may not appear unjust and unrighteous?"'

b   'No,' replied Glaucon, 'they are all bound to seem in a way both beautiful and ugly; and the same is true of the other things you mention.'

'And what about the many things which are double something else? If they are double one thing can't they be equally well regarded as half something else?'

'Yes.'

'And things which we say are large or small, light or heavy, may equally well be given the opposite epithet.'

'Yes; they may all be given both.'

'Then can we say that any of these many things *is*, any more than it *is not*, what anyone says it is?'

'They are ambiguous like the puzzles people ask at parties,' he replied, 'or the children's riddle about the eunuch hitting the bat and what he threw at it and what it was sitting on.[15]   *c* They have a similar ambiguity, and one can't think of them definitely either as being or as not-being, or as both, or as neither.'

'Can you think of any better way to treat them, then, than place them between being and not-being? They are not so dark as to be less real than what is not, or so luminously clear as to be more real than what is.'   *d*

'Precisely.'

'Our conclusion, therefore, it seems, is that the many conventional views held by most people about beauty and the rest hover somewhere between what is not and what fully is.'

'Yes.'

'And we agreed earlier that, if there appeared to be anything of the sort, it should be called the field of opinion and not of knowledge, the fluctuating intermediate realm being apprehended by the intermediate faculty.'

'Yes, we did.'

'Those then who have eyes for the multiplicity of beautiful   *e* things and just acts, and so on, but are unable, even with another to guide them, to see beauty itself and justice itself, may be said in all cases to have *opinions*, but cannot be said to know any of the things they hold opinions about.'

'That follows.'

'And what about those who have eyes for the eternal, unchanging things? They surely have knowledge and not opinion.'

'That follows too.'

'And they set their hearts on the field of knowledge, while the   *480 a* other type set theirs on the field of opinion – for, as you will remember, we said that their eyes and hearts were fixed on the beautiful sounds and colours and so on, and that they could not bear even the suggestion that there was such a thing as beauty itself.'

'Yes, I remember.'

'So we shall be making no mistake to call them lovers of opinion rather than lovers of wisdom or philosophers. Do you think they will be very annoyed with us for saying so?'

'Not if they take my advice,' he replied; 'they have no right to be annoyed at the truth.'

'And those whose hearts are fixed on the true being of each thing are to be called philosophers and not lovers of opinion?'

'Yes, certainly.'

2. The Qualities of Character Required in the Philosopher
The philosopher is shown to require, as philosopher, all the qualities that could be asked for in a good ruler.

BK VI   'Well, Glaucon,' I said, 'we can now see, at last, what a philosopher is and what he is not, but we've had to go a long
484 a   way round to find out.'

'I doubt if we could have done it more shortly,' he replied.

'I don't think we could. Though I think we could have managed better if it had been the only subject we were discussing,
b   and we hadn't so much else to get through before we can see the difference between a just life and an unjust.'

'Then where do we go from here?'

'The next question is this. If philosophers have the capacity to grasp the eternal and immutable, while those who have no such capacity are not philosophers and are lost in multiplicity and change, which of the two should be in charge of a state?'

'What would be a reasonable line to take?' he asked.

c   'To say that we will appoint as Guardians whichever of them seem able to guard the laws and customs of society.'

'Right.'

'And isn't it obvious whether it's better for a blind man or a clear-sighted one to guard and keep an eye on anything?'

'There's not much doubt about that,' he agreed.

'But surely "blind" is just how you would describe men who have no true knowledge of reality, and no clear standard[16] of

perfection in their mind to which they can turn, as a painter
turns to his model, and which they can study closely before they   *d*
start laying down rules in this world about what is admirable
or right or good where such rules are needed, or maintaining,
as Guardians, any that already exist.'

'Yes, blind is just about what they are.'

'Shall we make them Guardians then? Or shall we prefer the
philosophers, who have learned to know each true reality, and
have no less practical experience, and can rival them in all
departments of human excellence.'

'It would be absurd not to choose the philosophers, if they
are not inferior in all these other respects; for in the vital quality
of knowledge they are clearly superior.'

'Then oughtn't we to show how knowledge can be combined   485 *a*
with these other qualities in the same person?'

'Yes.'

'As we said at the beginning of our discussion, the first thing
is to find out what their natural character is. When we have
agreed about that we shall, I think, be ready to agree that they
can have those other qualities as well, and that they are the
people to put in charge of society.'

'Explain.'

'One trait in the philosopher's character we can assume is his
love of any branch of learning that reveals eternal reality, the   *b*
realm unaffected by the vicissitudes of change and decay.'

'Agreed.'

'He is in love with the whole of that reality, and will not
willingly be deprived even of the most insignificant fragment of
it – just like the lovers and men of ambition we described earlier
on.'[17]

'Yes, you are quite right.'

'Then if the philosopher is to be as we described him, must
he not have a further characteristic?'   *c*

'What?'

'Truthfulness. He will never willingly tolerate an untruth, but
will hate it, just as he loves truth.'

'That seems likely enough.'

'It's not only likely,' I replied, 'it is an absolutely necessary

characteristic of the lover that he should be devoted to everything closely connected with the object of his love.'

'True.'

'And is there anything more closely connected with wisdom
than truth?'

'No.'

'So it's hardly possible to combine in the same character a
d love of wisdom and a love of falsehood.'

'Quite impossible.'

'So the man who has a real love of learning will yearn for the
whole truth from his earliest years.'

'Certainly.'

'But we know that if a man's desires set strongly in one
direction, they are correspondingly less strong in other directions, like a stream whose water has been diverted into another
channel.'

'Surely.'

'So when the current of a man's desires flows towards the
acquisition of knowledge and similar activities, his pleasure will
e be in things purely of the mind, and physical pleasures will pass
him by – that is if he is a genuine philosopher and not a sham.'

'That most certainly follows.'

'And he will be self-controlled and not grasping about money.
Other people are more likely to worry about the things which
make men so eager to get and spend money.'

486 *a*   'True.'

'And of course, when you are distinguishing the philosophic
from the unphilosophic character there is something else you
must look for.'

'What is that?'

'You must see it has no touch of meanness; pettiness of mind
is quite incompatible with the constant attempt to grasp things
divine or human as a whole and in their entirety.'

'Very true.'

'And if a man has greatness of mind and the breadth of vision
to contemplate all time and all reality, can he regard human life
as a thing of any great consequence?'

'No, he cannot.'

'So he won't think death anything to be afraid of.'   b

'No.'

'And so mean and cowardly natures can't really have any dealings with true philosophy.'

'No, they can't.'

'And a well-balanced man, who is neither mean nor ungenerous nor boastful nor cowardly, can hardly be difficult to deal with or unjust.'

'Hardly.'

'So when you are looking for your philosophic character you will look to see whether it has been, from its early days, just and civilized or uncooperative and savage.'

'Certainly.'   c

'There's something else you won't overlook.'

'What is that?'

'Whether it learns easily or not. You can't expect anyone to have much love for anything which he does with pain and difficulty and little success.'

'No, you can't.'

'And can a man avoid being entirely without knowledge if he can't retain anything he's learnt, and has no memory at all?'

'How can he?'

'So he will labour in vain and in the end be driven to hate himself and the whole business of learning.'

'Inevitably.'

'So we can't include a forgetful man as one qualified for   d
philosophy; we must demand a good memory.'

'Yes, certainly.'

'Again, a nature that has no taste or style will tend inevitably to lack a sense of proportion.'

'It will.'

'And isn't a sense of proportion nearly related to truth?'

'Yes, it is.'

'So we want, in addition to everything else, a mind with a grace and sense of proportion that will naturally and easily lead it on to see the form[18] of each reality.'

'I agree.'

'Do you agree, then, that we have now been through a list of   e

characteristics, which all go together, and which the mind must
have if it is to have a sufficiently full apprehension of reality?'

'Yes, it must certainly have them all.'

'Can you, then, possibly find fault with an occupation for the
proper pursuit of which a man must combine in his nature good
memory, readiness to learn, breadth of vision and grace, and be
a friend of truth, justice, courage, and self-control?'

'Momus[19] himself could find no fault there.'

'Grant, then, education and maturity to round them off, and
aren't they the only people to whom you would entrust your
state?'

3. The Prejudice Against Philosophy and the Corruption of the Philosophic Nature in Contemporary Society

*Adeimantus objects that however well all this sounds in theory,
in practice philosophers are either useless or dangerous. Socrates
replies that the better type of philosopher is useless because
contemporary democratic society has no use for him, and so he
has no alternative but to stand aside from the corruption of
political life; and that the philosophic character is only dangerous when corrupted. Besides, there are plenty of charlatans who
will take the place of the true philosopher, and will bring out
the worst in the public they flatter.*

*Two things should be remembered in this section. First,
Plato's distrust of the working of democracy as he had seen it
at Athens; there are few more vivid condemnations of the ways
of democratic politicians than the similes of the sea-captain
(488a–e) and of the 'large and powerful animal' (493b). Today
we should also remember the operations of the 'mass media'.
Second, his dislike of the educational tradition represented by
the contemporary school of Isocrates. Isocrates continued the
tradition, started by the Sophists, of a general education centred
upon rhetoric, the art of public speaking and self-expression.
Plato, who, it should be remembered, also regarded his Academy
as a school for statesmen, insisted on a more rigorous intellectual*

discipline of the kind to be outlined in Book VII. Isocrates
thought Plato unrealistic, Plato thought Isocrates superficial.

Here Adeimantus interrupted. 'Of course no one can deny   b
what you have said, Socrates. But whenever people hear you
talking like this they have an uneasy feeling that, because they're
not very experienced in this procedure of question and answer,
each question in the argument leads them a little further astray,
until at the end of it all their small admissions are added up
and they come a cropper and are shown to have contradicted
themselves; they feel your arguments are like a game of draughts
in which the unskilled player is always in the end hemmed in   c
and left without a move by the expert. Like him they feel
hemmed in and left without anything to say, though they are
not in the least convinced by the conclusion reached in the
moves you have made in the game you play with words. Look
at our present discussion. It might well be said that it was
impossible to contradict you at any point in argument, but yet
that it was perfectly plain that in practice people who study
philosophy too long, and don't treat it simply as part of their
early education and then drop it, become, most of them, very
odd birds, not to say thoroughly vicious; while even those who   d
look the best of them are reduced by this study you praise so
highly to complete uselessness as members of society.'[20]

When he had finished, I asked him whether he thought these
charges untrue, to which he replied, 'I don't know; I'd like to
hear what you think.' I answered that, if he wanted to know,
they seemed to me perfectly true. 'Then how,' he asked, 'can
you possibly say that society's troubles will never cease until it   e
is ruled by philosophers, if you agree that they're useless
members of society?'

'To answer that question,' I said, 'I must give you an illustration.'

'A thing which, of course, you never normally do!'

'There you go,' I said, 'pulling my leg when you've landed   488 a
me with such a difficult point to prove. But you listen to my
illustration, and see just how greedy I am for comparisons. For

there's really no single thing one can use to illustrate the plight of the better type of philosopher in contemporary society; one must draw on several sources for one's illustrations in defence of him, like a painter combining two or more animals into a goat-stag or similar monster.

'Suppose the following to be the state of affairs on board a ship or ships. The captain[21] is larger and stronger than any of
b the crew, but a bit deaf and short-sighted, and similarly limited in seamanship. The crew are all quarrelling with each other about how to navigate the ship, each thinking he ought to be at the helm; they have never learned the art[22] of navigation and cannot say that anyone ever taught it them, or that they spent any time studying it; indeed they say it can't be taught and are
c ready to murder anyone who says it can. They spend all their time milling round the captain and doing all they can to get him to give them the helm. If one faction is more successful than another, their rivals may kill them and throw them overboard, lay out the honest captain with drugs or drink or in some other way, take control of the ship, help themselves to what's on board, and turn the voyage into the sort of drunken pleasure-
d cruise you would expect. Finally, they reserve their admiration for the man who knows how to lend a hand in controlling the captain by force or fraud; they praise his seamanship and navigation and knowledge of the sea and condemn everyone else as useless. They have no idea that the true navigator must study the seasons of the year, the sky, the stars, the winds and
e all the other subjects appropriate to his profession if he is to be really fit to control a ship; and they think that it's quite imposs-ible to acquire the professional skill needed for such control (whether or not they want it exercised) and that there's no such thing as an art of navigation. With all this going on aboard aren't the sailors on any such ship bound to regard the true
489 a navigator as a word-spinner and a star-gazer, of no use to them at all?'

'Yes, they are,' Adeimantus agreed.

'I think you probably understand, without any explanation, that my illustration is intended to show the present attitude of society towards the true philosopher.'

'Yes, I understand.'

'Then you must tell it to anyone who is surprised that society does not value its philosophers, and try first to convince him that it would be far more surprising if it did.'   *b*

'I will,' he said.

'And tell him it's quite true that the best of the philosophers are of no use to their fellows; but that he should blame, not the philosophers, but those who fail to make use of them. For it is not natural for the master to request the crew to be ruled by him or for the wise to wait on the rich (the author of that epigram was wrong[23]); the true and natural order is for the sick man, whether rich or poor, to wait on the doctor, and for those   *c* in need of direction to wait on him who can give it, if he's really any use, and not for him to beg them to accept direction.[24] And you won't be far wrong if you compare the politicians who at present rule us to the sailors in our illustration, and those whom they call useless visionaries to the true navigators.'

'That is very true.'

'These are the causes and conditions which make it difficult for the best of all pursuits to get a good reputation from men whose practice runs contrary to it. But far the most damaging   *d* reproach to philosophy is brought on it by those who pretend to practise it, and whom your critic has in mind when he says that most people who resort to it are vicious, and the best of them useless – a criticism with which I agreed, did I not?'

'Yes.'

'Well, we have explained the reason for the uselessness of the best of them.'

'Yes, we have.'

'Shall we go on to explain why the majority of them are necessarily corrupted, and show, if we can, that it's not philo-   *e* sophy's fault?'

'Yes, please do.'

'Let's begin our discussion by recalling how we described[25] the character that anyone who is to be a really good man must have. Its first requisite, if you remember, was truth, which he   490 *a* must pursue at all costs on pain of becoming an impostor and being excluded from true philosophy.'

'That was what we said.'

'This alone is a startling paradox in view of common opinion.'

'It certainly is,' he agreed.

'Then shall we not fairly plead in reply that our true lover of
b knowledge naturally strives for reality, and will not rest content
with each set of particulars which opinion takes for reality, but
soars with undimmed and unwearied passion till he grasps the
nature of each thing as it is,[26] with the mental faculty fitted to
do so, that is, with the faculty which is akin to reality, and which
approaches and unites with it, and begets intelligence and truth
as children, and is only released from travail when it has thus
attained knowledge and true life and fulfilment?'

'That is as fair a reply as we can make.'

'Then can such a man love falsehood? Must he not hate it?'
c 'He must.'

'And where truth gives the lead we shan't expect a company
of evils to follow.'

'How could they?'

'But we shall expect a just, sound character and self-discipline
as well.'

'Very true.'

'Then I don't think we need insist on a review of the company
of other qualities the philosophic nature must have. You will
remember we found that they also included courage, greatness
of mind, quickness to learn and a good memory. At that point
d you interrupted to say that, while everyone would be compelled
to agree with what we said, if he turned from the argument and
looked at the people we were talking about, he would say that
he saw that some philosophers were useless and others complete
rogues. In our attempt to find the cause of this reproach we are
now faced with the question, why are most philosophers rogues?
And that is why we have been compelled to bring our definition
of the nature of the true philosopher in again.'

e 'That is so,' he agreed.

'This, then, is the philosophic nature whose deterioration
we must examine; in most cases it is completely ruined, but
sometimes it survives, and then, as you said, men say it's no use,
491 a though quite harmless. After that we must examine the nature

of the characters[27] that imitate it and set out on a way of life for which they are quite unsuited and which is quite beyond them, and by their many mistakes bring philosophy into the universal disrepute you have described.'

'Tell me,' he said, 'about this deterioration.'

'I will try to describe it if I can,' I replied. 'I think everyone will agree that the combination of qualities we have required in the character of our ideal philosopher will occur, men being   b what they are, very seldom.'

'Very seldom indeed.'

'Yet think of the many powerful factors that may cause its deterioration in these rare characters.'

'What are they?'

'Most extraordinary of all is that each one of the qualities we praised in it – courage, self-discipline and the rest – corrupts its possessor and distracts him from philosophy.'

'I'm surprised to hear that.'

'What is more,' I went on, 'what are commonly called the   c good things of life all contribute to ruin and distract him – good looks, wealth, physical strength, powerful social and family connections, and all the rest – you know the type of thing I mean.'

'Yes,' he said. 'But I'd like to know more precisely what you're getting at.'

'Grasp it as a whole,' I replied, 'and it will be clear enough, and you won't think these preliminaries so odd.'

'How do you mean?'

'We know that any seed or growth, plant or animal, depends   d on the right nourishment and climate and soil; and the more robust it is the more the lack of them will hinder its proper growth, as a bad environment is more inimical to the good than to the indifferent.'

'True.'

'So it's reasonable to expect that very high natural quality will come off worse in an unfavourable environment than poor quality.'

'Yes, reasonable enough.'

'Well then, Adeimantus,' I said, 'on this principle, must we   e not say that the most gifted characters become particularly bad if they are badly brought up? Or do you suppose that great wrongs and unmixed wickedness are the product of a feeble nature rather than of a robust nature ruined by its upbringing? Is a weak nature likely to be responsible for anything of consequence, good or bad?

'No; I agree with you,' he said.

'The philosophic nature we have postulated, therefore, if it is properly taught, must in the course of its growth develop every excellence, but if it is sown and grows in unsuitable soil, the 492 *a* very opposite will happen, unless providence intervenes. Or do you share the common view that some of our young men are corrupted by Sophists? Can the influence of individual Sophists really corrupt them to any extent? Isn't it really the public who *b* say this who are themselves Sophists on a grand scale, and give a complete training to young and old, men and women, turning them into just the sort of people they want?'

'When do they do that?' he asked.

'When they crowd into the seats in the assembly or law courts or theatre, or get together in camp or any other popular meeting place, and, with a great deal of noise and a great lack of moderation, shout and clap their approval or disapproval of whatever *c* is proposed or done, till the rocks and the whole place re-echo, and redouble the noise of their boos and applause. Can a young man's heart remain unmoved by all this? How can his individual training stand the strain? Won't he be swamped by the flood of popular praise and blame, and carried away with the stream till he finds himself agreeing with popular ideas of what is admirable or disgraceful, behaving like the crowd and becoming one of them?'

d 'Yes, that's bound to happen,' he agreed.

'And yet we've still said nothing about the most compelling force of all.'

'What?' he asked.

'The punishments – disfranchisement, fines, or death – which these educational experts inflict on those who won't listen to them, imposing sanctions where persuasion has failed.'

'Yes, punish they certainly do.'

'Then what success can private teaching or any individual Sophist have against such pressure?'

'None, I'm afraid,' he said.   e

'None at all,' I agreed, 'and it's sheer folly to make the attempt. To produce a different type of character, educated for excellence on standards different from those held by public opinion, is not, never has been, and never will be possible – in terms, that is, of human possibility, and short of a miracle as they say. For, make   493 a
no mistake, to escape harm and grow up on the right lines in our present society is something that can fairly be attributed to divine providence.'

'I agree,' he said.

'Then I hope you will agree to this too.' When he asked what it was, I went on, 'All those individuals who make their living by teaching, and whom the public call "Sophists" and envy for their skill, in fact teach nothing but the conventional views held and expressed by the mass of the people when they meet; and this they call a science.[28] What I mean is this. Suppose a man was in charge of a large and powerful animal, and made a study   b
of its moods and wants; he would learn when to approach and handle it, when and why it was especially savage or gentle, what the different noises it made meant, and what tone of voice to use to soothe or annoy it. All this he might learn by long experience and familiarity, and then call it a science, and reduce it to a system and set up to teach it. But he would not really know which of the creature's tastes and desires was admirable   c
or shameful, good or bad, right or wrong; he would simply use the terms on the basis of its reactions, calling what pleased it good, what annoyed it bad. He would have no rational account to give of them, but would call the inevitable demands of the animal's nature right and admirable, remaining quite blind to the real nature of and difference between inevitability and goodness, and quite unable to tell anyone else what it was. He would make a queer sort of teacher, wouldn't he?'

'Very queer.'

'But is there really any difference between him and the man who thinks that the knowledge of the passions and pleasures of   d
the mass of the common people is a science, whether he be

painter, musician, or politician? If he keeps such company, and submits his poems or other productions, or his public services, to its judgement, he is going out of his way to make the public his master and to subject himself to the fatal necessity[29] of producing only what it approves. And have you ever heard any serious argument to prove that such productions have any genuine merit?'

e   'No, and I don't expect I shall.'

'Bearing all this in mind, let us recall our earlier distinction between beauty itself and particular beautiful things, and 494 a between what is in itself and the many particulars. Do you think the common man will allow it? Will he ever believe anything of the sort?'

'He certainly won't.'

'So philosophy is impossible among the common people.'

'Quite impossible.'

'And the common people must disapprove of philosophers.'

'Inevitably.'

'So also will all individuals who mix with the crowd and want to be popular with it.'

'That is obvious.'

'What hope can you see in all this that the philosophic nature will remain true to its vocation and persevere to the end? You b will remember that we agreed earlier that it must be quick to learn, have a good memory, and be brave and generous.' He agreed, and I went on, 'With such gifts a man is bound from childhood to take the lead among his fellows, especially if he is as gifted physically as mentally.'

'Yes, that's bound to happen.'

'And his friends and fellow-citizens will want to use him for their own purposes when he grows up.'

'Of course they will.'

c   'They will be very submissive when they ask favours or express their admiration, flattering in anticipation the power that will one day be his.'

'That is the way of the world,' he said.

'Then, in the circumstances, how do you expect him to behave?' I asked. 'Especially if his native country is a great one

and he is himself a man of wealth and family, and well-built
and good-looking into the bargain. Isn't he sure to be filled with
boundless ambition, and think himself capable of running the
affairs of Greece, and of all the world[30] besides; won't he become   *d*
very high and mighty and full of senseless ostentation and inane
pride?'[31]

'Yes, he will.'

'Suppose someone approaches him while he is falling into this
state, and gently tells him the truth – that he's completely lacking
in understanding, and won't acquire it unless he works for it
like a slave; do you think he'll find it easy to listen, beset with
so many evil influences?'

'No, he'll find it very difficult.'

'If, however,' I went on, 'his natural gifts and his natural bent
for reason make him susceptible to its influence, and incline and   *e*
draw him towards philosophy, what reaction must we expect
from his companions, who think they are going to be deprived
of his support and society? There's nothing they won't do or
say to prevent him from being won over, or to hinder his adviser   495 *a*
by private intrigue and public prosecution.'[32]

'That is inevitable.'

'Then how can he possibly be a philosopher?'

'He can't possibly.'

'Do you see, then,' I concluded, 'that we were quite right to
say that the very constituents of the philosophic nature were in
a way responsible, when it is badly brought up, for its fall from
its proper calling, to which riches and all other so-called goods
of the same kind also contribute?'

'Yes,' he agreed, 'we were quite right.'

'These, then, are the many influences that destroy the best
natures – which are rare enough in any case, as we said – and   *b*
spoil them for the highest of all pursuits. And it is men so gifted
who inflict the deepest injuries on communities and individuals,
and indeed, if their inclinations run that way, do them the
greatest good. Small natures never do much good or harm to
either.'

'Very true.'

'So Philosophy is abandoned by those who should be her true

c lovers, who leave her deserted and unwed to pursue a life that
does not really suit them, while she, like an abandoned orphan,
suffers at the hands of second-rate interlopers all the shame and
abuse which you have said her detractors accuse her of, when
they say that half her companions are worthless and the other
half downright wicked.'

'That is what is commonly said.'

'And quite rightly,' I replied. 'For when they see so good a
d piece of territory, with all its titles and dignities, unoccupied, a
whole crowd of squatters gladly sally out from the meaner
trades, at which they have acquired a considerable degree of
skill, and rush into philosophy, like a crowd of criminals taking
refuge in a temple. For philosophy, abused as it is, still retains a
far higher reputation than other occupations, a reputation
which these stunted natures covet, their minds being as cramped
e and crushed by their mechanical lives as their bodies are
deformed by manual trades. This all follows, doesn't it?'

'Yes.'

'They are for all the world like some bald-headed little tinker
who's just got out of prison and come into money, and who has
a bath and dresses himself up in a new suit, like a bridegroom,
and sets off to marry his boss's daughter because her family's
fallen on hard times.'

496 a 'The comparison is fair enough.'

'What sort of children are they likely to produce? A mean and
misbegotten lot, I think.'

'Inevitably.'

'And when men who are unfit for education have intimate
dealings (which they don't deserve) with philosophy, are not
the thoughts and opinions they produce fairly called sophistry,
with nothing legitimate nor any trace of true wisdom among
them?'

'Certainly.'

'So only a very small remnant survives, Adeimantus, of all
b those worthy to have any dealings with philosophy – perhaps
some honest man saved by the circumstance of exile from the
influences that would corrupt his natural loyalty to her, or some
great mind born in a petty state and so despising politics; and

there may be a gifted few who turn to philosophy from other occupations which they rightly despise. I suppose, too, that there are some who are handicapped like our friend Theages[33] who had every other temptation to desert philosophy, but was prevented by bad health from going into public life. My own divine sign,[34] I think, hardly counts, as hardly anyone before me has had it. This small company, then, when they have tasted the happiness of philosophy and seen the frenzy of the masses, understand that political life has virtually nothing sound about it, and that they'll find no ally to save them in the fight for justice; and if they're not prepared to join others in their wickedness, and yet are unable to fight the general savagery single-handed, they are likely to perish like a man thrown among wild beasts, without profit to themselves or others, before they can do any good to their friends or society. When they reckon all this up, they live quietly and keep to themselves, like a man who stands under the shelter of a wall during a driving storm of dust and hail; they see the rest of the world full of wrongdoing, and are content to keep themselves unspotted from wickedness and wrong in this life, and finally leave it with cheerful composure and good hope.'

'If they do that it will be no small achievement,' he said.

'Yes, but how much greater it might be in a suitable society, where they could develop more fully, to their own salvation and that of the community.'

4. The Philosopher Ruler Not Impossible

There is nothing inherently impossible in the idea of a philosopher ruler. Philosophers might gain political power, or an existing ruler might become a philosopher; and the public would soon be persuaded of the benefits of philosophic rule. But the philosophic training must be the right one, and the changes in society would have to be radical.

Plato's own attempts to carry his ideal into the world of practical politics on the lines suggested in this section have been referred to in the Introduction, pp. xviii ff.

'But I think we've said enough about the reasons for the bad reputation of philosophy and how unjust it is – or have you anything to add?'

'No, I've nothing more; but I'd like to know which of existing

b societies you think suits it.'

'There isn't one,' I replied; 'which is just my complaint. There's no existing form of society good enough for the philosophic nature, with the result that it gets warped and altered, like a foreign seed sown in alien soil under whose influence it commonly degenerates into the local growth. In exactly the same way the philosophic type loses its true powers, and falls into habits alien to it. If only it could find a social structure whose excellence matched its own, then its truly divine quality

c would appear clearly, and all other characters and ways of life stand revealed as merely human. But I know you're going to ask what this social structure is.'

'You're wrong,' he said, 'I'm not. I was going to ask whether it was the state whose foundation we have been describing.'

'In all other respects, it is,' I replied; 'but we did say at the time[35] that there must be in our state some authority with the

d same idea of how society should be constituted as that you embodied in your legislation.'

'Yes, that was what we said,' he agreed.

'But we did not make the point clear enough. I was afraid of what your criticisms had already shown to be a long and difficult demonstration; and the hardest part of it is still to come.'

'And what is that?'

'How a state can handle philosophy without destroying itself. All great undertakings are risky, and, as they say, what is worth while is always difficult.'

e 'None the less,' he said, 'we must clear the point up and so complete our demonstration.'

'It's not the will but the ability that may be lacking,' I rejoined. 'You'll see for yourself how ready I am to try. Watch me now, I'm going to be bold enough to risk saying that the state should tackle philosophy in a way quite opposite to the present.'

'Explain.'

'At present,' I said, 'those who do take it up are quite young,

and study it in the interval before they go on to set up house   498 a
and earn their living; they start on the most difficult part (I mean
abstract argument) and give it up when they've barely touched
it, and are then considered complete philosophers. Later in life,
if they accept an invitation to listen to a philosophic discussion
by others, they think it quite an event, the sort of thing one does
in one's spare time, and by the time they are old any spark they
have in them is extinguished even more finally than Heraclitus'   b
sun[36] – it will never be relit.'

'And what's the right way to approach it?' he asked.

'The exact opposite. When they are young, children should
only tackle the amount of philosophic training their age can
stand; while they are growing to maturity they should devote a
good deal of attention to their bodies, if they are to find them a
useful equipment for philosophy. When they are older and their
minds begin to mature, their mental training can be intensified.
Finally, when their strength begins to fail, and they are no longer   c
fit for political or military service, they can be given their head,
and devote all their main energies to philosophy – that is if their
life is to be a happy one and their final destiny after death to
match their life on earth.'

'You certainly speak boldly enough, Socrates,' said Adeimantus; 'but I think that the majority of your audience will be
all the bolder to contradict you, and remain quite unconvinced,
not least Thrasymachus.'

'Now don't start a quarrel between me and Thrasymachus,
when we've just become friends – not that we were ever really
enemies. I shan't give up trying till we have convinced him and   d
the rest of them, or at any rate done something to prepare them
for a future incarnation when they will meet these arguments
again.'

'That's rather a long time ahead.'

'Not so long compared with the whole of time. But there's no
reason to be surprised if we can't convince the majority of
people. They have never seen our words come true. They are
used to carefully matched phrases,[37] not the kind of spontaneous   e
argument we are having now; and as to a man who will live up
to our ideal of excellence and do his best to match it both in

word and deed, and who rules a state as good as himself – that,
499 a surely, is a thing of which they've never seen a single instance.'

'Never indeed.'

'Nor have they heard enough free and fair discussion, which
strains every nerve to discover the truth out of sheer desire for
knowledge, and gives a wide berth to subtle tricks of argument
whose only object is to make an effect or contest a point,
whether in law-court or lecture-room.'

'No, they've not,' he agreed.

'It was for these reasons and with all this in view,' I said, 'that
b we felt bound in all honesty, though with some trepidation, to
say that there would never be a perfect state or society or
individual until some chance compelled this minority of uncor-
rupted philosophers, now called useless, to take a hand in politics, willy-nilly, and compelled society to listen to them; or else
until providence inspired some of our present rulers and kings,
or their sons, with a genuine love of true philosophy. There is
c no reason to suppose that either or both of these things is
impossible; if there were, I think you will agree that there would
be some justification for laughing at us for day-dreaming.'

'Yes, there would.'

'We are therefore ready to maintain that, whether it be in the
infinity of past time, or in the future, or even at the present in
some foreign[38] country beyond our horizons, whenever men
skilled in philosophy are somehow forced to take part in politics,
d then the society we have described either exists or existed or
will exist, and the spirit of philosophy herself gain control. No
impossibility is involved. What we have described is admittedly
difficult, but it is not impossible.'

'I agree with you.'

'But you don't expect most people to do so?'

'Probably not.'

'You know, my dear Adeimantus,' I rejoined, 'you mustn't
e make accusations like that against the common run of men.
They'll change their minds if instead of bullying them you are
gentle with them, and try to remove their prejudice against
500 a learning and show them what you mean by philosophers, defining their character and habits in the terms we used just now and

showing that you don't mean what they think you mean. Or do
you think that people who are really amiable and good-tempered
will show spite or anger if you don't show it yourself? Let me say
at once that I don't think this sort of perversity is characteristic of
the majority of men, but only of comparatively few.'

'And of course I agree with you.'

'Do you agree too that the popular dislike of philosophy is   *b*
due to that disorderly gang of gate-crashers, their mutual abuse
and jealousy, and their unphilosophic preoccupation with personalities?'

'Very much so.'

'Because the true philosopher, as you know, Adeimantus,
whose mind is on higher realities, has no time to look at the
affairs of men, or to take part in their quarrels with all the   *c*
jealousy and bitterness they involve. His eyes are turned to
contemplate fixed and immutable realities, a realm where there
is no injustice done or suffered, but all is reason and order, and
which is the model which he imitates and to which he assimilates
himself as far as he can. For is there any way to stop a man
assimilating himself to anything with which he enjoys dealing?'

'No.'

'So the philosopher whose dealings are with the divine order
himself acquires the characteristics of order and divinity so far   *d*
as a man may; though as always he will have his detractors.'

'That is all very true.'

'Then if the philosopher is compelled to try to introduce the
standards which he has seen there, and weave them not into
himself only, but into the habits of men both in their private
and public lives, will he lack the skill to produce self-discipline
and justice and all the other ordinary virtues?'

'Certainly not.'

'And if the public discover that we are telling the truth about
philosophers, will they still be angry with them and disbelieve   *e*
us when we say that no state can find happiness unless the artists
drawing it use a divine pattern?'

'If they do make the discovery, they will stop being angry.
But what sort of drawing do you mean?'   501 *a*

'The first thing our artists must do,' I replied, ' – and it's not easy – is to wipe the slate of human society and human habits clean. For our philosophic artists differ at once from all others in being unwilling to start work on an individual or a city, or draw out laws, until they are given, or have made themselves, a clean canvas.'

'They are quite right.'

'After that the first step will be to sketch in the outline of the social system.'

'Yes, and then?'

b   'Our artist will, I suppose, as he works, look frequently in both directions, that is, at justice and beauty and self-discipline and the like in their true nature,[39] and again at the copy of them he is trying to make in human beings, mixing and blending traits to give the colour of manhood, and judging by that quality in men that Homer too called godly and godlike.'

'Quite right.'

'He will sometimes delete and draw again, of course, but will go on till he has made human nature as acceptable to God as

c   may be.'

'It should be a very beautiful picture.'

'Do you think,' I asked, 'we are beginning to persuade the would-be attackers of whose assault you warned us[40] of the skill of that artist in social constitutions[41] whose praises we sang to them, and into whose hands we were going to put our states, which made them so angry? Will they listen to us less impatiently now?'

'Certainly, if they have any sense.'

d   'What objections have they left to bring? Can they say that the philosopher does not love reality and truth?'

'That would be quite absurd.'

'Can they deny that the character we have described is at home with the best?'[42]

'No.'

'Or that such a character, given suitable scope, will make the perfectly good philosopher, if any will? Will they prefer the other lot whom we excluded?'

e   'Certainly not.'

'Will they still be angry when we say that until society is

controlled by philosophers there will be no end to the troubles of states or their citizens, and no realization in practice of the institutions[43] we have described in theory?'

'Less angry than they were perhaps.'

'Then do you mind if we go further and say that they are altogether reconciled and won over? That should shame them into agreement if anything will.'

502 a

'Very well then.'

'Then let us assume that we have convinced them so far,' I said. 'Do you think that any of them will object that kings' or rulers' sons cannot possibly have the philosophic character?'

'No; no one would say that.'

'And will anyone be able to argue that anyone so born must inevitably be corrupted? We admit that it is difficult to avoid corruption; but will anyone object that not a single individual could avoid it in the whole of time?'

b

'Hardly.'

'But one is enough for our purpose,' I said; 'if society obeys him, he can set all our doubts at rest.'

'He can.'

'Because once he has power and institutes all the laws and customs we have described, there's no impossibility in supposing that the citizens would be ready to carry them out.'

'None at all.'

'And would it be an impossible miracle if others agreed with our opinion?'

c

'I think not.'

'We have, then, already shown adequately enough in our discussion that our proposals, if practicable, are the best that can be devised.'

'Yes, we have.'

'The conclusion seems to be that our proposed legislation, if put into effect, would be the ideal, and that to put it into effect, though difficult, would not be impossible.'

'That is our conclusion.'

5. The Good as Ultimate Object of Knowledge

Plato proceeds to the education of the philosopher, with which the rest of this Part and the whole of the next Part are concerned.

1. *He begins with a reminder of the qualities of character which the philosopher must have, and goes on to emphasize that those qualities must be based on knowledge, ultimately on knowledge of the good, which for him means, as this passage makes clear, the form of the good. After dismissing briefly the views of those who believe the good is pleasure or knowledge, Socrates refuses to give a direct statement of his own view of it, and instead offers to describe it in a simile.*

'Well, then, that part of our job is done – and it's not been easy; we must now go on to the next, and ask about the studies and pursuits which will produce these saviours of our society. *d* What are they to learn and at what age are they to learn it?'

'Yes, that's our next question.'

'I didn't really gain anything,' I said, 'by being clever and putting off the difficulties about the possession of women, the production of children and the establishment of Rulers till later. I knew that my true society would give offence and be difficult to realize; but I have had to describe it all the same. I've dealt with the business about women and children, and now I've got *503 a* to start again on the Rulers. You will remember that we said they must love their country, and be tested both in pleasure and pain, to ensure that their loyalty remained unshaken by pain or fear or any other vicissitude; those who failed the test were to be rejected, but those who emerged unscathed, like gold tried in the fire, were to be established as rulers and given honours and rewards both in life and after death.[44] This is roughly what we *b* said, but we were afraid of stirring up the problems we are now facing, and our argument evaded the issue and tried to get by without being seen.'

'Yes, I remember,' he said.

'You know, I hesitated before to say the rash things I've said,'

I replied; 'but now let me be brave and say that our Guardians, in the fullest sense, must be philosophers.'

'So be it.'

'Think how few of them there are likely to be. The elements in the character which we said[45] they must have don't usually combine into a whole, but are normally found separately.'

'What do you mean?'   *c*

'Readiness to learn and remember, quickness and keenness of mind and the qualities that go with them, and enterprise and breadth of vision, aren't usually combined with readiness to live an orderly, quiet and steady life; their keenness makes such temperaments very unpredictable and quite devoid of steadiness.'

'True.'

'And again, steady, consistent characters on whom you can rely, and who are unmoved by fear in war, are equally unmoved   *d* by instruction. Their immobility amounts indeed to numbness and, faced with anything that demands intellectual effort, they yawn and sink into slumber.'

'That's all quite true.'

'But we demand a full and fair share of both sets of qualities from anyone who is to be given the highest form of education and any share of office or authority.'

'And rightly.'

'So the character we want will be a rare occurrence.'

'It will.'

'And we must not only test it in the pains and fears and   *e* pleasures we have already described, but also try it out in a series of intellectual studies which we omitted before, to see if it has the endurance to pursue the highest forms of knowledge,   504 *a* without flinching as others flinch in physical trials.'

'A fair test; but what,' he asked, 'are these highest forms of knowledge?'

'You remember,' I answered, 'that we distinguished[46] three elements in the mind, and then went on to deal with justice, self-control, courage and wisdom.'

'If I didn't remember that,' he said, 'I shouldn't have any claim to hear the rest of the argument.'

'Then do you remember what we said just before we dealt with these subjects?'[47]

'What?'

b   'We said that a really clear view of them could only be got by making a detour for the purpose, though we could give some indication on the basis of our earlier argument. You said that was good enough, and so our subsequent description fell short, in my view, of real precision; whether it was precise enough for you, is for you to say.'

'I thought you gave us fair measure, and so, I think, did the others.'

c   'My dear Adeimantus, in matters like this nothing is fair measure that falls short of the truth in any respect,' I replied. 'You can't use the imperfect as a measure of anything – though people are sometimes content with it, and don't want to look further.'

'Yes, but it's usually because they're too lazy.'

'A most undesirable quality in a Guardian of state and laws.'

'A fair comment.'

'Then he must take the longer way round,' I said, 'and must
d   work as hard at his intellectual training as at his physical; otherwise, as we've just said, he will never finally reach the highest form of knowledge, which should be peculiarly his own.'

'The highest?' he asked. 'But is there anything higher than justice and the other qualities we discussed?'

'There is,' I said. 'And we ought not to be content with the sight of a mere sketch even of these qualities, or fail to complete
e   the picture in detail. For it would be absurd, would it not, to devote all our energies to securing the greatest possible precision and clarity in matters of little consequence, and not to demand the highest precision in the most important things of all?'

'Quite absurd,' he agreed. 'But you can hardly expect to escape cross-questioning about what you call the highest form of knowledge and its object.'

'I don't expect to escape from you,' I returned; 'ask your questions. Though you've heard about it often enough, and
505 a   either don't understand for the moment, or else are deliberately giving me trouble by your persistence – I suspect it's the latter,

because you have certainly often been told that the highest form
of knowledge is knowledge of the form of the good, from which
things that are just and so on derive[48] their usefulness and value.
You know pretty well that that's what I have to say, and that
I'm going to add that our knowledge of it is inadequate, and
that if we are ignorant of it the rest of our knowledge, however
perfect, can be of no benefit to us, just as it's no use possessing
anything if you can't get any good out of it. Or do you think   *b*
there's any point in possessing anything if it's no good? Is there
any point in having all other forms of knowledge without that
of the good, and so lacking knowledge about what is good and
valuable?'[49]

'I certainly don't think there is.'

'And you know of course that most ordinary people think
that pleasure is the good, while the more sophisticated think it
is knowledge.'

'Yes.'

'But those who hold this latter view can't tell us what knowledge they mean, but are compelled in the end to say they mean
knowledge of the good.'

'Which is quite absurd.'

'An absurdity they can't avoid, if, after criticizing us for *not*
knowing the good, they then turn round and talk to us as if we   *c*
did know it; for they say it is "knowledge of the good" as if we
understood what they meant when they utter the word "good".'

'That's perfectly true.'

'Then what about those who define good as pleasure? Is their
confusion any less? Aren't they compelled to admit that there
are bad pleasures?'

'Of course they are.'

'And they thus find themselves admitting that the same things
are both good and bad, don't they?'

'Yes.'   *d*

'So it's obvious that the subject is highly controversial.'

'It is indeed.'

'Well, then, isn't it obvious too that when it's a matter of
justice or value many people prefer the appearance to the reality,
whether it's a matter of possession and action or of reputation;

but that no one is satisfied to have something that only *appears* to be good, but wants something that *really* is, and has no use here for appearances?'

'Absolutely true.'

'The good, then, is the end of all endeavour, the object on
e which every heart is set, whose existence it divines, though it finds it difficult to grasp just what it is; and because it can't handle it with the same assurance as other things it misses any value those other things have. Can we possibly agree that the
506 *a* best of our citizens, to whom we are going to entrust everything, should be in the dark about so important a subject?'

'It's the last thing we can admit.'

'At any rate a man will not be a very useful Guardian of what is right and valuable if he does not know in what their goodness consists; and I suspect that until he does no one can know them adequately.'

'Your suspicions are well founded.'

'So our society will be properly regulated only if it is in the
b charge of a Guardian who has this knowledge.'

'That must be so,' he said. 'But what about you, Socrates? Do you think that the good is knowledge or pleasure? Or do you think it's something else?'

'What a man!' I exclaimed. 'It's been obvious for some time that you wouldn't be satisfied with other people's opinions!'

'But I don't think it's right, Socrates,' he protested, 'for you
c to be able to tell us other people's opinions but not your own, when you've given so much time to the subject.'

'Yes, but do you think it's right for a man to talk as if he knows what he does not?'

'He has no right to talk as if he knew; but he should be prepared to say what it is that he thinks.'

'Well,' I said, 'haven't you noticed that opinion without knowledge is always a poor thing? At the best it is blind – isn't anyone who holds a true opinion without understanding like a blind man on the right road?'

'Yes.'

'Then do you want a poor, blind, halting display from me,
d when you can get splendidly clear accounts from other people?'

'Now, for goodness' sake don't give up when you're just at the finish, Socrates,' begged Glaucon. 'We shall be quite satisfied if you give an account of the good similar to that you gave of justice and self-control and the rest.'

'And so shall I too, my dear chap,' I replied, 'but I'm afraid it's beyond me, and if I try I shall only make a fool of myself and be laughed at. So please let us give up asking for the present what the good is in itself; I'm afraid that to reach what I think *e* would be a satisfactory answer is beyond the range of our present inquiry. But I will tell you, if you like, about something which seems to me to be a child of the good, and to resemble it very closely – or would you rather I didn't?'

'Tell us about the child and you can owe us your account of the parent,' he said.

'It's a debt I wish I could pay back to you in full, instead of *507 a* only paying interest[50] on the loan,' I replied. 'But for the present you must accept my description of the child of the good as interest. But take care I don't inadvertently cheat you by forging my account of the interest due.'

'We'll be as careful as we can,' he said. 'Go on.'

2. *The Simile of the Sun. This simile compares the Form of the Good to the Sun, and may be set out in tabular form as follows:*

Visible World	Intelligible World
The Sun	*The Good*
Source of { *growth and light*	*Source of* { *reality and truth,*
which gives	*which gives*
visibility to objects of sense	*intelligibility to objects of thought*
and	*and*
the power of seeing to the eye.	*the power of knowing to the mind.*
The faculty of sight.	*The faculty of knowledge.*

'I must first get your agreement to, and remind you of something we have said earlier in our discussion,[51] and indeed on many other occasions.'

b   'What is it?' he asked.

I replied, 'We say that there are many particular things that are beautiful, and many that are good, and so on, and distinguish between them in our account.'

'Yes, we do.'

'And we go on to speak of beauty-in-itself, and goodness-in-itself, and so on for all the sets of particular things which we have regarded as many; and we proceed to posit by contrast a single form, which is unique, in each case, and call it "what really is" each thing.'[52]

'That is so.'

'And we say that the particulars are objects of sight but not of intelligence, while the forms are the objects of intelligence but not of sight.'

'Certainly.'

c   'And with what part of ourselves do we see what we see?'

'With our sight.'

'And we hear with our hearing, and so on with the other senses and their objects.'

'Of course.'

'Then have you noticed,' I asked, 'how extremely lavish the designer of our senses was when he gave us the faculty of sight and made objects visible?'

'I can't say I have.'

'Then look. Do hearing and sound need something of another kind in addition to themselves to enable the ear to hear and the

d sound to be heard – some third element without which the one cannot hear or the other be heard?'

'No.'

'And the same is true of most, I might say all, the other senses. Or can you think of any that needs anything of the kind?'

'No, I can't.'

'But haven't you noticed that sight and the visible do need one?'

'How?'

'If the eyes have the power of sight, and its possessor tries to use this power, and if objects have colour, yet you know that he

e will see nothing and the colours will remain invisible unless a third element is present which is specifically and naturally adapted for the purpose.'

'What is that?' he asked.

'What you call light,' I answered.

'True.'

'Then the sense of sight and the visibility of objects are yoked by a yoke a long way more precious than any other – that is, if 508 a light is a precious thing.'

'Which it most certainly is.'

'Which, then, of the heavenly bodies[53] do you regard as responsible for this? Whose light would you say it is that makes our eyes see and objects be seen most perfectly?'

'I should say the same as you or anyone else; you mean the sun, of course.'

'Then is sight related to its divine source as follows?'

'How?'

'The sun is not identical with sight, nor with what we call the eye in which sight resides.'

'No.'   b

'Yet of all sense-organs the eye is the most sunlike.'

'Much the most.'

'So the eye's power of sight is a kind of infusion dispensed to it by the sun.'

'Yes.'

'Then, moreover, though the sun is not itself sight, it is the cause of sight and is seen by the sight it causes.'

'That is so.'

'Well, that is what I called the child of the good,' I said. 'The good has begotten it in its own likeness, and it bears the same relation to sight and visible objects in the visible realm that the good bears to intelligence and intelligible objects in the intelligible realm.'   c

'Will you explain that a bit further?' he asked.

'You know that when we turn our eyes to objects whose colours are no longer illuminated by daylight, but only by moonlight or starlight, they see dimly and appear to be almost blind, as if they had no clear vision.'

'Yes.'

d   'But when we turn them on things on which the sun is shining, then they see clearly, and obviously have vision.'

'Certainly.'

'Apply the analogy to the mind. When the mind's eye is fixed on objects illuminated by truth and reality, it understands and knows them, and its possession of intelligence is evident; but when it is fixed on the twilight world of change and decay, it can only form opinions, its vision is confused and its opinions shifting, and it seems to lack intelligence.'

'That is true.'

e   'Then what gives the objects of knowledge their truth and the knower's mind the power of knowing is the form[54] of the good. It is the cause of knowledge and truth, and you will be right to think of it as being itself known, and yet as being something other than, and even more splendid[55] than, knowledge and truth, splendid as they are. And just as it was right to think of light
509 *a*   and sight as being like the sun, but wrong to think of them as being the sun itself, so here again it is right to think of knowledge and truth as being like the good, but wrong to think of either of them as being the good, whose position must be ranked still higher.'

'You are making it something of remarkable splendour if it is the source of knowledge and truth, and yet itself more splendid than they are. For I suppose *you* can't mean it to be pleasure?' he asked.

'A monstrous suggestion,' I replied. 'Let us pursue our analogy further.'

b   'Go on.'

'The sun, I think you will agree, not only makes the things we see visible, but causes the processes of generation, growth and nourishment, without itself being such a process.'

'True.'

'The good therefore may be said to be the source not only of the intelligibility of the objects of knowledge, but also of their being and reality; yet it is not itself that reality, but is beyond it, and superior to it in dignity and power.'

c   'It really must be miraculously transcendent,' remarked Glaucon to the general amusement.

'Now, don't blame me,' I protested; 'it was you who made me say what I thought about it.'

'Yes, and please go on. At any rate finish off the analogy with the sun, if you haven't finished it.'

'I've not nearly finished it.'

'Then go on and don't leave anything out?'

'I'm afraid I must leave a lot out,' I said. 'But I'll do my best to get in everything I can in present circumstances.'

'Yes, please do.'

6. The Divided Line

The analogy of the Divided Line is, Plato makes clear, a sequel to the Sun simile, its purpose being to illustrate further the relation between the two orders of reality with which the Sun simile dealt. But it does so from a particular point of view, that of the states of mind (pathēmata: 511d) in which we apprehend these two orders or realms. The purpose of the Line, therefore, is not, primarily, to give a classification of objects. Both of the two states of mind correlated with the intelligible realm deal with the same kind of object (the forms), though each deals with them in a different way; and though in the physical world there is a difference between physical things and their shadows, that difference is used primarily to illustrate degrees of 'truth' or genuineness in what is apprehended – we know very little about a thing if our knowledge is confined to shadows or images of it or, for that matter, to its superficial appearance. The simile may be set out in the form of the table overleaf.

Broadly speaking, the mental states comprised by the four sub-divisions are: (A) Intelligence. Full understanding, culminating in the vision of ultimate truth. This understanding is reached by philosophy, or as Plato often calls it 'dialectic'; a term whose modern associations are quite misleading in interpreting the Republic, *but which, with that caution, remains a convenient translation. (B) Reason. The procedure of mathematics, purely deductive and uncritical of its assumptions. (C) Belief. Commonsense beliefs on matters both moral and physical, which are a fair practical guide to life but have not been fully thought out. (Later, in the* Timaeus, *Plato includes the natural sciences in this sub-section, as they can never reach ultimate truth, being concerned with a changeable world.) (D) Illusion. All the various illusions, 'secondhand impressions and opinions'*[56] *of which the minds of ordinary people are full. In this section 'illusion' merely appears as the perception of shadows and reflections. But the wider interpretation is demanded by the Cave simile, which elaborates in a more graphic form the classification set out in the Line. And it is also clearly implied in Book X (595 below) that all works of poetry and art are to be included in this sub-section.*

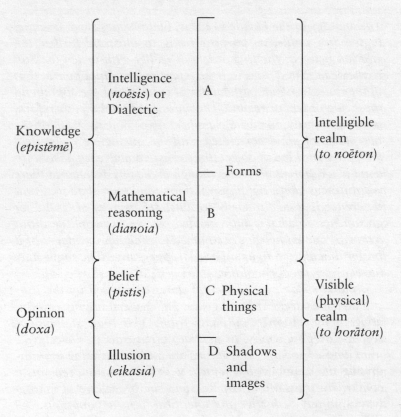

Knowledge (*epistēmē*)	Intelligence (*noēsis*) or Dialectic	A
	Mathematical reasoning (*dianoia*)	Forms — B
Opinion (*doxa*)	Belief (*pistis*)	C Physical things
	Illusion (*eikasia*)	D Shadows and images

Intelligible realm (*to noēton*)

Visible (physical) realm (*to horāton*)

To look forward for a moment, Plato is not entirely consistent in his use of terms (see Part VIII, note 23). In Part VII, section 2.1 ff. the contrast is frequently between doxa and gnosis, another word for knowledge. Noēsis is sometimes used of sub-section A of the Line, but, perhaps because the content of the whole 'region' AB is called noēton, it is also used of intellectual operations more generally. And at one place (534a) epistēmē is used of sub-section A. The content of CD, commonly referred to in the Line as to horāton, the visible, is in this diagram also called the physical world. Though there is an emphasis in the simile on purely visual terms, Plato instances animals, plants and manufactured objects as examples in sub-section C, and for example a donkey eating hay in a barn is not a purely visual object. Besides, it is made quite clear in Part VIII that CD is the world perceived by our senses (aisthēton), the world of material change (genesis). The diagram assumes that both noēsis and dianoia deal with forms and that dianoia has no separate type of object. It is sometimes claimed that Plato implies that there are special mathematical objects in sub-section B; but his language at 510d suggests rather that the mathematicians deal with forms, but in a not fully adequate way. See also Part VIII, note 9.

This brief dogmatic summary can hardly do justice to the problems raised by the Line and its two companion similes and to the controversies which they have occasioned. Some suggestions for further reading will be found in the endmatter (References and Sources, see especially Cross and Woozley, Chs. 9 and 10). But the reader should first study what Plato himself has to say about the way in which the similes are to be interpreted and linked: see especially 517b–d, and note 78, 532a–534b and cf. Appendix I.

'You must suppose, then,' I went on, 'that there are these two powers[57] of which I have spoken, and that one of them is supreme over everything in the intelligible order or region, the other over everything in the visible region – I won't say in the physical universe or you will think I'm playing with words.[58] At any rate you have before your mind these two orders[59] of things, the visible and the intelligible?'

'Yes, I have.'

[509] *d*

'Well, suppose you have a line divided into two unequal parts, and then divide the two parts again in the same ratio,[60] to represent the visible and intelligible orders. This gives you, in terms of comparative clarity and obscurity, in the visible order one sub-section of images (D): by "images" I mean first shadows, then reflections in water and other close-grained, polished surfaces, and all that sort of thing, if you understand me.'

510a

'I understand.'

'Let the other sub-section (C) stand for the objects which are the originals of the images – the animals around us, and every kind of plant and manufactured object.'

'Very good.'

'Would you be prepared to admit that these sections differ in that one is genuine,[61] one not, and that the relation of image to original is the same as that of the realm of opinion to that of knowledge?'

b   'I most certainly would.'

'Then consider next how the intelligible part of the line is to be divided.'

'How?'

'In one sub-section (B) the mind uses the originals of the visible order in their turn as images, and has to base its inquiries on assumptions[62] and proceed from them not to a first principle but to a conclusion: in the other (A) it moves[63] from assumption to a first principle which involves no assumption, without the images used in the other sub-section, but pursuing its inquiry solely by and through forms themselves.'

'I don't quite understand.'

c   'I will try again, and what I have just said will help you to understand. I think you know that students of geometry and calculation and the like begin by assuming there are odd and even numbers, geometrical figures and the three forms of angle, and other kindred items in their respective subjects; these they regard as known, having put them forward as basic assumptions which it is quite unnecessary to explain to themselves or anyone

d   else on the grounds that they are obvious to everyone. Starting from them, they proceed through a series of consistent steps to the conclusion which they set out to find.'

'Yes, I certainly know that.'

'You know too that they make use of and argue about visible figures,[64] though they are not really thinking about them, but about the originals which they resemble; it is *not* about the square or diagonal which they have drawn that they are arguing, but about the square itself or diagonal itself, or whatever the figure may be. The actual figures they draw or model, which themselves cast their shadows and reflections in water – these they treat as images only, the real objects of their investigation being invisible except to the eye of reason.'[65]   511 a

'That is quite true.'

'This type of thing I called intelligible, but said that the mind was forced to use assumptions in investigating it, and did not proceed to a first principle, being unable to depart from and rise above its assumptions; but it used as illustrations the very things (C) which in turn have their images and shadows on the lower level (D), in comparison with which they are themselves respected and valued for their clarity.'

'I understand,' he said. 'You are referring to what happens in   b
geometry and kindred sciences.'[66]

'Then when I speak of the other sub-section of the intelligible part of the line you will understand that I mean that which the very process of argument grasps by the power of dialectic; it treats assumptions not as principles, but as assumptions in the true sense, that is, as starting points and steps in the ascent to something which involves no assumption and is the first principle of everything; when it has grasped that principle it can again descend, by keeping to the consequences that follow from it, to a conclusion. The whole procedure involves nothing in the sensible world, but moves solely through forms to forms, and   c
finishes with forms.'

'I understand,' he said; 'though not fully, because what you describe sounds like a long job. But you want to distinguish that part (A) of the real and intelligible (A + B) which is studied by the science[67] of dialectic as having greater clarity than that (B) studied by what are called "sciences".[68] These sciences treat their assumptions as first principles and, though compelled to use reason[69] and not sense-perception in surveying[70] their *d* subject-matter, because they proceed in their investigations *from* assumptions and not *to* a first principle, they do not, you think, exercise intelligence on it, even though with the aid of a first principle it is intelligible.[71] And I think that you call the habit of mind of geometers and the like reason but not intelligence, meaning by reason something midway between opinion (C + D) and intelligence (A).'

'You have understood me very well,' I said. 'So please take it that there are, corresponding to the four sections of the line,
e these four states of mind; to the top section intelligence, to the second reason, to the third belief, and to the last illusion.[72] And you may arrange them in a scale, and assume that they have degrees of clarity corresponding to the degree of truth possessed by their subject-matter.'

'I understand,' he replied, 'and agree with your proposed arrangement.'

7. The Simile of the Cave

This is a more graphic presentation of the truths presented in the analogy of the Line; in particular, it tells us more about the two states of mind called in the Line analogy Belief and Illusion. We are shown the ascent of the mind from illusion to pure philosophy, and the difficulties which accompany its progress. And the philosopher, when he has achieved the supreme vision, is required to return to the cave and serve his fellows, his very unwillingness to do so being his chief qualification.

As Cornford pointed out, the best way to understand the simile is to replace 'the clumsier apparatus' of the cave by the cinema, though today television is an even better comparison. It is the moral and intellectual condition of the average man from which Plato starts; and though clearly the ordinary man knows the difference between substance and shadow in the physical world, the simile suggests that his moral and intellectual opinions often bear as little relation to the truth as the averagefilm or television programme does to real life.

'I want you to go on to picture the enlightenment or ignorance of our human condition somewhat as follows. Imagine an underground chamber like a cave, with a long entrance open to the daylight and as wide as the cave. In this chamber are men who have been prisoners there since they were children, their legs and necks being so fastened that they can only look straight ahead of them and cannot turn their heads. Some way off, behind and higher up, a fire is burning, and between the fire and the prisoners and above them runs a road, in front of which a curtain-wall has been built, like the screen at puppet shows between the operators and their audience, above which they show their puppets.'

'I see.'

'Imagine further that there are men carrying all sorts of gear along behind the curtain-wall, projecting above it and including figures of men and animals made of wood and stone and all sorts of other materials, and that some of these men, as you would expect, are talking and some not.'

'An odd picture and an odd sort of prisoner.'

'They are drawn from life,'[73] I replied. 'For, tell me, do you think our prisoners could see anything of themselves or their fellows except the shadows thrown by the fire on the wall of the cave opposite them?'

'How could they see anything else if they were prevented from moving their heads all their lives?'

'And would they see anything more of the objects carried along the road?'

'Of course not.'

'Then if they were able to talk to each other, would they not assume that the shadows they saw were the real things?'

'Inevitably.'

'And if the wall of their prison opposite them reflected sound, don't you think that they would suppose, whenever one of the passers-by on the road spoke, that the voice belonged to the shadow passing before them?'

'They would be bound to think so.'

'And so in every way they would believe that the shadows of the objects we mentioned were the whole truth.'[74]

'Yes, inevitably.'

'Then think what would naturally happen to them if they were released from their bonds and cured of their delusions. Suppose one of them were let loose, and suddenly compelled to stand up and turn his head and look and walk towards the fire;

d all these actions would be painful and he would be too dazzled to see properly the objects of which he used to see the shadows. What do you think he would say if he was told that what he used to see was so much empty nonsense and that he was now nearer reality and seeing more correctly, because he was turned towards objects that were more real, and if on top of that he were compelled to say what each of the passing objects was when it was pointed out to him? Don't you think he would be at a loss, and think that what he used to see was far truer[75] than the objects now being pointed out to him?'

'Yes, far truer.'

e 'And if he were made to look directly at the light of the fire, it would hurt his eyes and he would turn back and retreat to the things which he could see properly, which he would think really clearer than the things being shown him.'

'Yes.'

'And if,' I went on, 'he were forcibly dragged up the steep and rugged ascent and not let go till he had been dragged out into

516*a* the sunlight, the process would be a painful one, to which he would much object, and when he emerged into the light his eyes would be so dazzled by the glare of it that he wouldn't be able to see a single one of the things he was now told were real.'[76]

'Certainly not at first,' he agreed.

'Because, of course, he would need to grow accustomed to the light before he could see things in the upper world outside the cave. First he would find it easiest to look at shadows, next at the reflections of men and other objects in water, and later on at the objects themselves. After that he would find it easier to observe the heavenly bodies and the sky itself at night, and

b to look at the light of the moon and stars rather than at the sun and its light by day.'

'Of course.'

'The thing he would be able to do last would be to look

directly at the sun itself, and gaze at it without using reflections in water or any other medium, but as it is in itself.'

'That must come last.'

'Later on he would come to the conclusion that it is the sun that produces the changing seasons and years and controls everything in the visible world, and is in a sense responsible for everything that he and his fellow-prisoners used to see.'   *c*

'That is the conclusion which he would obviously reach.'

'And when he thought of his first home and what passed for wisdom there, and of his fellow-prisoners, don't you think he would congratulate himself on his good fortune and be sorry for them?'

'Very much so.'

'There was probably a certain amount of honour and glory to be won among the prisoners, and prizes for keensightedness for those best able to remember the order of sequence among the passing shadows and so be best able to divine their future   *d*
appearances. Will our released prisoner hanker after these prizes or envy this power or honour? Won't he be more likely to feel, as Homer says, that he would far rather be "a serf in the house of some landless man",[77] or indeed anything else in the world, than hold the opinions and live the life that they do?'

'Yes,' he replied, 'he would prefer anything to a life like   *e*
theirs.'

'Then what do you think would happen,' I asked, 'if he went back to sit in his old seat in the cave? Wouldn't his eyes be blinded by the darkness, because he had come in suddenly out of the sunlight?'

'Certainly.'

'And if he had to discriminate between the shadows, in compe-
tition with the other prisoners, while he was still blinded and   517 *a*
before his eyes got used to the darkness – a process that would take some time – wouldn't he be likely to make a fool of himself? And they would say that his visit to the upper world had ruined his sight, and that the ascent was not worth even attempting. And if anyone tried to release them and lead them up, they would kill him if they could lay hands on him.'

'They certainly would.'

'Now, my dear Glaucon,' I went on, this simile must be
b connected throughout with what preceded it.[78] The realm
revealed by sight corresponds to the prison, and the light of the
fire in the prison to the power of the sun. And you won't go
wrong if you connect the ascent into the upper world and the
sight of the objects there with the upward progress of the mind
into the intelligible region. That at any rate is my interpretation,
which is what you are anxious to hear; the truth of the matter
is, after all, known only to god.[79] But in my opinion, for what it
is worth, the final thing to be perceived in the intelligible region,
c and perceived only with difficulty, is the form of the good; once
seen, it is inferred to be responsible for whatever is right and
valuable in anything, producing in the visible region light and
the source of light, and being in the intelligible region itself
controlling source of truth and intelligence. And anyone who is
going to act rationally either in public or private life must have
sight of it.'

'I agree,' he said, 'so far as I am able to understand you.'

'Then you will perhaps also agree with me that it won't
be surprising if those who get so far are unwilling to involve
themselves in human affairs, and if their minds long to remain
d in the realm above. That's what we should expect if our simile
holds good again.'

'Yes, that's to be expected.'

'Nor will you think it strange that anyone who descends from
contemplation of the divine to human life and its ills should
blunder and make a fool of himself, if, while still blinded and
unaccustomed to the surrounding darkness, he's forcibly put on
trial in the law-courts or elsewhere about the shadows of justice
or the figures[80] of which they are shadows, and made to dispute
e about the notions of them held by men who have never seen
justice itself.'

'There's nothing strange in that.'

518 a   'But anyone with any sense,' I said, 'will remember that the
eyes may be unsighted in two ways, by a transition either from
light to darkness or from darkness to light, and will recognize
that the same thing applies to the mind. So when he sees a mind
confused and unable to see clearly he will not laugh without

thinking, but will ask himself whether it has come from a clearer world and is confused by the unaccustomed darkness, or whether it is dazzled by the stronger light of the clearer world *b* to which it has escaped from its previous ignorance. The first condition of life is a reason for congratulation, the second for sympathy, though if one wants to laugh at it one can do so with less absurdity than at the mind that has descended from the daylight of the upper world.'

'You put it very reasonably.'

'If this is true,' I continued, 'we must reject the conception of education professed by those who say that they can put into the mind knowledge that was not there before – rather as if they *c* could put sight into blind eyes.'

'It is a claim that is certainly made,' he said.

'But our argument indicates that the capacity for knowledge is innate in each man's mind, and that the organ by which he learns is like an eye which cannot be turned from darkness to light unless the whole body is turned; in the same way the mind as a whole must be turned away from the world of change until its eye can bear to look straight at reality, and at the brightest of all realities which is what we call the good. Isn't *d* that so?'

'Yes.'

'Then this turning around of the mind itself might be made a subject of professional skill,[81] which would effect the conversion as easily and effectively as possible. It would not be concerned to implant sight, but to ensure that someone who had it already was not either turned in the wrong direction or looking the wrong way.'

'That may well be so.'

'The rest, therefore, of what are commonly called excellences[82] of the mind perhaps resemble those of the body, in that *e* they are not in fact innate, but are implanted by subsequent training and practice; but knowledge, it seems, must surely have a diviner quality, something which never loses its power, but *519a* whose effects are useful and salutary or again useless and harmful according to the direction in which it is turned. Have you never noticed how shrewd is the glance of the type of men commonly called bad but clever? They have small minds, but their sight is sharp and piercing enough in matters that concern them; it's not that their sight is weak, but that they are forced to serve evil, so that the keener their sight the more effective that evil is.'

'That's true.'

'But suppose,' I said, 'that such natures were cut loose, when
b they were still children, from all the dead weights natural to this world of change and fastened on them by sensual indulgences like gluttony, which twist their minds' vision to lower things, and suppose that when so freed they were turned towards the truth, then this same part of these same individuals would have as keen a vision of truth as it has of the objects on which it is at present turned.'

'Very likely.'

'And is it not also likely, and indeed a necessary consequence of what we have said, that society will never be properly governed either by the uneducated, who have no knowledge of the
c truth, or by those who are allowed to spend all their lives in purely intellectual pursuits? The uneducated have no single aim in life to which all their actions, public and private, are to be directed; the intellectuals will take no practical action of their own accord, fancying themselves to be out of this world in some kind of earthly paradise.'

'True.'

'Then our job as lawgivers is to compel the best minds to attain what we have called the highest form of knowledge, and to ascend to the vision of the good as we have described, and
d when they have achieved this and see well enough, prevent them behaving as they are now allowed to.'

'What do you mean by that?'

'Remaining in the upper world, and refusing to return again to the prisoners in the cave below and share their labours and rewards, whether trivial or serious.'

'But surely,' he protested, 'that will not be fair. We shall be compelling them to live a poorer life than they might live.'

e 'The object of our legislation,' I reminded him again, 'is not the special welfare of any particular class in our society, but of

the society as a whole;[83] and it uses persuasion or compulsion   520 a
to unite all citizens and make them share together the benefits
which each individually can confer on the community; and its
purpose in fostering this attitude is not to leave everyone to
please himself, but to make each man a link in the unity of the
whole.'

'You are right; I had forgotten,' he said.

'You see, then, Glaucon,' I went on, 'we shan't be unfair to
our philosophers, but shall be quite fair in what we say when
we compel them to have some care and responsibility for others.   b
We shall tell them that philosophers born in other states can
reasonably refuse to take part in the hard work of politics; for
society produces them quite involuntarily and unintentionally,
and it is only just that anything that grows up on its own should
feel it has nothing to repay for an upbringing which it owes to
no one. "But," we shall say, "we have bred you both for your
own sake and that of the whole community to act as leaders
and king-bees in a hive; you are better and more fully educated
than the rest and better qualified to combine the practice of
philosophy and politics. You must therefore each descend in   c
turn and live with your fellows in the cave and get used to seeing
in the dark; once you get used to it you will see a thousand times
better than they do and will distinguish the various shadows,
and know what they are shadows of, because you have seen the
truth about things admirable and just and good. And so our
state and yours will be really awake, and not merely dreaming
like most societies today, with their shadow battles and their
struggles for political power, which they treat as some great
prize. The truth is quite different: the state whose prospective   d
rulers come to their duties with least enthusiasm is bound to
have the best and most tranquil government, and the state whose
rulers are eager to rule the worst." "[84]

'I quite agree.'

'Then will our pupils, when they hear what we say, dissent
and refuse to take their share of the hard work of government,
even though spending the greater part of their time together in
the pure air above?'

'They cannot refuse, for we are making a just demand of just   e men. But of course, unlike present rulers, they will approach the business of government as an unavoidable necessity.'

'Yes, of course,' I agreed. 'The truth is that if you want a well-governed state to be possible, you must find for your future rulers some way of life they like better than government; for only then will you have government by the truly rich, those, that is, whose riches consist not of gold, but of the true happiness of a good and rational life. If you get, in public affairs, men whose life is impoverished and destitute of personal satisfactions, but who hope to snatch some compensation for their own inadequacy from a political career, there can never be good government. They start fighting for power, and the consequent internal and domestic conflicts ruin both them and society.'

'True indeed.'

b   'Is there any life except that of true philosophy which looks down on positions of political power?'

'None whatever.'

'But what we need is that the only men to get power should be men who do not love it, otherwise we shall have rivals' quarrels.'

'That is certain.'

'Who else, then, will you compel to undertake the responsibilities of Guardians of our state, if it is not to be those who know most about the principles of good government and who have other rewards and a better life than the politician's?'

'There is no one else.'

PART VIII
EDUCATION OF THE
PHILOSOPHER

Having described the Philosopher Ruler, Plato proceeds to the further education, beyond that described in Part III, necessary to produce him. This further education consists of five mathematical disciplines – arithmetic, plane and solid geometry, astronomy, and harmonics – followed by a training in pure philosophy or 'Dialectic' in Plato's sense. Though some concessions are made to practical utility, the main stress throughout is on the training of the mind, with the vision of the Good as its ultimate objective; and mathematics is to be studied without any immediate practical or scientific aim in view.

As the opening sentences make clear, the education outlined in this Part is to be understood in terms of Sun, Cave, and Line; the point is re-emphasized towards the end of Part VIII, section 3.

1. Preliminary

The type of study required must be one that will provoke the mind to thought.

'Then would you like us to consider how men of this kind are to be produced, and how they are to be led up to the light, like the men in stories who are said to have risen from the underworld to heaven?' [521]c

'I should like it very much.'

'It's not a thing we can settle by spinning for it,'[1] I said. 'What is at issue is the conversion of the mind from a kind of twilight to the true day, that climb up into reality which we shall say is true philosophy.'

'Yes, of course.'

d   'So we must try to find out what sort of studies have this effect.'

'We must.'

'Well, Glaucon,' I asked, 'what should men study if their minds are to be drawn from the world of change to reality? Now it occurs to me that we said our rulers must be trained for war when they were young.'

'We did.'

'Then the subject we're looking for must be relevant in war too.'

'How do you mean?'

'It mustn't be useless to soldiers.'

'Not if we can avoid it.'

'Well, we've already arranged² for their physical training and
e   their education in literature and music.'

'We have.'

'And of these two, physical training is concerned with the world of change and decay, for the body, which it looks after, grows and declines.'

'Yes, clearly.'

522   'So it won't be the study we are looking for.'

'No.'

'Then what about the education in literature and music which we described earlier on?'

'That,' he reminded me, 'was the complement of their physical education. It gave a training by habituation, and used music and rhythm to produce a certain harmony and balance of character and not knowledge; and its literature, whether fictional or factual, had similar effects. There was nothing in it to produce the effect you are seeking.'

b   'Your memory's quite correct,' I said, 'we shan't find what we want there. But where on earth shall we find it, Glaucon? The more practical forms of skill³ don't seem very elevating –'

'Certainly not. But if we exclude them, as well as physical and literary education, what else is there left?'

'Well, if we can't think of anything outside them, we must find some feature they all share.'

'What do you mean?'

'For example, there is one thing that all occupations, practical, intellectual, or scientific, make use of – one of the first things we must all learn.'

'What?'

'Something quite ordinary – to tell the difference between one, two and three; in a word, to count and calculate. Is it not true that every practical or scientific activity must be able to do that?'

'Yes, it must,' he agreed.

'And war as much as any other?'

'Necessarily so.'

'I wonder if you have noticed what a silly sort of general Agamemnon is made to look on the stage when Palamedes claims to have invented number, and so organized the army at Troy and counted the ships and everything else. It implies that nothing had been counted before and that Agamemnon, apparently, did not know how many feet he had, if he couldn't count. What sort of general do you think he made?'

'A pretty odd one,' he said, 'if it's really true.'

'So we shall require that a soldier must learn, as well as other things, how to calculate and count.'

'Yes, of course, if he's to be able to organize an army, indeed to be human at all.'

'I wonder, then,' I asked, 'if you would agree with me about this branch of study?'

'In what way?'

'That it is probably one of the subjects we are looking for, which naturally leads to thought,[4] though no one makes proper use of its great power to draw men to reality.'

'How do you mean?'

'I'll try to explain what I have in mind,' I said, 'and show you how I distinguish in my own mind between things that have the drawing power I mean and things that have not. If you will follow me and tell me where you agree and disagree, we can then see more clearly whether I have the right idea.'

'Explain.'

'Right,' I said. 'You see, there are some perceptions which
_b_ don't call for any further exercise of thought, because sensation
can judge them adequately, but others which demand the exercise of thought because sensation cannot give a trustworthy
result.'

'You obviously mean things seen at a distance, or drawn in
perspective.'

'No, you haven't quite got my meaning,' I replied.

'Then what do you mean?' he asked.

'By perceptions that don't call for thought I mean those that
_c_ don't simultaneously issue in a contrary perception; those that
do call for thought are those that do so issue in the sense that in
them sensation is ambiguous between two contraries, irrespective of distance. But you will understand more clearly if I put it
as follows. Here, we say, are three fingers, the middle, third,
and little one.'

'Yes.'

'And you can assume you've got what I call a close view of
them. But there's a further point I'd like you to consider.'

'What is it?'

'Each of them looks as much a finger as any other, and it
_d_ makes no difference whether it's in the middle or at either end,
whether it's white or black, fat or thin, and so on. There is
nothing here to force the mind of the ordinary man to ask
further questions or to think what a finger is; for at no stage has
sight presented the finger to it as being also the opposite of a
finger.'

'No, it hasn't.'

'So there's nothing in this sort of perception likely to call for
_e_ or stimulate thought.'

'Nothing.'

'But what about the size of the fingers? Can sight distinguish
properly whether they are large or small? Does it matter which
one is in the middle or at the end? And can touch distinguish
thickness and thinness or degrees of hardness and softness?
Aren't all the senses in fact deficient in their perception of such

qualities? Don't they operate as follows – touch, for example, which is concerned with hardness, must also be concerned with softness, and reports to the mind that to its perception the same object is both hard and soft.'   524 *a*

'Yes.'

'Then must not the mind find it difficult in such cases to understand what this sense means by hard, if it says the same thing is soft as well? Or again, what light and heavy mean, if the sense concerned indicates that what is heavy is light and what is light is heavy?'

'Yes; this sort of message puzzles the mind and needs investigation.'   *b*

'It's probably in this sort of case, then,' I said, 'that the mind calls in reasoning⁵ and thought, and tries to investigate whether one object has been reported to it or two.'

'Certainly.'

'And if the answer is two, is not each of the pair a separate entity?'

'Yes.'

'And if each is a separate entity, and between them they make up two, then the mind will perceive two separate entities; for if they weren't separate it wouldn't perceive two but one.'   *c*

'That is correct.'

'But sight, we said, perceives large and small as qualities which are not distinct but run into each other.'

'Yes, so we said.'

'And to clear the matter up thought must adopt the opposite approach and look at large and small as distinct and separate qualities – a reverse process to that of sensation.'

'True.'

'And from that there follows the question, what then *are* large and small?'

'That's perfectly true.'

'And that is how we came to use the terms *the intelligible* and *the visible*.'⁶   *d*

'Correct.'

'This was what I was trying to say just now, when I said that

we are called on to use our reason[7] when our senses receive
opposite impressions, but that when they do not there is nothing
to awaken thought.'

'Yes, I understand now,' he said, 'and agree with you.'

2. The Five Mathematical Studies

*Mathematics has, pre-eminently, the characteristics required in
section 1, and Plato proceeds to list five mathematical disciplines
which the Philosopher Ruler must study.*

I. Arithmetic

'Then in which category do you think the unit and number
fall?'

'I don't know.'

'Well, work it out from what we have said,' I told him. 'If our
perception of the unit, by sight or any other sense, is quite
e unambiguous, then it does not draw the mind towards reality
any more than did our perception of a finger. But if it is always
combined with the perception of its opposite, and seems to
involve plurality as much as unity, then it calls for the exercise
of judgement and forces the mind into a quandary in which it
must stir itself to think, and ask what unity in itself is; and if
that is so, the study of the unit is among those that lead the mind
525 *a* on and turn it to the vision of reality.'

'Well, the perception of unity by sight most certainly has this
characteristic; for we see the same thing both as a unit and as
an unlimited plurality.'

'And if that's true of the unit,' I said, 'it must be true of
number as a whole.'

'It must.'

'And number is the concern of counting and calculation.'

'Of course.'

b 'So both will lead the mind on towards truth.'

'Yes, they are extraordinarily effective for the purpose.'

'And so they should be included among the studies we are

looking for. Soldiers must study them so that they can organize their armies, and philosophers so that they can, as they must, escape from this transient world to reality; otherwise they will never be able to calculate.'[8]

'That is so.'

'And our Guardians are both soldiers and philosophers.'

'Of course.'

'We can, then, properly lay it down that arithmetic shall be a subject for study by those who are to hold positions of responsibility in our state; and we shall ask them not to be amateurish in their approach to it, but to pursue it till they come to understand, by pure thought, the nature of numbers – they aren't concerned with its usefulness for commercial transactions, as if they were merchants or shopkeepers, but for war and for the easier conversion of the soul from the world of becoming to that of reality and truth.'

'Excellent.'

'You know,' I said, 'now that we have mentioned the study of arithmetic, it occurs to me what a subtle and widely useful instrument it is for our purpose, if one studies it for the sake of knowledge and not for commercial ends.'

'How is that?' he asked.

'As we have just said, it draws the mind upwards and forces it to argue about numbers in themselves, and will not be put off by attempts to confine the argument to collections of visible or tangible objects. You must know how the experts in the subject, if one tries to argue that the unit itself is divisible, won't have it, but make you look absurd by multiplying it if you try to divide it, to make sure that their unit is never shown to contain a multiplicity of parts.'

'Yes, that's quite true.'

'What do you think they would say, Glaucon, if one were to say to them, "This is very extraordinary – what are these numbers you are arguing about, whose constituent units are, so you claim, all precisely equal to each other, and at the same time not divisible into parts?"[9] What do you think their answer would be to that?'

'I suppose they would say that the numbers they mean can be

c

d

e

526 a

apprehended by reason,[10] but that there is no other way of handling them.'

'You see therefore,' I pointed out to him, 'that this study looks
b as if it were really necessary to us, since it so obviously compels the mind to use pure thought in order to get at the truth.'

'It certainly does have that effect,' he agreed.

'Another point – have you noticed how those who are naturally good at calculation are nearly always quick at learning anything else, and how the slow-witted, if trained and practised in calculation, always make progress and improve in speed even if they get no other benefit?'

c 'That is true.'

'Yet I suppose there's hardly any form of study which comes harder to those who learn or practise it.'

'That is true.'

'For all these reasons, then, we must retain this subject and use it to train our ablest citizens.'

'I agree.'

II. Plane Geometry

As with arithmetic the emphasis is on intellectual training, not practical usefulness, with the vision of the form of Good as the ultimate objective.

'That's one subject settled then. Next let us see if the one that follows it is of any use to us.'

'Do you mean geometry?' he asked.

'Exactly.'

d 'It's obviously useful in war,' he said. 'If a man knows geometry it will make all the difference to him when it comes to pitching camp or taking up a position, or concentrating on deploying an army, or any other military manoeuvre in battle or on the march.'

'For that sort of purpose,' I replied, 'the amount of geometry or calculation needed is small. What we want to find out is whether the subject is on the whole one which, when taken

further, has the effect of making it easier to see the form of the   *e*
good. And that, we say, is the tendency of everything which
compels the mind to turn to the region of ultimate blessedness
which it must spurn no effort to see.'

'You are right,' he said.

'So it will be useful if, and only if, it compels us to contemplate
reality rather than the realm of change.'

'That's our view.'

'Well, then, no one with even an elementary knowledge of   527 *a*
geometry will dispute that it's a science quite the reverse of what
is implied by the terms its practitioners use.'

'Explain.'

'The terms are quite absurd, but they are hard put to it to
find others. They talk about "squaring" and "applying" and
"adding" and so on, as if they were *doing* something and their
reasoning had a practical end, and the subject were not, in fact,
pursued for the sake of knowledge.'

'Yes, that's very true.'   *b*

'And we must further agree . . .'

'To what?'

'. . . that the objects of that knowledge are eternal and not
liable to change and decay.'

'Yes, there's no question of that: the objects of geometrical
knowledge are eternal.'

'Then it will tend to draw the mind to the truth and direct the
philosophers' reason upwards, instead of downwards, as we
wrongly direct it at present.'

'It is sure to.'

'Then you must be sure to require the citizens of your ideal   *c*
state not to neglect geometry. It has considerable incidental
advantages too.'

'What are they?' he asked.

'Its usefulness for war, which you have already mentioned,' I
replied; 'and there is a certain facility for learning all other
subjects in which we know that those who have studied geometry lead the field.'

'They are miles ahead,' he agreed.

'So shall we make this the second subject our young men must study?'

'Yes.'

III. Solid Geometry

Though work was being done on solid geometry in Plato's day, the subject was still, as he makes clear, relatively undeveloped.

d   'And the third should be astronomy. Or don't you agree?'

'Yes, I certainly agree. A degree of perception in telling the seasons, months and years is useful not only to the farmer and sailor but equally to the soldier.'

'You amuse me,' I said, 'with your obvious fear that the public will disapprove if the subjects you prescribe don't seem useful. But it is in fact no easy matter, but very difficult for people to believe that there is a faculty in the mind of each of us which these studies purify and rekindle after it has been ruined and blinded by other pursuits, though it is more worth preserving than any eye since it is the only organ by which we perceive

e   the truth. Those who agree with us about this will give your proposals unqualified approval, but those who are quite unaware of it will probably think you are talking nonsense, as they won't see what other benefit is to be expected from such studies. Make up your mind which party you are going to reason

528 a   with – or will you ignore both and pursue the argument largely for your own satisfaction, though without grudging anyone else any profit he may get from it?'

'That's what I'll do,' he replied; 'I'll go on with the discussion chiefly for my own satisfaction.'

'Then you must go back a bit,' I said, 'as we made a wrong choice of subject to put next to geometry.'

'How was that?'

'We proceeded straight from plane geometry to solid bodies

b   in motion without considering solid bodies first on their own. The right thing is to proceed from second dimension to third, which brings us, I suppose, to cubes and other three-dimensional figures.'

'That's true enough,' he agreed, 'but the subject is one which doesn't seem to have been explored yet, Socrates.'

'For two reasons,' I replied. 'There is no state which sets any value on it, and so, being difficult, it is not pursued with energy; and the pursuit is not likely to be successful without a director, who is difficult to find and, even if found, is unlikely to be obeyed in the present intolerant mood of those who study the subject. But, under the general direction of a state that sets a *c* value on it, their obedience would be assured, and investigations pressed forward continuously and energetically till the problems were cleared up. Even now, with all the neglect and inadequate treatment it has suffered from the public and from students who do not understand its real uses, the subject is so attractive that it makes progress in spite of all handicaps, and it would not be surprising if a solution of its problems were to appear.'

'Yes, it has very great attractions,' he said. 'But explain more *d* clearly what you said just now. You said geometry dealt with plane surfaces.'

'Yes.'

'Then you first said astronomy came next, but subsequently went back on what you had said.'

'More haste less speed,' I said. 'In my hurry I overlooked solid geometry, which should come next, because it's so absurdly undeveloped, and put astronomy, which is concerned with solids in motion, after plane geometry.' *e*

'Yes, that's what you did,' he agreed.

'Then let us put astronomy fourth, and assume that the neglect of solid geometry would be made good under state encouragement.'

IV. Astronomy

In reading Plato's disparagement of observation here two things should be remembered.

(1) 'Plato's primary purpose here is not to advance physical science; but to train the mind to think abstractly' (Cornford, p. 241). (2) Mathematical astronomy was still only just beginning, and until the astronomer has his mathematical tools he

can make no progress; it was the insistence, in the Academy, on
the essentially mathematical nature of the problems that led to
the rapid progress of astronomy in the two hundred years after
Plato's death. Plato himself later gave a higher place to observa-
tion in the Laws *and* Epinomis; *and it should not be forgotten*
that in the Myth of Er (Part XI, section 3, 616b ff.) and later in
the Timaeus *he did try to account in physical terms for the*
movements of the heavenly bodies.

'That is fair enough,' he said. 'And since you have just been
attacking me for commending astronomy for low motives, let
529 a me approve of it now on your principles; for it must be obvious
to everyone that it, of all subjects, compels the mind to look
upwards and leads it from earth to the heavens.'

'Perhaps I'm an exception,' I said, 'for it isn't obvious to me.'

'Why?'

'I think that, as it's at present handled by those who use it as
an introduction to philosophy, it makes us look down, not up.'

'What do you mean?' he asked.

'I think you've a really high-class idea of the study of "higher
things",' I replied. 'Perhaps you think that anyone who puts his
b head back and gazes at a painted ceiling learns something and
is using his mind and not his eyes. You may be right, and I may
be just simple minded, but I can't believe that the mind is made
to look upwards except by studying the real and the invisible. If
anyone tries to learn anything about the world of sense whether
by gaping upwards or blinking downwards,[11] I don't reckon
c that he really *learns* – there is no *knowledge*[12] to be had of such
things – nor do I reckon his mind is directed upwards, even if
he's lying on his back or floating on the sea.'

'I'm guilty,' he said, 'and deserve to be scolded. But how else
do you mean that astronomy ought to be studied if it's to serve
our purpose?'

'Like this,' I said. 'The stars that decorate the sky, though we
rightly regard them as the finest and most perfect of visible
d things, are far inferior, just because they are visible, to the true
realities; that is, to the true relative velocities, in pure numbers
and perfect figures, of the orbits and what they carry in them,[13]

which are perceptible to reason and thought but not visible to the eye. Do you agree?'

'Yes.'

'Well, then,' I went on, 'we ought to treat the visible splendours of the sky as illustrations to our study of the true realities, just as one might treat a wonderful and carefully drawn design by Daedalus or any other artist or draughtsman. Anyone who knew anything about geometry, and saw such a design, would admire the skill with which it was done, but would think it absurd to study it in the serious hope of learning the truth about proportions such as equal or double.'

'It would be absurd to hope for that,' he agreed.

'Isn't the true astronomer in the same position when he watches the movements of the stars?' I asked. 'He will think that the heavens and heavenly bodies have been put together by their maker as well as such things can be; but he will also think it absurd to suppose that there is an always constant and absolutely invariable relation of day to night, or of day and night to month, or month to year, or, again, of the periods of the other stars to them and to each other. They are all visible and material, and it's absurd to look for exact truth in them.'

'I agree now you put it like that,' he said.

'We shall therefore treat astronomy, like geometry, as setting us problems for solution,' I said, 'and ignore the visible heavens, if we want to make a genuine study of the subject and use it to convert the mind's natural intelligence to a useful purpose.'

'You are demanding a lot more work than astronomy at present involves,' he said.

'We shall make other demands like it, I think, if we are to be any use as lawgivers. But,' I asked, 'can you suggest any other suitable study?'

'Not at the moment.'

V. Harmonics

Which is to be treated on the same principles as Astronomy.

d 'All the same, there are not one but several species of motion,' I said. 'I suppose that an expert could enumerate them all; but even I can distinguish two of them.'

'What are they?'

'The one we've been talking about and its counterpart.'

'What's that?'

'I think we may say that, just as our eyes are made for astronomy, so our ears are made for the movements of harmony, and that the two are, as the Pythagoreans[14] say, and as we should agree, Glaucon, sister sciences. Isn't that so?'

'Yes.'

e 'And as the work involved is considerable we will consult them on the subject, and perhaps on others too. But all through we must maintain the principle we have laid down.'

'Which principle?'

'As we said when dealing with astronomy just now, our pupils must not leave their studies incomplete or stop short of the final
531 *a* objective. They can do this just as much in harmonics as they could in astronomy, by wasting their time on measuring audible concords and notes against each other.'

'Lord, yes, and pretty silly they look,' he said. 'They talk about "intervals" of sound, and listen as carefully as if they were trying to hear a conversation next door. And some say they can distinguish a note between two others, which gives them a minimum unit of measurement, while others maintain that there's no difference between the notes in question. They
b all prefer to use their ears instead of their minds.'

'You mean those people who torment the strings and try to wring the truth out of them by twisting them on pegs. I might continue the metaphor[15] and talk about strokes of the bow, and accusations against the strings and their shameless denials – but I'll drop it, because I'm not thinking so much of these people as
c of the Pythagoreans, who we said would tell us about harmonics. For they do just what the astronomers do; they look for numeri-

cal relationships in audible concords, and never get as far as formulating problems and examining which numerical relations are concordant, which not, and why.'

'But that would be a fearsome job,' he protested.

'A useful one, none the less,' I said, 'when the object is to discover what is valuable and good, though useless if pursued for any other end.'

'That may well be.'

3. Dialectic

The mathematical studies are only the preliminary to dialectic. We are reminded of the Line and Cave (Part VII, sections 6 and 7). Dialectic is the exercise of pure thought, the highest section of the Line; its object is the vision of the good, the last stage in the ascent from the Cave, when the eye can look at the sun itself. Plato does not profess to give here a full account of dialectic (533a), but we learn some important things about it. It is a process of rational argument ('dialectic' means discussion); it is critical of assumptions (such as those of the mathematician), which it 'destroys' and relates to a first principle (533c); it tries to grasp what 'each thing is in itself' (i.e. its form; 533b); it culminates in coherent knowledge (537c) and in an apprehension of the form of the good (532a–b, 534b–c).

'Yes,' I said, 'for it's only if we can pursue all these studies   *d* until we see their common ground and relationship, and can work out how they are akin, that they contribute to our purpose and the trouble we spend on them is not lost.'

'So I should imagine. But it means a great deal of work, Socrates.'

'And you don't suppose it's more than a beginning, do you?' I asked. 'The subjects we've described are only a prelude to the main theme we have to learn. For you don't think that people who are good at them are skilled in dialectic, do you?'   *e*

'Heavens, no, though I have come across a few exceptions.'

'And can they ever acquire any of the knowledge we say they must have if they can't argue logically?'[16]

'No, they can't.'

532 a 'But isn't this just the theme which dialectic takes up? It is of course an intellectual theme, but can be represented in terms of vision, as we said, by the progress of sight from shadows to the real creatures themselves, and then to the stars themselves, and finally to the sun itself. So when one tries to get at what each thing is in itself by the exercise of dialectic, relying on reason without any aid from the senses, and refuses to give up until one

b has grasped by pure thought what the good is in itself, one is at the summit of the intellectual realm,[17] as the man who looked at the sun was of the visual realm.'

'That's perfectly true.'

'And isn't this progress what we call dialectic?'

'Yes.'

'The prisoners in our cave,' I went on, 'were released and turned round from the shadows to the images which cast them and to the fire, and then climbed up into the sunlight; there they

c were still unable to look at animals and plants and at the light of the sun, but could see[18] reflections in water and shadows of things (real things, that is, and not mere images throwing shadows in the light of a fire itself derivative compared with the sun). Well, the whole study of the sciences we have described has the effect of leading the best element in the mind up towards the vision of the best among realities, just as the body's clearest

d organ was led to the sight of the brightest of all things in the material and visible world.'[19]

'I quite agree with all you've said myself,' said Glaucon; 'I think it's difficult to accept completely, but in another way hard to deny. However, as this isn't the only occasion on which we shall hear about it and we may often have to return to it in the future, let us assume your account of it is correct and go on to deal with the main theme itself as thoroughly as we have dealt with the prelude. Tell us what sort of power dialectic has, and

e what forms of it there are and the paths they follow; for these would seem to lead to our destination, where we shall find rest and reach the end of our journey.'

'My dear Glaucon,' I said, 'you won't be able to follow me   533 a
further, not because of any unwillingness on my part, but
because what you'd see would no longer be an image of what
we are talking about but the truth itself, that is, as I see it; one
ought not at this point to claim certainty, though one can claim
that there is something of the kind to see, don't you think?'

'Yes indeed.'

'And should we add it is only the power of dialectic that can
reveal it, and then only to someone experienced in the studies
we have just described? There is no other way, is there?'

'We can claim that with certainty.'

'Well, at any rate no one can deny that it is some further   b
procedure (over and above those we have been describing)
which sets out systematically to determine what each thing
essentially is in itself.[20] Of other skilled activities[21] some are
concerned with human opinions or desires, or with growing or
making things, or devoted to looking after them when they are
grown or made; as for the rest, geometry and the like, though
they have some hold on reality, we can see that they are only   c
dreaming about it; they can never wake and look at it as it is, so
long as they leave the assumptions they use undisturbed and
cannot account for them. For if one's starting point is something
unknown, and one's conclusion and intermediate steps are made
up of unknowns also, how can the resulting consistency ever by
any manner of means become knowledge?'

'It can't possibly.'

'Dialectic, in fact, is the only procedure which proceeds by
the destruction of assumptions to the very first principle,[22] so as   d
to give itself a firm base. When the eye of the mind gets really
bogged down in a morass of ignorance, dialectic gently pulls it
out and leads it up, using the studies we have described to help
it in the process of conversion. These studies we have often,
through force of habit, referred to as branches of *knowledge*,
but we really need another term, to indicate a greater degree of
clarity than opinion but a lesser degree than knowledge – we   e
used the term "reason" earlier on. But I don't think we shall
quarrel about a word – the subject of our inquiry is too important for that.'

'We certainly shan't.'

'So we shall be content to use any term provided it conveys the degree of clarity of a particular state of mind.'

'Yes.'

534 a 'Then let us be content with the terms[23] we used earlier on for the four divisions of our line – calling them, in order, pure knowledge (A), reason, belief, and illusion. The last two we class together as opinion, the first two as knowledge (A + B), opinion being concerned with the world of becoming, knowledge (A + B) with the world of reality. Knowledge (A + B) stands to opinion as the world of reality does to that of becoming, and pure knowledge (A) stands to belief and reason to illusion as knowledge (A + B) stands to opinion. The relation of the realities corresponding to knowledge (A + B) and opinion and the two-fold divisions into which they fall we had better omit if we're not to involve ourselves in an argument even longer than we've already had.'

b 'Yes,' said Glaucon; 'and I agree about your other points, so far as I can follow you.'

'So you agree in calling a man a dialectician who can take account of the essential nature of each thing; and in saying that anyone who is unable to give such an account of things either to himself or to other people has to that extent failed to understand them.'

'I can hardly do otherwise.'

'Then doesn't the same apply to the good? If a man can't
c define the form of the good and distinguish it clearly in his account from everything else, and then battle his way through all objections, determined to give them refutation based on reality and not opinion,[24] and come through with his argument unshaken, you wouldn't say he knew what the good in itself was, or indeed any other good. Any shadowy notion such a man gets hold of is the product of opinion rather than knowledge, and he's living in a dream from which he will not awake on this
d side of the other world, where he will finally sleep for ever.'

'With all that I agree emphatically.'

'Well, then, if you ever really had the job of bringing up and educating these imaginary children of yours, you would not, I take it, let them reach positions of high responsibility in society while they're still like irrational lines.'[25]

'No.'

'So you will lay it down that they must devote themselves especially to this discipline, which will enable them to ask and answer questions with the highest degree of understanding.'

'With your help I will.'

e

'Then you agree that dialectic is the coping-stone that tops our educational system; it completes the course of studies and there is no other study that can rightly be placed above it.'

'I agree.'

For a summary of the philosophical passages in the Republic *and a comparison with the* Phaedrus *and* Symposium *see Appendix I.*

4. Selection and Curriculum

Plato first emphasizes the moral and, more particularly, intellectual virtues necessary in those who are to embark on the course outlined. He then specifies the length of time needed for each stage and the age at which it should be started. The first stage, described in Part III, lasts till the age of eighteen. From eighteen to twenty there are two years of physical training and military service. Then, between the ages of twenty and thirty, selected candidates are put through the mathematical disciplines; that stage is followed (after further selection) by five years' dialectic, any earlier introduction to which is, we are reminded, very dangerous; then follow fifteen years' practical experience in subordinate offices, after which those who have survived all these tests are fully qualified Philosopher Rulers and divide their time between philosophy (which they prefer) and ruling.

'All you have to do now, then,' I went on, 'is to make an allocation, showing who should study these subjects and how.'

535 a

'Yes, that's all.'

'Do you remember the kind of people we picked when you were choosing our Rulers?'[26]

'Of course I do.'

'In most respects we should pick those with the same natural qualities – we should prefer the steadiest and bravest and, so far

b as possible, the best-looking. But we shall also look not only for moral integrity and toughness, but for natural aptitude for this kind of education.'

'And how would you distinguish that?'

'Well, my dear chap,' I said, 'they need intellectual eagerness, and must learn easily. For the mind shirks mental hardship more than physical; it touches it more nearly, whereas physical labour it can share with the body.'

'True.'

c 'They must have good memories, determination and a fondness for hard work. How, otherwise, will they be ready to go through with such an elaborate course of study on top of their physical training?'

'They won't, unless they have every natural advantage.'

'Which explains what is wrong with philosophy today and why it has a bad reputation; as we said before,²⁷ it is taken up by those unworthy of it. Philosophy should be wooed by true men, not bastards.'

'How do you mean?' he asked.

d 'First of all,' I said, 'anyone who takes it up must have no crippling inhibitions about hard work. He mustn't be only half inclined to work, and half not – for instance, a man who is very fond of hunting and athletics and all kinds of physical exercise, but has no inclination to learn, listen and inquire, and dislikes all intellectual effort of that kind. And there are people just as crippled in the opposite way.'

'That's very true.'

'We shall regard as equally handicapped for the pursuit of

e truth a mind which, while it detests deliberate lying, and will not abide it in itself and is indignant to find it in others, cheerfully acquiesces in conventional misrepresentations²⁸ and feels no indignation when its own ignorance is shown up, but wallows

536 *a* in it like a pig in a sty.'

'I entirely agree.'

'We must be as careful to distinguish genuine and bastard in dealing with all the various kinds of human excellence – discipline, courage, breadth of vision, and the rest. Lack of the knowledge needed for such discrimination on the part of an individual or a community merely leads to the unwitting employment of people who are unsound and bogus in some way whether as friends or rulers.'

'That is very true.'

'We must avoid these mistakes,' I went on. 'If we pick those   *b*
who are sound in limb and mind and then put them through our long course of instruction and training, Justice herself can't blame us and we shall preserve the constitution of our society; if we make any other choice the effect will be precisely the opposite, and we shall plunge philosophy even deeper in ridicule than it is at present.'

'Which would be a shameful thing to do.'

'It would,' I agreed. 'But I'm not sure I'm not being slightly ridiculous at the moment myself.'

'How?'

'I was forgetting that we are amusing ourselves with an   *c*
imaginary sketch, and was getting too worked up. I had in mind as I spoke the unjust abuse which philosophy suffers, which annoyed me, and my anger at the critics made me speak more seriously than I should.'

'Oh, come!' he said, 'you didn't sound to me too serious.'

'Well, that's how I felt as I was speaking. However, don't let's forget that when we were making our earlier choice,[29] we chose elderly men; but that won't do now. We mustn't let Solon[30]   *d*
persuade us that there are a lot of things one can learn as one grows old; one is less able to learn then than to run. The time for all serious effort is when we are young.'

'Undoubtedly.'

'Arithmetic and geometry and all the other studies leading to dialectic should be introduced in childhood,[31] though we mustn't exercise any form of compulsion in our teaching.'

'Why?' he asked.

'Because a free man ought not to learn anything under duress.   *e*
Compulsory physical exercise does no harm to the body, but compulsory learning never sticks in the mind.'

'True.'

'Then don't use compulsion,' I said to him, 'but let your
537 a children's lessons take the form of play. You will learn more
about their natural abilities that way.'

'There's something in what you say.'

'Do you remember,' I reminded him, 'that we said that our
children ought to be taken on horseback to watch fighting, and,
if it was safe, taken close up and given their taste of blood, like
hound puppies?'

'Yes, I remember.'

'Well, we must enrol in a select number those who show
themselves most at home in all these trials and studies and
dangers.'

b   'At what age?' he asked.

'As soon as their necessary physical training is over. During
that time, whether it be two or three years, they won't be able
to do anything else; physical fatigue and sleep are unfavourable
to study. And one of the most important tests is to see how they
show up in their physical training.'

'Of course.'

'After that time, then, at the age of twenty, some of them will
be selected for promotion, and will have to bring together the
c disconnected subjects they studied in childhood and take a
comprehensive view of their relationship with each other and
with the nature of reality.'

'That is the only way to acquire lasting knowledge.'

'And also the best test of aptitude for dialectic, which is the
ability to take the comprehensive view.'

'I agree.'

'You will have to keep these requirements in view and make
d a further choice among your selected candidates when they pass
the age of thirty. Those who show the greatest perseverance in
their studies, in war, and in their other duties, will be promoted
to higher privileges, and their ability to follow truth into the
realm of pure reality, without the use of sight or any other sense,
tested by the power of dialectic. And here, my friend, you will
have to go to work very carefully.'

'Why particularly?'

'Haven't you noticed the appalling harm done by dialectic at   *e*
present?'

'What harm?'

'It fills people with indiscipline.'

'Oh, yes, I've noticed that.'

'And does it surprise you?' I asked. 'Aren't you sorry for the
victims?'

'Why should I be?'

'Well, imagine an adopted[32] child who has been brought up   538 *a*
in a large, rich and powerful family, with many hangers-on;
when he grows up he discovers that he is not the child of his
so-called parents, but can't discover who his real parents are.
Can you imagine how he will feel towards the hangers-on and
his supposed parents, first while he still doesn't know they aren't
his real parents, and then when he does? Shall I tell you what I
should expect?'

'Yes, do.'

'Well, I should expect that, so long as he didn't know they   *b*
weren't his real parents, he would respect his mother and father
and other supposed relations more than the hangers-on, be
more concerned with their needs, and less inclined to do or say
anything outrageous to them, or to disobey them in matters of
importance.'

'Very likely.'

'But when he discovered the truth, I should expect him to
give up respecting them seriously and devote himself to the
hangers-on; their influence with him would increase, he'd associate with them openly and live by their standards, and, unless his   *c*
natural instincts were particularly decent, he'd pay no more
attention to his previously reputed father and relations.'

'That's all very likely. But,' he asked, 'what bearing has the
illustration on those who take up philosophic discussions?'

'This. There are certain opinions about what is right and
honourable in which we are brought up from childhood, and
whose authority we respect like that of our parents.'

'True.'

'And there are certain habits of an opposite kind, which have   *d*
a deceitful attraction because of the pleasures they offer, but

which no one of any decency gives in to, because he respects the
authority of the beliefs of his fathers.'

'True again.'

'Yes,' I said, 'but what happens when he is confronted with
the question, "What do you mean by 'honourable'?" When he
gives the answer tradition has taught him, he is refuted in
argument, and when that has happened many times and on
many different grounds, he is driven to think that there's no
difference between honourable and disgraceful, and so on with
all the other values, like right and good, that he used to revere.

e What sort of respect for their authority do you think he'll feel
at the end of it all?'

'He's bound to show less respect and obedience.'

'Then when he's lost any respect or feeling for his former
beliefs but not yet found the truth, where is he likely to turn?

539 *a* Won't it be to a life which flatters his desires?'

'Yes, it will.'

'And so we shall see him become a rebel instead of a con-
former.'

'Inevitably.'

'Yet all this is a natural consequence of starting on philosophic
discussions in this way, and, as I've just said, there's every reason
for us to excuse it.'

'Yes, and be sorry about it,' he agreed.

'Then if you want to avoid being sorry for your thirty-year-
olders, you must be very careful how you introduce them to
such discussions.'

'Very careful.'

b 'And there's one great precaution you can take, which is to
stop their getting a taste of them too young. You must have
noticed how young men, after their first taste of argument, are
always contradicting people just for the fun of it; they imitate
those whom they hear cross-examining each other, and themselves cross-examine other people[33] like puppies who love to
pull and tear at anyone within reach.'

'They like nothing better,' he said.

'So when they've proved a lot of people wrong and been
c proved wrong often themselves, they soon slip into the belief

that nothing they believed before was true; with the result that
they discredit themselves and the whole business of philosophy
in the eyes of the world.'

'That's perfectly true,' he said.

'But someone who's a bit older,' I went on, 'will refuse to
have anything to do with this sort of idiocy; he won't copy those
who contradict just for the fun of the thing, but will be more
likely to follow the lead of someone whose arguments are aimed
at finding the truth. He's a more reasonable person and will get
philosophy a better reputation.'   *d*

'True.'

'In fact all we've been saying has been said in the attempt to
ensure that only men of steady and disciplined character shall be
admitted to philosophic discussions, and not anyone, however
unqualified, as happens at present.'

'I entirely agree.'

'Then suppose twice as long is spent on an exclusive, continuous and intensive study of philosophy as we proposed should
be spent on the corresponding physical training, will that be
enough?'

'Do you mean six years or four?'   *e*

'It doesn't matter,' said I; 'make it five. After that they must
be sent down again into the Cave we spoke of, and compelled
to hold any military or other office suitable for the young, so
that they may have as much practical experience as their fellows. 540 *a*
And here again they must be tested to see if they stand up to
temptations of all kinds or give way to them.'

'And how long do you allow for this stage?'

'Fifteen years. And when they are fifty, those who have come
through all our practical and intellectual tests with distinction
must be brought to their final trial, and made to lift their mind's
eye to look at the source of all light, and see the good itself,
which they can take as a pattern for ordering their own life as   *b*
well as that of society and the individual. For the rest of their
lives they will spend the bulk of their time in philosophy, but
when their turn comes they will, in rotation, turn to the weary
business of politics and, for the sake of society, do their duty as
Rulers, not for the honour they get by it but as a matter of

necessity. And so, when they have brought up successors like
themselves to take their place as Guardians, they will depart to
the islands of the blest,[34] and the state will set up a public

c memorial to them and sacrifice to them, if the Pythian Oracle
approves, as divinities, or at any rate as blessed and godlike.'

'It's a fine picture you have drawn of our Rulers, Socrates.'

'And some of them will be women,' I reminded him. 'All I
have said about men applies equally to women, if they have the
requisite natural capacities.'

'Of course,' he agreed, 'if they are to share equally in everything with the men, as we described.'

d 'Well, then, do you agree that the society and constitution we
have sketched is not merely an idle dream, difficult though its
realization may be? The indispensable condition is that political
power should be in the hands of one or more true philosophers.
They would despise all present honours as mean and worthless,

e and care most for doing right and any rewards it may bring;
and they would regard justice as being of paramount importance, and, throughout their reorganization of society, serve and
forward it.'

'How would they proceed?'

'They would begin by sending away into the country all

541 *a* citizens over the age of ten; having thus removed the children
from the influence of their parents' present way of life, they
would bring them up on their own methods and rules, which
are those which we have been describing. This is the best and
quickest way to establish our society and constitution, and for
it to prosper and bring its benefits to any people among which
it is established.'

'Yes, that's much the best way; and I think, Socrates,' he
added, 'that you have explained very well how such a society
would come into existence, if ever it did.'

'Then haven't we said enough about this state of ours and the
corresponding type of man? For it's surely obvious what kind
of man we shall want.'

'Perfectly obvious,' he agreed. 'And I agree with you that
there's no more to be said.'

PART IX
IMPERFECT SOCIETIES

Plato now returns to the point at which he broke off to describe the provisions for women and children and the training of the Philosopher Ruler (449a–e), and proceeds to describe four imperfect types of society – Timarchy, Oligarchy, Democracy, and Tyranny. They are described as if they occurred in that order in a historical series; but Plato is concerned with a moral degeneration, and the historical framework should not be taken too literally. To each society there corresponds a type of individual, whose description follows immediately after that of the society. The origin and character of these individual types and of the society to which they correspond are described quite independently (the origin of democracy, for example, is different from that of the 'democratic man') and not all individuals in each society can be of the type corresponding to it (there can, for example, strictly speaking only be one 'tyrant' in a tyranny); but the traits in the individual will be those admired in the society to which he corresponds, he will be its ideal man, and the description of this ideal serves to throw further light on the society.

1. Recapitulation

Enumeration of the four imperfect societies to be described. The brief recapitulation of Plato's ideal society with which this section begins may be compared with a similar summary at the beginning of the Timaeus *17–20 (Timaeus and Critias, Penguin, pp. 29–32), though there is no formal connection between the dialogues.*

BK VIII   'Well that's that. What we have agreed, Glaucon, is that in the
perfect state women and children should be held in common,
543 *a*   that men and women should share the same education and the
same occupations both in peace and war, and that they should
be governed[1] by those of their number who are best at philosophy and war.'

'That is what we have agreed.'

b   'We have agreed too that, when our Rulers are appointed,
they will take the soldiers and settle them in accommodation of
the kind we described, where there are no private quarters but
everything is common to all; and besides these arrangements
for accommodation you will remember what we said about
property.'

'Yes,' he said, 'it was that they should possess none of the
things other men now do; they were to train for war and act as
c   Guardians over the community, in return for which they were
to get their keep as their annual wage, and devote themselves to
the care of their fellow-Guardians and the whole state.'

'That is right,' I said. 'But now we've dealt with all that, tell
me, where were we when we started off on it? Let us pick up
the track again.'

'That's easy. You were talking, rather as you were just now,
as if you had finished your description of the state, and were
d   saying that the state you had described and the individual corres-
544 *a*   ponding to it were what you would call good – though as we
have now seen you could do something much better in the way
of a description of them. Anyhow, you were saying that if this
was the right kind of state, the others must be wrong. And, I
remember, you said that the others were four in number, and
that it was worth discussing how they and the characters corresponding to them were at fault, so that, having examined the
various types of character and agreed which was best and which
worst, we could then consider whether the best was the happiest,
and the worst the most miserable, or not. I was just asking
b   what the four kinds of society were when Polemarchus and

Adeimantus interrupted, and your reply to them has brought us to where we now are.'

'You've a very good memory,' I said.

'Well, let's go back, like a wrestler practising the same hold again, and I will ask you the same question and you try to give me the answer you were going to give.'

'I will if I can.'

'Well, I'm particularly anxious myself to hear what these four kinds of society are.'

'There's no difficulty about that,' I replied. 'The ones I mean   c
have names in common use. There is your much admired Cretan or Spartan type; secondly, and second in common estimation, though it's burdened with many evils, there is the type called oligarchy; thirdly, and by contrast, follows democracy; and finally comes tyranny, often thought the finest and most out-standing of all, but really the most diseased. Do you know of any other type of society which can be reckoned a distinct species? There are hereditary monarchies, and states where kingship is bought, but these and other similar examples are   d
really crosses between our four types, and are to be found as frequently among barbarians as Greeks.'

'Yes, there are many odd variations.'

'You realize, I suppose,' I went on, 'that there must be as many types of individual as of society? Societies aren't made of sticks and stones, but of men whose individual characters, by turning the scale one way or another, determine the direction of   e
the whole.'

'Yes; society must be formed of individuals.'

'Then, if there are five types of society, there must presumably be five types of individual character.'

'Yes.'

'But we have already described as truly just and good the type corresponding to our ideal society where the best rule.'

'Yes, we have.'

'What we must do next, then, is to go through the inferior   545 a
types, the competitive and ambitious man who corresponds to the Spartan form of society, and then the other three, the oligar-chic and democratic and tyrannic. Thus we can contrast the

worst type of man with the best, and complete our inquiry into
the relative happiness and unhappiness which pure justice and
pure injustice bring to their possessor, and know whether we
are to pursue injustice with Thrasymachus, or justice with the
b   argument we are examining.'

'That is just what we want to do.'

'We began our discussion of moral qualities by examining
them in society before we examined them in the individual,
because it made for greater clarity. Shall we do the same thing
now? We will take first the ambitious society – I know no
current name for it; let us call it "timarchy" or "timocracy" –
c   we will examine it and then look at the corresponding individual
beside it; we will then deal similarly with oligarchy and the
oligarchic man, go on to take a look at democracy and the
democratic man, and finally come to the society governed by a
tyranny, and look at it and the tyrannical character. We can
then try to form a proper judgement on the question before us.'

'Yes; that would be the logical order in which to look at them
and reach a decision.'

2. Timarchy

*In this description Plato has Sparta in mind; it is not easy to
relate it to anything in our experience. The Spartans were, in
effect, a military aristocracy living in a serf-population, and the
characteristics attributed here to Timarchy are those which
common opinion at Athens would have attributed to Sparta.*

*The section opens with an account of how Timarchy origi-
nates from the ideal state. The details are explained in the notes;
the principle is that the change is due to social strife, however
that may start.*

'Then let us try,' I said, 'to describe how our ideal state turns
into a timocracy. The answer is perhaps simple. Change in any
d   society starts with civil strife among the ruling class; as long as
the ruling class remains united, even if it is quite small, no
change is possible.'

'That is true.'

'Then how will change take place in our state? How will Auxiliaries and Rulers come to fall out with each other or among themselves? Shall we invoke the Muses, like Homer, and ask them to tell us "how the quarrel first began"? Let us imagine that they are talking to us in a rather dramatic, high-flown fashion, pretending to be very much in earnest, though they are really only teasing us as if we were children.'

'How?'

'Like this. – It will be difficult to bring about any change for the worse in a state so constituted; but since all created things must decay, even a social order of this kind cannot last for all time, but will decline. And its dissolution will be as follows. Not only for plants that grow in the earth, but for animals that live on it, there are seasons of fertility and infertility of both mind and body, seasons which come when their periodic motions come full circle, a period of longer duration for the long-lived, shorter for the short-lived. And though the Rulers you have trained for your city are wise, reason and observation will not always enable them to hit on the right and wrong times for breeding; some time they will miss them and then children will be begotten amiss. For the divine creature there is a period contained in a perfect number. For the human creature it is the smallest number in which certain multiplications, dominating and dominated, comprising three distances and four terms, give a final result, by making like and unlike, increasing and decreasing, which is commensurate and rational. Their basic ratio of four to three, coupled with five, and multiplied by three, yields two harmonies, of which one is the product of equal factors and of a hundred multiplied the same number of times, while the other is the product of factors of which some are equal, some unequal, that is, *either* a hundred squares of diagonal of rational number, each diminished by one, *or* a hundred squares of irrational number, each diminished by two, *and* one hundred cubes of three.[2]

'This whole geometrical number, controlling the process, determines the quality of births, and when the Guardians ignore this and mate brides and bridegrooms inopportunely, the

e

546 a

b

c

d

resulting children will be neither gifted nor lucky. The best of
them will be appointed to office by their elders, but won't really
be worthy of it, and so when they come to hold the posts their
fathers held will start neglecting us, though they are Guardians,
and undervalue the training, first of the mind and then of the
body, with the result that your young men will be worse educated. In the next generation Rulers will be appointed who have
e lost the true Guardian's capacity to distinguish the metals from
which the different classes of your citizens, like Hesiod's, are
547 *a* made – gold, silver, bronze, and iron; and when iron and silver
or bronze and gold are mixed, an inconsistent and uneven
material is produced, 'whose irregularities, wherever they occur,
must engender war and hatred. That, then, is the pedigree of
strife, wherever it happens.'

'And we shall assume their answer is right,' he said.

b   'As indeed it must be, coming from the Muses,' I replied.

'And what will the Muses say next?' he asked.

'Once internal strife has started, the two elements[3] pull in
different directions; the iron and bronze towards private profit
and property in land and houses and gold and silver, the other
two, the silver and gold, having true riches in their own hearts,
towards excellence and the traditional order of things. The
violence of their opposition is resolved in a compromise under
which they distribute land and houses to private ownership,
c while the subjects whom they once guarded as freemen and
friends, and to whom they owed their maintenance, are reduced
to the status of serfs and menials, and they devote themselves to
war and holding the population in subjection.'

'I agree; that is the origin of the change.'

'And will not the resultant society,' I asked, 'lie between the
ideal and oligarchy?'

'Yes.'

'So much for the change. What will be its results? Isn't it clear
d that a constitution midway between our earlier society and
oligarchy will have some of the features of each as well as certain
peculiarities of its own?'

'Yes.'

'Then do you think it will resemble our earlier society in

features such as these – respect for authority, the soldier-class abstaining from agriculture, industry, or business, the mainten-ance of the common messes, and the attention paid to physical and military training?'

'Yes.'

'Its own peculiar characteristics, on the other hand, will be,   *e* for example, a fear of admitting intelligent people to office, because intelligence is no longer combined with simplicity and sincerity; it will prefer the simpler, hearty⁴ types, who prefer   548 *a* war to peace. It will admire the tricks and stratagems which are needed in war, which will be its constant occupation.'

'Yes.'

'A feature it will share with oligarchy,' I went on, 'will be its love of money. There will be a fierce and secret passion for gold and silver, now that there are private strongrooms to hide it in, and now that there are the four walls of their private houses – expensive nests in which they can spend lavishly on their wives and anything else they choose.'   *b*

'That is very true.'

'They will also be mean about money, because though they love it they may not acquire it openly; but they will be ready enough to spend other people's money for their own satisfaction. They will enjoy their pleasures in secret, avoiding the law like truant children; the reason being that they have been educated by force rather than persuasion, owing to neglect of the true principles of a rational philosophic education and an over-   *c* valuation of physical at the expense of intellectual⁵ training.'

'The society you are describing is very much of a mixture of good and evil,' he said.

'Yes, it is,' I agreed. 'But it has one salient feature, due to its emphasis on the strenuous element in us⁶ – ambition and the competitive spirit.'

'Very true.'

'So much, then, for the origin and nature of this kind of society,' I said. 'We have only sketched it in outline without filling in the details, because an outline is enough to enable us   *d* to distinguish the most just and most unjust types of men, and because it would be an interminable labour to go through all types of society and the individual characters corresponding to them in detail.'

'You are quite right.'

3. The Timarchic Character

Ambitious, energetic, athletic, but a prey to inner uncertainty and conflict.

'Then what about the individual corresponding to the society we have just sketched? What is he like and how is he produced?'

'I suspect,' said Adeimantus, 'that he's rather like Glaucon here as far as the competitive spirit goes.'

e   'Yes, perhaps he is,' I replied. 'But there are other features in which he's not so like him.'

'What are they?'

'He must be rather more self-willed, and rather less well-educated, though not without an interest in the arts; ready to listen, but quite incapable of expressing himself. He will be
549 *a*   harsh to his slaves, because his imperfect education has left him without a proper sense of his superiority to them; he will be polite to his fellow-freemen and obey the authorities readily. He will be ambitious to hold office himself, regarding as qualifications for it not the ability to speak or anything like that, but military achievements and soldierly qualities, and he'll be fond of exercise and hunting.'

'That's the spirit of the society he's living in.'

b   'When he's young,' I continued, 'he will despise money, but the older he grows the keener he will get about it. His nature has a touch of avarice and there are flaws in his character because he has lost his best safeguard.'

'And what is that?' asked Adeimantus.

'A blend of reason and a properly trained imagination,'[7] I said. 'That is the only thing whose presence will preserve the excellence of its possessor intact through life.'

'A fair answer.'

'Well, then, that's the type of young man corresponding to the timocratic society.'

'Agreed.'   c

'And this is roughly how he's produced. Suppose a young man, whose father is a good man but lives in a badly run state and avoids office and honours and law-suits and all the bother attached to them, being quite content with a back seat to save himself trouble –'

'How does that produce our type?'

'When he hears his mother complaining that *her* husband isn't one of the bosses, and that she is slighted by other women   d because of it; she sees that her husband is not very keen on making money, but avoids the wranglings and bickerings of politics and the law, which he treats very lightly, and keeps his own counsel, while he doesn't take her unduly seriously, though he does not neglect her. All this annoys her and she says that the boy's father isn't a real man and is far too easy-going, and drones on with all the usual complaints women make in the   e circumstances.'

'And a dreary lot of them there are too,' said Adeimantus.

'And, as you know,' I went on, 'servants who seem quite loyal will sometimes repeat the same sort of thing to the children behind their master's back. And if they see the father failing to prosecute someone who owes him money or has done him some wrong, they tell the son that when he grows up he must have   550a his rights and be more of a man than his father. The boy hears the same sort of thing outside and sees how those who mind their own business are publicly called silly and not thought much of, while those who don't get all the honour and glory. He hears and sees all this, and on the other hand listens to what his father has to say, and sees his way of life from close to and contrasts it with other people's; as a result he is torn in two directions, his father's influence fostering the growth of his   b rational nature, and that of the others his desire and his ambition.[8] And since he's not really at heart a bad chap, but has merely got into bad company, he takes a middle course between the two, and resigns control of himself to the middle element and its competitive spirit, and so becomes an arrogant and ambitious man.'

'You seem to me to have given a very complete account of his genesis,' he said.

c   'In that case,' I replied, 'the description of our second society and individual is done.'

'It is.'

4. Oligarchy

A society in which wealth is the criterion of merit and the wealthy are in control. The appearance of a 'drone' class of criminals and malcontents.

'We must go on, as Aeschylus says, to "another man matched with another state", or rather, if we are to follow our plan, to the state first?'

'Proceed.'

'Well, I suppose that the next kind of society is an oligarchy.'

'And what sort of régime do you mean by an oligarchy?'

'A society where it is wealth[9] that counts,' I said, 'and in
d   which political power is in the hands of the rich and the poor have no share of it.'

'I understand.'

'We must first describe how oligarchy originates from timocracy – though heaven knows,' I added, 'it's obvious enough even to a blind man.'

'Tell us how.'

'The accumulation of wealth in private hands is what destroys timarchy. The men find ways to become extravagant, and for this reason pervert the law and disobey it, and the women follow their example.'

'That's all likely enough.'

e   'And mutual observation and jealousy stamps the same character on the ruling class as a whole.'

'Likely again.'

'The further they go in the process of accumulating wealth,

the more they value it and the less they value goodness. For aren't wealth and goodness related like two objects in a balance, so that when one rises the other must fall?'

'Emphatically yes.'

'So the higher the prestige of wealth and the wealthy, the lower that of goodness and good men will be.'   551 a

'Obviously.'

'And we practise what we admire and neglect what we despise.'

'We do.'

'And so there is a transition from the ambitious, competitive type of man to the money-loving businessman, honour and admiration and office are reserved for the rich, and the poor are despised.'

'That is so.'

'At this stage they introduce legislation, the characteristic mark of an oligarchy, which prescribes a certain minimum   b amount of property – greater or less according to the narrowness of the oligarchy – as a necessary qualification for office, a measure they force through by armed violence, if they have not already got their way by terrorism. Do you agree?'

'Yes.'

'Then that is, briefly, how an oligarchy is set up.'

'Yes, but what sort of a society is it?' he asked. 'What are its characteristic faults?'   c

'In the first place,' I replied, 'the principle which characterizes it is unsound. For consider, if one chose ships' captains on grounds of wealth, and never gave a poor man a command, even if he was the better sailor –'

'You would have some pretty bad navigation.'

'And isn't the same true of any other form of authority?'

'Personally I should agree.'

'Except in politics?' I asked. 'Or is it true in politics too?'

'It is truest of all about politics,' he replied, 'for political authority is the most difficult and the most important.'

'That, then, is one very serious fault in oligarchy.' He agreed,   d and I went on, 'But there is another hardly less serious.'

'What?'

'That it inevitably splits society into two factions, the rich and the poor, who live in the same place and are always plotting against each other.'

'Heaven knows that's just as serious.'

'Its probable inability to wage war is another discreditable feature. The oligarchs can't do this because they must either arm the people, whom they fear worse than the enemy, or, if they don't, have the thinness of their ranks[10] shown up by the stress of battle; and at the same time they are too grasping to want to pay the expenses of a war.'

'Yes, that's another discreditable feature.'

'Then what about the fact that the same people engage in many different occupations, farming, business, and war? We condemned this once; do we think it right now?'

'Certainly not.'

'Then we come to the worst defect of all, which makes its first appearance in this form of society.'

'What is it?'

'That a man can sell all he has to another and live on as a member of society without any real function; he's neither businessman nor craftsman nor cavalryman nor infantryman,[11] but merely one of the so-called indigent poor.'

'It's the first form of society in which this happens,' he agreed.

'And there is certainly nothing to prevent it in oligarchies; otherwise you would not get the sharp division between the very rich and the very poor.'

'True.'

'There's another point. When our pauper was rich, did he perform any of the useful social functions we've just mentioned simply by spending his money? Though he may have appeared to belong to the ruling class, surely in fact he was neither ruling, nor serving society in any other way; he was merely a consumer of goods.'

'That is all he was,' he agreed, 'a mere consumer, whatever he seemed to be.'

'Don't you think we can fairly call him a drone? He grows up in his own home to be a plague to the community, just as a drone grows in its cell to be a plague to the hive.'

'An apt comparison, Socrates.'

'Then would you agree, Adeimantus, that all winged drones have been created by god without stings, but that our two-footed ones vary, some having no stings and some very formidable ones; and that the stingless type end their days as beggars, the stinging type as what we call criminals?'

d

'Yes, entirely.'

'Obviously, then,' I went on, 'in any state where there are beggars there are also, hidden away somewhere about the place, thieves and pick-pockets and temple robbers and all such practitioners of crime.'

'Obviously.'

'And do you find beggars in an oligarchy?'

'Most people are beggars except the ruling class.'

'Then we may suppose there are also plenty of stinging drones, in the shape of criminals whom the government is careful to hold in restraint.'

e

'We may indeed,' he agreed.

'And the reason for their existence is lack of education, bad upbringing and a bad form of government.'

'It is.'

'That, then, is what the oligarchic society is like, and those, or even worse than those, are its faults,' I said.

553 *a*

'You have hit it off pretty well,' he agreed.

'And so we may regard our account of this type of constitution, in which power is linked with property, and of which oligarchy is the common name, as complete. Let us proceed to the corresponding individual, his origin and character.'

'Yes, let us.'

5. The Oligarchic Character

His sole object is to make money.

'The transition from timarchic to oligarchic man takes place, I think, as follows.'

'Go on.'

'The timarchic man has a son who at first admires his father and follows in his footsteps; then he sees him suddenly wrecked
b in some political disaster – he has, perhaps, spent all his substance and energy in some military command or other position of authority, only to be brought into court by informers and put to death, or exiled, or outlawed with the loss of all his property.'

'That might well happen.'

'The son sees all this,' I continued, 'and, frightened by his sufferings and the loss of property, incontinently dethrones
c courage and ambition from the place they have held in his heart. Reduced to poverty, and forced to earn his living, by slow and painful economy and hard work he succeeds in amassing a fortune; so won't he proceed to elevate the element of desire and profit-seeking to the throne, and let it govern like an oriental despot with tiara, chain, and sword?'

'Yes.'

d 'While reason and ambition squat in servitude at its feet,[12] reason forbidden to make any calculation or inquiry but how to make more money, ambition forbidden to admire or value anything but wealth and the wealthy, or to compete for anything but the acquisition of wealth and whatever leads to it.'

'There's no transition quicker or more violent than that from ambition to avarice,' he said.

e 'And isn't the man we have described our oligarchic type?' I asked.

'He certainly developed from the type corresponding to the society from which oligarchy developed,' he replied.

'Then let's see if he has similar characteristics.'

554 a 'Go on.'

'The first similarity is in the overriding importance he gives to money.'

'Of course.'

'Again, he is economical and hard-working, satisfying only his necessary wants and indulging in no other expenses, but repressing his other desires as pointless.'

'True again.'

'Yes, he's rather a squalid character,' I said, 'always on the make and putting something by – a type commonly much

admired. And again, surely, we see the similarity to our oligar- *b*
chic society.'

'I agree,' he said; 'money is what both chiefly value.'

'Yes, because I don't suppose he ever gave any attention to
his education.'

'I should think not; otherwise he wouldn't have promoted a
blind[13] actor to play his chief part.'

'A good point. Now, tell me,' I went on, 'I suppose that his
lack of education will breed desires in him, like the pauper and *c*
criminal drones, which his general carefulness will keep under
restraint.'

'Yes, certainly.'

'And do you know where to look if you want to see these
criminal desires at work?'

'Where?'

'In his handling of the guardianship of orphans, or of any
other matter where he has plenty of scope for dishonesty.'

'True.'

'There it becomes quite clear that the high reputation for
honesty which he has in other business transactions is due
merely to a certain respectable constraint which he exercises *d*
over his evil impulses, for fear of their effect on his concerns as
a whole. There's no moral conviction, no taming of desire by
reason, but only the compulsion of fear.'

'Very true.'

'And what is more, you are pretty sure to find evidence of the
presence of these drone desires when a man of this kind is
spending other people's money.'

'Oh, very much so.'

'This sort of man, then, is never at peace in himself, but has a
kind of dual personality, in which the better desires on the whole
master the worse.'   *e*

'True.'

'He therefore has a certain degree of respectability, but comes
nowhere near the real goodness of an integrated and balanced
character.'

'I agree.'

'And, being a mean fellow, he's a poor competitor personally

for any success or ambitious achievement in public life; he's
unwilling to spend money in the struggle for distinction, and
scared of stirring up a whole lot of expensive desires to fight on
the side of his ambition. So, like a true oligarch, he fights with
only part of himself, and though he loses the battle he saves his
money.'

'Yes, that's true.'

'Then need we hesitate any longer to say that the grasping
money-maker corresponds to the oligarchic society?'

'No.'

6. Democracy

*Equality of political opportunity and freedom for the individual
to do as he likes are, for Plato and Aristotle, the salient characteristics of democracy. Plato is writing, of course, about democracy
in the ancient city-state, and has Athens particularly in mind
(cf. Introduction, pp. xxiii ff.); translation into terms of modern
experience must bear this in mind. Compare also the account of
the transition from democracy to tyranny, 562a ff., for further
characteristics of democracy.*

'Our next subject, I suppose, is democracy. When we know
how it originates, and what it is like, we can again identify and
pass judgement on the corresponding individual.'

'That would be consistent with the procedure we've been
following.'

'Then doesn't oligarchy change into democracy in the following way, as a result of lack of restraint in the pursuit of its
objective of getting as rich as possible?'

'Tell me how.'

'Because the rulers, owing their power to wealth as they do,
are unwilling to curtail by law the extravagance of the young,
and prevent them squandering their money and ruining themselves; for it is by loans to such spendthrifts or by buying up
their property that they hope to increase their own wealth and
influence.'

'That's just what they want.'

'It should then be clear that love of money and adequate self-discipline in its citizens are two things that can't coexist in any society; one or the other must be neglected.'   *d*

'That's pretty clear.'

'This neglect and the encouragement of extravagance in an oligarchy often reduces to poverty men born for better things.'

'Yes, often.'

'Some of them are in debt, some disfranchised, some both, and they settle down, armed with their stings, and with hatred in their hearts, to plot against those who have deprived them of their property and against the rest of society, and to long for revolution.'   *e*

'Yes, they do.'

'Meanwhile the money-makers, bent on their business, don't appear to notice them, but continue to inject their poisoned loans wherever they can find a victim, and to demand high rates   556 *a* of interest on the sum lent, with the result that the drones and beggars multiply.'

'A result that's bound to follow.'

'Yet even when the evil becomes flagrant they will do nothing to quench it, either by preventing men from disposing of their property as they like, or alternatively by other suitable legislation.'

'What legislation?'

'It's only a second best, but it does compel some respect for decent behaviour. If contracts for a loan were, in general, made by law at the lender's risk, there would be a good deal less   *b* shameless money-making and a good deal less of the evils I have been describing.'

'Much less.'

'But as it is the oligarchs reduce their subjects to the state we have described, while as for themselves and their dependants – their young men live in luxury and idleness, physical and   *c* mental, become idle, and lose their ability to resist pain or pleasure.'

'Indeed they do.'

'And they themselves care for nothing but making money, and have no greater concern for excellence than the poor.'

'True.'

'Such being the state of rulers and ruled, what will happen when they come up against each other in the streets or in the course of business, at a festival or on a campaign, serving in the navy or army? When they see each other in moments of danger, the rich man will no longer be able to despise the poor man; the poor man will be lean and sunburnt, and find himself fighting next to some rich man whose sheltered life and superfluous flesh make him puff and blow and quite unable to cope. Won't he conclude that people like this are rich because their subjects are cowards, and won't he say to his fellows, when he meets them in private, "This lot are no good; we've got them where we want them"?'

'I'm quite sure he will.'

'When a person's unhealthy, it takes very little to upset him and make him ill; there may even be an internal cause for disorder. The same is true of an unhealthy society. It will fall into sickness and dissension at the slightest external provocation, when one party or the other calls in help from a neighbouring oligarchy or democracy; while sometimes faction fights will start without any external stimulus at all.'

557 a   'Very true.'

'Then democracy originates when the poor win, kill or exile their opponents, and give the rest equal civil rights and opportunities of office, appointment to office being as a rule by lot.'[14]

'Yes,' he agreed, 'that is how a democracy is established, whether it's done by force of arms or by frightening its opponents into withdrawal.'

'What sort of a society will it be?' I asked, 'and how will its affairs be run? The answer, obviously, will show us the character of the democratic man.'

'Obviously.'

'Would you agree, first, that people will be free? There is liberty and freedom of speech in plenty, and every individual is free to do as he likes.'

'That's what they say.'

'Granted that freedom, won't everyone arrange his life as pleases him best?'

'Obviously.'

'And so there will be in this society the greatest variety of   *c* individual character?'

'There's bound to be.'

'I dare say that a democracy is the most attractive of all societies,' I said. 'The diversity of its characters, like the different colours in a patterned dress, make it look very attractive. Indeed,' I added, 'perhaps most people would, for this reason, judge it to be the best form of society, like women and children when they see gaily coloured things.'

'Very likely.'

'And, you know, it's just the place to go constitution-hunting.'   *d*

'How so?'

'It contains every possible type, because of the wide freedom it allows, and anyone engaged in founding a state, as we are doing, should perhaps be made to pay a visit to a democracy and choose what he likes from the variety of models it displays, before he proceeds to make his own foundation.'

'It's a shop in which he'd find plenty of models on show.'   *e*

'Then in democracy,' I went on, 'there's no compulsion either to exercise authority if you are capable of it, or to submit to authority if you don't want to; you needn't fight if there's a war, or you can wage a private war in peacetime if you don't like peace; and if there's any law that debars you from political or judicial office, you will none the less take either if they come your way. It's a wonderfully pleasant way of carrying on in the   558 *a* short run, isn't it?'

'In the short run perhaps.'

'And isn't there something rather charming about the good-temper of those who've been sentenced in court? You must have noticed that in a democracy men sentenced to death or exile stay on, none the less, and go about among their fellows, with no more notice taken of their comings and goings than if they were invisible spirits.'

'I've often seen that.'

'Then they're very considerate in applying the high principles   *b*

we laid down when founding our state; so far from interpreting
them strictly, they really look down on them. We said that no
one who had not exceptional gifts could grow into a good
man unless he were brought up from childhood in a good
environment and trained in good habits. Democracy with a
grandiose gesture sweeps all this away and doesn't mind what
the habits and background of its politicians are; provided they
c profess themselves the people's friends, they are duly honoured.'

'All very splendid.'

'These, then, and similar characteristics are those of democracy. It's an agreeable anarchic form of society, with plenty of
variety, which treats all men as equal, whether they are equal
or not.'

'The description is easy to recognize.'

7. The Democratic Character

Versatile but lacking in principle. Desires necessary and
unnecessary.

'Then let us look at the corresponding individual. Should we
first look at his origin, as we did with the society?'

'Yes.'

d 'Won't it be like this? Our mean oligarchic character may
have a son, whom he will bring up in his own ways.'

'So far, so good.'

'He will forcibly restrain himself from those pleasures that
lead to expense rather than profit, the "unnecessary" pleasures
as they have been called.'

'Yes, obviously.'

'Then do you think that, if we are to avoid arguing in the
dark, we had better define the difference between necessary and
unnecessary desires?'

'Yes, I think so.'

e 'Desires we can't avoid, or whose satisfaction benefits us, can
fairly be called necessary, I think. We are bound by our very
559 a nature to want to satisfy both, are we not?'

'Certainly.'

'And so may surely with justice use the term "necessary" to describe them.'

'Yes.'

'But we can call "unnecessary" all desires which can be got rid of with practice, if we start young, and whose presence either does us no good or positive harm. Isn't that a fair enough description?'

'Fair enough.'

'Shall we give examples of each, to get a general idea of what we mean?'

'I think we should.'

'Would you say that the desire to eat enough for health and fitness, and the desire for the bread and meat requisite for the purpose, was necessary?'   b

'Yes, I think so.'

'And the desire for bread is necessary on both counts, because it benefits us and because it is indispensable to life.'

'Yes.'

'And the desire for meat so far as it conduces to fitness.'

'Certainly.'

'But the desire for a more varied and luxurious diet is one which, with discipline and training from an early age, can normally be got rid of, and which is physically harmful and psychologically damaging to intelligence and self-discipline. May it not therefore rightly be called unnecessary?'

'Quite rightly.'   c

'The first kind of desire we could also call acquisitive, because of its practical usefulness, the second kind wasteful.'

'True.'

'And does not the same hold good of sex and the other desires?'

'Yes.'

'Then what we called the drone type will, as we said, be swayed by a mass of such unnecessary pleasures and desires, the   d thrifty oligarchic type by necessary ones.'

'Yes.'

'Let's go back to the question how the democratic man origin-

ates from the oligarchic. This generally happens, I think, as
follows.'

'How?'

'When a young man, brought up in the narrow[15] economical
way we have described, gets a taste of the drones' honey and gets
into brutal and dangerous company, where he can be provided
e with every variety and refinement of pleasure, with the result that
his internal oligarchy starts turning into a democracy.'

'That's bound to happen.'

'In society the change took place when one party brought in
sympathizers from outside to help it. Will the change in our
young man be brought about when one or other type of desire
in him gets assistance from kindred and similar desires outside
him?'

'Yes, certainly.'

'And I take it that if the oligarchic element in him gets support
from a counter-alliance of the remonstrances and criticisms
560 *a* either of his father or of other members of his family, the result
is a conflict of factions and a battle between the two parts of
himself.'

'True enough.'

'And sometimes the democratic element gives way to the
oligarchic, and some of his desires are destroyed and some
driven out; and a certain sense of decency is produced in the
young man's mind and internal order restored.'

'Yes, that sometimes happens.'

'Alternatively the exiled desires are succeeded by others akin
to them, which are nursed in secret because of his father's
b ignorance of how to bring him up properly, and grow in number
and strength.'

'This is the normal course of events.'

'These drag him back to his old associates, and breed and
multiply in secret.'

'True again.'

'In the end they capture the seat of government, having discovered that the young man's mind is devoid of sound knowledge and practices and true principles, the most effective
safeguards the mind of man can be blessed with.'

'Far the most effective.'

'The vacant citadel in the young man's mind is filled instead by an invasion of pretentious fallacies and opinions.'

'Very much so.'

'And back he goes to live with the Lotus-eaters.[16] If his family send help to the economical element in him, the pretentious invaders shut the gates of the citadel, and will not admit the relieving force, nor will they listen to the individual represen-   *d* tations of old and trusted friends. They make themselves masters by force of arms, they call shame silliness and drive it into disgrace and exile; they call self-control cowardice and expel it with abuse; and they call on a lot of useless desires to help them banish economy and moderation, which they maintain are mere provincial parsimony.'

'All very true.'

'They expel the lot and leave the soul of their victim swept   *e* clean, ready for the great initiation[17] which follows, when they lead in a splendid garlanded procession of insolence, licence, extravagance, and shamelessness. They praise them all extravagantly and call insolence good breeding, licence liberty, extravagance generosity, and shamelessness courage. Do you agree,' I   561 *a* asked, 'that that's how a young man brought up in the necessary desires comes to throw off all inhibitions and indulge desires that are unnecessary and useless?'

'Yes, your description is very clear.'

'For the rest of his life he spends as much money, time and trouble on the unnecessary desires as on the necessary. If he's lucky and doesn't get carried to extremes, the tumult will subside   *b* as he gets older, some of the exiles will be received back, and the invaders won't have it all their own way. He'll establish a kind of equality of pleasures, and will give the pleasure of the moment its turn[18] of complete control till it is satisfied, and then move on to another, so that none is underprivileged and all have their fair share of encouragement.'

'That's true.'

'If anyone tells him that some pleasures, because they spring from good desires, are to be encouraged and approved, and others, springing from evil desires, to be disciplined and   *c* repressed, he won't listen or open his citadel's doors to the truth, but shakes his head and says all pleasures are equal and should have equal rights.'

'Yes, that's just how he feels and just what he does.'

'In fact,' I said, 'he lives from day to day, indulging the pleasure of the moment. One day it's wine, women and song,[19] the next water to drink and a strict diet; one day it's hard physical train-

d ing, the next indolence and careless ease, and then a period of philosophic study. Often he takes to politics and keeps jumping to his feet and saying or doing whatever comes into his head. Sometimes all his ambitions and efforts are military, sometimes they are all directed to success in business. There's no order or restraint in his life, and he reckons his way of living is pleasant, free and happy, and sticks to it through thick and thin.'

e   'A very good description of the life of one who believes in liberty and equality,' he commented.

'Yes,' I said, 'and I think that the versatility of the individual, and the attractiveness of his combination of a wide variety of characteristics, match the variety of the democratic society. It's a life which many men and women would envy, it contains patterns of so many constitutions and ways of life.'

'It does indeed.'

562 *a*   'This, then, is the individual corresponding to the democratic society, and we can fairly call him the democratic man.'

'Agreed.'

8. Tyranny[20]

The conflict of rich and poor in democracy, and the tyrant's rise as popular champion; his private army and the growth of oppression.

'We've still got the most splendid society and individual of all to describe,' I said, 'tyranny and the tyrant.'

'Yes, we have.'

'Well, my dear Adeimantus, what is the nature of tyranny? It's obvious, I suppose, that it arises out of democracy.'

'Yes.'

'Then isn't it true that tyranny arises out of democracy in the same sort of way that democracy arises out of oligarchy?' *b*

'How do you mean?'

'The main objective of oligarchy, for the sake of which it was established, was, I think we agreed, wealth.'

'Yes.'

'And its fall was due to the excessive desire for wealth, which led to the neglect of all other considerations for the sake of making money.'

'True.'

'Then does not democracy set itself an objective, and is not excessive desire for this its downfall?'

'And what is this objective?'

'Liberty,' I said. 'You must have heard it said that this is the greatest merit of a democratic society, and that for that reason *c* it's the only society fit for a man of free spirit to live in.'

'It's certainly what they often say.'

'Then, as I was just saying, an excessive desire for liberty at the expense of everything else is what undermines democracy and leads to the demand for tyranny.'

'Explain.'

'A democratic society in its thirst for liberty may fall under the influence of bad leaders, who intoxicate it with excessive *d* quantities of the neat spirit; and then, unless the authorities are very mild and give it a lot of liberty, it will curse them for oligarchs and punish them.'

'That is just what a democracy does.'

'It goes on to abuse as servile and contemptible those who obey the authorities and reserves its approval, in private life as well as public, for rulers who behave like subjects and subjects who behave like rulers. In such a society the principle of liberty is bound to go to extremes, is it not?' *e*

'It certainly is.'

'What is more,' I said, 'it will permeate private life and in the end infect even the domestic animals with anarchy.'

'How do you mean?'

'Well,' I said, 'it becomes the thing for father and son to

change places, the father standing in awe of his son, and the son neither respecting nor fearing his parents, in order to assert what he calls his independence; and there's no distinction between citizen and alien and foreigner.'

'Yes, these things do happen.'

'They do,' I said, 'and there are other more trivial things. The teacher fears and panders to his pupils, who in turn despise their teachers and attendants; and the young as a whole imitate their elders, argue with them and set themselves up against them, while their elders try to avoid the reputation of being disagreeable or strict by aping the young and mixing with them on terms of easy good fellowship.'

'All very true.'

'The extreme of popular liberty is reached in this kind of society when slaves – male and female – have the same liberty as their owners – not to mention the complete equality and liberty in the relations between the sexes.'

'Let's have the whole story while we're at it, as Aeschylus[21] says.'

'Right,' I said; 'you shall. You would never believe – unless you had seen it for yourself – how much more liberty the domestic animals have in a democracy. The dog comes to resemble its mistress, as the proverb has it,[22] and the same is true of the horses and donkeys as well. They are in the habit of walking about the streets with a grand freedom, and bump into people they meet if they don't get out of their way. Everything is full of this spirit of liberty.'

'You're telling me!' he said. 'I've often suffered from it on my way out of town.'

'What it all adds up to is this,' I said; 'you find that the minds of the citizens become so sensitive that the least vestige of restraint is resented as intolerable, till finally, as you know, in their determination to have no master they disregard all laws, written or unwritten.'

'Yes, I know.'

'Well, this is the root from which tyranny springs,' I said; 'a fine and vigorous beginning.'

'Vigorous indeed; but what happens next?' he asked.

'The same disease which afflicted and finally destroyed oligarchy afflicts democracy, in which it has more scope, still more virulently and enslaves it. Indeed, any extreme is liable to produce a violent reaction; this is as true of the weather and plants and animals as of political societies.'

564 a

'It's what one would expect.'

'So from an extreme of liberty one is likely to get, in the individual and in society, a reaction to an extreme of subjection.'

'Likely enough.'

'And if that is so, we should expect tyranny to result from democracy, the most savage subjection from an excess of liberty.'

'That's quite logical.'

'But I haven't answered your question, which was, what is the disease whose growth enslaves democracy and oligarchy alike?'

b

'Yes, that's what I asked.'

'You remember me talking about a class of thriftless idlers, whom I compared to drones, their energetic leaders to drones with stings, the more inert mass of followers to drones without stings.'

'An apt comparison too.'

'Whenever these two elements appear in society they cause trouble,' I said, 'as phlegm and bile do in the body. The good doctor and the good lawgiver must make provision against both in advance, just as the bee-keeper who knows his job will try to prevent drones being bred at all, and if they are bred cut them out at once, cells and all.'

c

'A very necessary operation.'

'Then, in order that we may be in a better position to make the judgement we want let us proceed as follows.'

'How?'

'Let us suppose a democratic society falls into three groups, as indeed it does. First comes the group we have mentioned, larger than in an oligarchy because of the freedom it gets.'

d

'Granted.'

'And indeed a good deal more energetic.'

'How is that?'

'In an oligarchy it is despised and kept from power, and so lacks practice and strength. In a democracy practically all the leaders are drawn from it. Its more energetic elements do the talking and acting, the remainder sit buzzing on the benches

e   and won't let anyone else speak, so that all public business, with trifling exceptions, is in their hands.'

'Quite true.'

'Then there's a second group which continually emerges from the mass.'

'What is that?'

'Everyone's on the make, but the steadiest characters will generally be most successful in making money.'

'Very likely.'

'And the drones find them a plentiful and most convenient source to extract honey from.'

'There's not much to be extracted from poor men.'

'And so this group, on which the drones batten, are called the rich.'

'That's about it.'

565 *a*   'The third group is the mass of the people, who earn their own living, take little interest in politics, and aren't very well off. They are the largest class in a democracy, and once assembled are supreme.'

'Yes,' he said, 'but they won't assemble often unless they are given their share of honey.'

'They get their share all right,' I replied. 'Their leaders rob the rich, keep as much of the proceeds as they can for themselves, and distribute the rest to the people.'

b   'Yes, that's how they get their share.'

'Those whom they've plundered are forced to defend themselves, by speaking in the Assembly and doing the best they can elsewhere.'

'They can't avoid it.'

'They are then accused by their rivals of plotting against the people and being reactionaries and oligarchs, even though in fact they may have no revolutionary intentions.'

'That's true.'

'In the end, when they see the people trying to wrong them,

not with intent, but out of ignorance and because they've been misled by the slanders spread by their leaders, why then they've no choice but to turn oligarchs in earnest, not because they want to, but again because the drones' stings have poisoned them.'

'Perfectly true.'

'There follow impeachments and trials in which the two parties bring each other to court.'

'There do indeed.'

'In this struggle don't the people normally put forward a single popular leader, whom they nurse to greatness?'

'Yes, as a rule.'

'Then it should be clear,' I said, 'that this leadership is the root from which tyranny invariably springs.'

'Perfectly clear.'

'Then how does the popular leader start to turn into a tyrant? Isn't it, clearly, when he starts doing what we hear about in the story about the shrine of Zeus Lykaeus in Arcadia?'

'What is the story?'

'That the man who tastes a single piece of human flesh, mixed in with the rest of the sacrifice, is fated to become a wolf. Surely you've heard the tale?'

'Yes, I have.'

'The same thing happens with the popular leader. The mob will do anything he tells them, and the temptation to shed a brother's blood is too strong. He brings the usual unjust charges against him, takes him to court and murders him, thus destroying a human life, and getting an unholy taste of the blood of his fellows. Exiles, executions, hints of cancellation of debts and redistribution of land follow, till their instigator is inevitably and fatally bound either to be destroyed by his enemies, or to change from man to wolf and make himself tyrant.'

'That is an inevitable necessity.'

'It is he who leads the class war against the owners of property.'

'It is.'

'And if he's exiled, and then returns in spite of his enemies, he returns a finished tyrant.'

'Obviously.'

b   'And if they are unable to banish him, or set the citizens
against him and kill him, they form a secret conspiracy to
assassinate him.'

'That's what usually happens,' he agreed.

'Then follows the notorious gambit which all tyrants produce
at this stage of their career, the demand for a personal bodyguard
to preserve their champion for the people.'

c   'True indeed.'

'And this the people grant him without misgiving, because
they fear for his safety.'

'True again.'

'This is the time for anyone who is rich, and under suspicion
of being an enemy of the people as well, to act on the oracle
given to Croesus, and

> flee by Hermus' pebbled shore,
> nor fear the shame of coward more.'[23]

'He certainly won't get a second chance to be ashamed.'

'No,' I agreed, 'it'll be death if he's caught.'

'Certain death.'

'Meanwhile there's clearly no question of our champion
d   "measuring his towering length in the dust";[24] he overthrows
all opposition and grasps the reins of state, and stands, no longer
champion, but the complete tyrant.'

'That's the inevitable conclusion,' he agreed.

'Then shall we describe the happy condition of this man, and
of the state in which a creature like him is bred?'

'Yes, please, let us.'

'In his early days he has a smile and a kind word for everyone;
e   he says he's no tyrant, makes large promises, public and private,
frees debtors, distributes land to the people and to his own
followers, and puts on a generally mild and kindly air.'

'He has to.'

'But I think we shall find that when he has disposed of his
foreign enemies by treaty or destruction, and has no more to
fear from them, he will in the first place continue to stir up war
in order that the people may continue to need a leader.'

'Very likely.'

'And the high level of war taxation will also enable him to   567 a
reduce them to poverty and force them to attend to earning their
daily bread rather than to plotting against him.'

'Clearly.'

'Finally if he suspects anyone of having ideas of freedom and
not submitting to his rule, he can find an excuse to get rid of
them by handing them over to the enemy. For all these reasons
a tyrant must always be provoking war.'

'Yes, he must.'   b

'But all this lays him open to unpopularity.'

'Inevitably.'

'So won't some of the bolder characters among those who
helped him to power, and now hold positions of influence, begin
to speak freely to him and to each other, and blame him for
what is happening?'

'Very probably.'

'Then, if he is to retain power, he must root them out, all of
them, till there's not a man of any consequence left, whether
friend or foe.'

'That's obvious.'

'So he must keep a sharp eye out for men of courage or vision
or intelligence or wealth; for, whether he likes it or not, it is his
happy fate to be their constant enemy and to intrigue until he   c
has purged them from the state.'

'A fine kind of purge,' he remarked.

'Yes,' I returned, 'and the reverse of a purge in the medical
sense. For the doctor removes the poison and leaves the healthy
elements in the body, while the tyrant does the opposite.'

'Yet it seems inevitable, if he's to remain in power.'

'He is compelled to make the happy choice,' I said, 'between   d
a life with companions most of whom are worthless and all of
whom hate him, and an inevitable death.'

'That is his fate.'

'And the greater the unpopularity of this policy, the larger
and the more trustworthy must his bodyguard be.'

'Inevitably.'

'Where will he look for men on whom he can rely?' I asked.

'They will flock to him of their own accord,' he answered, 'if he pays them.'

'In the dog's name!'[25] I exclaimed, 'do you mean another
e   mixed swarm of drones from abroad?'

'That's what I mean.'

'But won't he also want to recruit on the spot?'

'How will he do that?'

'By robbing the citizens of their slaves, freeing them, and enrolling them in his bodyguard.'

'That's true; and very faithful members of it they will be.'

'What an enviable lot the tyrant's is,' I exclaimed, 'if these are
568 *a*   the trusty friends he must employ after destroying his earlier supporters.'

'Well, that's how it is,' he said.

'And I suppose these newly made citizens, whose company he keeps, admire him very much, though all decent men detest and avoid him.'

'Of course.'

'No wonder, then, that tragedy in general and Euripides in particular among tragedians have such a reputation for wisdom.'

'How so?'

'Because of that profound remark of his about tyrants being
b   "wise because they keep company with the wise." He meant, no doubt, by the wise the companions we've described.'[26]

'Yes, and what is more he calls tyranny godlike, and praises it in many other ways. But so do the other poets.'

'And therefore,' I said, 'the tragic poets will perhaps, in their wisdom, forgive us and states whose constitution is like ours, if we refuse to admit them because they sing the praises of tyranny.'

c   'I think those who have any wits will forgive us,' he said.

'Yes, and I expect they will make a tour of other states, where they will hire actors, with their fine persuasive voices, to play their works to large audiences, and sway them over to tyranny or democracy.'

'I expect so.'

'They will, of course, get money for their services and make a great reputation, particularly, one would expect, with tyrants, but also, though to a lesser degree, with democracies. But the higher up our series of constitutions they go, the more their reputation fails them, as if it were short of breath and couldn't *d* climb farther.'

'Very true.'

'But we are digressing,' I said. 'We must go back to what we were saying about our tyrant's private army. How is he to maintain the changing ranks of this splendid and motley gang?'

'Obviously he'll use any temple treasures there are, so long as they last, and the property of his victims.[27] That will enable him to tax the people less.'

'And when these sources fail?'   *e*

'Then he and his gang, boy-friends and girl-friends, will live on his parents' estate.'

'I see,' I said. 'You mean that the people who have bred him will have to maintain him and his crew.'

'They will have no option.'

'No option?' I said. 'But what if they get annoyed and say that it's not right for a father to keep his son when he's grown up – it's the son should keep the father: and that they never *569 a* intended, when they bred him and set him up, that when he grew great *they* should be enslaved to their own slaves, and have to keep him and his servile rabble; on the contrary, *he* was to be *their* champion and free them from the power of the wealthy and so-called upper classes? What if they then order him and his partisans to leave the country, like a father ordering his son out of the house with his riotous friends?'

'Then,' said he with emphasis, 'people will find out soon enough what sort of a beast they've bred and groomed for *b* greatness. He'll be too strong for them to turn out.'

'What?' I exclaimed. 'Do you mean that the tyrant will dare to use violence against the people who fathered him, and raise his hand against them if they oppose him?'

'Yes,' he said, 'when he has disarmed them.'

'So the tyrant is a parricide,' said I, 'and little comfort to his old parent. In fact, here we have real tyranny, open and avowed, and the people find, as the saying is, that they've jumped out of

the frying-pan of subjection to free men into the fire of subjection
c to slaves, and exchanged their excessive and untimely freedom
for the harshest and bitterest of servitudes, where the slave is
master.'

'That is exactly what happens.'

'Well,' I said, 'I think we can fairly claim to have given an
adequate description of how democracy turns to tyranny and
what tyranny is like.'

'I think we can.'

9. The Tyrannical Character

Its essential similarity to the criminal type.[28]

BK IX   'We've still to describe the individual of tyrannical character
and see how he develops from the democratic man, what he's
571 a like, and whether his life is a happy or miserable one.'

'Yes, we're still left with him.'

'There's something else I want to do too.'

'What?'

'I don't think our classification of the nature and number of
the desires is complete. And as long as that's incomplete the
b object of our investigation will remain obscure.'

'Well, now's your chance.'

'Good. What I want to get clear about is this. I think that
some of the unnecessary pleasures and desires are lawless and
violent. Perhaps we are all born with them, but they are disciplined by law and by a combination of reason and the better
desires till in some people they are got rid of altogether, or
c rendered few and feeble, though in some they retain their
numbers and strength.'

'But what are the desires you mean?'

'The sort that wake while we sleep, when the reasonable and
humane part of us is asleep and its control relaxed, and our
fierce bestial nature, full of food and drink, rouses itself and has
its fling and tries to secure its own kind of satisfaction. As you
know, there's nothing too bad for it and it's completely lost to

all sense and shame. It doesn't shrink from attempting inter- *d*
course (as it supposes) with a mother or anyone else, man, beast
or god, or from murder or eating forbidden food. There is, in
fact, no folly nor shamelessness it will not commit.'

'That's perfectly true.'

'But a man of sound and disciplined character, before he goes
to sleep, has wakened his reason and given it its fill of intellectual argument and inquiry; his desires he has neither starved *e*
nor indulged, so that they sink to rest and don't plague the
highest part of him with their joys and sorrows, but leave it to *572 a*
pursue its investigations unhampered and on its own, and to its
endeavours to apprehend things still unknown to it, whether
past, present or future; the third, spirited, part of him he calms
and keeps from quarrels so that he sleeps with an untroubled
temper. Thus he goes to rest with the other two parts of him
quietened, and his reasoning element stimulated, and is in a
state to grasp the truth undisturbed by lawless dreams and *b*
visions.'

'That's exactly what happens.'

'We've been digressing, I know, but my point is this – that
even in the outwardly most respectable of us there is a terribly
bestial and immoral type of desire, which manifests itself particularly in dreams. Do you think I'm talking sense, and do you
agree?'

'Yes, I agree.'

'Then let's go back to the character of our democratic man.
He was produced, you remember, by an early upbringing under
an economical father, whose desires centred entirely on *c*
business, and who had no use for the "unnecessary" desires for
either amusement or elegance.'

'Yes, I remember.'

'But he got into the company of men with more sophisticated
tastes and desires of the kind we described, took to their ways
because of his dislike of his father's meanness, and was driven
to all sorts of excesses; yet at heart he was a better man than
his corrupters, and so effected what he thought was a very
reasonable compromise between the competing attractions of *d*
the two lives, getting the best of both and avoiding both mean-

ness and extravagance – in fact, he turned into a democratic character from an oligarchic.'

'Yes, I still think that's true.'

'Suppose, then,' I went on, 'he has in due course a son whom he brings up in his own ways.'

'Suppose it.'

e 'Suppose, further, that the same thing happens to the son as to the father; he's drawn towards complete licence (which his tempters call complete liberty), his father and family support moderation,[29] and his tempters come in on the other side. And when the wicked wizards who want to make him a tyrant despair of keeping their hold on the young man by other means,

573 a they contrive to implant a master passion in him to control the idle desires that divide his time between them, like a great winged drone – unless you can think of a better description for such a passion?'

'No – that describes it very well.'

'The other desires buzz round it, loading it with incense and perfume, flowers and wine, and all the pleasures of a dissolute life, on which they feed and fatten it until at last they produce in it the sting of mania. Then the master passion runs wild and takes madness into its service; any opinions or desires with a

b decent reputation and any feelings of shame still left are killed or thrown out, until all discipline is swept away, and madness usurps its place.'

'A very complete description of the genesis of the tyrannical man.'

'Isn't this the reason,' I asked, 'why the passion of sex has for so long been called a tyrant?'

'Maybe.'

c 'And isn't there also a touch of the tyrant about a man who's drunk?'

'Yes.'

'And the madman whose mind is unhinged imagines he can control gods and men and is quite ready to try.'

'That's certainly true.'

'Then a precise definition of a tyrannical man is one who,

either by birth or habit or both, combines the characteristics of drunkenness, lust, and madness.'

'Certainly.'

'So much, then, for his origin. And how does he live?'

'I must pass the ball back to you; you tell me.'   *d*

'I will,' I said. 'When a master passion within has absolute control of a man's mind, I suppose life is a round of extravagant feasts and orgies and sex and so on.'

'It's bound to be.'

'And there will be a formidable extra crop of desires growing day by day and night by night and needing satisfaction.'

'There will indeed.'

'So whatever income he has will soon be expended,' I said, and, when he agreed, added, 'and next of course he'll start   *e* borrowing and drawing on capital.'

'Yes.'

'When these sources fail, his large brood of fierce desires will howl aloud, and he will inevitably be stung to madness by them, and still more by the master passion under which they all do armed service, and will cast about to find someone to rob by   574 *a* force or fraud.'

'That's sure to happen,' he said.

'Plunder he must have from all available sources or his life will be torment and agony.'

'He must.'

'In his own life it's always been the later pleasure that has had the better of it at the expense of the earlier, and so he considers that his mother and father, as the older generation, should take second place to him and that, when his share of the family estate is exhausted, he should help himself to their property.'   *b*

'Of course.'

'If they don't give in to him, I suppose he'll try first to get his way by fraud and deceit.'

'I suppose so.'

'And if he can't, will he proceed to robbery and violence?'

'I think he will.'

'And if his old mother and father put up a resistance and

show fight, will he feel any scruple about playing the tyrant to them?'

'I wouldn't give much for his parents' chances,' said Adeimantus.

c   'Do you really mean that he will strike his own mother and his ageing father, to whom he is bound by ties of birth and long affection, and, if they're all under the same roof, subordinate them to his latest mistress or his latest young favourite, who have no claims on him at all?'

'That is just what I mean.'

'What a lucky thing it is,' I said, 'to have a tyrant for a son!'

'A real bit of luck,' he agreed.

d   'And I suppose that when he comes to the end of his father's and mother's resources, having by now a pretty considerable swarm of pleasures collected in himself, he'll start by burgling a house or holding someone up at night, and go on to clean out a temple. Meanwhile the older beliefs about honour and dishonour, which he was brought up to accept as right, will be overcome by others, once held in restraint but now freed

e   to become the bodyguard of his master passion. When he was still democratically minded and under the influence of the laws and his father, they only appeared in his dreams; but under the tyranny of the master passion he becomes in his waking life what he was once only occasionally in his dreams, and there's

575 a   nothing, no taboo, no murder, however terrible, from which he will shrink. His passion tyrannizes over him, a despot without restraint or law, and drives him (as a tyrant drives a state) into any venture that will profit itself and its gang, a gang collected partly from the evil company he keeps and partly from impulses within himself which these same evil practices have freed from restraint. Do you think that's the sort of life he will lead?'

'Yes, I think so.'

'And if there are only a few characters of this kind in a state

b   and the bulk of the people are law-abiding, they will emigrate and take service with a tyrant elsewhere, or else fight as mercenaries in any war there is going on. In times of complete peace, they stay at home and commit a lot of minor crimes.'

'Such as?'

'They become thieves, burglars, pick-pockets, footpads, temple robbers, and kidnappers; or, if they have a ready tongue, they turn informers and false witnesses or take bribes.'

'I suppose you call all these minor crimes so long as the *c* criminals are few.'

'Minor is a relative term,' I replied, 'and so far as the welfare or wickedness of the community goes, crimes like these don't come anywhere near tyranny. But when the criminals and their followers increase in numbers and become aware of their strength, the folly of the people helps them to produce a tyrant, and they pick the man who is at heart the completest and most absolute tyrant.'

'Yes,' he said, 'for he's likely to be best fitted for tyranny.'

'And if the people submit to him, well and good. If not, he'll *d* punish his country, if he can, just as he punished his parents. He will bring his home country, his once dear motherland as the Cretans call it, under the control of the gang of upstart followers whom he introduces, and keep it in subjection to them. Which was the object of all his ambitions, was it not?'

'Yes, it was.' *e*

'Men of his kind behave in the same sort of way in private life, before they have gained power. Their companions are parasites in every way subservient to them, and they are themselves always prepared to give way and put on the most extravagant *576 a* act of friendship if it suits their purpose, though once that purpose is achieved their tune changes.'

'It does indeed.'

'So tyrannical characters pass their lives without a friend in the world; they are always either master or slave, and never taste true friendship or freedom.'

'True.'

'So we shall be right to call them faithless men.'

'We shall.'

'And if our definition of justice was correct, perfect specimens of injustice.' *b*

'And our definition was quite correct.'

'We can sum it all up by saying that the worst type of man

behaves as badly in his waking life as we said some men do in their dreams.'

'We can.'

'And that is just what happens when a natural tyrant gains absolute power, and the longer he holds it the truer he runs to type.'

'That is inevitable,' said Glaucon, who took up the argument at this point.

10. The Types of Character and Their Degrees of Happiness

Having sketched the four types of imperfect society and the four corresponding types of character, Plato proceeds to rank them in order of happiness, and in particular to contrast the perfectly just man, the Philosopher Ruler, with the completely unjust man, the Tyrant, thereby answering the original question asked by Glaucon and Adeimantus.

1. On the evidence provided by the descriptions given it is shown that they rank in happiness in the order in which they were discussed, with the tyrant as the most unhappy.

'Now isn't it clear,' I asked, 'that the wickedest man will also
c prove to be the unhappiest? And that therefore, in fact, the longer and more extensive a tyrant's power, the greater and more lasting his unhappiness really is, whatever most people may think?'

'It must be so.'

'And does not the tyrannical man correspond to the state governed by a tyranny, the democratic man to a democratic state, and so on?'

'Yes.'

'And so in excellence and happiness the relations between the different types of individual will correspond to the relations between the different types of state?'

'Of course.'   *d*

'Then what is the relative excellence of a state governed by a tyrant and one governed by philosopher kings as we first described?'

'They are opposite extremes,' he replied; 'one is the best and one the worst possible.'

'I won't ask you which is which,' I said, 'as I think that is obvious. But would you make the same judgement about their relative happiness and unhappiness? And we must not be over-awed by the sight of the tyrant himself and his immediate following, but examine the whole society, plunging in and hav-   *e* ing a thorough look round before giving our answer.'

'That's a fair challenge. And it is obvious that there is no more unhappy society than that ruled by a tyrant, and none happier than our philosopher kingship.'

'It would, I think, be fair for us to make the same challenge when dealing with the corresponding individuals. We should   577 *a* expect the true judge to have an understanding that can pene-trate below the surface into the man's character, and not be overawed like a child by the pomp and circumstance of the tyrant's life, but see through them. He will then be competent to form a judgement, to which we should listen, particularly if he has also lived with a tyrant and seen how he behaves in his own house and with his own family – the best place to catch him stripped of all his dramatic paraphernalia – as well as seeing   *b* him in the emergencies of public life.[30] So should we ask him to tell us about the relative happiness and unhappiness of the tyrant's life compared with the others?'

'That's a very fair challenge too.'

'Then shall we pretend that we ourselves have the necessary judgement and experience, so that we may have someone to answer our questions?'

'All right.'

'Let us approach the question by dealing with the character-   *c* istics of the state and of the individual one by one, in the light of the analogy between them.'

'What characteristics?'

'To begin with the state, is a state ruled by a tyrant in a condition of freedom or slavery?'

'It is in complete slavery.'

'And yet it contains some who are masters and free men.'

'Yes, but they are a minority. The mass of the people and the best elements in it are miserable slaves without rights.'

d   'Well, then,' I said, 'if the individual is analogous to the state, he must be similarly placed. His mind will be burdened with servile restrictions, because the best elements in him will be enslaved and completely controlled by a minority of the lowest and most lunatic impulses.'

'Yes, that must be so.'

'Then is such a man in a condition of freedom or slavery?'

'Of slavery, obviously.'

'And is not the state enslaved to a tyrant least able to do as it wishes?'

'Yes.'

e   'So the mind in which there is a tyranny will also be least able to do what, as a whole, it wishes, because it is under the compulsive drive of madness, and so full of confusion and remorse.'

'Of course.'

'Is a state under a tyranny rich or poor?'

'Poor.'

578 a   'So the corresponding character must be poverty-stricken and unsatisfied.'

'Yes.'

'Both state and individual, again, must be haunted by fear.'

'They must be.'

'And will there be any state in which you will find more complaints and anguish and mourning and pain?'

'There will not.'

'Will not the same be true of the corresponding individual under the mad tyranny of his desires and passions?'

'It will.'

b   'With all these reasons and many others in mind, you decided that the state ruled by a tyrant was the unhappiest of all.'

'And wasn't I right?' he asked.

'Perfectly right,' I answered. 'And with all these reasons in mind, what have you to say about the tyrannical man?'

'He's clearly far the unhappiest of all men.'

'There,' I said, 'you are wrong.'

'Why?' he asked.

'I think,' I said, 'that you will perhaps agree –'

'Well?'

'– that the tyrannical individual is even unhappier if he's not left to live as a private citizen, but has the misfortune to be thrust by circumstances to supreme power.'   c

'I should guess from what we've already said that that is true.'

'Yes,' I said, 'but we are concerned with the most important of issues, the choice between a good and an evil life, and guessing isn't good enough; we must examine the arguments thoroughly.'

'Yes, you're quite right.'

'Then consider. I think we ought to start from the following considerations.'   d

'Well, what are they?'

'Let us consider a wealthy private slave-owner with a large number of slaves. The control of large numbers is a point of likeness to tyranny; the difference is one of degree.'

'Yes.'

'Such slave-owners, as you know, don't live in fear of their slaves.'

'Why should they?'

'There's no reason at all; but do you know why?'

'Because the individual has the support of society as a whole.'

'Exactly,' I said. 'But imagine now that some god were to   e
take a single man who owned fifty or more slaves and were to transport him and his wife and children, his goods and chattels and his slaves, to some desert place where there would be no other free man to help him; wouldn't he be in great fear that he and his wife and children would be done away with by the slaves?'

'In very great fear indeed.'

'So he'd have to curry favour with some of these very slaves,   579 a
make them large promises, and give them their freedom, much against his will, till he became the parasite of his own servants.'

'It would be his only alternative to destruction,' he said.

'Then suppose the god surrounded him with a lot of neighbours who would not tolerate the claims of any man to control another, and would punish with utmost severity anyone attempting to do so.'

b   'That would make his predicament still worse, because he would be surrounded by enemies on all sides.'

'Yet this is just the sort of predicament in which the tyrant is imprisoned. He is naturally a prey to fears and passions of every sort, as we have described; and he's the only person in the state who can't travel abroad or attend the festivals the ordinary free man loves to see, much as in his heart he longs to, but must lurk in the shelter of his home, like a woman, and envy the
c   freedom with which other men can travel and see things worth seeing.'

'Very true.'

'The tyrannical character, therefore, whom you judged to be the most wretched of men because of the harvest of evils produced by the disorder prevailing within him, is in all these ways still worse off when he ceases to be a private citizen, and is compelled by fate to become a real tyrant and to control others though he cannot control himself. It's just as if you compelled
d   an invalid or paralytic to spend his life on military service or in athletic competitions instead of living quietly at home.'

'Yes, that's a very apt comparison, Socrates.'

'And so, my dear Glaucon, will you agree that the actual tyrant's condition is utterly wretched, and his life harder than the one you thought hardest?'

'I entirely agree.'

'So, whatever people may think, the truth is that the real
e   tyrant is really a slave of the most abject kind dependent on scoundrels. He can never satisfy his desires, and behind his multitudinous wants you can see, if you know how to survey it as a whole, the real impoverishment of his character; his life is haunted by fear and – if the condition of the state he rules is any
580 *a* guide, as we know it is – torn by suffering and misery. Do you agree?'

'Very much so,' he replied.

'Add to all that what we said before, that his power will make him still more envious, untrustworthy, unjust, friendless, and godless, a refuge and home for every iniquity, and you can see that he's a source of misery above all to himself, but also to his neighbours.'

'No one who has any sense could deny it.'

'Come on, then,' I said, 'you must act as final judge for us, and give us your verdict how these five types – the philosopher *b* king, the timocratic, the oligarchic, the democratic and the tyrannical man – stand in order of happiness.'

'The verdict is easy,' he replied. 'I rank the competitors in the order of their appearance, not only in happiness but also in degree of excellence.'

'Then shall we hire a herald,' I asked, 'or shall I proclaim the judgement of the son of Ariston myself – that the supremely happy man is the one who is justest and the best, that is, the philosopher king who is sovereign over himself, and that the *c* supremely wretched man is the one who is unjustest and worst, that is, again, the man who is most tyrannical and who tyrannizes completely both over himself and over his own country?'

'You may proclaim it,' he said.

'And may I add,' I asked, 'that the judgement remains true whether their true characters are known to men and gods or not?'

'You may.'

2. *On the basis of the threefold classification of the elements in the human mind made earlier (Part v, section 2 ff.), it is shown that the life of the just man and the philosopher is pleasanter than any other.*

'Well, there is one of our proofs,' I said. 'Let us see what you *d* make of the second one.'

'What is it?'

'We divided the mind of the individual into three elements, corresponding to the three classes in the state. This makes a further proof possible.'

'And how does it proceed?'

'As follows. Each of the three elements has its own particular pleasures, and similarly its own desires and its own governing principles.'[31]

'How do you mean?'

'We saw,' I said, 'that one element in a man gives him understanding, another spirit and enterprise, while the third shows itself in too many forms for us to be able to describe it in a *e* single word. We accordingly called it after its most salient characteristics, "desire", because of the violence of the desires for food and drink and sex and the like, or "acquisitiveness", because wealth is the means of satisfying desires of this kind.'

581 *a*   'And we were quite right,' he said.

'Now if we want, for purposes of clarity, to settle on a single heading under which to refer to this third element in the mind, would it not be best to say that its pleasures and affections were centred in gain? So we could correctly describe it by saying that its motive was love of profit or gain.'

'Yes, I think we could.'

'Similarly the element of spirit is entirely devoted to the achievement of success and reputation.'

'Certainly.'

'Could we not therefore appropriately say that its motives are ambition and love of honour?'

b   'Very appropriately.'

'And of course it is obvious that the element of understanding is solely directed to the discovery of the truth, and is least concerned with wealth or reputation.'

'That's absolutely clear.'

'And so we may say that the corresponding motives here are love of knowledge and wisdom.'

'I agree.'

'Then in the human mind does not one or other of these three *c* sets of motives predominate, according to circumstances?'

'It does.'

'That is why we divide men into three basic types, according to whether their motive is knowledge, success or gain.'

'Surely.'

'And each type, of course, has its appropriate pleasures.'

'Yes, certainly.'

'If you asked each of these three types in turn which of the three lives was the pleasantest, he would, of course, give the highest praise to his own. Will the money-maker set any value on the pleasures of honour or knowledge compared with his *d* profits, unless they have a cash value?'

'None at all.'

'And what about the man who loves honour?' I asked. 'Doesn't he think the pleasures of money-making rather vulgar, and those of learning, unless they bring him honour, mere idle nonsense?'

'True.'

'And what are we to suppose the philosopher thinks of other pleasures compared with that of knowing the truth and being *e* always engaged in the pursuit of it? Won't he rank them far lower, regarding them as "necessary" in the strict sense, things he'd do without if they weren't unavoidable?'

'There can be no doubt of that.'

'When therefore there is dispute about the three types of pleasure and three types of life, and they are being compared simply on the grounds of the amount of pleasure they give and *582 a* without any reference to how admirable or how good or bad they are, how are we to know what is the truth?'

'I'm sure I don't know,' he said.

'Look at it in this way. What do we need if we are to judge fairly? Can you suggest any better standards than experience, intelligence, and reason?'

'Certainly not.'

'Then look. Which of the three men we have described has the greatest experience of all three types of pleasure? Is the gain-lover's knowledge of the truth such that you would rank his experience of the pleasures of knowledge above the philosopher's experience of the pleasures of gain?' *b*

'Far from it,' he said. 'The philosopher cannot help tasting the pleasures of gain from his earliest years; but the gain-lover is under no necessity to taste or experience the sweetness of the pleasure of knowing the truth – indeed, he would find it difficult to do so even if he wished.'

'Then the philosopher has the advantage over the gain-lover in his experience of both kinds of pleasure.'

'A very considerable advantage.'

c   'And how does he compare with the man who loves honour? Has he less experience of the pleasures of honour than the ambitious man of the pleasures of knowledge?'

'No. Honour comes to all, if they attain the object of their several efforts, for the rich man and the brave man and the wise man are all widely respected. All three therefore have experience of the pleasures of honour; but only the philosopher can taste the pleasure of contemplating reality and truth.'

d   'As far as experience goes, then,' I said, 'the philosopher is in the best position to judge.'

'Much the best.'

'And he is the only one in whom intelligence is joined with experience.'

'True.'

'And besides, it is the philosopher, and not either of the other two, who has the necessary tools.'

'What do you mean?'

'We said our judgement must be reached through reason.'

'Yes.'

'And rational argument is the philosopher's special tool.'

'That's true.'

'Now, if wealth and profit were our best criteria, the prefer-
e ences and dislikes of the gain-lover would inevitably contain the highest degree of truth.'

'Inevitably.'

'And if our criteria were honour, success and courage, the same would be true of the man of honour and ambition.'

'Obviously.'

'But since we are judging by experience, intelligence and reason . . . ?'

'It follows that truth is to be found in the preferences of the philosopher and man of reason.'

583 a   'Of the three types of pleasure, therefore, the pleasantest is that which belongs to the element in us which brings us know-

ledge, and the man in whom that element is in control will live the pleasantest life.'

'It must be so,' he agreed. 'The wise man speaks with authority when he prefers his own life.'

'And which life and which type of pleasure will his judgement rank second?'

'Obviously that of the ambitious, soldierly type. It is nearer his own than the money-maker's is.'

'So the pleasures of gain come last, I suppose.'

'Of course they do.'

3. *The philosopher's pleasures are the most real of all pleasures: all others are to some extent mixed with pain and therefore illusory, particularly the pleasures of the tyrant.*

'Well, the just man has beaten the unjust in two successive   b
rounds; now for the third, before which wrestlers at the Olympic
Games invoke Olympian Zeus the Saviour. Look – I think
I've heard some wise man say that only the pleasures of the
intelligence are entirely true and unadulterated, and all others
an empty sham.[32] A fall in this final round should settle the
matter.'

'It should. But tell me how you mean.'

'I will explain,' I said, 'but you must help by answering my   c
questions.'

'You have only to ask them.'

'Tell me, then,' I asked, 'is not pleasure the opposite of pain?'

'Most certainly.'

'And is there not a state in which we feel neither enjoyment, nor pain?'

'There is.'

'It will lie between the two, I suppose, giving the mind rest from both. Do you agree?'

'Yes.'

'Do you remember,' I went on to ask, 'what patients always say when they are ill?'

'What?'

'That there is nothing pleasanter than health, though they
d   had not realized its supreme pleasure till they were ill.'

'Yes, I remember.'

'And haven't you heard people in pain saying that there is no
greater pleasure than relief from pain?'

'I have.'

'You must, in fact, have noticed many similar cases in
which the pain we suffer makes us glorify freedom and rest from
pain as the highest pleasure, rather than any positive enjoyment.'

'Perhaps,' he suggested, 'it is because in those circumstances
rest is welcomed as definitely pleasurable.'

e   'Then when enjoyment ceases,' I replied, 'the rest from pleasure will be painful.'

'Maybe.'

'In that case rest, which we said was our intermediate state
between pleasure and pain, will itself at times be both, pleasure
and pain.'

'Apparently.'

'But can something which is neither of two things be both of
them?'

'I think not.'

'What is more, both pleasure and pain when they occur are
processes of mental *change*,[33] are they not?'

'Yes.'

'But didn't we see just now that to feel neither pleasure nor
584 *a*   pain is to be in a state of *rest* between the two?'

'We did.'

'Then can it be right to suppose that absence of pain is pleasure
or absence of enjoyment pain?'

'No, it can't.'

'It cannot therefore, in fact, be so. The state of rest must
appear pleasant by contrast with previous pain or painful by
contrast with previous pleasure; but, judged by the standard of
true pleasure, neither *appearance* can be genuine, but must be
some sort of conjuring trick.'

'That is what the argument indicates.'

b   'To rid you of any lingering idea you may still have that pleasure really is the cessation of pain, and pain the cessation of pleasure, look at pleasures that don't follow pain.'

'Where do I look for them and what are they?' he asked.

'There are a lot of them,' I answered, 'but the best example, if you think of it, is the pleasures of smell. These are very intense, come quite suddenly without any previous pain, and leave no pain behind when they cease.'

'That's perfectly true.'

'So we must not let ourselves believe that pure pleasure con-   c
sists in relief from pain, or pure pain in the cessation of pleasure.'

'Agreed.'

'And yet,' I went on, 'the majority of the intensest pleasures, so called, which we experience through the body, are of this kind, being in some sense relief from pain.'[34]

'Yes, they are.'

'And the same applies, does it not, to the pleasures and pains of anticipation that precede them?'

'Yes.'

'Do you know what I think the character of these pleasures is   d
and what they most closely resemble?'

'No, tell me.'

'Do you agree that in the natural world there is a top, a bottom, and a middle?'

'Yes.'

'Then won't anyone who rises from the bottom to the middle think he has risen towards the top? And as he stands in the middle and looks down to where he came from, won't he think he's at the top, never having seen the real top?'

'I don't see how he could think anything else.'

'And suppose he then went down again, he would suppose he   e
was going down to the bottom, and would be right.'

'Yes.'

'And would not all this happen to him because he had no experience of what top, middle, and bottom really were.'

'Obviously.'

'Then is it surprising that the views of men who lack experience of the truth should be as unsound about pleasure and pain and the neutral state between them as they are about a good

585 a   many other things? When they are subjected to pain, they will think they are in pain and their pain will be real. But they will be convinced that the transition from pain to the neutral state brings satisfaction and pleasure, whereas in fact their lack of experience of true pleasure leads them to make a false contrast between pain and the absence of pain, just as someone who had never seen white might similarly contrast grey with black.'

'That's none of it in the least surprising,' he said. 'In fact, it would be surprising if it were otherwise.'

'Then consider; aren't hunger and thirst and the like states of
b   physical depletion?'

'Of course.'

'And ignorance and empty-headedness states of mental depletion?'

'Certainly.'

'And they can be satisfied by replenishing the body with food and the mind with understanding?'

'They can.'

'And don't we get truer replenishment from replenishing what is more rather than what is less real?'

'Yes, obviously.'

'Then which group has a fuller share of pure reality, things like bread, meat and drink and food generally, or things like
c   judgement, knowledge, understanding and, in brief, all excellencies of mind? Put the question this way – which do you think is more truly real, something which belongs to the realm of unchanging and eternal truth, exists in it and is of its nature, or something which belongs to the realm of change and mortality, exists in it and is of its nature?'

'That which belongs to the unchanging realm is much more real.'

'And is the reality of the unchanging any more real than it is knowable?'

'No.'

'Nor true?'

'Nor true.'[35]

d   'And a lesser degree of truth means a lesser degree of reality?'

'Necessarily.'

'So in general the sort of thing that supplies the needs of the body is less true and less real than the sort of thing that supplies the needs of the mind.'

'Much less.'

'And isn't the same true of the body itself as compared with the mind?'

'I should say so.'

'But the more real the means of replenishment and the thing replenished, the greater, presumably, the reality of the replenishment.'

'I agree.'

'It follows that, if we experience pleasure when our natural needs are suitably replenished, the more real the thing replenished and the means of replenishment, the more genuine and truly real the consequent enjoyment and pleasure; whereas when there is a lesser degree of reality the less truly and certainly we are satisfied and the less reliable and less true our pleasure.'

'That is inevitable.'

'Those, therefore, who have no experience of wisdom and goodness, and do nothing but have a good time, spend their life straying between the bottom and middle in our illustration, and never rise higher to see or reach the true top, nor achieve any real fulfilment or sure and unadulterated pleasure. They bend over their tables, like sheep with heads bent over their pasture and eyes on the ground, they stuff themselves and copulate, and in their greed for more they kick and butt each other with hooves and horns of steel, and kill each other because they are not satisfied, as they cannot be while they fill with unrealities a part of themselves which is itself unreal and insatiable.'

'My dear Socrates,' said Glaucon, 'you sound as if you were delivering an oracle on the life of the common man.'

'And are not the pleasures of such a life inevitably mixed with pain, and so an empty sham[36] and mere phantoms of true pleasure? Both owe their apparent intensity to mutual contrast, and breed mad desires in the hearts of fools, who fight about them as Stesichorus said the heroes fought at Troy about a mere phantom of Helen because they were ignorant of the truth.'[37]

'Something of the sort is inevitable.'

e

586 a

b

c

'Then what about the element of spirit? Isn't it inevitably the same story again, when a man seeks his fill of honour or success or ambition without sense or reason, and in the achievement of
d satisfaction the desire for honour and success leads to envy and violence, ambition to discontent?'

'Yes, inevitably again.'

'I think, then,' I said, 'that we may venture to conclude that if our desire for gain and our ambition will follow the guidance of knowledge and reason, and choose and pursue only such pleasures as wisdom indicates, the pleasures they achieve will be the truest of which they are capable, because truth is their guide, and will also be those proper to them – for isn't what is
e proper to a thing what is best for it?'

'Yes, that's certainly so.'

'Then if the mind as a whole will follow the lead of its philosophic element, without internal division, each element will be just and in all other respects perform its own function, and in addition will enjoy its own particular pleasures, which
587 a are the best and truest available to it.'

'Absolutely true.'

'But when either of the other two elements is in control, it cannot achieve its own proper pleasure, and compels the other two to pursue a false pleasure that is not their own.'

'True.'

'And won't this effect be produced most markedly by the elements furthest removed from philosophy and reason?'

'Very much so.'

'And is not what is furthest removed from reason furthest removed also from law and order?'

'Obviously.'

'And didn't we see that the passionate and tyrannical desires
b were the furthest from law and order?'

'Much the furthest.'

'And the orderly and kingly desires the nearest?'

'Yes.'

'So the tyrant is furthest removed from man's true and proper pleasure, the philosopher king nearest it.'

'Necessarily.'

'And the tyrant therefore leads the most unpleasant, the philosopher king the most pleasant of lives.'

'That necessarily follows.'

4. *Finally it is shown that the tyrant is 729 times more unhappy than the philosopher king.*[38]

'Do you know,' I asked, 'just how much unhappier the tyrant is than the philosopher king?'

'No, tell me.'

'There appear to be three types of pleasure,' I replied, 'one genuine, two spurious.[39] The tyrant, in his flight from law and reason, trespasses beyond the bounds of the spurious types, surrounding himself with an armed gang of slavish pleasures, and the degree of his inferiority is not easy to describe. One might do it as follows.'

'How?'

'The tyrant was third in order from the oligarch, the democratic type intervening between them.'

'Yes.'

'So (if our argument is correct) the pleasure he enjoys will be a phantom three times further from reality than the oligarch's.'

'True.'

'The oligarch, again, was third in order from the philosopher king (assuming philosopher kingship and the rule of the best to be identical[40]).'

'He was.'

'So the distance of the tyrant's pleasure from true pleasure can be expressed numerically as three times three.'

'So it seems.'

'The tyrant's phantom pleasure is, therefore, in spatial terms a plane number.'[41]

'Exactly.'

'Square this and then cube it and it becomes obvious how great the distance is.'[42]

'Obvious to a mathematician anyway!'

'Conversely, you will find, if you work out the cube, that the

e   measure of difference between the two in terms of true pleasure
is that the philosopher king lives seven hundred and twenty-nine
times more pleasantly than the tyrant, and the tyrant the same
amount more painfully than the philosopher king.'

'What a terrific calculation,' he exclaimed, 'and all to show
how much difference there is between the just and unjust man
588 *a*   in terms of pleasure and pain!'

'But it's quite correct,' I replied, 'and fits human life, if human
life is measured by days and nights and months and years.'[43]

'As of course it is.'

'And if the good and just man is so much superior to the bad
and unjust man in terms of pleasure, will not his superiority be
infinitely greater in terms of grace and beauty of life and of
excellence?'

'Infinitely greater,' he replied emphatically.

11. Conclusion

*Wrongdoing and injustice therefore cannot pay, and goodness
brings its own reward. But it is doubtful if the ideal society
described, where goodness would have full scope, will ever exist
on earth.*

b   'So far so good,' I said. 'Having got so far in the argument,
let us recall what it was that started us off. It was, I think,
the assertion that wrongdoing paid the man who combined
complete injustice with a reputation for justice.'[44]

'That was it.'

'Well, now that we have agreed what the effects of just and
unjust conduct are, we can have a word with its author.'

'What shall we say?' he asked.

'Let us construct a model of the human personality, to show
him what his assertion really implies.'

c   'What sort of model?'

'Like one of those composite beasts in the old myths, Chi-
maera and Scylla and Cerberus and all the rest, which combine
more than one kind of creature in one.'

'I know the stories.'

'Imagine a very complicated, many-headed sort of beast, with heads of wild and tame animals all round it, which it can produce and change at will.'

'Quite a feat of modelling,' he replied; 'but fortunately it's   *d*
easier to imagine than it would be to make.'

'Add two other sorts of creature, one a lion, the other a man. And let the many-headed creature be by far the largest, and the lion the next largest.'

'That's rather easier to imagine.'

'Then put the three together and combine them into a single creature.'

'Done.'

'Then give the whole the external appearance of one of the three, the man, so that to eyes unable to see anything beneath the outer shell it looks like a single creature, a man.'   *e*

'That is done too.'

'Then let us point out that to say that it pays this man to do wrong and not to do right, is to say that it pays him to give the many-headed beast a good time, and to strengthen it and the lion and all its qualities, while starving the man till he becomes   589 *a*
so weak that the other two can do what they like with him; and that he should make no attempt to reconcile them and make them friends, but leave them to snarl and wrangle and devour each other.'

'That is just what it means to approve injustice and wrong-doing.'

'On the other hand, to say that it pays to be just is to say that we ought to say and do all we can to strengthen the man within us, so that he can look after the many-headed beast like a farmer,   *b*
nursing and cultivating its tamer elements and preventing the wilder ones growing, while he makes an ally of the lion and looks after the common interests of all by reconciling them with each other and with himself.'

'That, again, is exactly what it means to approve of justice.'

'The glorification of injustice is therefore wrong on all counts, and the glorification of justice right. For, whether you look to   *c*
pleasure or profit or reputation, to praise justice is to tell the

truth, to disparage it to talk in ignorance of what you are disparaging, and entirely unsound.'

'Yes, I agree.'

'But let us deal gently with our opponent; his mistake isn't deliberate. "My dear chap," let us say to him, "what is the origin and purpose of the conventional notions of fair and foul? Does not the one subject the beast in us to our human, or perhaps I should say our divine, element, while the other enslaves our

d   humaner nature to the beast?" He's bound to agree with that, isn't he?'

'Yes, if he listens to me.'

'Then on this reckoning,' I asked, 'can it possibly pay anyone to make money by doing wrong, if the result of his so doing is

e   to enslave the best part of himself to the worst? No one would say it paid to sell his son or daughter as a slave to harsh and wicked masters, however high the price; if one ruthlessly enslaves the divinest part of oneself to the most godless and abominable, is it not a miserable piece of bribery, with results

590 *a*   far more fatal than Eriphyle's sale of her husband's life for a necklace?'[45]

'If I may answer for him,' said Glaucon, 'I should say it was far more fatal.'

'And why has self-indulgence always been censured? Isn't it because it gives too much freedom to the monstrous multiform creature within us?'

'Obviously.'

'And are not obstinacy and bad temper censured for increas-

b   ing and intensifying the strength of the lion and dragon in us to too high a pitch?'

'Certainly.'

'Similarly are not luxury and effeminacy censured for relaxing it till it grows slack and cowardly?'

'Yes.'

'And we blame flattery and meanness when they subordinate the spirited element in us to the unruliness of the beast, and when, to gratify the beast's greed and love of money, they school the lion to put up with insults and turn it into an ape.'

c   'True.'

'And why do we despise manual work as vulgar? Isn't it because it indicates a certain weakness in our higher nature, which is unable to control the animal part of us, and can only serve and learn how to pander to it?'

'Yes, I think so.'

'To ensure that people of this type are under the same authority as the highest type, we have said that they should be subjected to that highest type, which is governed by its divine *d* element; but this control is not exercised, as Thrasymachus thought, to the detriment of the subject, but because it is better for every creature to be under the control of divine wisdom. That wisdom and control should, if possible, come from within; failing that it must be imposed from without, in order that, being under the same guidance, we may all be friends and equals.'[46]

'That is all very right.'

'And this is plainly the intention of the law, in the support it *e* gives to all citizens, and of the control we exercise over children, not letting them run free till we have established some kind of constitutional government in them, and have educated the best *591 a* in them to be their guardian and ruler and to take over from the best in us: then we give them their freedom.'

'That is clearly so.'

'Then how, my dear Glaucon,' I asked, 'can we possibly argue that it pays a man to be unjust or self-indulgent or do anything base that will bring him more money and power but make him a worse man?'

'We can't possibly.'

'And how can it pay him to escape the punishment of wrong-doing by not being found out? If he escapes doesn't he merely *b* become worse? And if he's caught and punished isn't the beast in him calmed and tamed, and his humaner part set free? And doesn't that mean that he is making the best of his natural gifts, and, by forming a character in which self-control and justice and understanding are combined, getting something worth more than physical strength and health and good looks, just as the mind is worth more than the body?'

'Perfectly true.'

c   'This, then, will be the object of the intelligent man's life-long
endeavours. The only studies he will value will be those that
form his mind and character accordingly.'

'That's clear enough.'

'And as for his physical condition and training – he won't live
for the indulgence of brutish and irrational pleasures, indeed he
won't even make health his primary concern; strength and health
and good looks will mean nothing to him unless they conduce
d   to self-control, and we shall always find him attuning his body
to match the harmony of his mind and character.'

'He must if he's to be a true musician.'[47]

'And won't he observe the same principle of harmony and
order in acquiring wealth? He won't be dazzled, will he, by
popular ideas of happiness and make endless troubles for himself
by piling up a fortune?'

'I should think not.'

e   'Because, in so far as he is able to save or spend, he will do so
under the watchful guidance of the principles of self-government
in his own heart; and his only concern will be to prevent them
being upset either because he possesses too much or too little.'

'Exactly.'

592 a   'He will follow the same principles over honours, private or
public. If he thinks they will make him a better man he will
accept and enjoy them, if he thinks they will destroy the order
within him, he will avoid them.'

'If that is his object, he won't enter politics,' he said.

'Oh yes, he will,' I replied, 'very much so, in the society where
he really belongs; but not, I think, in the society where he's
born, unless some miracle happens.'

'I see what you mean,' he said. 'You mean that he will do so
in the society which we have been describing and which we have
b   theoretically founded; but I doubt if it will ever exist on earth.'

'Perhaps,' I said, 'it is laid up as a pattern in heaven, where
he who wishes can see it and found it in his own heart.[48] But it
doesn't matter whether it exists or ever will exist; in it alone,
and in no other society, could he take part in public affairs.'

'I expect you are right.'

PART X
THEORY OF ART

This part has the appearance of an appendix, written to justify against anticipated or actual criticism the attack on the poets in Books II and III (Part III). It has sometimes been suggested that it should not be taken too seriously. But the claims made for the poets by Greek opinion were often extravagant. They treated the works of Homer and the poets as their Bible, and in Plato's Ion Homer is claimed as a teacher of everything from carpentry to morals and generalship. It is such claims that Plato has primarily in mind, but there is nothing to suggest that he is not serious, though he is often characteristically ironical; and the general contention in section 1 that poetry is illusion fits well into the scheme of the Divided Line (Part VII, section 6, above). See Cross and Woozey, ch. 12.

1. Art and Illusion

The Greek word mimesis, *'representation', used in Part III to describe dramatic as opposed to narrative poetry, is now used to describe artistic creation as a whole, and interpreted to mean a rather literal imitation.[1] The productions both of the painter and the poet are imitations of a life which has itself only secondary reality, and neither painter nor poet have any knowledge of what they imitate. Pictures and poems are secondhand, unreal, and tell us nothing about life.*

'You know,' I said, 'among all the excellent features of our ideal state, there's none I rank higher than its treatment of poetry.'

'Why exactly?'

'Because it excluded all dramatic representation.[2] Now that we have distinguished the various elements in the mind, we can
b see even more clearly how essential it is to exclude it.'

'What do you mean?'

'Between ourselves – and you mustn't give me away to the tragedians and other writers of the kind – such representations definitely harm the minds of their audiences, unless they're inoculated against them by knowing their real nature.'

'What exactly have you in mind?'

'I must tell you, I suppose; yet the love and respect I've always had from a boy for Homer makes me hesitate – for I think he's
c the original master and guide of all the great tragic poets. But one must not respect an individual more than the truth, and so, as I say, I must tell you.'

'You must,' he said.

'Listen, then; or, rather, answer my questions.'

'Ask away.'

'Can you tell me in general terms what representation *is*? I'm not sure that I know, myself, exactly how to describe its purpose.'

'Then it's not very likely I shall!'

596 a   'Oh, I don't know,' I said. 'It isn't always the sharpest eyes that see things first.'

'True enough,' he replied. 'But with you here, if I did see anything, I shouldn't much want to say so. You must use your own eyes.'

'Then shall we start by following our usual procedure? You know that we always postulate in each case a single form for each set of particular things, to which we apply the same name?'[3]

'Yes, I know.'

b   'Then let us take any set you choose. For example, there are many particular beds and tables.'

'Yes.'

'But there are only two forms, one of bed and one of table.'

'Yes.'

'Then we normally say that the maker of either of these kinds of furniture has his eye on the appropriate form when he makes the beds and tables we use; and similarly with other things. For no craftsman could possibly make the form itself, could he?'

'No.'

'Well now, I wonder what you would call a craftsman of the following kind.'

'Describe him.'   c

'One who can make all the objects produced by other particular crafts.'

'He would be a wonderfully clever man.'

'Just a minute, and you'll be more surprised still. For this same craftsman can not only make all artificial objects, but also create all plants and animals, himself included, and, in addition, earth and sky and gods, the heavenly bodies and everything in the underworld.'

'An astonishing exhibition of skill!' he exclaimed.   d

'You don't believe me?' I asked. 'Tell me, do you think that a craftsman of this sort couldn't exist, or (in one sense, if not in another) create all these things? Do you know that there's a sense in which you could create them yourself?'

'What sense?'

'It's not difficult, and can be done in various ways quite quickly. The quickest way is to take a mirror and turn it round in all directions; before long you will create sun and stars and   e earth, yourself and all other animals and plants, and furniture and the other objects we mentioned just now.'

'Yes, but they would only be reflections,' he said, 'not real things.'

'Quite right,' I replied, 'and very much to the point. For a painter is a craftsman of just this kind, I think. Do you agree?'

'Yes.'

'You may perhaps object that the things he creates are not real; and yet there *is* a sense in which the painter creates a bed, isn't there?'

'Yes,' he agreed, 'he produces an appearance of one.'

'And what about the carpenter? Didn't you agree that what   597 a he produces is not the form of bed which according to us is what a bed really is,[4] but a particular bed?'

'I did.'

'If, then, what he makes is not "what a bed really is", his product is not "what is", but something which *resembles* "what is" without *being* it. And anyone who says that the products of the carpenter or any other craftsman are ultimately real can hardly be telling the truth, can he?'

'No one familiar with the sort of arguments we're using could suppose so.'

'So we shan't be surprised if the bed the carpenter makes is a
b   shadowy thing compared to reality?'

'No.'

'Then shall we try to discover just what the activity of representation is, on the basis of this example?'

'Yes, please.'

'We have seen that there are three sorts of bed. The first exists in nature, and we would say, I suppose, that it was made by god. No one else could have made it, could they?'

'I think not.'

'The second is made by the carpenter.'

'Yes.'

'And the third by the painter?'

'Granted.'

'So painter, carpenter, and god are each responsible for one kind of bed.'

'Yes.'

c   'God, then, created only one real bed-in-itself in nature, either because he wanted to or because some necessity prevented him from making more than one; at any rate he didn't produce more than one, and more than one could not possibly be produced.'

'Why?'

'Because, suppose he created two only, another would emerge whose form the other two shared, and it, not the other two, would be the real bed-in-itself.'

'That's true.'

d   'And I suppose that god knew it, and as he wanted to be a real creator of a real bed, and not just a carpenter making a particular bed, produced in nature a single bed-in-itself.'

'I suppose so.'

'Then do you think we might call him author of its nature or some such name?'

'We could do so with justice; for it and all other things in nature[5] are his creation.'

'And what about the carpenter? Doesn't he manufacture a bed?'

'Yes.'

'And what about the artist? Does he make or manufacture?'

'No.'

'Then what does he do?'

'I think that we may fairly claim that he represents what the   *e*
other two make.'

'Good,' said I. 'Then you say that the artist's representation stands at third remove from reality?'

'I do.'

'So the tragic poet, if his art is representation, is by nature at third remove from the throne of truth; and the same is true of all other representative artists.'

'So it seems.'

'We are agreed about representation, then. But, tell me, which does the painter try to represent? The thing-itself as it is in   598 *a*
nature or the things the craftsman makes?'

'The things the craftsman makes.'

'As they are, or as they appear? There is still that distinction to make.'

'I don't understand,' he said.

'What I mean is this. If you look at a bed, or anything else, sideways or endways or from some other angle, does it make any difference to the bed? Isn't it merely that it *looks* different, without *being* different? And similarly with other things.'

'Yes, it's the same bed, but it looks different.'

'Then consider – when the painter makes his representation,   *b*
does he do so by reference to the object as it actually is or to its superficial appearance?[6] Is his representation one of an apparition[7] or of the truth?'

'Of an apparition.'

'The art of representation is therefore a long way removed

from truth, and it is able to reproduce everything because it has little grasp of anything, and that little is of a mere phenomenal appearance. For example, a painter can paint a portrait of a shoemaker or a carpenter or any other craftsman without

c understanding any of their crafts; yet, if he is skilful enough, his portrait of a carpenter may, at a distance, deceive children or simple people into thinking it is a real carpenter.'

'Yes, it may.'

'In all such cases,' I went on, 'we should bear the following considerations in mind. When someone tells us that he has met

d someone who is a master of every craft and has a more exact understanding about all subjects than any individual expert, we must answer that he is a simple-minded fellow who seems to have been taken in by the work of a charlatan, whose apparent omniscience is due entirely to his own inability to distinguish knowledge, ignorance, and representation.'

'Very true.'

'We must go on to examine the claims of the tragedians and their chief, Homer. We are told that they are masters of all

e forms of skill, and know all about human excellence and defect and about religion; for – so the argument runs – a good poet must, if he's to write well, know all about his subject, otherwise he can't write about it. We must ask ourselves whether those who have met the poets have, when they see or hear their works, failed to perceive that they are representations at the third remove from reality, and easy to produce without any know-

599 a ledge of the truth, because they are appearances and not realities; or are they right, and do good poets really know about the subjects on which the public thinks they speak so well?'

'It's a question we should certainly examine.'

'Suppose, then, a man could produce both the original and the copy. Do you think he would seriously want to devote himself to the manufacture of copies and make it the highest object in life?'

b 'No, I don't.'

'Of course not. If he really knew about the things he represented, he would devote himself to them and not to their representations; he would try to leave behind him the memory of many deeds well done, and be more anxious to be praised himself than to write in praise of others.'

'I agree; his reputation and effectiveness would both be greater.'

'We won't, then, expect Homer or any of the poets to explain medicine or any similar skilled activity to us; for example, if they claim to be real doctors and not merely to imitate doctors' talk, we won't ask them to name any poet, ancient or modern, who has performed cures like Aesculapius, or founded a school of medicine to follow him as he did. But we *have* a right to cross-question Homer when he tries to deal with matters of such supreme importance as military strategy, political adminis-tration and human education. "My dear Homer," we shall say, "if our definition of representation is wrong and you are not merely manufacturing copies at third remove from reality, but are a stage nearer the truth about human excellence, and really capable of judging what kind of conduct will make the indi-vidual or the community better or worse, tell us any state whose constitution you have reformed, as Lycurgus did at Sparta and others have done elsewhere on a larger or smaller scale. What city attributes the benefit of its legal system to your skill? Italy and Sicily owe theirs to Charondas, we owe ours to Solon. Tell us who is similarly indebted to you."'

'I don't think,' said Glaucon, 'that Homer's most devoted admirers could claim there was anyone.'

'Well, then, is there any record of a successful war being fought in Homer's day either under his command or with his advice?'

'No.'

'Then had he any practical skill? Is he said to have invented any ingenious technical or practical devices like Thales of Miletus or Anacharsis the Scythian?'[8]

'He did nothing of that sort.'

'Well, if he did no public service, do we hear of him founding a school of his own, where enthusiastic pupils came to hear him while he lived and to hand on a Homeric way of life to their successors? That was how Pythagoras got his great reputa-tion, and his successors still talk of a Pythagorean way of life which distinguishes them in the eyes of the world from other people.'

'We hear nothing of that sort about Homer. Indeed, if the stories about Homer are true, his friend Creophylus is an even more absurd example of education than his name[9] suggests, as he is said to have paid very little attention to Homer in his own
c   day, when he was still alive.'

'Yes, that's the story,' I said. 'But do you think, Glaucon, that if Homer had really been able to bring men the benefits of education, instead of merely representing it, he would not have had many enthusiastic followers and admirers? Protagoras of Abdera and Prodicus of Ceos[10] and a whole lot of other individual teachers have managed to persuade their contemporaries
d   that no one who has not studied under *them* is fit to manage either private or public affairs; and they are so admired for this expert knowledge that their pupils are almost ready to carry them about shoulder-high. Would the contemporaries of Homer and Hesiod have let them continue as wandering minstrels, if they had really been able to make them better men? Wouldn't they have clung to them like solid gold and tried to keep them at home, and if they wouldn't stay, gone to school with them
e   wherever they were till they had learnt what they could from them?'

'I think that's perfectly true, Socrates.'

'We may assume, then, that all the poets from Homer downwards have no grasp of truth but merely produce a superficial likeness of any subject they treat, including human excellence. For example, as we said just now, the painter paints what looks
601 a   like a shoemaker, though neither he nor his public know about shoe-making, but judge merely by colour and form.'

'True.'

'In the same way the poet can use words and phrases as a medium to paint a picture of any craftsman, though he knows nothing except how to represent him, and the metre and rhythm and music will persuade people who are as ignorant as he is, and who judge merely from his words, that he really has something to say about shoemaking or generalship or whatever it may be. So great is the natural magic of poetry. Strip it of its

poetic colouring, reduce it to plain prose, and I think you know *b*
how little it amounts to.'

'Yes, I've noticed that.'

'Like a face which relied on the bloom of youth for its charm,
and whose lack of beauty is plain to see when youth deserts it.'

'Yes.'

'Now to another point. The artist who makes a likeness of
a thing knows nothing about the reality but only about the
appearance – that was what we said, wasn't it?'   *c*

'Yes.'

'But that is only half the story. Let us look at it more fully.'

'Go on.'

'The painter may paint a picture of bridle and bit.'

'Yes.'

'But aren't they made by the harness-maker and smith?'

'Yes.'

'Then does the painter know what the bridle and bit ought
to be like? Isn't this something that even the makers – the
harness-maker and the smith – don't know, but only the horse-
man who knows how to use them?'

'True.'

'Isn't the same thing always true?'

'Your meaning?'

'You always have the three techniques – use, manufacture, *d*
and representation.'

'Yes.'

'And isn't the quality, beauty and fitness of any implement or
creature or action judged by reference to the use for which man
or nature produced it?'

'Yes.'

'It must follow, then, that the user of a thing has the widest
experience of it and must tell the maker how well it has performed its function in the use to which he puts it. For example,
the flute-player reports to the flute-maker on the performance
of his flutes, and will give specifications for their manufacture *e*
which the flute-maker will follow.'

'Of course.'

'The player, in fact, knows about the merits and defects of his instruments, and the manufacturer will rely on the player's judgement?'

'Yes.'

'The maker of an implement, therefore, has a correct *belief*[11]
602 *a* about its merits and defects, but he is obliged to get this by associating with and listening to someone who *knows*. And the person with the relevant knowledge is the user.'

'That is so.'

'What about the artist and his representations? Has he the user's direct experience of the things he paints to enable him to know whether or not his pictures are good or right? Or has he the correct opinion that springs from enforced acquaintance with and obedience to someone who knows what he ought to paint?'

'He has neither.'

'So the artist has neither knowledge nor correct opinion about the goodness or badness of the things he represents.'

'Apparently not.'

'So the poet too, as artist, will be beautifully ill-informed about the subjects of his poetry.'

'Completely.'

b   'None the less he'll go on writing poetry, in spite of not knowing whether what he produces is good or bad: and what he will represent will be anything that appeals to the taste of the ignorant multitude.'

'What else can he do?'

'Well,' I concluded, 'we seem to be pretty well agreed that the artist knows little or nothing about the subjects he represents and that the art of representation is something that has no serious value; and that this applies above all to all tragic poetry, epic or dramatic.'

'Yes, entirely agreed.'

We have in this section (Part X, section 1) two trios: three 'makers', God who makes the Form, the craftsman who makes, e.g., the bed 'with his eye on the form', and the artist who copies what the craftsman has made; three skills, that of the user, of the maker, and of the artist. The two trios are not entirely

*consistent with each other: in the one the craftsman-maker has
his 'eye on the form', in the other he takes his instructions from
the user, whose knowledge of the* true function *of what is made
is presumably equivalent to the knowledge of its* form. *The
parallel with Parts* VII–VIII *is again not exact. But we have (a)
the realm of Forms which is the object of knowledge, (b) the
realm of ordinary experience in which we have true belief (*pistis*)
or true opinion (*doxa*) and on a lower level the copies, images
or ghosts (note 7 above) made by the artist, which recall the
images of sub-section D of the Line and the* shadows *seen by
the prisoners in the Cave. Compare Crombie, vol. II, pp.* 103–4.

2. The Appeal of Art and Poetry

*Art and poetry appeal to, and represent, the lower, less rational
part of our nature.*

'Now, look here,' I said; 'we have said that this process of [602] *c*
representation deals with something at third remove from the
truth, haven't we?'

'Yes.'

'Then on what part of the human being does it exercise its
power?'

'What do you mean by part?'

'Something like this. The apparent size of an object, as you
know, varies with its distance from our eye.'

'Yes.'

'So also a stick will look bent if you put it in the water, straight   *d*
when you take it out, and deceptive differences of shading can
make the same surface seem to the eye concave or convex; and
our minds are clearly liable to all sorts of confusions of this
kind. It is this natural weakness of ours that the scene-painter
and conjuror and their fellows exploit with magical effect.'

'True.'

'Measuring, counting, and weighing have happily been discovered to help us out of these difficulties, and to ensure that
we should not be guided by apparent differences of size, quantity

and heaviness, but by calculations of number, measurement, and weight.'

'Of course.'

'And these calculations are performed by the element of
e   reason in the mind.'

'Yes, that's true.'

'Yet when reason informs us, as the result of frequent measurements, that one thing is greater than or less than or equal to another, it may be contradicted by appearances.'

'It may be.'

'Yet we said that the same part of us cannot hold different opinions about the same thing at the same time.'

'And we were quite right.'

603 a   'So the part of the mind which contradicts the measurements cannot be the same as the part which agrees with them.'

'No.'

'But the part which relies on measurement and calculation must be the best part of us.'

'Of course.'

'So is not the part which contradicts them an inferior one?'

'Inevitably.'

'That was the conclusion I had in mind when I said that the work of the painter and of all other representative artists was far removed from the truth and associated with elements in us
b   equally far removed from reason, in a fond liaison without health or truth.'

'Absolutely true.'

'So representative art is an inferior child born of inferior parents.'

'I suppose so.'

'And does this apply to the visual arts only, or also to the art which appeals to the ear which we call poetry?'

'I should think it probably applies to poetry too.'

'We mustn't rely on probabilities drawn from painting,' I said, 'but consider the part of the mind to which dramatic poetry
c   appeals, and ask what serious worth it has.'

'Yes, that's what we should do,' he agreed.

'Then let us put it like this,' I went on: 'drama represents human beings in action, either voluntarily or under compulsion; in that action they fare, as they think, well or ill, and experience joy or sorrow. Is that a fair summary?'

'Yes.'

'And does a man remain at unity in himself in all these experiences? We saw that there could be conflict and contrary opinions about the same objects in the realm of vision; isn't there a similar conflict and internal struggle in the realm of action? There is really no need to ask the question, because, as I remember, we have already earlier in our discussion[12] agreed well enough that our mind is full of innumerable conflicts of this sort.'

'We were quite right about that.'

'Yes, but there's an omission we must now make good.'

'What is it?'

'Didn't we then say[13] that a good man who loses his son, or anything else dear to him, will bear the misfortune more equably than other people?'

'Yes.'

'Now consider: is it because he will feel no grief? Or is that impossible, and is it because he will moderate his sorrow?'

'The second alternative is nearer the truth.'

'Then tell me, will he be more inclined to resist and fight against his grief when his fellows can see him, or when he is alone by himself?'

'Much more inclined when others can see him.'

'On the other hand, when he is alone he will not mind saying and doing things which he would be ashamed to let other people hear or see.'

'That is true.'

'Reason and principle demand restraint, while his very feeling of sorrow prompts him to give way to grief.'

'True.'

'And the simultaneous presence of opposite impulses about the same thing implies that there are two elements in his nature.'

'Of course.'

'Of these, one is prepared to obey the direction of principle.'

'How do you mean?'

'Well, of course, custom and principle say that it is best, so far as we can, to bear misfortune patiently and without com-
c plaint; for we cannot tell whether it will turn out well or ill, and nothing is gained by impatience, nor is anything in human life of great consequence; besides, grief prevents us getting just the help we need.'

'And what is that?'

'That of deliberation,' I said, 'which reflects on what has happened and then makes what reason picks as the best move that the fall of the dice allows. We must learn not to hold our
d hurts and waste our time crying, like children who've bumped themselves, but to train our mind to cure our ills and rectify our lapses as soon as it can, banishing sorrow by healing it.'

'That is the right way to deal with misfortune.'

'And the highest part of us is ready to follow this reasoning.'

'Yes, obviously.'

'The other part of us, which remembers our sufferings and is never tired of bemoaning them, we may, I think, call irrational and lazy and inclined to cowardice.'

'Yes, we may.'

e 'And this recalcitrant element in us gives plenty of material for dramatic representation; but the reasonable element and its unvarying calm are difficult to represent, and difficult to understand if represented, particularly by the motley audience gathered in a theatre, to whose experience it is quite foreign.'

605 a 'Very true.'

'The dramatic poet will not therefore naturally turn to this element, nor will his skill be directed to please it, if he wants to win a popular reputation; but he will find it easy to represent a character that is unstable and refractory.'

'Obviously.'

'Then we can fairly take the poet and set him beside the painter. He resembles him both because his works have a low
b degree of truth and also because he deals with a low element in the mind. We are therefore quite right to refuse to admit him to a properly run state, because he wakens and encourages and strengthens the lower elements in the mind to the detriment of reason, which is like giving power and political control to the

worst elements in a state and ruining the better elements. The dramatic poet produces a similarly bad state of affairs in the mind of the individual, by encouraging the unreasoning part of it, which cannot distinguish greater and less but thinks the same things are now large and now small, and by creating images far removed from the truth.'

'I agree.'

3. The Effects of Poetry and Drama

Poetry, dramatic poetry in particular, has a bad effect on its audiences, who learn to admire and imitate the faults it represents. We cannot, therefore, allow poets in our ideal state.

'The gravest charge against poetry still remains. It has a terrible power to corrupt even the best characters, with very few exceptions.'

'It is indeed terrible if it can do that.'

'Then listen. When we hear Homer or one of the tragic poets representing the sufferings of a hero and making him bewail them at length, perhaps with all the sounds and signs of tragic grief, you know how even the best of us enjoy it and let ourselves be carried away by our feelings; and we are full of praises for the merits of the poet who can most powerfully affect us in this way.'

'Yes, I know.'

'Yet in our private griefs we pride ourselves on just the opposite, that is, on our ability to bear them in silence like men, and we regard the behaviour we admired on the stage as womanish.'

'Yes, I'm aware of that.'

'Then is it really right,' I asked, 'to admire, when we see him on the stage, a man we should ourselves be ashamed to resemble? Is it reasonable to feel enjoyment and admiration rather than disgust?'

'It seems most unreasonable,' he said.

'Particularly,' I added, 'if you look at it in this way.'

'How?'

c

d

e

606 a

'If you consider that the poet gratifies and indulges the instinctive desires of a part of us, which we forcibly restrain in our
private misfortunes, with its hunger for tears and for an unin-
hibited indulgence in grief. Our better nature, being without
b adequate intellectual or moral training, relaxes its control over
these feelings, on the grounds that it is someone else's sufferings
it is watching and that there's nothing to be ashamed of in
praising and pitying another man with some claim to goodness
who shows excessive grief; besides, it reckons the pleasure it gets
as sheer gain, and would certainly not consent to be deprived of
it by condemning the whole poem. For very few people are
capable of realizing that what we feel for other people must
infect what we feel for ourselves, and that if we let our pity for
the misfortunes of others grow too strong it will be difficult to
restrain our feelings in our own.'

c   'That is very true.'

'Does not the same argument apply to laughter as to pity?
For the effect is similar when you enjoy on the stage – or even
in ordinary life – jokes that you would be ashamed to make
yourself, instead of detesting their vulgarity. You are giving rein
to your comic instinct, which your reason has restrained for fear
you may seem to be playing the fool, and bad taste in the theatre
may insensibly lead you into becoming a buffoon at home.'

'It may indeed.'

d   'Poetry has the same effect on us when it represents sex and
anger, and the other desires and feelings of pleasure and pain
which accompany all our actions. It waters them when they
ought to be left to wither, and makes them control us when we
ought, in the interests of our own greater welfare and happiness,
to control them.'

'I can't deny it,' he said.

e   'And so, Glaucon,' I continued, 'when you meet people who
admire Homer as the educator of Greece, and who say that in
the administration of human affairs and education we should
study him and model our whole lives on his poetry, you must
607 *a* feel kindly towards them as good men within their limits, and
you may agree with them that Homer is the best of poets and

first of tragedians. But you will know that the only poetry that should be allowed in a state is hymns to the gods and paeans in praise of good men; once you go beyond that and admit the sweet lyric or epic muse, pleasure and pain become your rulers instead of law and the rational principles commonly accepted as best.'

'Quite true.'

'Our defence, then, when we are reminded that we banished poetry from our state, must be that its character was such as to give us good grounds for so doing and that our argument required it. But in case we are condemned for being insensitive and bad mannered, let us add that there is an old quarrel between philosophy and poetry. One can quote many examples of this ancient antagonism: remarks about the "bitch that growls and snarls at her master", and "a reputation among empty-headed fools", or "the crowd of heads that know too much" and the "subtle thinkers" who are "beggars" none the less.[14] However, let us freely admit that if drama and poetry written for pleasure can prove to us that they have a place in a well-run society, we will gladly admit them, for we know their fascination only too well ourselves; but it would be wicked to abandon what seems to be the truth. I expect you feel the fascination of poetry yourself, don't you,' I asked, 'especially when it's Homer exercising it?'

'I do indeed.'

'It is only fair, then, that poetry should return, if she can make her defence in lyric or other metre.'

'Yes.'

'And we should give her defenders, men who aren't poets themselves but who love poetry, a chance of defending her in prose and proving that she doesn't only give pleasure but brings lasting benefit to human life and human society. And we will listen favourably, as we shall gain much if we find her a source of profit as well as pleasure.'

'Yes, we shall gain a lot.'

'But if they fail to make their case, then we shall have to follow the example of the lover who renounces a passion that is doing him no good, however hard it may be to do so. Brought up as we have been in our own admirably constituted[15] societies, we are bound to love poetry, and we shall be glad if it proves to have high value and truth; but in the absence of such proof we shall, whenever we listen to it, recite this argument of ours to ourselves as a charm to prevent us falling under the spell of a childish and vulgar passion. Our theme shall be that such poetry has no serious value or claim to truth, and we shall warn its

b   hearers to fear its effects on the constitution of their inner selves, and tell them to adopt the view of poetry we have described.'

'I entirely agree.'

'Yes, my dear Glaucon,' I said, 'because the issues at stake, the choice between becoming a good man or a bad, are even greater than they appear, and neither honour nor wealth nor power, nor poetry itself, should tempt us to neglect the claims of justice and excellence of every kind.'

'I agree,' he said; 'your argument convinces me, as I think it would anyone else.'

There is a parallel to Plato's treatment of poetry and art in Tolstoy, What is Art? *(p. 50). 'To evoke in oneself a feeling one has once experienced, and having invoked it in oneself, then, by means of movements, lines, colours, sounds or forms expressed in words, so to transmit that feeling that others may experience the same feeling – this is the activity of art. Art is a human activity, consisting in this, that one man consciously, by means of certain external signs, hands on to others the feelings he has lived through, and that other people are infected by these feelings, and also experience them.'*

Both Plato and Tolstoy think that the poet and artist in some way infect *those who read or see their productions with the feelings which those productions portray, and since the feelings portrayed are often morally questionable, such portrayal must be treated with the greatest caution. Both, in consequence, make a pretty clean sweep of the traditionally great artists and writers. Plato eliminates Homer and the tragedians; Tolstoy's list is even more detailed and comprehensive, ranging from Sophocles to Shakespeare, and including Beethoven and Wagner (ibid., pp. 122–3). Plato adds (605c–606d) a further criticism based on his analysis of the mind (opening note to Part v, section 2 above), as he considers that poetry and art appeal to the mind's lower elements.*

PART XI
THE IMMORTALITY OF
THE SOUL AND THE
REWARDS OF GOODNESS

1. The Soul Immortal

The soul is immortal because its own specific fault, moral wickedness, cannot destroy it.

[608] c 'Yet, you know,' I said, 'we haven't yet described the chief rewards and prizes that goodness can win.'

'If they're greater than those we've described already, they must be enormous.'

'Can anything really great grow in a short time?' I asked. 'For the span from youth to old age is surely short enough compared to the whole of time.'

'A mere nothing,' he agreed.

'Then ought not a thing that is immortal to concern itself with
d the whole of time rather than with so short a span?'

'I suppose so,' he replied, 'but what of it?'

'Don't you know,' I asked, 'that our soul is immortal and never perishes?'

He looked at me in astonishment, and exclaimed, 'Good Lord, no! Are you prepared to maintain it is?'

'I ought to be,' I said. 'And so ought you; there's nothing difficult about it.'

'There is for me; but I should like to hear you explain it if it's so easy.'

'I will.'

'Go on.'

'You use the terms good and evil, don't you?'

'I do.'

'I wonder if you think of them in the same way that I do.'   *e*

'How is that?'

'I call anything that harms or destroys a thing evil, and anything that preserves and benefits it good.'

'I agree.'

'Then hasn't each individual thing its own particular good and evil? So most things are subject to their own specific form   609 *a* of evil or disease; for example, the eyes to ophthalmia and the body generally to illness, grain to mildew, timber to rot, bronze and iron to rust, and so on.'

'Yes.'

'And is not their effect to flaw anything they attack, and finally to disintegrate and destroy it altogether?'

'Yes.'

'A thing's specific evil or flaw is therefore what destroys it, and nothing else will do so. For what is good is not destructive,   *b* nor what is neutral.'

'That is true.'

'If, therefore, we find anything whose specific evil can mar it, but cannot finally destroy it, we shall know that it must by its very nature be indestructible.'

'So it would seem.'

'Then, is there anything which makes the soul evil?'

'Yes, there certainly is – all the things we have been describing, injustice, indiscipline, cowardice, and ignorance.'   *c*

'Do any of them finally destroy it? We must not make the mistake of thinking that, because injustice is a flaw in the soul, the unjust or foolish man, when he is caught doing wrong, is destroyed by his injustice. We must rather look at it like this. The body's particular flaw is disease, which weakens and destroys it, till finally it ceases to be a body at all; and the result of the destructive presence of their particular evil is, in all the other   *d* instances we quoted, annihilation, is it not?'

'Yes.'

'Let us examine the soul in the same way. Do injustice and other forms of evil by their persistent presence in it destroy and weaken it, till they finally kill it and sever it from the body?'

'No, certainly not.'

'But it would be quite illogical to suppose that anything could be destroyed by the specific evil of something else, but not by its own.'

'Quite illogical.'

e   'For you know, of course, Glaucon,' I went on, 'that it would not be right to suppose that the death of the body was due to the badness of its food, which might be old or rotten or have any other characteristic defect; if any such defect in the food set up a process of deterioration in the body, we should say that the body had been killed by its own particular evil, disease, of

610*a* which the bad food was the occasion. But we ought not ever to say that the body, which is one kind of thing, has been killed by the badness of its food, which is another kind of thing, unless the bad food has produced the body's own specific kind of evil.'

'That is quite true,' he agreed.

'It follows by the same reasoning,' I continued, 'that unless a bodily flaw can produce in the soul one of the soul's own flaws, we cannot suppose that it will destroy it in the absence of such a flaw, as that would imply that the specific evil of one thing could destroy another quite different thing.'[1]

'Yes, that follows.'

'Either we must refute this argument, therefore, or, so long as

b   it remains unrefuted, we must maintain that the soul remains quite unaffected by fever or disease or injury, or even by the body being cut to fragments – unless, that is, someone can prove to us that any of these experiences makes the soul more unjust or wicked than it was. We cannot admit that either the soul or anything else can be destroyed by the presence in it of another

c   thing's specific evil in the absence of its own.'

'At any rate no one will ever prove that death makes the soul more wicked.'

'But even if anyone is brave enough to tackle our argument,' I said, 'and, in an attempt to avoid admitting the immortality of the soul, maintains that men become worse and more wicked when they die, we shall still claim that, if it is true, it is their wickedness which is fatal to them; it's like a naturally deadly

disease which sooner or later, according to the violence of the   *d*
attack, kills those who suffer from it, rather than the execution
of a criminal by the external forces of the law.'

'If wickedness really is fatal to its possessor,' Glaucon
exclaimed emphatically, 'there's nothing very terrible about it;
it merely ends his troubles. The truth is surely just the opposite.
It's other people that wickedness kills, if it can, while so far
removed is it from being fatal to its possessor that it makes him   *e*
full of life and tirelessly energetic as well.'

'You are quite right,' I agreed. 'And if its own particular fault
and its own particular evil has no power to destroy or kill the
soul, it is not likely to be an exception to the general rule
that nothing can be destroyed by an evil adapted to destroy
something else, but only by one adapted to destroy itself.'[2]

'No, that's hardly likely, I should think.'

'Then if there's no evil that can destroy it, either its own or
another's, it must exist for ever; that is to say, it must be   611 *a*
immortal.'

'It must be.'

'We can take that, then, as proved,' I said. 'And if so, it
follows that the same souls have always existed. Their number
cannot be decreased, because no soul can die, nor can it increase;
any increase in the immortal must be at the expense of mortality,
and if that were possible, everything would in the end be
immortal.'

'True.'

'But that is something which our argument forbids us to
believe. Nor should we believe, either, that in its essential nature   *b*
the soul is diverse and variable and full of internal conflicts.'

'Why do you say that?' he asked.

'Because we were thinking just now of the soul as composed
of a number of parts which do not fit perfectly together.[3] In that
case it could hardly be immortal.'

'No, it hardly could.'

'Well then, our recent argument and the others prove conclusively that the soul is immortal. But if we want to see it as it really
is, we should look at it, not as we do now, when it is deformed   *c*
by its association with the body and other evils, but in the pure

state which reason reveals to us. We shall then find that it is a thing of far greater beauty, and shall be able to distinguish far more clearly justice and injustice and all the other qualities we have talked about. We have described truly enough the soul as

d we at present see it. But we see it in a state like that of Glaucus the sea-god, and its original nature is as difficult to see as his was after long immersion had broken and worn away and deformed his limbs, and covered him with shells and seaweed and rock, till he looked more like a monster than what he really was. That is the sort of state we see the soul reduced to by countless evils. For the truth we must look elsewhere.'

'Where?' Glaucon asked.

e 'To the soul's love of wisdom,' I said. 'Think how its kinship with the divine and immortal and eternal makes it long to associate with them and apprehend them; think what it might become if it followed this impulse whole-heartedly and was lifted by it out of the sea in which it is now submerged, and if it

612 *a* shed all the rocks and shells which, because it feeds on the earthly things that men think bring happiness, encrust it in wild and earthy profusion.[4] Then one really could see its true nature, composite or single or whatever it may be. However, as it is, we have, I think, described well enough its character and experience in this mortal life.'

'Quite well enough,' he agreed.

2. The Rewards of Goodness in this Life

The purpose of the whole argument has been to show that goodness is its own reward, irrespective of consequences. But, now that has been proved, we may add that in fact the good man is rewarded by society in this life.

'And now,' I said, 'I think our argument has fulfilled the conditions you laid down, and, in particular, has avoided men-

b tioning the rewards and reputation which justice brings, as you complained Homer and Hesiod do.[5] We have found that justice is itself the best thing for our true self[6] and that we should act justly whether or not we have Gyges' ring, and a cap of invisibility into the bargain.'

'That's perfectly true.'

'That being so, Glaucon,' I asked, 'can there be any objection if we go on and describe the rewards which justice and excellence of every kind bring at the hands of men and gods, in this life   *c* and the next?'

'No objection at all.'

'Then you must give up the concession I made in our argument.'

'What was that?'

'I agreed that the good man should have a reputation for wickedness and the wicked man for goodness; you said that, though it might in fact be impossible for either men or gods to be so deceived, yet you wanted the concession for the purposes of the argument so that we could judge between justice and injustice in themselves, without their consequences. Don't you   *d* remember?'

'I can hardly deny it,' he said.

'Then, now that judgement has been given,' I said, 'I want to ask that we should agree to restore Justice her good name with gods and men; she can then gather the rewards gained from appearances and give them to her possessor, just as we have seen her faithfully giving the benefits of the reality to those who really hold to her.'⁷

'That's a fair request.'   *e*

'Then will you first grant that neither the just nor the unjust man's character is hidden from the gods?'

'Yes.'

'If so, then, as we agreed at the beginning,⁸ they will love one and hate the other.'

'That's true.'

'And the man they love may expect, may he not, all the blessings heaven can give him, except in so far as there is   613 *a* necessary punishment due to him for offences committed in a former life?'

'Yes.'

'So we must assume that, if the just man is poor or ill or

suffering from any other apparent misfortune, it is for his ultimate good in this life or the next. For the gods will never neglect
b the man whose heart is set on justice and who is ready, by
pursuing excellence, to become as like god as man is able.'

'If he is like them, they are not likely to neglect him.'

'On the other hand, we must suppose that the reverse of all
this is true of the unjust man.'

'Most certainly.'

'These, therefore, are the rewards the just man receives from
the gods.'

'I should certainly agree.'

'And what about men?' I asked. 'If the truth be told, isn't it
this – that the clever rogue is rather like a runner who does well
over the first half of the course, but then flags? He is very quick
off the mark, but in the end is humiliated and runs off with his
c tail between his legs⁹ without any prize. The real runner stays
the course and carries off the prize in triumph. Isn't the same
thing true in general of the just man? In any action, in dealings
with others, or in life itself, isn't he the man who in the end gets
both the rewards and the good name among his fellows?'

'Yes.'

'Then will you allow me to say about him all that you said
d about the unjust man?¹⁰ That is, that the just man, when he
grows old, will, if he wishes, hold positions of authority in the
state, marry whom he likes and marry his children to whom he
likes, and so on, as you said of the unjust man. Conversely the
unjust man will, in general, even if he gets away with it when he
is young, be caught at the end of the course and humiliated; his
old age will be miserable, he will be an object of contempt to
e citizen and foreigner alike, and will be whipped and suffer all
those punishments you so rightly called brutal – torture and
branding; there is no need for me to repeat them. Will you let
me say all this?'

'Yes, you may fairly say it.'

3. The Myth of Er

The Good Man's rewards in the life after death. The responsibility of the individual and the doctrine of transmigration. This concluding section of the dialogue is cast in the form of a myth, as is Plato's habit when he wishes to convey religious or moral truths for which plain prose is inadequate. Much of the detail is borrowed from contemporary sources, probably Orphic.

'These, then,' said I, 'are the prizes and rewards and gifts which the just man receives from gods and men while he is still alive, over and above those which justice herself brings him.'   614 *a*

'And very sure and splendid they are,' he replied.

'Yet they are nothing in number and magnitude when compared to the things that await the just man and unjust man after death; you must hear about these too, so that our discussion may pay in full what it owes to both of them.'

'There are few things I would hear more gladly.'   *b*

'What I have to tell won't be like Odysseus' tale to Alcinous,[11] I continued, 'but the story of a brave man, Er, son of Armenius, a native of Pamphylia. He was killed in battle, and when the dead were taken up on the tenth day the rest were already decomposing, but he was still quite sound; he was taken home and was to be buried on the twelfth day, and was lying on the funeral pyre, when he came to life again and told the story of what he had seen in the other world. He said that when his soul   *c* left his body it travelled in company with many others till they came to a wonderfully strange place, where there were, close to each other, two gaping chasms in the earth, and opposite and above them two other chasms in the sky. Between the chasms sat Judges, who having delivered judgement, ordered the just to take the right-hand road that led up through the sky, and fastened the evidence for the judgement in front of them, while they ordered the unjust, who also carried the evidence of all that they had done behind them, to take the left-hand road that led   *d* downwards. When Er came before them, they said that he was to be a messenger to men about the other world, and ordered

him to listen to and watch all that went on in that place. He
then saw the souls, when judgement had been passed on them,
departing some by one of the heavenly and some by one of the
e earthly chasms; while by the other two chasms some souls rose
out of the earth, stained with the dust of travel, and others
descended from heaven, pure and clean. And the throng of souls
arriving seemed to have come from a long journey, and turned
aside gladly into the meadow and encamped there as for a
festival; acquaintances exchanged greetings, and those from
615 *a* earth and those from heaven inquired each other's experiences.
And those from earth told theirs with sorrow and tears, as they
recalled all they had suffered and seen on their underground
journey, which lasted a thousand years, while the others told of
the delights of heaven and of the wonderful beauty of what they
had seen. It would take a long time to tell you the whole story,
Glaucon, but the sum of it is this. For every wrong he has done
to anyone a man must pay the penalty in turn, ten times for each,
b that is to say, once every hundred years, this being reckoned as
the span of a man's life. He pays, therefore, tenfold retribution
for each crime, and so for instance those who have been responsible for many deaths, by betraying state or army, or have cast
others into slavery, or had a hand in any other crime, must pay
tenfold in suffering for each offence. And correspondingly those
who have done good and been just and god-fearing are rewarded
c in the same proportion. He told me too about infants who died
as soon as they were born, or who lived only a short time, but
what he said is not worth recalling. And he described the even
greater penalties and rewards of those who had honoured or
dishonoured gods or parents or committed murder. For he said
that he heard one soul ask another where Ardiaeus the Great
was. (This Ardiaeus was the tyrant of a city in Pamphylia some
thousand years before, who had killed his old father and elder
d brother and done many other wicked things, according to the
story.) "He has not come, and he never will," was the reply.
"For this was one of the terrible things we saw. We were near
the mouth of the chasm and about to go up through it after all
our sufferings when we suddenly saw him and others, most of
them tyrants, though there were a few who had behaved very

wickedly in private life, whom the mouth would not receive   *e*
when they thought they were going to pass through; for whenever anyone incurably wicked like this, or anyone who had not
paid the full penalty, tried to pass, it bellowed. There were some
fierce and fiery-looking men standing by, who understood the
sound, and thereupon seized some and led them away, while
others like Ardiaeus they bound hand and foot and neck, flung   616 *a*
them down and flayed them, and then impaled them on thorns
by the roadside; and they told the passers-by the reason why
this was done and said they were to be flung into Tartarus."
And Er said that the fear that the voice would sound for them
as they went up was the worst of all the many fears they
experienced; and when they were allowed to pass in silence their
joy was great.

'These, then, are the punishments and penalties and the
corresponding rewards of the other world.'

*The paragraph which follows gives, in brief and allusive form,
a picture of the structure of the universe, in which the rings on
the spindle-whorl are the orbits of the planets and the sphere of
the fixed stars. A brief note on the details is given in Appendix II.*

'After seven days spent in the meadow the souls had to set   *b*
out again on the eighth and came in four days to a place from
which they could see a shaft of light stretching from above
straight through[12] earth and heaven, like a pillar, closely resem-
bling a rainbow, only brighter and clearer; this they reached
after a further day's journey and saw there in the middle of the
light stretching from the heaven the ends of the bonds of it,[13] for
this light is the bond of heaven and holds its whole circumference   *c*
together, like the swifter[14] of a trireme. And from these ends
hangs the spindle of Necessity, which causes all the orbits to
revolve; its shaft and its hook are of adamant, and its whorl a
mixture of adamant and other substances. And the whorl is   *d*
made in the following way. Its shape is like the ones we know;
but from the description Er gave me we must suppose it to
consist of a large whorl hollowed out, with a second, smaller

one fitting exactly into it, the second being hollowed out to hold a third, the third a fourth, and so on up to a total of eight, like a nest of bowls. For there were in all eight whorls, fitting one
e inside the other, with their rims showing as circles from above and forming the continuous surface of a single whorl round the shaft, which was driven straight through the middle of the eighth. The first and outermost whorl had the broadest rim; next broadest was the sixth, next the fourth, next the eighth, next the seventh, next the fifth, next the third, and last of all the second. And the rim of the largest and outermost was many-coloured, that of the seventh was the brightest, the eighth was illuminated by the seventh, from which it takes its colour,
617 *a* the second and fifth were similar to each other and yellower than the others, the third was the whitest, the fourth reddish and the sixth second in whiteness. The whole spindle revolved with a single motion, but within the movement of the whole the seven inner circles revolved slowly in the opposite direction to that of the whole, and of them the eighth moved fastest, and
b next fastest the seventh, sixth and fifth, which moved at the same speed; third in speed was the fourth, moving as it appeared to them with a counter-revolution; fourth was the third, and fifth the second. And the whole spindle turns in the lap of Necessity. And on the top of each circle stands a siren, which is carried round with it and utters a note of constant pitch, and the eight notes together make up a single scale. And round about
c at equal distances sit three other figures, each on a throne, the three Fates, daughters of Necessity, Lachesis, Clotho, and Atropos; their robes are white and their heads garlanded, and they sing to the sirens' music, Lachesis of things past, Clotho of things present, Atropos of things to come. And Clotho from time to time takes hold of the outermost rim of the spindle and helps to turn it, and in the same way Atropos turns the inner rims with her left hand, while Lachesis takes inner and outer
d rims with left and right hand alternately.

'On their arrival the souls had to go straight before Lachesis. And an Interpreter first marshalled them in order and then took from the lap of Lachesis a number of lots and patterns of life and, mounting on a high rostrum, proclaimed: "This is the word

of Lachesis, maiden daughter of Necessity. Souls of a day, here
you must begin another round of mortal life whose end is death.
No Guardian Spirit will be allotted to you; you shall choose
your own. And he on whom the lot falls first shall be the first to   *e*
choose the life which then shall of necessity be his. Excellence
knows no master; a man shall have more or less of her according
to the value he sets on her. The fault lies not with God, but with
the soul that makes the choice." With these words he threw the
lots among them, and each picked up that which fell beside him,
all except Er himself, who was forbidden to do so. And as each   618 *a*
took up his lot he saw what number he had drawn. Then the
Interpreter set before them on the ground the different patterns
of life, far more in number than the souls who were to choose
them. They were of every conceivable kind, animal and human.
For there were tyrannies among them, some life-long, some
falling in mid-career and ending in poverty, exile and beggary;
there were lives of men famed for their good looks and strength   *b*
and athletic prowess, or for their distinguished birth and family
connections, there were lives of men with none of these claims
to fame. And there was a similar choice of lives for women.
There was no choice of quality of character since of necessity
each soul must assume a character appropriate to its choice; but
wealth and poverty, health and disease were all mixed in varying
degrees in the lives to be chosen.

'Then comes the moment, my dear Glaucon, when everything   *c*
is at stake. And that is why it should be our first care to abandon
all other forms of knowledge, and seek and study that which
will show us how to perceive and find the man who will give us
the knowledge and ability to tell a good life from a bad one and
always choose the better course so far as we can; we must reckon
up all that we have said in this discussion of ours, weighing the
arguments together and apart to find out how they affect the
good life, and see what effects, good or ill, good looks have when
accompanied by poverty or wealth or by different dispositions of   *d*
character, and what again are the effects of the various blends of
birth and rank, strength and weakness, cleverness and stupidity,
and all other qualities inborn or acquired. If we take all this into
account and remember how the soul is constituted, we can   *e*

choose between the worse life and the better, calling the one
that leads us to become more unjust the worse, and the one that
leads us to become more just the better. Everything else we can
let go, for we have seen that this is the best choice both for living
and dead. This belief we must retain with an iron grip when we
619 a enter the other world, so that we may be unmoved there by the
temptation of wealth or other evils, and avoid falling into the
life of a tyrant or other evil-doer and perpetrating unbearable
evil and suffering worse, but may rather know how to choose
the middle course, and avoid so far as we can, in this life and
the next, the extremes on either hand. For this is the surest way
b to the highest human happiness.

'But to return. Er told us that the Interpreter then spoke as
follows: "Even for the last comer, if he chooses wisely and lives
strenuously, there is left a life with which he may be well content.
Let him who chooses first look to his choice, and him who
chooses last not despair." When he had spoken, the man with
the first lot came forward and chose the greatest tyranny he
c could find. In his folly and greed he chose it without examining
it fully, and so did not see that it was his fate to eat his children
and suffer other horrors; when he examined it at leisure, he beat
his breast and bewailed his choice, ignored the Interpreter's
warning, and forgot that his misfortunes were his own fault,
blaming fate and heaven and anything but himself. He was
one of the souls who had come from heaven, having lived his
previous life in a well-governed state, but having owed his
goodness to habit and custom and not to philosophy; and
d indeed, broadly speaking, the majority of those who were caught
in this way came from heaven without the discipline of suffering,
while those who came from earth had suffered themselves and
seen others suffer and were not so hasty in their choice. For this
reason and because of the luck of the draw there was a general
change of good for evil and evil for good. Yet it is true also that
anyone who, during his earthly life, faithfully seeks wisdom and
whose lot does not fall among the last may hope, if we may
e believe Er's tale, not only for happiness in this life but for a
journey from this world to the next and back again that will not

lie over the stony ground of the underworld but along the smooth road of heaven.

'And to see the souls choosing their lives was indeed a sight, Er said, a sight to move pity and laughter and wonder. For the most part they followed the habits of their former life. And so he saw the soul that had once been Orpheus[15] choose the life of a swan; it was unwilling to be born of a woman because it hated all women after its death at their hands. The soul of Thamyris[16] chose the life of a nightingale, and he saw a swan and other singing birds choose the life of a man. The twentieth soul to choose chose a lion's life; it was the soul of Ajax,[17] son of Telamon, which did not want to become a man, because it remembered the judgement of the arms. It was followed by Agamemnon,[18] who also because of his sufferings hated humanity and chose to be an eagle. And Atalanta's[19] turn came somewhere about the middle, and when she saw the great honours of an athlete's life she could not resist them and chose it. After her he saw Epeius,[20] son of Panopeus, taking on the role of a skilled craftswoman, and right among the last the buffoon Thersites[21] putting on the form of an ape. And it so happened that it fell to the soul of Odysseus to choose last of all. The memory of his former sufferings had cured him of all ambition and he looked round for a long time to find the uneventful life of an ordinary man; at last he found it lying neglected by the others, and when he saw it he chose it with joy and said that had his lot fallen first he would have made the same choice. And there were many other changes from beast to man and beast to beast, the unjust changing into wild animals and the just into tame in every kind of interchange.

'And when all the souls had made their choice they went before Lachesis in the order of their lots, and she allotted to each its chosen Guardian Spirit, to guide it through life and fulfil its choice. And the Guardian Spirit first led it to Clotho, thus ratifying beneath her hand and whirling spindle the lot it had chosen; and after saluting her he led it next to where Atropos spins, so making the threads of its destiny irreversible; and then, without turning back, each soul came before the throne of

620 a

621 a Necessity and passing before it waited till all the others had
       done the same, when they proceeded together to the plain of
       Lethe through a terrible and stifling heat; for the land was
       without trees or any vegetation.

       'In the evening they encamped by the Forgetful River, whose
       water no pitcher can hold. And all were compelled to drink a
       certain measure of its water; and those who had no wisdom to
       save them drank more than the measure. And as each man
  b   drank he forgot everything. They then went to sleep and when
       midnight came there was an earthquake and thunder, and like
       shooting stars they were all swept suddenly up and away, this
       way and that, to their birth. Er himself was forbidden to drink,
       and could not tell by what manner of means he returned to his
       body; but suddenly he opened his eyes and it was dawn and he
       was lying on the pyre.

       'And so, my dear Glaucon, his tale was preserved from perish-
  c   ing, and, if we remember it, may well preserve us in turn, and
       we shall cross the river of Lethe safely and shall not defile our
       souls. This at any rate is my advice, that we should believe the
       soul to be immortal, capable of enduring all evil and all good,
       and always keep our feet on the upward way and pursue justice
       with wisdom. So we shall be at peace with the gods and with
       ourselves, both in our life here and when, like the victors in the
       games collecting their prizes, we receive our reward; and both
  d   in this life and in the thousand-year journey which I have
       described, all will be well with us.'

APPENDIX I
THE PHILOSOPHICAL
PASSAGES IN THE
REPUBLIC

The philosophical passages in the *Republic* are of first importance for the understanding of Plato's philosophy. The three best known, the similes of the Sun, the Divided Line and the Cave, run consecutively, and we are explicitly told to connect the third of them, the Cave, with 'what has preceded it' (517*b*, Part VII, note 78). I have suggested (Part VII, section 5(2)) that this phrase must be interpreted to cover also the philosophical passages which occur earlier in Part VII and especially in section 2(1). In addition, the section on Dialectic in Part VIII (section 3: cf. note 23) explicitly refers back to the Cave and Line and seems to be intended as a summary of the philosophical teaching of the dialogue.

It is not easy to keep all these passages in mind at once, and the table on the following pages is intended to set them out visually together in skeleton form, in the belief that the first step to understanding them is to study them together. The horizontal divisions do not reproduce the proportions of the Line, partly for typographical reasons and partly because their significance is still a matter of argument. Plato can hardly have failed to notice that sub-section B = sub-section C; but we are given no hint of what this may mean, though we are warned not to embark on interpretations beyond those we are given for fear of landing ourselves in a long argument (534*a*, and Part VIII, note 23). The main horizontal division in the table is that between knowledge and the operations of the intellect or intelligence on the one hand and 'opinion' on the other, with the corresponding fields or realms of reality which they apprehend.

The four sub-divisions in the Line refer to mental operations and do not necessarily recur in the fields corresponding to them. *Noēsis* and *dianoia* seem to be two ways of dealing with forms and not to correspond to two different types of 'object' apprehended; *pistis* and *eikasia* do in a sense correspond to a difference of object, but the 'objects' of *eikasia* can have no *independent* existence from those of *pistis*, of which they are derivations (shadows, reflections). The sub-divisions are not therefore always easy to trace when not explicitly referred to, and we might doubt their importance but for their emphatic final reappearance (534*a*), after references to the Cave (532*b*) and Line (533*c*), in the Educational programme (531*d* ff.).

The Good appears regularly as the culmination of the scheme and is shown at the head of the vertical columns *in italics* to indicate its pre-eminence.

In Col. III i.C the phrase 'Commonsense assurance' as a rendering of *pistis* is taken from Cross and Woozley.

The last entries in Col. III i.D and Col. V i.D are bracketed because they are an interpretation and not a direct reference to anything Plato says, though Col. IV 2 (last entry) provides some justification for them (cf. Cross and Woozley, pp. 220–21).

'Mathematical Objects' in Col. III 2 are shown in brackets because there seems to be no direct reference to them in the text and most commentators think they had no place in this stage of Plato's thought.

What the table does bring out, I hope, is that Plato does not, at each stage, mention all the details of his philosophy; Col. I, for example, has only a single horizontal division, and as already mentioned, the fourfold division occurs irregularly after its introduction. On the other hand, when all the passages are considered together a reasonably consistent pattern emerges, even if details remain uncertain.

In these passages in the *Republic* the emphasis is largely intellectual. There is a long training in the disciplines of mathematics and of 'dialectic', which comprises what we should call logic and philosophy. But Socrates has hinted (506*d*) that the apprehension of the Form of the Good, the final objective of the

philosophic process, is something of which it is difficult to give
a direct description, and has substituted (507*a*–521*a*) the three
similes of Sun, Line and Cave. We find a less intellectual
approach in the *Phaedrus* and *Symposium* (translations of both
which dialogues are available in Penguin). It has been called by
Simone Weil the way of salvation through feeling. In the
Phaedrus the soul again has three parts or elements (cf. Part v,
section 2 ff. above), and is compared to a winged chariot with
two horses and a driver; there is a good horse corresponding to
the *thumoeides* of the *Republic*, an unruly horse corresponding
to the *Republic*'s 'appetite', and a driver, the *Republic*'s reason.
The soul is immortal and in its disembodied state joins at one
point a great procession and sees 'what is outside the heavens'
(247*b*), the whole realm of the Forms, of which it retains some
recollection which may be awakened by its perceptions when it
is embodied in this life, in particular by perceptions of beauty.
(Compare the myth of Er in the *Republic*, Part XI, section 3.)
The same thought recurs in the *Symposium*, where the driving
force is *Éros*, the love of beauty in all forms and the impulse to
all creative activity, ranging from its simplest form in physical
reproduction to its higher levels in artistic and literary creation,
and culminating in philosophy. The process is described by
Socrates in the form of an account which he says was given
to him by a 'wise woman', a priestess called Diotima. The
culmination of the process is a final vision or revelation, and
Diotima describes the way to it as follows:

'"Anyone who wants to pursue this goal correctly must begin by
turning to physical beauty, and then if he gets the right guidance fall
in love with a particular individual and with him produce thoughts of
beauty. He must then perceive that the beauty in one individual is
similar to that in another, and that if beauty of form is what he is
pursuing it is stupid not to recognize that the beauty exhibited by all
individuals is the same. With that recognition he becomes the lover of
all physical beauty, and his passion for a single individual slackens as
something of small account. The next stage is for him to reckon beauty
of mind more valuable than beauty of body, and if he meets someone
who has an attractive mind but little bodily charm, to be content to

love and care for him and produce thoughts which improve the young; this again will compel him to look for beauty in habits of life and customs and to recognize that here again all beauty is akin, and that bodily beauty is a poor thing in comparison. From ways of life he must proceed to forms of knowledge and see their beauty too, and look to the fullness of beauty as a whole, giving up the slavish and small-minded devotion to individual examples, whether a boy or man or way of life, and turning instead to the great sea of beauty now before his eyes. He can then in his generous philosophic love beget great and beautiful words and thoughts, and be strengthened to glimpse the one supreme form of knowledge, whose object is the beauty of which I will now speak . . . For anyone who has been guided so far in his pursuit of love, and surveyed these beauties in right and due order, will at this final stage of love suddenly have revealed to him a beauty whose nature is marvellous indeed, which is the culmination of all his efforts." ' (210a–e)

The conception of an intelligible realm beyond the range of ordinary sense-perception and yet in some way dependent on it which we find in the *Republic* fits in well with the higher realm of the *Phaedrus* and *Symposium*. In them the supreme Form is beauty; in the *Republic* it is the good. The *Phaedrus* and *Symposium* add passion and feeling to the more intellectual austerity of the *Republic*, but the personal experience in which both processes culminate is something which eludes exact verbal expression and Plato has to resort to simile and myth.

Col. I The philosopher, knowledge & reality		II The Sun	III The Line	
1. Cognitive state	2. Field of operation		1. State of mind (*pathēma* 511d)	2. Field of Operation
Knowledge: *epistēmē*, 477b or *gnōsis*, 477a Infallible 477e	The forms (*idea* 479a *eidos* 476a); each single 476a. Beauty itself, justice itself, etc. 476a. What is, being (*to on, ousia* 478a, 479c) cf. 485b eternal reality	*The form of the good* 508e Beauty itself etc. 507b apprehended by intelligence and knowledge (*nous, gnōsis* 508d) The good is source of being, reality and intelligibility (509b, 508d)	A. Intelligence (*noēsis, nous*) Upward movement to a first principle (*archē*) thence back to conclusions (511a, b). Deals with forms only (511c) B. Reasoning (*dianoia*) Downward movement from assumptions to conclusion, as in geometry and kindred *technai* (511a, b, d). Uses visible figures as illustrations (510d–e, 511a)	*The first principle (archē) of everything* (511a, b) A. The forms 511c B. Mathematical postulates etc. 510c–511b (Mathematical objects? 526a)
Opinion: *doxa*, 477b Intermediate between *epistēmē* & *agnoia* Fallible, 477e Ignorance *agnoia* 477b, 478c *agnōsia* 477a	The multiplicity of actions, objects, things: 476a, 476c, 479e. These 'share in' (*metechein*) the corresponding form. They are subject to change (485b) and 'hover between being and not-being' 479a–d What is not (*to mē on* 478c 479c)	The visible sun Particular beautiful etc. things (507b). The twilight world of change (coming-to-be: *genesis*) apprehended by opinion (*doxa*): 508d The sun is cause of coming-to-be and growth as well as of visibility (509b)	C. Belief (*pistis*): 511d–e. 'Commonsense assurance' D. Illusion (*eikasia*): 511d–e (Sophist, poet, artist: cf. Part x)	C. Animals, plants, manufactured objects (510a) Models or drawings of geometrical figures 510d–e D. Images, shadows, reflections of originals in C (510a)

Vertical labels in column II: Knowledge: *epistēmē* / Opinion: *doxa*

Vertical labels in column III: Intelligible realm (*noētos topos* 509d) / Visible realm (*boratos topos* 509d)

IV The Cave		V The educational curriculum		
1. Simile	2. Interpretation	1. Activity	2. Field of operation	3. Summary (533e–534a)
The Sun (516b) A. Real physical things (516a–b)	*The Good* 517b–c	A. Dialectic (531d) which completes the philosopher's studies (532a, 534e)	*The form of the good* (526d, 534c)	A. Knowledge (*epistēmē*)
	The education of the philosopher (the upward progress of the mind 517b) *[outside the Cave]*	B. The five mathematical studies, corresponding to the escape from the cave and looking at shadows and reflections (532b–c)	The intelligible realm (*noēton* 524c); eternal and unchanging (527b)	
B. Shadows and reflections of real things (516a)				B. Reasoning (*dianoia*) *[Noēsis]*
The fire (514b) C. Artificial models of real things in A (514c: cf. 517d images, 532b likenesses) D. Shadows thrown by the models in C, or echoes caused by their carriers (515a–b)	The visible realm 517a–b C. Images of justice (517d) D. Shadows of these images (517d) *[inside the Cave]*	C. The first stage of education (521e–522a) (D. cf. The misleading activities of sophist, poet, artist)	The visible realm (*horaton*), subject to change (*genesis*): 524c, 527b	C. Belief (*pistis*) D. Illusion (*eikasia*) *[Doxa]*

APPENDIX II
THE SPINDLE OF
NECESSITY

This passage has been much discussed, but the following points are generally agreed:

(1) The 'Spindle of Necessity' is intended, however imperfectly, to give a picture of the working of the Universe.

(2) Plato thought that the universe was geocentric, with the fixed stars on a sphere or band at the outside, the earth at the centre, and the orbits of the sun, moon, and planets between earth and stars.

(3) The rims of the whorl are intended to represent these orbits, and have the following equivalences:

1. The fixed stars	5. Mercury
2. Saturn	6. Venus
3. Jupiter	7. Sun
4. Mars	8. Moon

Thus, for example, we are told that 'the fourth (Mars) was reddish' and 'the eighth (Moon) was illuminated by the seventh (Sun)'.

(4) The breadth and relative motion of the rims represent the distances and relative speeds of the planets, though it is difficult to be certain about details (cf. Cornford, *Plato's Cosmology*, p. 88).

(5) The singing sirens are Plato's version of the Pythagorean doctrine of the 'harmony of the spheres', which Aristotle describes as follows:

'It seems to some thinkers that bodies so great must inevitably produce a sound by their movement: even bodies on the earth do so, although they are neither so great in bulk nor moving at so high a speed, and as for the sun and the moon, and the stars, so many in number and enormous in size, all moving at a tremendous speed, it is incredible that they should fail to produce a noise of surpassing loudness. Taking this as their hypothesis, and also that the speeds of the stars, judged by their distances, are in the ratios of the musical consonances, they affirm that the sound of the stars as they revolve is concordant. To meet the difficulty that none of us is aware of this sound, they account for it by saying that the sound is with us right from birth and has thus no contrasting silence to show it up; for voice and silence are perceived by contrast with each other, and so all mankind is undergoing an experience like that of a coppersmith, who becomes by long habit indifferent to the din around him' (*De Caelo*, 11, 9, trans. Guthrie, Loeb edition).

In the more detailed interpretation of the passage there is much uncertainty, and the Greek itself is far from unambiguous. There are those (e.g. J. S. Morrison,* *JHS*, 1955, p. 59f.; *Parmenides and Er*) who prefer to translate the word here rendered 'through' by 'across', and to suppose that the phrase refers to a straight band of light running across the heavens. This makes it more difficult to understand what is meant by 'from above'; but in any case it is not easy to see quite *where* the souls are and *what* it is they see 'in the middle of the light' (or 'down the middle of the light').

The 'pillar' and 'rainbow' do not help much. Though the natural meaning of 'pillar' is something standing upright, it could be used to illustrate a straight band of light; the reference to the rainbow appears to be to its colour, but the rainbow is also a band of light running across the sky. We are left with the two other illustrations, the swifter and the spindle.

Morrison and Williams, *Greek Oared Ships*, pp. 294–8, have shown pretty conclusively what a 'swifter' (Greek *hypozōma*) is. It is a rope running longitudinally round a ship, from stem

---

*I am grateful to Mr Morrison for several discussions on this passage, in which we could never reach an agreed solution.

to stern, whose purpose was 'to subject the outside skin to a constricting tension which would keep the structure from working loose under the stress of navigation under oar and sail' (p. 298). There is a clear parallel with the light which 'holds the circumference together'. In addition the ends of the swifter were brought inboard at the stern where there was a device for tightening them. Similarly the ends of the 'bands of heaven' are brought in, though exactly where or how is not clear. But the illustration certainly seems, so far, to indicate that there is a *band* of light running *round* the heaven, whose ends are brought in and somehow fastened, and which holds the whole heaven together.

But Plato proceeds at once to the second illustration of the spindle. Fig. 1 shows a spindle. Essentially it consists of shaft and weight or whorl. The function of the weight is to keep the thread spinning: the shaft is needed not only as an axis of revolution but also for winding the thread when it has become too long. To hold the thread while the next length is spun there must be something to which to fasten it, the function of the hook in this passage. The primary purpose of the comparison is to illustrate, from a familiar object, a system in which the heavenly bodies go round the earth in rings. The description of the whorl makes this fairly clear, and the main weakness of the comparison is that it makes no provision for the inclination of the axis of the ecliptic, in which sun, moon and planets move, to that of the fixed stars. The armillary sphere in the *Timaeus* (Plato: *Timaeus and Critias* (Penguin)) is a more satisfactory illustration. But there are further problems. Nothing is said about the position or shape of the earth. It must be at the centre of the system, with the heavenly bodies revolving round it. Once the heavenly bodies have been thought of as three dimensional, it is a fairly obvious step to think of them as spheres: if the moon is not a disc it must be a ball. And it is plausible therefore to suppose the earth to be spherical, as it undoubtedly is in the *Timaeus* and as it is commonly supposed to be in the *Phaedo* (though Mr Morrison has challenged the supposition and holds that the earth is a hemisphere with flat surface in both *Phaedo* and the *Republic: Phronesis IV*, 1959, pp. 101–9; *Classical*

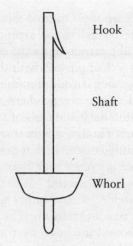

Fig. 1 Greek Spindle

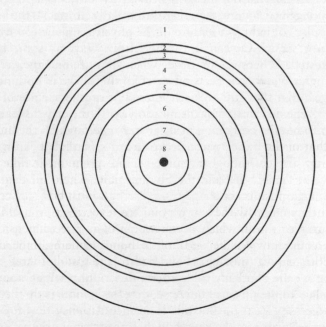

Fig. 2 The Rim on the Whorl (after Adam)

Quarterly lxii, pp. 46 ff.). Granted a central earth of spherical or other shape there remains the problem of the spindle shaft. Does it correspond to anything in the physical universe? If the spindle of Necessity 'hangs from the ends of the band of heaven' one would suppose that it does. It is true that the spindle is only a model; but a good model reproduces the main features of its original, and in the *Timaeus* there is an axis 'stretched through the whole' (40 BC). Though this in turn may be a reflection of the more sophisticated model in that dialogue, it is none the less a not unreasonable inference that Plato thought of the universe as turning on *some* sort of axis.

We are left therefore with a rather unsatisfactory inconsistency between the two illustrations. The swifter suggests a band of light running round the heavens, the spindle an axis round which they pivot. If the ends of the band when brought in could form a pillar of light that was also an axis it would reconcile the two illustrations, but the evidence hardly allows one to speak with certainty. In any event there are still obscurities. If the band (or pillar) of light is a feature of the physical universe, why do we not see it? Or can it be the Milky Way, as some have suggested? Where are the souls when they see and then reach the light, whether it be band or column? There is nothing to suggest that they are ever anywhere but on the surface of the earth. The description of the meadow, with the chasms leading *up* into heaven and *down* into earth, *beneath* which the unjust soul's journey takes place, leaves no doubt that it is on the earth's surface, though at some remote point on it (like the grove of Persephone and the Elysian plain, where incidentally Rhadamanthus is, in the *Odyssey*). If the earth were spherical then they might well be at a point from which they could see features of the universe which we cannot. But even so, just where and how are the 'ends' of the bands brought inboard (to use the nautical metaphor) and tied to the spindle? At a later point we are suddenly told, after a description which appears to relate to the physical universe, that the spindle is on the 'lap of Necessity' (617*b*). But this is an inconsistency that follows the introduction of the Fates and their traditional occupation of spinning; it is good symbolism to put the universe on the lap of

Necessity, and so the inconsistency of making her sit within the system on her lap is overlooked. It is, indeed, well to remember that this passage occurs in a myth, that in his myths Plato often gives symbolic meaning precedence over precision of detail, and that there are therefore likely in the detail to be features that are strictly speaking irreconcilable.

Hilda Richardson's article 'The Myth of Er', *Classical Quarterly* xx, 1926, p. 119, is perhaps still as good a treatment as any of the whole section (Part xi, section 3). Further references are given in the list of References and Sources.

Notes

PART I: INTRODUCTION

1. See note 4.
2. The festival was in honour of Bendis, the Thracian equivalent of Artemis.
3. The precise meaning of the Greek phrase is uncertain, but it must refer to the approach of death.
4. The Greek word translated as 'doing right' is *dikaiosunē*, commonly translated as 'justice', which is the main theme of the *Republic*, whose subtitle is 'about *dikaiosunē*'. But 'justice' is, as Cross and Woozley say (p. vi), 'a thoroughly unsuitable word to use as a translation of the Greek word'. *Dikaiosunē* has a less legal and more moral meaning than 'justice'; it is in fact the most general Greek word for 'morality', both as a personal quality and as issuing in right action. So Liddell and Scott translates the corresponding epithet *dikaios* as 'observant of duty to god and man, righteous'. Normally in this translation the two words are rendered by 'justice', 'right action', and 'just', 'right'. But the Greek meaning is uncomfortably wide and occasional variants are used, indicated when appropriate by footnotes. Similar remarks apply to words of opposite meaning – *adikia* 'injustice', 'wrongdoing', *adikos* 'unjust', 'wrong'. But here there is the further complication of a verb *adikein*, 'to do wrong' or 'injustice' (intrans.) or to 'wrong' or 'injure' (trans.).
5. Seventh-century lyric poet: notice the appeal to a poet on an issue of this kind, and cf. opening notes to Part III and section 1.
6. *Technē*: see closing note to section 2.
7. *Odyssey*, XIX, 395.
8. Or 'unjust . . . just': *adikos . . . dikaios*, see note 4.
9. Socrates is taking Polemarchus' point which is about *injuring* or *damaging* one's enemies. He is not thinking of punishment; though the later part of this argument anticipates the penal reformers.

10. *Aretē*: see note 35. The Greek has simply 'by reference to the excellence of . . .'. The judgement is a comparative one between two states of the horse, and it is interesting that Plato speaks of it as being made in the light of what we think a horse *ought to be*, its 'excellence'; hence the use of the word 'standard' here, though *aretē* is *also* a quality of character.

11. *Aretē*.

12. The Seven Wise Men.

13. The first three of them were tyrants, the typical bad men of Greek tradition: the last took bribes from Persia, the traditional enemy.

14. For section 3 (Thrasymachus) and the following section 4 (Glaucon and Adeimantus) see Guthrie, *History of Greek Philosophy*, vol. III, pp. 88–99.

15. A reference to the provision in Athenian law whereby a defendant, if found guilty, could propose an alternative penalty to that demanded by the prosecution.

16. The Sophists charged for their instruction: Introduction, p. xvii.

17. *Dikaiosunē*.

18. *Dikaion*.

19. Doctor and patient, captain and crew.

20. *Technē*.

21. *Technē*.

22. Lit: 'any further *aretē*' (note 35). Each *technē* is a self-contained activity, operating in a particular field, and needing nothing to supplement it.

23. *Technē*.

24. The Greek word is *epistēmē*, indicating knowledge or any organized body of knowledge.

25. Or 'render an account of'.

26. Cf. 342*a–c*.

27. *Technē*.

28. *Technē*.

29. Cross and Woozley, p. 22.

30. See 344*c*.

31. *Aretē*: see note 35.

32. *Kakia*, the opposite of *aretē*: a strong word for radical defect or wickedness.

33. In the following passage Plato makes considerable use of a word (*pleonektein*) that means 'get the better of', 'outdo', 'do better than', which is difficult to reproduce in translation. The English 'compete', used several times here, has something of the same flavour in that competition aims at getting the better of someone else or outdoing him. But no single English word will really serve.

Plato's argument is that in all skilled activity (*technē*) which involves knowledge (*epistēmē*, note 24) the practitioners aim at getting the right result and not at outdoing each other. The musician must get his instrument *in tune* and does not in the process try to do better than other musicians. There is no competition but only a right result. The argument is then transferred by analogy to justice and injustice. In the *Gorgias* (483, 508) Plato similarly argues that *pleonexia* is the basic fault of the unjust man.

34. *Epistēmē* cf. note 33.

35. Greek *aretē*, traditionally translated 'virtue'. But the Greek word has a wider connotation than the rather moralistic sense in which 'virtue' is today used in English. It and the corresponding epithet *agathos* are 'the most powerful' words of commendation used of a man' (A. W. H. Adkins, *Merit and Responsibility*, p. 31). They convey a meaning of excellence, effectiveness irrespective of the sphere in which it is exercised. So to call the just man 'wise and good' (above) is to imply that he has both the knowledge and the effectiveness to arrange his life to the best advantage (whatever that may be). The English 'good' has many of the ambiguities of the corresponding Greek *agathos* (though not all) in that you can have a good tool or horse as well as a good man, and things can be 'good' in a moral or material sense. In this translation 'good' normally translates *agathos* and 'excellence' *aretē*. Here 'goodness' is used for *aretē* because it is the characteristic attribute of the good (*agathos*) man.

36. See Guthrie, *A History of Greek Philosophy*, III, p. 90, note 4. T. is here disclaiming responsibility for the argument since S. will not allow him to conduct it in his own way.

37. Book I, 343*c*–*e*, 347*e*, H 348*a*–*d*.

38. *Aretē*.

39. Lit: 'is': because the just man has just been shown to be 'wise and good' (cf. 350*c*.).

40. See note 39.

41. *Aretē*: the ambiguity excellence/virtue – goodness should be remembered here (see note 35).

42. Greek *psuchē*. The Greek word is used to cover, as appears from this passage, both the principle of life (its original meaning was the breath of life) and the seat of mental functions, like those listed in the next words. So it sometimes means personality or character. But it can also carry the religious and moral connotation of the English word 'soul': it is the immortality of the *psuchē* which is dealt with in Book x (Part XI, section 1 ff.).

43. See above, 350*c*.

44. Perhaps a reference to Socrates' customary profession of ignorance.

45. *Adikein*: see note 4.

46. This paragraph has been seen as a form, or anticipation, of the Social Contract theories of the 17th/18th centuries. But there are differences as well as similarities. Both have a historical element (not perhaps to be taken too seriously): in both the basis of social arrangements is a contract, explicit or implicit (though this contractual element is not much stressed by Glaucon). But whereas the 17th/18th centuries were interested in the problem of sovereignty – why should I obey the political authorities? – Glaucon is concerned to find a basis for *moral* (rather than political) obligation, which he founds on mutual agreement.

47. *Adikein – dikaiosunē*.

48. See note 47.

49. *Septem contra Thebas*, 1. 592.

50. These two lines follow immediately that quoted above from the *Septem*: ll. 593–4.

51. In the Greek, 'brother should stand by brother'.

52. *Works and Days*, 232.

53. *Odyssey*, xix, 109.

54. Possibly Eumolpus. Musaeus and Eumolpus were both authors of poems which expounded Orphic beliefs.

55. *Works and Days*, 287.

56. *Iliad*, IX, 497.

57. *Frag.* 213.

58. *Frag.* 86–9.

59. *Psuchē*: see note 42. 'Character' might be a better rendering here.

PART II: PRELIMINARIES

1. See G. Vlastos in *Classical Philology*, 1968, pp. 291 ff.

2. Possibly in 409 BC – in which case it is one of Plato's anachronisms: but possibly in 424 BC.

3. Greek *polis*, 'city-state', translated in this version as 'community', 'state' or 'society'.

4. *Technē*: see closing note to Part I, section 2.

5. The Greeks reclined so at meals.

6. I.e. acquisitiveness.

7. *Technē*.

8. Lit: 'well-born': the Greek word has the ambiguity of the English 'noble' in earlier usage, i.e. 'well-born' or 'of high quality'.

9. *Psuchē*: the mental qualities corresponding to the physical.

10. There is a play on words here in the Greek. The two words used, *philosophos* and *philomathés*, both indicate love of learning or knowledge. So the dog who *knows* his master becomes a philosopher.

PART III: EDUCATION: THE FIRST STAGE

1. Greek *mousikē*. There is no English equivalent. The word covers the secondary or literary education referred to in the opening heading to Part III. Paul Shorey, in the Loeb translation (Heinemann, 1930–35), comments that the word covers 'playing the lyre, music, poetry, letters, culture, philosophy according to the context'. Throughout this Part it is translated as 'education' or 'stage of education' (to distinguish it from the further stage described in Part VIII) because it is with its educational aspect that Plato is concerned. But the reader should remember the wider overtones behind the Greek word so translated. *Mousikē* is the sphere of the Muses, of whom there were nine, presiding between them over all the arts, literary, plastic, graphic, musical, and even (in philosophy) intellectual. 'Mind and character' in this passage translates *psuchē*.

2. The Greek word *pseudos* and its corresponding verb meant not only 'fiction' – stories, tales – but also 'what is not true' and so, in suitable contexts, 'lies': and this ambiguity should be borne in mind.

3. There is a Greek proverb, 'The beginning is everything'.

4. Lit: 'rather than their bodies with their hands'. A rather obscure phrase, but the intention seems to be to emphasize the importance of training mind and character (*psuchē*) as against body (*sōma*).

5. Ouranos (the sky), the original supreme god, was castrated by his son Cronos to separate him from Gaia (mother earth). Cronos was in turn deposed by Zeus in a struggle in which Zeus was helped by the Titans.

6. Such a robe was woven by Athenian maidens for presentation to Athene.

7. Hephaestos, who (according to a late source) is said by Pindar to have bound her to her throne.

8. *Iliad*, I, 586–94.

9. *Iliad*, XX, 1–74; XXI, 385–513.

10. Plato tends to use 'gods' (plural) or 'god' (singular) indifferently. When he speaks of 'god' we must not interpret him in terms of simple monotheism. He thought that the myths of Greek polytheism were crude and misleading, as he says in this section. He does seem to have

believed (like most Greeks) in a *supreme* god, but he would not have regarded that belief as precluding the existence of a *multiplicity* of spiritual powers of whom many could rank as (subordinate) gods. This is the sort of theology we meet in the *Timaeus* and *Laws*.

11. The reader of the following passage should bear the following ambiguities in mind: (1) the Greek word for good (*agathos*) can mean (a) morally good, (b) beneficial or advantageous; (2) the Greek word for evil (*kakos*) can also mean harm or injury; (3) the adverb of *agathos* (*eu* – well) can imply either morally right or prosperous. The word translated 'cause of' could equally well be rendered 'responsible for'.

12. *Iliad*, XXIV, 527. Quotations from Homer are generally taken from the translations by Dr Rieu in the Penguin series. At times (as here) the version quoted by Plato differs slightly from the accepted text.

13. Source unknown.

14. *Iliad*, IV, 69 ff. and XX, 1–74.

15. *Frag.* 160.

16. *Psuchē.*

17. *Odyssey*, XVII, 485.

18. A minor sea-god capable of transforming himself into all sorts of shapes.

19. Mother, by Peleus, of Achilles. She was a sea-nymph and to win her in marriage Peleus had to wrestle with her while she assumed all kinds of shapes to avoid him.

20. The quotation is from a lost play of Aeschylus.

21. See note 2: *pseudos* can mean both 'falsehood' and 'fiction'. English cannot keep the ambiguity, but the reader should remember that a single Greek word lies behind the two words used in this passage.

22. *Iliad*, II, 1–34: a dream promising, untruthfully, the early capture of Troy.

23. *Frag.* 350.

24. *Odyssey*, XI, 489.

25. *Iliad*, XX, 64.

26. *Iliad*, XXIII, 103.

27. *Odyssey*, X, 495.

28. *Iliad*, XVI, 856.

29. *Iliad*, XXIII, 100.

30. *Odyssey*, XXIV, 6.

31. *Iliad*, XXIV, 10.

32. *Iliad*, XVIII, 23.

33. *Iliad*, XXII, 414.

34. *Iliad*, XVIII, 54.

35. *Iliad*, XXII, 168.

36. *Iliad*, XVI, 433.

37. *Iliad*, I, 599.

38. See above, 382*a–e*, 383*a–b*.

39. *Odyssey*, XVII, 383.

40. *Iliad*, IV, 412.

41. *Iliad*, III, 8; and IV, 431.

42. *Iliad*, I, 225.

43. *Odyssey*, IX, 8.

44. *Odyssey*, XII, 342.

45. *Iliad*, XIV, 294 ff.

46. *Odyssey*, VIII, 266 ff.

47. *Odyssey*, XX, 17.

48. Proverbial.

49. *Iliad*, IX, 515; XIX, 278.

50. *Iliad*, XXII, 15, 20.

51. *Iliad*, XXI, 130; XXIII, 140.

52. *Iliad*, XXIV, 14 XXIII, 175.

53. Theseus carried off Helen, who was rescued by her brothers, the Dioscuri. Theseus and Peirithous together tried to abduct Persephone, goddess of the underworld.

54. Aeschylus, *Niobe*.

55. Perhaps 'the inherent advantages it brings' would make the meaning more explicit: cf. 367*e*.

56. The Greek word (*mimēsis*) covers both 'imitation' or 'copying' and dramatic and artistic representation in the widest sense. Plato will play on this ambiguity in the opening note to Part X ff.

57. Cornford, op. cit., p. 78.

58. Apollo: see 394*a*.

59. *Iliad*, I, 15.

60. Lit: 'good at representation' (*mimēsis*).

61. Lit: 'represent many things'.

62. Plato argues as if the principle of 'one man one job' which he has laid down (370*c*) implied that a man should not 'give many representations' (*mimēsis*) in the dramatic or literary sense.

63. 'Rhapsodes', who gave public recitations of poetic works, particularly of Homer.

64. The reader should remember (a) the 'dramatic' nature of the recitations required of the Greek schoolboy (cf. Part III, section heading 1 (c)); (b) that Plato assumes rather than proves that one is liable to become like the characters one acts (he will say more about this in Part X) and that it is therefore bad for his Guardians to act, as we might say, out of their true character; (c) that in Part X he will argue that even

watching drama (and presumably hearing or reading poetry) can have the same effects as acting in it.

65. *Mimēsis*.

66. The Guardians – their military function is still to the fore. The paragraph makes it clear that, though he is dealing primarily with education, Plato would have excluded from his state all poetry of the type to which he objects.

67. Lit: 'and in the same way'.

68. Marsyas, a Phrygian, challenged Apollo to a musical contest. His instrument was the flute, Apollo's the lyre. Apollo won and Marsyas was flayed alive.

69. Glaucon swears 'By Zeus', the chief Olympian god; Socrates, who always avoided such oaths, swears the oath traditionally ascribed to him, 'By the dog'.

70. A well-known fifth-century musician.

71. Cf. 397*b*.

72. The Greek word translated 'goodness of character' can equally mean 'good nature', or as we might say 'goodness of heart'. But the Greek word also commonly means 'silly', 'naïve'. The word translated 'lack of awareness of the world' means more literally 'silliness', 'lack of wit'. Plato is trying to ground aesthetic judgements on moral judgements, and is guarding himself against the charge that people of good character are often, in a rather simple-minded way, unaware of the realities of life.

73. Lit: 'damage in their *psuchē*'.

74. There may be a reference here to Plato's 'Theory of Forms'. The word translated 'qualities' is *eidos*, one of the words used by Plato for the forms: cf. opening note to Part VII, section 2.

75. See above, 398*e*.

76. Son of Apollo and god of healing: patron of doctors.

77. Sixth-century lyric poet.

78. *Iliad*, IV, 218.

79. The story occurs in Aeschylus and Euripides as well as in Pindar (*Agamemnon* 1022, *Alcestis* 3).

80. Greek *dikastēs*. The Athenian *dikastai*, sitting in panels, acted both as judge and jury.

81. Cf. note 72.

82. Lit: 'the man whose *psuchē* is good is a good one'.

83. *Thūmos*: see note to Part II, section 3.

84. *Mousicē*: see note 1.

85. *Mousikē*.

86. 'the one . . . the other': Plato uses the terms *mousicē* and *gumnasticē*

(physical training) which he has used throughout this Part. 'Energy and initiative': *thumoeides*.
87. *Mousikē*.

PART IV: GUARDIANS AND AUXILIARIES

1. *Polis*.
2. See note 3.
3. The Greek word means to 'cast a spell on', 'to bewitch' (*goēteuō*). 'Propaganda' would be a somewhat free translation – but its means of operation are very much those described in this passage, and the operations of the ad-man and the mass-media are not a bad modern parallel. They are the spell-binders of the modern world.
4. Lit: to support and help the Rulers in their decisions. 'To enforce the decisions of the Rulers' (Cornford). See opening note to Part IV, section 1.
5. Cf. the whole treatment of fiction, 377 ff. The myth or story he proceeds to tell follows the principles which he has laid down for myth and fiction generally.
6. i.e. the Auxiliaries.
7. 'We shall tell our people in mythical language', J. L. Davies and D. J. Vaughan, *The Republic of Plato*, 3rd edn (Macmillan, 1866).
8. *Polis*.
9. On promotion and demotion between classes, see note in Part VI, section 2.
10. The Myth was addressed to all three classes, and the previous sentence appears, again, to refer to all three. In this sentence there is no change of subject in the Greek, yet in it and in all that follows Plato is clearly speaking of the Guardians (or Rulers) only, who are as we have seen (opening note to Part II, section 3) his main concern.
11. See Part IX, opening notes.
12. Reading ἀργούς for γεωργούς in 421*b*2.
13. Cornford, op. cit., p. 109.
14. More literally: 'the individual will be not many but one, and the state grow to be one, not many'.
15. The first mention of the so-called 'community of wives and children' in the *Republic*; see opening note to Part VI, section 2.
16. *Politeia*: a derivation of *polis*, meaning system of government, constitution under which a state operates.
17. Lit: growth, but the context shows that the process is one of improvement.

18. Cf. *Odyssey*, 1, 351.

19. *Mousikē*.

20. There is a play on words in the Greek. The *Guardians* must build their *guard*house here because it is the most important point to defend.

21. In the next few sentences Plato uses a number of derivations of the Greek word *nomos* which are very difficult to reproduce in English. *Nomos* has meanings which cover positive law, convention, custom, social order in the widest sense: breaches of *nomos* may be illegal, against custom or convention, immoral, or, more generally, socially disruptive to a greater or lesser extent. The group of Greek derivations are here rendered by disorder, disorderly, better regulated, respect for order, orderly. Davies and Vaughan use 'loyal' instead of 'respect for order', so bringing out another *nuance* of the Greek.

22. A play in Greek on *paidia*, play, amusement, and *paideia*, education. Both concern children, *paides*.

23. Proverbial: like our 'birds of a feather'.

24. In what follows Plato has Athens in mind.

25. As we might say, neither the ordinary doctor nor the quack can help them.

PART V: JUSTICE IN STATE AND INDIVIDUAL

1. See 368*b*–*c*.

2. 'This is apparently the first passage in Greek literature where the doctrine of four cardinal virtues . . . is expressly enunciated' (see Adam, *The* Republic *of Plato*). It is a fairly large assumption that this quartet covers the field to be surveyed. Justice is the quality to be defined; but cf. Part I, note 4. Wisdom covers the virtues and qualities of the mind (understanding, intelligence, etc.). Courage has much the same meaning in English as the Greek original: but for Plato there are overtones from *thūmos*, cf. Part II, note to section 3 and Part V, note to section 2. The word translated 'self-discipline' means in origin 'sound sense', and has two main meanings in ordinary Greek usage: (a) 'prudence', good sense; (b) 'temperance', moderation, or, in the words of H. G. Liddell and R. L. Scott, *A Greek–English Lexicon* (Clarendon Press), 'control over the sensual desires'. The older translations 'prudence' and 'temperance' are hardly suitable today, and in view of Plato's insistence on the element of control (being master of oneself, 430*d* ff.), self-control, self-restraint, or *self-discipline* seem the best alternatives.

3. Cf. 429*c*.

4. Strictly speaking, only the Rulers can have true courage, because true courage must be based on full knowledge, which only they have. This will appear more fully later.

5. *Psuchē*.

6. The reference is to ordinary conversation, and not to any earlier passage in the dialogue. The Greek phrase, here given the conventional translation 'mind your own business', is almost exactly translated by the current (1974) catch-phrase 'doing your own thing'. It has a positive content – 'getting on with and doing your own job' – as well as the more negative meaning so often attached to the English phrase 'not interfering with other people'. A strictly literal translation would be 'doing the things that belong to (*possessive genitive*) oneself'. At 441e the translation 'performing its proper function' is used: cf. Cross and Woozley, p. 110.

7. Reading παρέχει with Adam.

8. Cf. Field, *The Philosophy of Plato*, p. 96; for Butler see A. Duncan-Jones, *Butler's Moral Philosophy* (Pelican).

9. *Psuchē*.

10. Plato refers to this longer treatment again in Book VI (504a), and, in fact, gives it in Books VI–VII.

11. *Psuchē*.

12. This argument is, to us, rather oddly expressed. We should more naturally say (what Plato in any case means) 'if you are hot you want a cold drink' and so on. But Plato wants to make the point that when thirsty we simply want to drink, and that the quality of the drink (hot or cold, long or short) is a kind of *addition* to the simple basic desire (see note 13, below). This way of thinking of qualities as separate entities is not without relevance to the theory of Forms (see Part VII, section 2).

13. Cornford puts the same point in different words when he says that Plato's object here is 'to distinguish thirst as a mere blind craving for drink, from a more complex desire whose object includes the pleasure or health expected to result from drinking' (Cornford, p. 131). In particular, there is the Socratic argument, referred to in this passage, that all desire is directed towards 'the good'. 'It is necessary to insist that we do experience blind cravings which can be isolated from any judgement about the goodness of their object' (Cornford, loc. cit.).

14. *Technē*.

15. *Thūmos*.

16. As it stands this sentence overstates the case. A few sentences below Plato makes the proviso that the second element is reason's 'natural auxiliary, unless corrupted by bad upbringing'. It is an essential feature

of his moral theory that different elements predominate to different degrees in different types of character (see Books VIII–IX), and that the control of reason is not always perfect. Reason's 'natural auxiliary' may be 'corrupted', and the three elements in the mind may 'interfere with each other' and try to 'do each other's business'. Perhaps in such cases reason is 'corrupted' too; it is not easy to define Plato's meaning precisely. But this should not prevent us from seeing the simple facts of the conflict of motives that he is trying to describe.

17. See 390d: *Odyssey*, XX, 17.

18. *Thūmos*.

19. See note 6. I have used 'perform its function' here because the context seems to require a more positive description than 'minding one's own business'.

20. Cf. 434e–435b.

21. *Aretē*: excellence or virtue, *kakia*: wickedness or defect. See opening note to Part V and Part I, note 35.

PART VI: WOMEN AND THE FAMILY

1. See above, 423e–424a.

2. Lit: 'gold-smelting', proverbial of those who 'fail in any speculation' (Liddell and Scott).

3. Notice the recurrent animal analogy throughout this part of the argument.

4. The Greeks always exercised naked, and the nakedness is merely a consequence of the proposal that women should take part in athletics at all. Women took part in physical training at Sparta; see Introduction, p. xxi.

5. Aristophanes in the *Ecclesiazusae* ('Women in Parliament') had already made fun of ideas similar to those which Plato expresses in this section, and Plato probably had him in mind.

6. 'The musician Arion, to escape the treachery of Corinthian sailors, leapt into the sea and was carried ashore at Taenarum by a dolphin. Herodotus, I, 24' (Cornford).

7. The technique of debate or argument was given much attention in the discussions started by the Sophists, and Plato often accuses his opponents of using it to score points rather than as an instrument of serious discussion.

8. *Genos*: natural kind.

9. Lit: occupation connected with the administration of the state (or society: *polis*).

10. More literally: the things (faculties, powers) of the body adequately serve the mind ... are in conflict with it.

11. Lit: occupation of those who administer the state (society: *polis*).

12. See Part II, section 3.

13. *Aretē*, see Part I, note 35.

14. With Adam and Shorey. Pindar, *Frag.* 209.

15. *Kalon – aischron.*

16. See note 15 above.

17. Compare the *Laws*, 804d, where Plato says that children 'belong to the state rather than to their parents'.

18. See 382b–d, 389b.

19. The words used ('the best possible flock', 'the Guardian herd') seem deliberately to recall the analogy with stock breeding. And the word translated 'nursery' at 460c means literally a pen or fold for rearing young animals.

20. This phrase and others on the following pages raise the question whether and how far Plato sanctioned infanticide. See note on Promotion, Demotion and Infanticide in Part VI, section 2.

21. Lit: 'number of men', i.e., presumably the number of the Guardian class.

22. I.e. at the marriage festivals.

23. See note on Promotion, Demotion and Infanticide in Part VI, section 2.

24. Perhaps a quotation from a victory ode, referring to a racehorse put to stud after its racing career was over.

25. I.e. the alternatives are abortion (not uncommon in the ancient world) or infanticide: see note on Promotion, Demotion and Infanticide in Part VI, section 2.

26. 'The majority of ancient writers ... denied that children were born in the eighth month of pregnancy' (Adam). Plato's months here are, of course, lunar months.

27. The details of these sentences are a little difficult to disentangle. Plato is dealing with the unions of the over-age; but the rules he lays down for them will, *a fortiori*, apply to the Guardians generally, and the last sentence has this wider application.

He first explains what is meant by father, mother, son, daughter, etc., under his system. What he does is to substitute relationships between *groups* for those between individuals; the basic group comprises all those mated at a particular marriage festival, who will be related collectively as fathers and mothers to all children born as a result of that festival. (We must suppose these festivals to take place at regular intervals and to last for a definite time, say a week or fortnight.) Other relationships are worked out on the same principle and Plato adds, for completeness, a definition of brother and sister. Granted these definitions, it should, as he points out, be easy enough to avoid the relationships he wishes to prevent.

It will be noticed that it is the father–daughter, son–mother type of relationship which he forbids. It was this type of incest about which the Greeks felt particularly strongly. Brother–sister unions were, they knew, practised in Egypt, and their own custom allowed marriage between uncle and niece, aunt and nephew, and half-brother and half-sister. In the last sentence, as the reference to the lot makes clear, Plato is thinking of his marriage festivals, and 'brother' and 'sister' are probably used in his special sense. It would, indeed, restrict the possibilities of mating unduly if brothers and sisters in that sense could not marry – parents are producing children for thirty (men) and twenty (women) years. But he has not precluded unions between brother and sister in the normal sense, and here probably allows them as a special case of brother and sister in his own sense. Children of the same parents would not, in his state, know that they were blood relations, as he has explained above, and such relationship would in any event, under his scheme, have no significance. The reference to Delphi has no special importance. The sanction of Delphi is needed because marriage is a religious institution; it might be asked 'once for all to approve the whole scheme of marriage laws, or it might be formally invoked at each festival' (Cornford, *Republic*, p. 159).

28. The Greek word is the normal one for a master of slaves or an absolute ruler or owner.

29. There is an ambiguity here in the Greek which cannot be reproduced in English. The Greek word *archon* means 'ruler' in a general sense, but is also used of the constitutionally appointed magistrates at Athens, and so here of the 'authorities' in a democratic form of government.

30. Proverbial, of making the best of what you have.

31. More fully, 'nothing against the nature of woman as compared with man'.

32. Plato seems to have forgotten that under his arrangements there will be young women as well, though he remembers them again a few sentences below.

33. *Iliad*, VIII, 311.

34. *Iliad*, VIII, 162.

35. Cf. Hesiod, *Works and Days*, 122.

36. The Greek 'daimon' was a spirit intermediate between gods and men.

37. This is a plain indication, if one is needed, that there will be slaves in Plato's state, though they will not be Greeks.

38. Greek custom allowed the recovery and burial of his dead by an enemy after a battle.

PART VII: THE PHILOSOPHER RULER

1. Plato here uses, whether deliberately or not, language that recalls his Theory of Forms (see section 2, Definition of the Philosopher). Particular things 'share in' or 'partake of' (*metechein*) the forms which they exemplify; and the form is a pattern (*paradeigma*) to which particulars approximate. *Paradeigma* is here represented by the English 'ideal pattern', 'ideally', 'ideal', as the emphasis is on the way in which example falls short of pattern, the actual fails to reproduce the perfection of the ideal.

2. See closing note to Part 1, section 3.

3. More precisely, 'the human race' (or 'species'). While it is no doubt improper, as it is unnecessary, to read a wider humanitarianism into these words, there is no reason to suppose Plato to mean anything other than what he says, which is that the principle he is laying down applies to *all* human beings wherever they are: cf. note 38 below.

4. Cf. closing note to Part 1, section 3.

5. *Eidos*; see opening note for section 2 above, p. 192. This passage is commonly taken as referring to the 'forms'. I have used a non-committal word in the translation to bring out the point that the word Plato uses has in itself no special connotation.

6. *Metechein*; see opening note to section 2 above, p. 195.

7. *Einai*: see opening note to section 2 above, p. 196. In this sub-section (VII, 2.1) *einai* (in its verbal or participial use) is translated by *is* or *being*, in order to avoid commitment to any more definite English interpretation and to retain the ambiguity of the Greek in what is a key passage.

8. 'Something that wasn't there' would bring out a further implication of the Greek: cf. opening note to section 2 above, p. 196.

9. Greek, *dunamis*: power, capacity, capability, potentiality. A few lines later it is used with a meaning which seems best expressed by 'faculty', and accordingly is so translated here. But 'faculty' must not be interpreted to imply the many technical and semi-technical meanings the word has acquired, but in its basic sense, 'aptitude for any special kind of action' (*OED*).

10. The Greek word (*gignōskō*) has a suggestion of knowledge by direct personal acquaintance.

11. *Gignōskō.*

12. For consistency 'opinion' is here used to translate *doxa* (and its verbal form *doxazein*). But in these sentences some prefer 'belief' ('believe'). They then read literally: 'Someone who believes relates his belief to something. Or is it possible to believe, but believe nothing?' Knowledge and opinion (belief) each have, in their own field, a grasp of reality, knowledge a certain grasp, opinion an uncertain. The standing of 'ignorance' (*agnoia*) is less clear (see Crombie, II, pp. 56–66).

13. See 477*b.*

14. See 477*a, b.*

15. A man who was not a man (a eunuch) threw a stone that was not a stone (a pumice-stone) at a bird that was not a bird (a bat) sitting on a twig that was not a twig (a reed).

16. *Paradeigma.*

17. See 474*c*–475*e.*

18. *Idea.*

19. The god of criticism and mockery.

20. *Polis.*

21. The Greek *nauklēros* meant, more strictly, 'ship-owner'. But here he is clearly in charge, and as Professor Guthrie has pointed out to me 'ship-owner', with its suggestion of Mr Onassis, could be more misleading.

22. Or 'science', *technē.*

23. Simonides, 'being asked on one occasion . . . whether it was better to be a man of genius or rich, replied "Rich, for men of genius are found at the court of the rich"' (Adam).

24. More literally 'control', 'government'.

25. See 485*a*–487*a.*

26. I.e. the forms, beauty itself, etc.

27. *Psuchē.*

28. Greek *sophia*, traditionally translated 'wisdom'. It also means 'cleverness' or 'skill'. The word translated 'system' (493*b*) is *technē.*

29. The Greek uses a proverbial expression, 'the necessity of Diomede', but its precise meaning is uncertain.

30. Lit: 'the barbarians'.

31. Plato is commonly supposed to have Alcibiades in mind in this passage but he must have felt these temptations himself: cf. Introduction, pp. xv–xvi.

32. If Plato is thinking of Alcibiades above, he must be thinking of Socrates here.

33. Mentioned in the *Apology*, 33*e.* 'Handicapped', lit: 'the bridle of Theages', which became proverbial.

34. 'A kind of voice' (*Apology*, 31c) which sometimes forbade him to do things.

35. See 412*a* above.

36. Heraclitus said there was 'a new sun every day.'

37. Cf. Part VII, section 3 heading.

38. Lit: 'barbarian': cf. note 3 above.

39. Lit: 'the just in nature', or 'the naturally just': a reference to the forms.

40. See 474*a* above.

41. Greek *politeia*, translated 'social system' above. The word refers to social and constitutional arrangements, *polis* to city, state, or society more generally.

42. Or 'akin to the best'; 'allied to perfection' (Cornford, and Davies and Vaughan).

43. *Politeia*.

44. See 412*b* ff.

45. See 484*a*–487*a*.

46. Part V, section 2 ff.

47. See Part V, note 10.

48. Lit: 'borrow'.

49. *Kalos*: 'beautiful', 'fair', 'fine', 'valuable'.

50. The Greek for 'interest' (the 'offspring' of a loan) is the same as for 'child'.

51. See 476*d*.

52. This is a difficult sentence of which variant translations are given. The version above follows Adam and adopts his emendation *καὶ ἰδέαν* for *καὶ ἰδεαν*. For the last phrase the modern philosopher might well say 'what x really is'.

53. Plato says 'gods'; he believed the heavenly bodies were divine.

54. *Idea*.

55. *Kalos*.

56. J. E. Raven, *Classical Quarterly* (Jan.–April 1953), p. 18.

57. The form of the good and the sun.

58. The Greek words for 'visible' and for 'physical universe' (or more literally 'heaven') bear some resemblance to each other, and it has been suggested that there was some connection between them.

59. *Eidos*: a good example of Plato's non-technical use of the term, to mean 'kind', 'sort', 'type' (as also at 511*a*, 'type of thing'). The technical (theory of 'forms') use is a natural sequel because things of a particular *kind* have a particular *form*.

60. See diagram in the opening note to section 6.

61. Lit: true.

62. Greek *hypothesis*, of which the English 'hypothesis' is a transliteration. But the English word means 'something that may be true but needs testing': the Greek word 'something *assumed* for the purpose of argument.'

63. 510*b*6, omit τό.

64. *Eidos*, non-technical again.

65. The translation is intended to bring out the strong visual metaphor. More literally, 'seeking to see those very things that one cannot see except with the reason'. The word translated 'reason' (*dianoia*) will be appropriated later in the passage as a quasi-technical term to designate the mathematical reasoning of sub-section B. 'As images': as we might say 'as illustrations'.

66. *Technē*: see note 68.

67. *Epistēmē*: see Part I, note 24.

68. Lit: 'the so-called *technai*'. The wide range of meaning of *technē* was noted in the closing note to Part I, section 2. Here the reference is to sub-section B of the line, and *technē* has already (note 66) been used in the phrase 'geometry and kindred *technai*', which describes its contents. Plato certainly does not mean the arts or practical skills (cf. 522*b* ff.), and Adam's 'mathematical sciences' gets the reference right. For more detail see Part VIII, section 2, where cf. note 19.

69. *Dianoia*.

70. A strongly visual word – 'gazing at'. So also the word translated 'studied' has a basic meaning 'looked at', 'contemplated'.

71. Plato uses 'intelligible' to describe the whole section A + B, which is the 'intelligible order' or 'region'. But here he seems to be referring to sub-section A only and to be indicating the deficiency of sub-section B, which is none the less dealing with material which if rightly handled is 'intelligible' in the full (A) sense. The meaning of the phrase is, however, uncertain. It reads literally 'it is intelligible (*noēton*) with (with the aid of? in conjunction with?) a (first) principle' or 'and has a first principle'. The interpretation here suggested gives a particular meaning to this more general wording: cf. again Part VIII, note 19.

It is worth adding that, at 511*a* and 511*e*, Plato emphasizes degrees of *clarity*, linked at 511*e* with *truth*; and that his four 'states' or 'habits' of mind are said to entail different degrees of clarity and truthfulness of apprehension, which need not correspond to a difference of object. Both shadow and object throwing it are in a sense physical things; it is our fault if we confuse them. If we speak of shadow and reflection as less true or genuine than their original this is really a comment on our own tendency to misapprehend them. Similarly, here, the mathematician has, compared to the philosopher, a defective apprehension of the same realities (the forms).

72. The words used for 'belief' and 'illusion' do not (with the possible exception of a use of *pistis* in Book x; see 601e) occur elsewhere in Plato in the sense in which they are used here. *Pistis*, 'belief', conveys overtones of assurance and trustworthiness: 'commonsense assurance' (Cross and Woozley, p. 226). *Eikasia*, 'illusion', is a rare word whose few occurrences elsewhere in Greek literature give us little guidance. It can mean 'conjecture', 'guesswork', and some prefer so to translate it here. But 'illusion' is perhaps more appropriate for a 'state of mind'.

73. Lit: 'like us'. How 'like' has been a matter of controversy. Plato can hardly have meant that the ordinary man cannot distinguish between shadows and real things. But he does seem to be saying, with a touch of caricature (we must not take him too solemnly), that the ordinary man is often very uncritical in his beliefs, which are little more than a 'careless acceptance of appearances' (Crombie, *An Examination of Plato's Doctrines*).

74. Lit: 'regard nothing else as true but the shadows'. The Greek word *alēthēs* (true) carries an implication of genuineness, and some translators render it here as 'real'.

75. Or 'more real'.

76. Or 'true', 'genuine'.

77. *Odyssey*, xi, 489.

78. I.e. the similes of the Sun and the Line (though 474c–480a must surely also be referred to). The detailed relations between the three similes have been much disputed, as has the meaning of the word here translated 'connected'. Some interpret it to mean a detailed correspondence ('every feature . . . is meant to fit' – Cornford), others to mean, more loosely, 'attached' or 'linked to'. That Plato intended some degree of 'connection' between the three similes cannot be in doubt in view of the sentences which follow. But we should remember that they are similes, not scientific descriptions, and it would be a mistake to try to find too much detailed precision. Plato has just spoken of the prisoners 'getting their hands' on their returned fellow and killing him. How could they do that if fettered as described at the opening of the simile (514a)? But Socrates was executed, so of course they must.

This translation assumes the following main correspondences:

Tied prisoner in the cave	Illusion
Freed prisoner in the cave	Belief
Looking at shadows and reflections in the world outside the cave and the ascent thereto	Reason

| Looking at real things in the world outside the cave | Intelligence |
| Looking at the sun | Vision of the form of the good. |

79. Cf. Part III, note 10.

80. Cf. 514b–c above.

81. *Technē*.

82. *Aretē*.

83. Cf. 420b and 466a above.

84. Socrates takes up here a point made to Thrasymachus at 347b.

PART VIII: EDUCATION OF
THE PHILOSOPHER

1. The reference is to a children's game in which a shell was spun to decide which side ran away and which gave chase.

2. In Part III. 'Literature and music' translates *mousikē*.

3. *Technai*: here used to refer to the practical crafts and skills.

4. *Noēsis*. There may be a reference to sub-section A of the Line: mathematical studies (sub-section B) 'lead on' to dialectic or *noēsis*. But the reference back to the Line at note 6 suggests that the word is here being used of intellectual operations more generally (A + B: *noēton*), as opposed to those of opinion (C + D: *doxaston*). Throughout this section 'thought' is used to translate *noēsis* (or its corresponding verb).

5. Or 'calculation'.

6. Cf. diagram, in opening note to Part VII, section 6.

7. *Dianoia*.

8. The Greek word can mean both 'reason' and 'calculate arithmetically'. Plato likes to use it in the wider sense of philosophical reasoning, yet without entirely losing its mathematical flavour.

9. The language of the previous paragraph ('numbers themselves', 'the unit itself') is that of the theory of forms. It is less clear what are the numbers referred to in this sentence. Some have supposed them to be entities intermediate between forms and particulars; see opening note to Part VII, section 6. But though Plato did hold some such view later in his life, this sentence is very slender evidence for it in the *Republic*.

10. *Dianoia*: Line sub-section B.

11. 'blinking downwards': the word is commonly taken in this context to refer to the eyes, but more usually refers to the mouth. Perhaps 'whether by looking up with his mouth open or down with it shut.'

12. *Epistēmē.*

13. A very difficult phrase to translate, and I have no great confidence in the version here given. I have translated *phorai* as 'orbits' as it is used of the movements of the heavenly bodies, and Plato here seems to be speaking of some ideal mathematical relationships between these orbits. 'What they carry'; i.e. probably the heavenly bodies themselves, frequently thought of as carried round in the orbit, like the stone in a ring. (The sun, moon and planets are carried on rings in the *Timaeus*.)

But if the detail is obscure, what Plato is trying to convey is perhaps clearer. In his day the data of observational astronomy were still very imperfect, and the problem of the astronomer was to find some mathematical way of accounting for them. What Plato is saying is that the solution of this mathematical problem is the important thing rather than observational detail. And in any case for Plato, as Shorey (Loeb II, p. 183, note f) says, 'no material object perfectly embodies the ideal and abstract mathematical relation'. Plato goes on to elaborate the point in the next two sentences, and in the then state of observational astronomy the mathematical emphasis was the right one.

14. The Pythagoreans were the first to discover that the notes in the scale could be expressed as numerical ratios.

15. Greek law allowed the torture of slaves for the purpose of extracting evidence from them.

16. Lit: 'give and take a rational account' (*logos*). Dialectic for Plato always worked by argument, and typically by question and answer – 'give and take'.

17. *Intellectual* realm': *noēton*, here A + B. 'What each thing is in itself', i.e. the forms. 'Pure thought': *noēsis*, Line sub-section A.

18. I prefer Ast's θέα to the O.C.T. θεῖα, but if Adam's explanation of θεῖα is correct (a 'half-technical Platonic phrase for reflections of natural objects produced by natural lights'), the meaning is not substantially different.

19. There is a clear parallel here between the climb up the 'steep and rugged ascent' out of the Cave plus the looking at shadows and reflections in the world outside which follows, and the study of the branches of mathematics described immediately above in section 2. Plato calls these mathematical studies 'sciences' again (*technai*: see Part VII, note 68). The same parallel occurs again on the following page.

20. I.e. the forms, e.g. beauty in itself, etc.

21. *Technai.* The passage brings out well the ambivalence of *technē* between purely practical and intellectual skills. Cf. Adam's note.

22. Cf. 511*b*: 'the first principle of everything'.

23. Plato, as we have seen, never developed a rigid technical terminol-

ogy; and at 533e has in effect said that he has no wish to do so. But his use of words in this paragraph is none the less confusing. *Epistēmē* is twice used for sub-section A of the Line (instead of *noēsis*): it is here translated 'pure knowledge (A)' to mark the particular use. *Noēsis*, earlier used of sub-section A, is then used of the whole section A + B, perhaps because this whole section can also be called *noēton*, the 'intelligible realm' (Part VII, section 6, opening note): it is here translated 'knowledge (A + B)'. Thus

Knowledge: *noēsis*		Opinion: *doxa*	
A	B	C	D
Pure thought	Reason	Belief	Illusion
epistēmē	*dianoia*	*pistis*	*eikasia*

In spite of this confusing use of terms the passage is of some importance. It firmly connects the educational course to be followed by the philosopher with the Line and Sun (see the reference to the good-in-itself, 534c) and, surely, makes it clear that the whole of these two Parts (VII and VIII) were conceived as a unity. Though Plato proceeds by stages, we are therefore justified in interpreting earlier in the light of later, especially when, as here, Plato makes an explicit connection.

What we learn from this passage, his final summary, is the following. He is still mainly concerned with the relative *reliability* of different methods of perception and argument. The main contrast (as it was on 474c ff.) is between knowledge, dealing with the intelligible realm (*epistēmē–noēton*), and opinion (*doxa*) dealing with what is here called the realm of change (*genesis*), i.e. the physical world (it has been called earlier at 532d the *material* world). Within each of these two realms there are two sub-divisions, whose relation in terms of reliability is again referred to here. Too much significance should not be attached to the proportions, taken from the Line, A + B:C + D::A:C and B:D. Plato probably means simply to draw attention to the sub-divisions, and point out that A in the one realm has the same degree of greater reliability than C in the other, as has B than D. He is careful *not* to work out correspondences between the different modes of perception and their 'objects'. This has always been a difficult point of interpretation, and he is perhaps indicating that we should not go beyond what he actually says. The attempt to do so has certainly led commentators into a 'multiplicity of arguments', as Plato warns us.

24. 'Reality' (*ousia, einai*) with its overtones of truth, 'opinion' (*doxa*) with its overtones of appearance, seeming, unreliability.

25. A reference to 'irrational' numbers, commonly illustrated by the incommensurability of the diagonal and side of a square (hence 'lines' here). The Greeks regarded such incommensurabilities as something of a mathematical scandal, and Plato here suggests that it is similarly scandalous that anyone who is 'irrational', in the sense 'unable to reason', should hold positions of responsibility.

26. See 375*a* ff., 484*a* ff.

27. See 495*a* ff.

28. This goes a little beyond the Greek, which says 'involuntary false-hood'. What must be meant is the kind of misapprehension which we absorb 'involuntarily', i.e. without thinking. Compare Crombie's 'care-less acceptance of appearances', describing sub-section D of the Line.

29. See 412*c*.

30. Solon said 'I go on learning many things as I grow old'; more colloquially, 'One learns a lot as one grows older.'

31. This, in effect, adds elementary mathematics to the curriculum of Part III.

32. The Greek word suggests an element of fraud, the child having in some way been palmed off on the parents; 'supposititious'.

33. Socrates was blamed because the young followed his example in this way: *Apology*, 23*c*.

34. The Greek heaven.

PART IX: IMPERFECT SOCIETIES

1. Lit: 'their kings should be': the philosopher kings.

2. The interpretation of this obscure passage has a long history, reviewed by A. Diès, 'Le nombre de Plato' in *Mémoires présentés à l'Académie des Inscriptions et Belles-Lettres*, XIV, 1940. Much turns on whether the sentence ending 'commensurate and rational' defines a different number from that defined in the remainder of the passage. Adam (Vol. II, commentary pp. 204 ff. and Appendix 1 to Book VIII) thought that it did. He supposed the number to be $3^3 + 4^3 + 5^3 = 216$, the period of the 'mortal creature', 216 days being considered by the Greeks to be the minimum period of gestation. He then supposed that the rest of the passage refers to the 'divine creature', whose number is 3600^2, the number of days in a 'Great Year' (the time it takes the heavenly bodies to return to the same relative positions). He thus gave the passage a certain cosmic significance, the microcosm (man) being

linked in some way (not very clear) with the macrocosm of the cosmos. But the run of the Greek is rather against this interpretation. The passage appears to be devoted entirely to the 'human creature' after a brief sentence in which the divine creature is merely referred to and then not mentioned again. And Diès has shown that the passage can be interpreted without introducing a second number. For details the reader should consult his article. Briefly, the numbers 3, 4 and 5 were considered important because they defined the smallest right-angled triangle with sides of rational number; and the calculations are, for the first sentence, $(3 \times 4 \times 5)_1 (3 \times 4 \times 5)^2{}_2 (3 \times 4 \times 5)^{3-}{}_3 (3 \times 4 \times 5)^4 = 12,960,000$ (Adam's 3600^2). Here then are three steps ('distances') between the brackets ('terms'), and the fourth bracket gives the 'final result'. The various combinations in the second sentence all again give the same figure [$36^2 \times 100^2$, and 4800 (arrived at in two ways) × 2700]. Diès, relying no doubt on what Plato says about the Muses (545e), believes that the passage is a *'plaisanterie de mathématicien'* (loc. cit., p. 10), and if he is right no very elaborate cosmic significance, like that suggested by Adam, should be read into it. What the passage as a whole is saying is that no mortal institutions can last for ever, and that the process of decline from the ideal is started by a generation of Guardians wrongly bred because of failure to observe the appropriate procedure, a failure whose occurrence is in some way controlled by an elaborate mathematical formula.

3. We are concerned at this stage with a dissension between two elements in the governing class, i.e. the Guardians (Rulers plus Auxiliaries), who have become corrupted and into the gold and silver of whose composition (cf. the allegory at 415a–d) iron and bronze have entered, with the result that they no longer maintain their former way of life or relation to the third class.

4. *Thumoeides*.

5. *Mousicē*.

6. *Thumoeides*.

7. As Shorey notes, the words here used, *logos* and *mousikē*, are untranslatable; on *mousicē*, see Part III, note 1. It is not easy to give an informative rendering. Jowett's 'philosophy ("reason", 1970 edn) tempered with music' is quaintly obscure, but Cornford's 'thoughtful and cultivated mind' hardly suggests a telling phrase. The reader should remember that the education outlined in Part VIII was a largely intellectual one, training the reason, while that outlined in Part III operated mainly through the arts. Both elements, Plato is here saying, are necessary.

8. The three 'parts' of the mind, see opening note to Part V, section 2.

9. More strictly 'property qualification'. A property qualification for office was a common feature of Greek oligarchies: cf. 551*b*.

10. A play on words in the Greek. Oligarchy is the 'rule of the few' (*oligoi*), and if they try to fight their own battles their *fewness* is shown up.

11. Greek cavalry and infantry (hoplites) normally had to provide and pay for their own weapons.

12. Throughout this passage Plato is still speaking in terms of the three elements distinguished in Part V, section 2 ff.: reason, the *thumoeides* which includes courage and ambition, and appetite comprising the instinctive desires and including the desire for money.

13. Wealth was proverbially a blind god to the Greeks.

14. Aristotle (*Politics*, 1317*b*21) notes as a characteristic of democracy 'election by lot either to all magistracies or to all that do not need experience and skill'.

15. Or 'uncultivated'.

16. *Odyssey*, IX, 82 ff. Proverbial of those who abandon home and family ties.

17. Plato uses language which recalls the mystery religions, in particular the procession from Athens to Eleusis. 'Splendid': the root meaning is 'clear' or 'bright' and there may be a reference to the fact that the procession, being an evening one, was torchlit.

18. There is a reference in the Greek to the appointment to office by lot.

19. Lit: 'getting drunk to the sound of the flute'. The justification for the rather corny translation is that at drinking parties the flutes were commonly played by girls: Alcibiades in the *Symposium* arrives rather drunk and leaning on a flute-girl. A more contemporary version might be 'pot and pop'.

20. I have used the traditional 'tyrant' and 'tyranny' to translate the Greek words of which they are, in fact, transliterations. As Cornford points out, the essential feature of the Greek 'tyrant' was that he was an absolute and sole ruler, and he accordingly uses the more neutral word 'despot'. But already in Plato's day the use of the word implied a certain moral disapproval, and tyrant is therefore a suitable translation.

21. *Frag.* 351 (Nauk). 'Let us say what comes to our lips, whatever it may be': perhaps 'Let's say what's on the tip of our tongue'.

22. Cf. 'like mistress, like maid'.

23. Herodotus, I, 55.

24. *Iliad*, XVI, 776.

25. See Part III, note 69.

26. The quotation comes in fact from Sophocles, not Euripides (Adam: ad loc.). But Euripides was commonly regarded as *sophos*, 'wise', with

its strong overtones in Greek of 'clever', and did end his days at the court of Archelaus of Macedon. The passage as a whole is evidence more of Plato's distrust of poets than of anything else.

27. Reading καὶ τὰ τῶν ἀπολομένων with Adam.

28. Cf. Henry Fielding, *The Life of Mr Jonathan Wild the Great* (1743).

29. Cf. 559e–560e.

30. Plato on his first visit to Sicily had lived with Dionysius I.

31. Perhaps 'and any one of the three may be in control' ('may govern the soul': Cornford).

32. The Greek word is used of producing an *illusion* of depth, etc. by means of shading (or shadow: the same word as that used of the shadows in Line and Cave) in a picture, or more particularly in the painting of stage scenery (which is *sham* and, having nothing behind it, *empty*).

33. Or 'motion': cf. 585a ff. on depletion and replenishment.

34. E.g. the pleasure of eating is preceded by the pain of hunger.

35. Both text and meaning of 585c7–12 are disputed: see notes by Adam and Cornford.

36. See note 32 above.

37. In Euripides' *Helen*, Helen tells how Hera gave Paris a phantom in place of the true Helen. While Greeks and Trojans fought for this phantom, she herself lived in Egypt, waiting for Menelaus. The story first appears in a fragment of the early-sixth-century poet Stesichorus.

38. M. Diès regards this passage as '*plaisanterie de mathématicien*': cf. note 2 above.

39. Corresponding to the three elements in the mind and to the first three political types – philosopher king, timocrat, and oligarch.

40. Cf. 544e.

41. The Greeks often represented numbers spatially, and a 'plane' number is one that can be represented by a plane figure the product of whose sides yields the number in question; here, $3 \times 3 = 9$.

42. We are given no reason why 9 should be cubed, but Adam notes 'the calculations are inspired by a desire to reach the total 729': see note 43 below. Nettleship (*Lectures*, p. 332) suggests that we must measure the difference in three dimensions.

43. The precise meaning is uncertain. But Philolaus, the Pythagorean, held that there were $364\frac{1}{2}$ days in the year; there are presumably the same number of nights, and $364\frac{1}{2} \times 2 = 729$. Philolaus also believed in a 'great year' of 729 months. Plato may not be entirely serious (note 38 above), but for him, as for many Greeks, this sort of numerical formula always had a certain fascination.

44. Cf. 360e–361d.

45. Wife of Amphiaraus, bribed with a necklace by Polynices to send her husband on the fatal expedition of the Seven against Thebes.

46. In this paragraph Plato uses the Greek word both for slave, translated 'subjected', 'subject', and for political control, translated 'governed', 'control'.

47. *Mousikos*: cf. Part III, note 1.

48. The literal translation of this well-known phrase is 'and seeing it, establish himself'. The alternative translations commonly given are 'establish himself as its citizen', or 'establish himself accordingly', i.e. 'establish it in himself'. The second alternative, here followed, seems to make better sense.

PART X: THEORY OF ART

1. In visual terms what we should call an extreme photographic realism. Such extreme realism, both in theory and practice, was not uncommon in the early fourth century, and is effectively criticized by Aristotle in the *Poetics*.

2. See Part III, section 1c.

3. I.e. the same name as we give to the form: see J. A. Smith, 'General Relative Clauses in Greek', *Classical Review*, 31: 3 (1917), pp. 68–71. Smith argues that this passage must not be interpreted to suggest that Plato thought that wherever there is a common name there is a single form. As Professor Guthrie has said, 'For Plato the kinds or classes (*eidē*) into which particulars fall are objectively determined by their nature (*eidē* or *phuseis*), and it is to them that the eternal Forms (also *eidē*) correspond.'

4. Cf. 507*b*, and opening note to Part VII, section 2.

5. Perhaps 'all other essential natures'; the reference is to the forms which are said to exist 'in nature' because they are what is ultimately real.

6. Lit: 'its appearance as it appears'.

7. The Greek word normally means an apparition or ghost.

8. Both numbered among the Seven Sages. Thales of Miletus was the first of the Greek philosophers: Anacharsis was credited with various practical inventions, and Thales had a reputation for practical skill as well as philosophy.

9. 'Beefeater' is perhaps the nearest rendering in English. He is said to have been an epic poet from Chios. Adam quotes 'I am a great eater of beef, and I believe that does harm to my wits' (*Twelfth Night*, 1. iii.90).

10. Two of the best-known fifth-century Sophists.

11. *Pistis*, the word used of sub-section C of the Line. In the next sentence the wider form *doxa*, opinion, is used: see Part VII, note 71.

12. Cf. Part V, section 2 ff.

13. Cf. 387*d–e*.

14. The sources of these quotations are unknown.

15. Ironical.

PART XI: THE IMMORTALITY OF THE SOUL
AND THE REWARDS OF GOODNESS

1. More literally the second half of this sentence reads, 'we cannot suppose that the soul is destroyed by an alien evil without any flaw of its own, one thing by the evil of another thing'.

2. The latter part of this sentence reads more literally '. . . *kill the soul*, an evil appointed for the destruction of something else will hardly destroy the soul or anything else for which it is not appointed'. 'Adapted': 'arranged', 'ordered', 'appointed', express each in a different way the idea that each type of thing has its own appropriate evil linked with it, and can only be destroyed by that evil.

3. Cf. 602*e–*603*e*, Part V, section 2.

4. In the *Timaeus*, 69*d* the two lower 'parts' of the soul are said to be mortal.

5. See 366*b–e*.

6. Lit: 'the soul itself'.

7. I.e. She can reward the reputation for justice as well, as the argument has shown her reward the reality.

8. 352*ab*.

9. The Greek has 'with ears on shoulders', of which, as Shorey notes, the English idiom is the equivalent.

10. See 362*a–c*.

11. *Odyssey*, IX–XII, where Odysseus tells his adventures to Alcinous, king of Phaeacia. Proverbial of a long story. But there is also a play on words: Alci-noos means 'stout-hearted', 'brave', as Er was.

12. Perhaps 'across': see Appendix II.

13. Probably of the heaven, but possibly of the light: the Greek is ambiguous.

14. See Appendix II, p. 377.

15. Singer and religious teacher, torn in pieces by Maenads, women followers of Dionysus.

16. Another singer, blinded because he challenged the Muses.

17. After the death of Achilles the Greeks adjudged his arms to Odysseus, in preference to Ajax. Ajax committed suicide in disappointment.
18. Victor of Troy, murdered by his wife Clytemnestra on his return.
19. Arcadian princess and huntress. Her suitors had to race with her and were killed if defeated.
20. Maker of the Trojan horse.
21. From the *Iliad*.

References and Sources

I. TEXT, EDITIONS, COMMENTARIES

Greek text: Oxford Classical Texts: *Plato*, Vol. IV, ed. J. Burnet (Oxford, 1962).

J. Adam, *The* Republic *of Plato* (2nd edition, with an introduction by D. A. Rees; Cambridge, 1963). This is a reprint of the original edition of 1902, with a useful introduction dealing with specific topics and work done on them since Adam's day.

R. L. Nettleship, *Lectures on the* Republic *of Plato* (Macmillan, paperback, 1963). A nineteenth-century commentary, still of value.

W. K. C. Guthrie, *A History of Greek Philosophy*, Vol. IV (Cambridge, 1975). Contains a clear and useful summary and analysis of the whole of the *Republic*.

R. C. Cross and A. D. Woozley, *Plato's* Republic (Macmillan, 1964). A philosophical commentary dealing with the *Republic* topic by topic. A useful general guide.

Julia Annas, *An Introduction to Plato's* Republic (Oxford, 1981).

Cross and Woozley have a useful bibliography, as has also Rees. See also Crombie (v. below).

II. POLITICAL AND GENERAL: CURRENT CONTROVERSY

W. Fite, *The Platonic Legend* (Scribner, 1934). The first of Plato's modern critics.

R. H. S. Crossman, *Plato Today* (2nd edn, London, 1959).

K. R. Popper, *The Open Society and its Enemies*, Vol. I: *The Spell of Plato* (Routledge & Kegan Paul, 5th edn, 1966).

These are the best-known modern attacks on Plato and on the *Republic* in particular. See Introduction, p. xlvii ff.

R. B. Levinson, *In Defense of Plato* (Harvard, 1953). This is far the most detailed and elaborate defence of Plato. A much shorter statement can be found in J. Wild, *Plato's Modern Enemies and the Theory of Natural Law* (Chicago University Press, 1953, pp. 9–59) and there is useful material in H. D. Rankin, *Plato and the Individual* (Methuen, 1964).

J. R. Bambrough, *Plato, Popper and Politics* (Cambridge, 1967) contains a collection of essays by critics and defenders.

A more general selection of articles and extracts, some of them dealing with the *Republic*, can be found in the two volumes *Plato* in the series *Modern Studies in Philosophy* (Macmillan, 1972), edited by G. Vlastos, and designed to illustrate 'contemporary interpretations of major philosophers'. Two general introductory works are F. M. Cornford, *Before and After Socrates* (Cambridge, 1960), and G. C. Field, *The Philosophy of Plato* (2nd edn, London, 1969).

III. ETHICS

A. W. H. Adkins, *Merit and Responsibility* (Oxford, 1960). This is subtitled *A Study in Greek Values* and deals with the history, down to the fourth century BC, of the various moral ideas held by the Greeks and dealt with by Plato.

J. Gould, *The Development of Plato's Ethics* (Cambridge, 1955).

IV. EDUCATION

H. I. Marrou, *A History of Education in Antiquity* (paperback Mentor, 1964). The best general history of the subject.

W. Barclay, *Educational Ideals in the Ancient World* (Collins, 1959).

R. L. Nettleship, *The Theory of Education in Plato's* Republic (Oxford, 1935).

The reader interested to glance forward to the later history of higher education in the ancient world should consult M. L. Clarke, *Higher Education in the Ancient World* (Routledge & Kegan Paul, 1971).

V. PHILOSOPHY

See Cornford (Ch. 3) and Field (Chs. 2 and 3), op cit., and J. E. Raven, *Plato's Thought in the Making* (Cambridge, 1965). These are the best general introduction. More elaborate is I. M. Crombie, *An Examination of Plato's Doctrines*, 2 vols. (Routledge & Kegan Paul, 1962), and on the theory of forms, W. D. Ross, *Plato's Theory of Ideas* (Oxford, 1951).

There is an extensive literature on Sun, Line and Cave, a selection of which will be found in Cross & Woozley's bibliography. See in particular J. E. Raven, 'Sun, Divided Line and Cave' (*Classical Quarterly*, 1953) and (not in C. & W.) John Ferguson, 'Sun, Line and Cave again' (*Classical Quarterly*, 1963) Part I, pp. 188–91.

VI. POETRY AND ART

For a rather different view of poetic and artistic inspiration taken by Plato elsewhere see the *Ion*, the *Phaedrus* (244a–256a) and the *Symposium* (201d–212c). The *Phaedrus* and *Symposium* are both published in Penguin. For the *Ion*, see B. Jowett, *The Dialogues of Plato*, 4th edn, Vol. 1.

For an account of the various Greek views on the subject in the late fifth and early fourth century, see T. B. L. Webster, 'Greek Theories of Art and Literature down to 400 BC' (*Classical Quarterly*, 1939), and for literary criticism in the ancient world generally G. M. A. Grube, *The Greek and Roman Critics* (Methuen, 1965).

See also R. G. Collingwood, *The Principles of Art* (Oxford, 1963); Tolstoy, *What is Art?*, trans. Aylmer Maude (Walter Scott Ltd, 1899).

VII. RELIGION

W. K. C. Guthrie, *The Greeks and their Gods* (Methuen, 1950). A 'religious companion to the Greek classics'.

VIII. ASTRONOMY

Reference has been made in the Appendix to F. M. Cornford *Plato's Cosmology* (Kegan Paul, 1937) in which there is a brief treatment of the astronomy of the Myth of Er. The standard general history of Greek astronomy is still T. L. Heath, *Aristarchus of Samos* (Oxford, 1913).

J. L. E. Dreyer, *History of Astronomy, Thales to Kepler* (Dover Pubs., 1953) covers a wider field and is a classic on the subject.

D. R. Dicks, *Early Greek Astronomy to Aristotle* (London, 1970) covers the relevant ground, but has been criticized for inaccuracy of detail (see J. S. Morrison, *Classical Review*, June 1971).

PENGUIN ⓟ CLASSICS

The Classics Publisher

'Penguin Classics, one of the world's greatest series' JOHN KEEGAN

'I have never been disappointed with the Penguin Classics. All I have read is a model of academic seriousness and provides the essential information to fully enjoy the master works that appear in its catalogue' MARIO VARGAS LLOSA

'Penguin and Classics are words that go together like horse and carriage or Mercedes and Benz. When I was a university teacher I always prescribed Penguin editions of classic novels for my courses: they have the best introductions, the most reliable notes, and the most carefully edited texts' DAVID LODGE

'Growing up in Bombay, expensive hardback books were beyond my means, but I could indulge my passion for reading at the roadside bookstalls that were well stocked with all the Penguin paperbacks ... Sometimes I would choose a book just because I was attracted by the cover, but so reliable was the Penguin imprimatur that I was never once disappointed by the contents.

Such access certainly broadened the scope of my reading, and perhaps it's no coincidence that so many Merchant Ivory films have been adapted from great novels, or that those novels are published by Penguin' ISMAIL MERCHANT

'You can't write, read, or live fully in the present without knowing the literature of the past. Penguin Classics opens the door to a treasure house of pure pleasure, books that have never been bettered, which are read again and again with increased delight' JOHN MORTIMER

READ MORE IN PENGUIN

In every corner of the world, on every subject under the sun, Penguin represents quality and variety – the very best in publishing today.

For complete information about books available from Penguin – including Puffins and Penguin Classics – and how to order them, write to us at the appropriate address below. Please note that for copyright reasons the selection of books varies from country to country.

In the United Kingdom: *Please write to* Dept EP, Penguin Books Ltd, Bath Road, Harmondsworth, West Drayton, Middlesex UB7 0DA

In the United States: *Please write to* Consumer Services, Penguin Putnam Inc., 405 Murray Hill Parkway, East Rutherford, New Jersey 07073-2136. *VISA and MasterCard holders call 1-800-631-8571 to order Penguin titles*

In Canada: *Please write to* Penguin Books Canada Ltd, 10 Alcorn Avenue, Suite 300, Toronto, Ontario M4V 3B2

In Australia: *Please write to* Penguin Books Australia Ltd, 487 Maroondah Highway, Ringwood, Victoria 3134

In New Zealand: *Please write to* Penguin Books (NZ) Ltd, Private Bag 102902, North Shore Mail Centre, Auckland 10

In India: *Please write to* Penguin Books India Pvt Ltd, 11, Community Centre, Panchsheel Park, New Delhi 110017

In the Netherlands: *Please write to* Penguin Books Netherlands bv, Postbus 3507, NL-1001 AH Amsterdam

In Germany: *Please write to* Penguin Books Deutschland GmbH, Metzlerstrasse 26, 60594 Frankfurt am Main

In Spain: *Please write to* Penguin Books S. A., Bravo Murillo 19, 1°B, 28015 Madrid

In Italy: *Please write to* Penguin Italia s.r.l., Via Vittoria Emanuele 451a, 20094 Corsico, Milano

In France: *Please write to* Penguin France, 12, Rue Prosper Ferradou, 31700 Blagnac

In Japan: *Please write to* Penguin Books Japan Ltd, Iidabashi KM-Bldg, 2-23-9 Koraku, Bunkyo-Ku, Tokyo 112-0004

In South Africa: *Please write to* Penguin Books South Africa (Pty) Ltd, P.O. Box 751093, Gardenview, 2047 Johannesburg

PLATO
The Last Days of Socrates

'Nothing can harm a good man either in life or after death'

The trial and condemnation of Socrates on charges of heresy and corrupting young minds is a defining moment in the history of classical Athens. In tracing these events through four dialogues, Plato also developed his own philosophy, based on Socrates' manifesto for a life guided by self-responsibility. *Euthyphro* finds Socrates outside the court-house, debating the nature of piety, while *The Apology* is his robust rebuttal of the charges of impiety and a defence of the philosopher's life. In the *Crito*, while awaiting execution in prison, Socrates counters the arguments of friends urging him to escape. Finally, in the *Phaedo*, he is shown calmly confident in the face of death, skilfully arguing the case for the immortality of the soul.

Hugh Tredennick's landmark 1954 translation has been revised by Harold Tarrant, reflecting changes in Platonic studies, with an introduction and expanded introductions to each of the four dialogues.

Translated by HUGH TREDENNICK *and* HAROLD TARRANT
With an introduction and notes by HAROLD TARRANT

Early Greek Philosophy

The Pre-Socratics, the first heroes of Western philosophy and science, paved the way for Plato, Aristotle and all their successors.

Democritus' atomic theory of matter, Zeno's dazzling 'proofs' that motion is impossible, Pythagorean insights into mathematics, Heraclitus' haunting and enigmatic epigrams – all form part of a revolution in human thought which relied on reasoning to justify its conclusions and forged the first scientific vocabulary.

Although none of their original writings have come down to us complete, patient detective work enables us to reconstruct the crucial questions they asked and their absorbing answers. Here Jonathan Barnes brings together the surviving Pre-Socratic fragments in their original contexts, allowing modern readers to get to grips with these pioneering thinkers, whose ideas remain at the centre of philosophical debate. The revised edition of the collection has been updated to take account of further research and a major new papyrus of Empedocles.

Revised edition
Translated and edited by JONATHAN BARNES

SEUTONIUS
The Twelve Caesars

'Too many rulers are a dangerous thing'

As private secretary to the Emperor Hadrian, Suetonius gained access to the imperial archives and used them (along with eye-witness accounts) to produce one of the most colourful biographical works in history. *The Twelve Caesars* chronicles the public careers and private lives of the men who wielded absolute power over Rome, from the foundation of the empire under Julius Caesar and Augustus, to the decline into depravity and civil war under Nero, and the recovery that came with his successors. A masterpiece of anecdote, wry observation and detailed physical description, *The Twelve Caesars* presents us with a gallery of vividly drawn – and all too human – individuals.

Robert Graves's celebrated translation, sensitively revised by Michael Grant, captures all the wit and immediacy of Suetonius' original.

'Graves has given us *The Twelve Caesars* in a good, dry, no-nonsense style ... Suetonius, in holding up a mirror to those Caesars of diverting legend, reflects not only them but ourselves: half-tempted creatures, whose great moral task is to hold in balance the angel and the monster within' GORE VIDAL

Translated by ROBERT GRAVES
Revised with an introduction by MICHAEL GRANT